In the Shadow of Katyn

"Stalin's Terror"

by Stanisław Swianiewicz

© Copyright 2002
Witold & Maria Cornelia Swianiewicz

All rights reserved. No part of this publication may be reproduced, stored in a retrieval system, or transmitted in any form or by any means, electronic, mechanical, photocopying, internet, recording or otherwise, except brief passages for reviews, without the prior permission of the publisher.

Originally written and published in Polish under the title: *W CIENIU KATYNIA*
Institut Littéraire, Paris 1976
Second print in Poland under the auspices of Solidarity, in 1981, Officyna Liberałów
Third print in Polish: Czytelnik, Warsaw, 1990

First Russian edition published in 1989
Translated from Polish and annotated by Vitaly Abramkin
Under the title: *V TENI KATYNI*
By Overseas Publications Interchange Ltd.
8 Queen Anne's Gardens, London W4 1TU, England
First English edition published in 2002
Translated from P.notated by Witold Swianiewicz
Under the *E SHADOW OF KATYN*

Copyri anisław Swianiewicz, 1976
Copyright © ut Littéraire: for the Polish language
Copyright © Russ edition Overseas Publications Interchange

Published by:Distributed by:
Witold PublishingBunker To Bunker Books
3735 Frigate Road, Pender Island1428 - 9th Avenue S.E.
B. C. V0N 2M2   CanadaCalgary, Alberta T2G 0T5

Canadian Cataloguing in Publication Data

Swianiewicz, Stanisław
In the Shadow of Katyn
Translation of: W Cieniu Katynia.
Includes bibliographical references and index

ISBN 1-894255-16-X

1. Swianiewicz, Stanisław. 2. Katyn Forest massacre, 1940
3. World War, 1939-1945- -Personal narratives, Polish.
4. Forced labor- -Soviet Union. I. Title
D804.S65S94 2002   940.54'05'094727   C2002-910303-7

Second Printing 2004

Book Production: Northwest Printing, Calgary, Alberta, Canada.
Back Cover photos: Courtesy Asp Rymsza, ASP RYMSZA
Charków, Katyn, Miednoje – Polish War Cemeteries, Gdynia 2000
Maps: Witold Swianiewicz

Printed in Canada

Pamięci żony mojej Olimpii
ten opis przeżyć poświęcam.

I dedicate this description of the cycle of
events to the memory of my wife, Olimpia.

Acknowledgments:

I wish to express my gratitude to my friends, Walter Oleszkowicz, and his daughter, Kathy Oleszkowicz, who have assisted me with the English edition of my father's book.

Special thanks go to my wife, Maria, for her tremendous input and resourcefulness in making this work come to fruition.

TABLE OF CONTENTS

i	Title Page	91	Lubyanka
v	Table of Contents	92	Psychoanalysis in solitary confinement
vi	Maps: - Poland Campaign (1939)		
vii	- NKVD Camps (1940-42)	102	Cell No. 41
viii	- Road to Freedom (1942)	106	My case
ix	Translator's Note - Witold Swianiewicz	112	My prison companions
xiii	Stanisław Swianiewicz, the author	118	Butyrki and the end of the investigation
xvii	Photos (1917-1970)		
xxi	Author's Foreword	123	The Verdict
		125	Transport to the North
	I THE APPROACHING STORM	129	My GULAG experiences
1	The Polish-German problem	131	NKVD as an Enterprise
4	Tactics of the Ministry of Foreign Affairs	132	Minorities
		137	Doctors
6	My impressions from Germany	140	One who was rejoicing
13	Expansion without resistance	146	The Anarchist
16	Doom over Poland	147	Release from the camps
18	Moods in Poland		
			V KUYBYSHEV
23	**II MOBILIZATION**	158	The Embassy
		162	The case of Ehrlich and Alter
	III FROM PIOTRKÓW TO KATYN	167	The mystery of Leon Kozłowski
28	Piotrków Trybunalski	170	The case of Rola-Janicki
32	Reorganization of the Division	174	Ksawery Pruszyński
33	Dorohusk near the Bug River		
36	The day of dramatic news	189	**VI JOURNEY TO TEHRĀN**
38	The battle near Tomaszów Lubelski		
39	Concentration near Suchowola	212	**VII REPORT ON THE MISSING OFFICERS**
42	Doubts and decisions		
47	Soldiers		
51	Old Soldier		**VIII KATYN FROM THE PERSPECTIVE OF THIRTY YEARS**
53	Captivity		
55	Putyvl		
62	Kozelsk	224	Unraveled aspects of Katyn
71	Near Katyn		
74	Copy of Document: - Order by Beria to transfer prisoner of war Swianiewicz, and translation	236	**IX THE DIALECTICS OF KATYN**
		242	**X DID KHRUSHCHEV WANT TO PUBLISH THE TRUTH ABOUT KATYN?**
	IV FROM KATYN TO KUYBYSHEV		
77	Internal NKVD prison in Smolensk		
80-83	Copy of Document: - Four page letter from Beria to Stalin with request to execute Polish prisoners of war, and translations	246	**XI KATYN AND THE SOVIET-GERMAN ALLIANCE**
		252	**XII RUSSIA vis-à-vis POLAND**
84	Prison Commander		
87	Transport to Moscow	256	Epilog
88	Copy of Document: - Order to send S. Swianiewicz from Smolensk to Moscow, and translation	260	Index of Names
		265	Chronology

THE CAMPAIGN IN POLAND, SEPTEMBER 1939

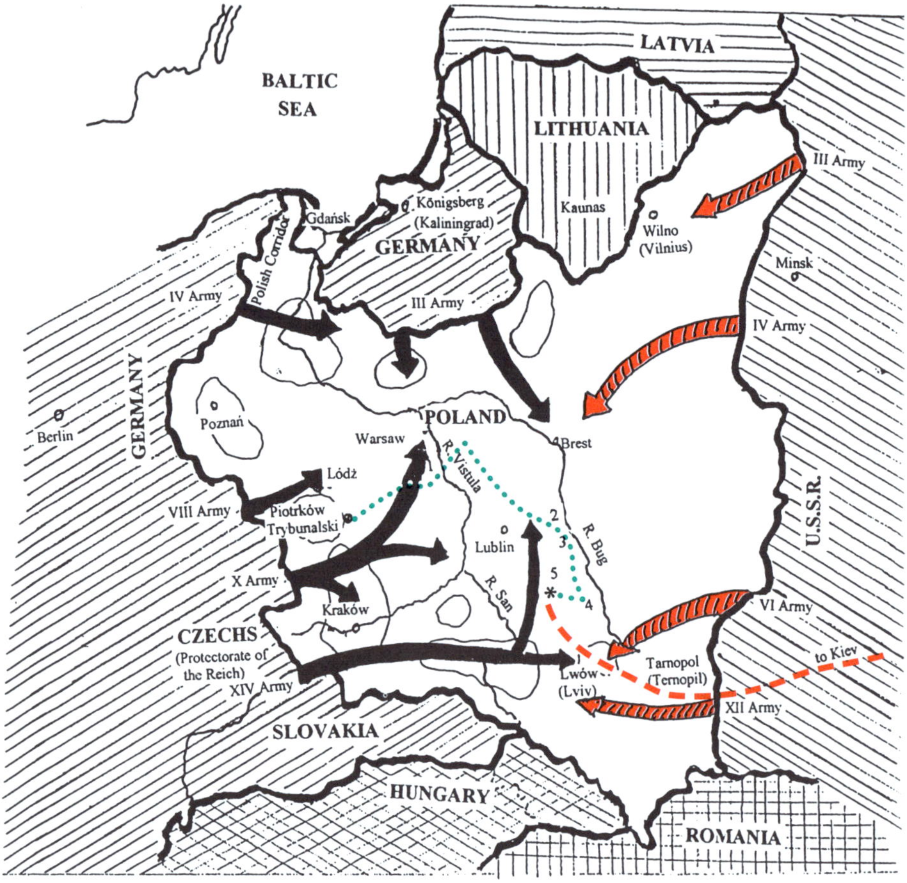

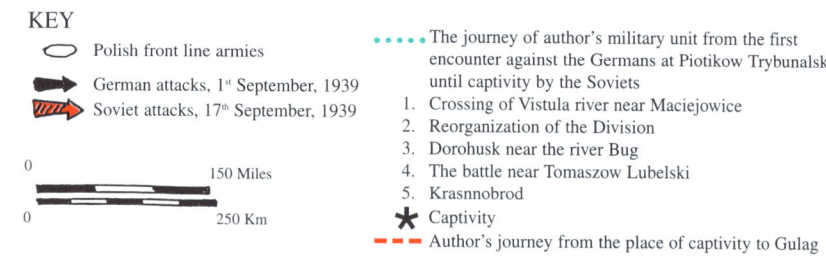

Political borders are those of September 1st, 1939

KEY

- ◯ Polish front line armies
- ➤ German attacks, 1st September, 1939
- ▥➤ Soviet attacks, 17th September, 1939

• • • • The journey of author's military unit from the first encounter against the Germans at Piotikow Trybunalski until captivity by the Soviets

1. Crossing of Vistula river near Maciejowice
2. Reorganization of the Division
3. Dorohusk near the river Bug
4. The battle near Tomaszow Lubelski
5. Krasnnobrod

✱ Captivity

– – – Author's journey from the place of captivity to Gulag

MAP OF NKVD CAMPS WHERE POLISH PRISONERS OF WAR WERE KEPT, AND THEIR PLACES OF BURIAL

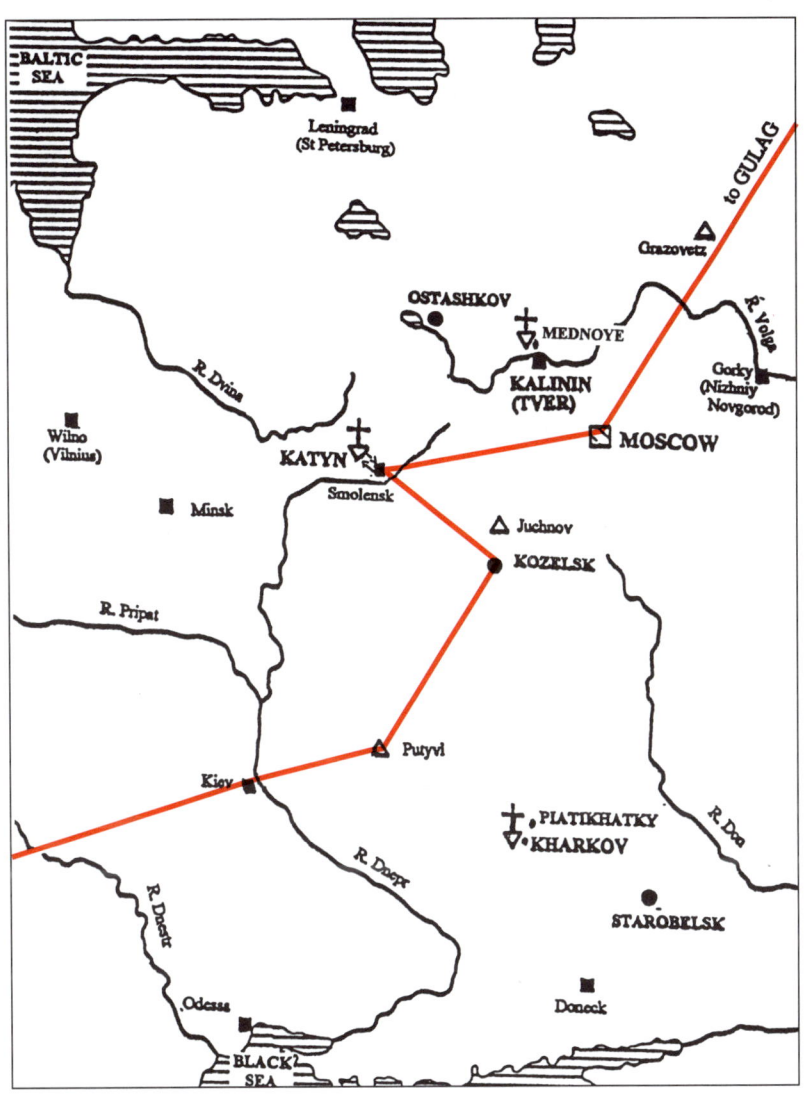

Key
● Polish officers camps   ☦ Places of execution   △ Transit camps

Note
Polish officers from the camp of Kozelsk were executed at Katyn Forest and buried there.

Polish officers from the camp of Ostashkov were executed in the NKVD cellars at Kalinin and then buried near the village of Mednoye.

Polish officers from the camp of Starobelsk were executed in the NKVD cellars at Kharkov and then buried near the village of Piatikhatky.

ROAD TO FREEDOM

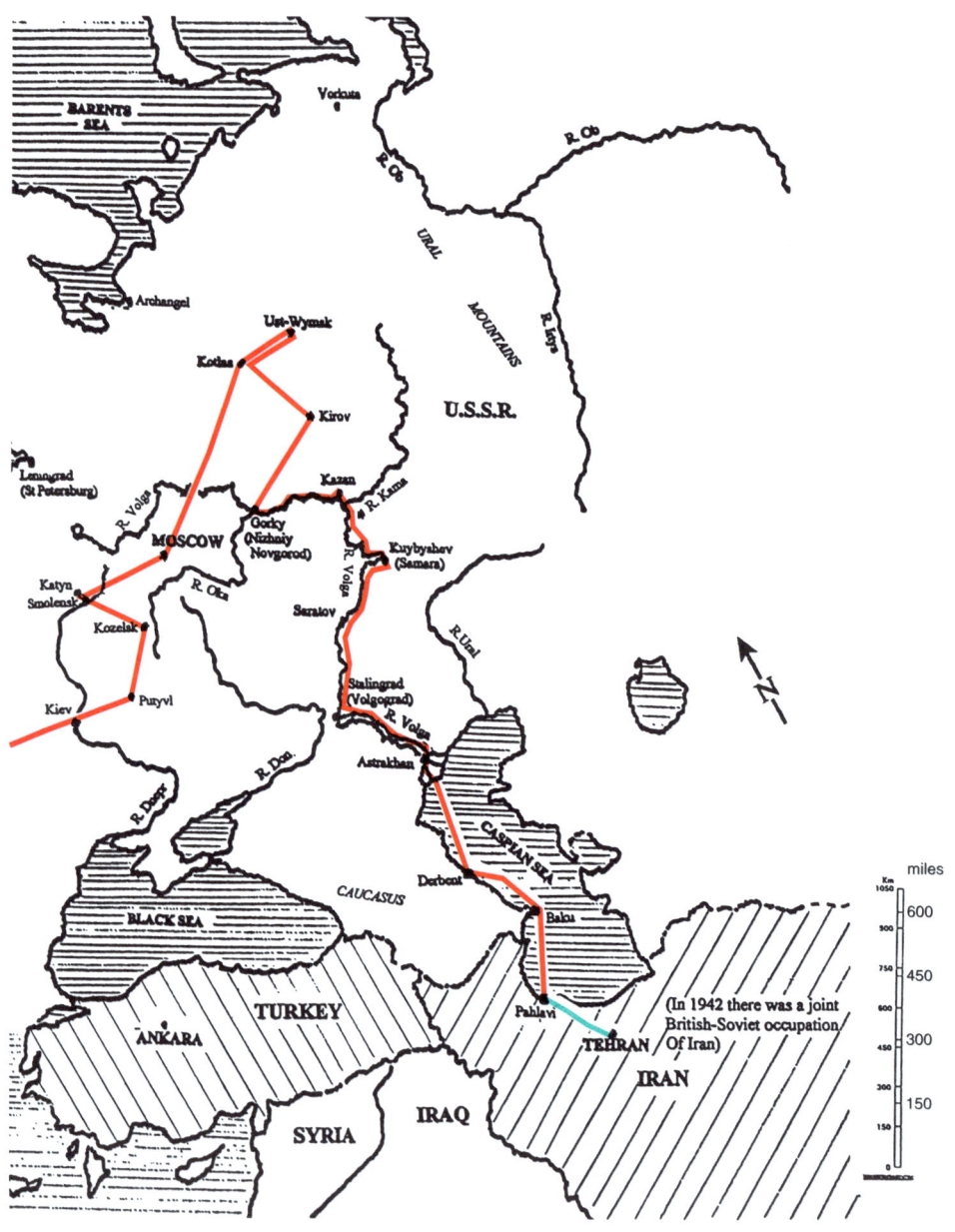

Translator's Note

The book *W Cieniu Katynia* (In the Shadow of Katyn), first published in 1976, is an important historical document that I have translated in its entirety. Additional footnotes and documents bring up to date many previously unknown – yet important – facts, thereby considerably exceeding the scope of the original text.

In the Shadow of Katyn deals with an episode in the history of Eastern Europe during the Second World War, but also encompasses history from well before World War I (1914-1918), through World War II (1939-1945), and includes events more than half a century beyond. Since World War II, the western press and many governments have been very timid in describing the events that took place in Eastern Europe for fear of offending the Soviet Union.

Before World War II, Poland was an independent country and free to enter into any alliances it desired. Poland had a military agreement with France, signed in 1921; and in April of 1939, Poland exchanged with Great Britain reciprocal guarantees of independence and integrity, and at the end of August 1939, a close alliance was signed between Poland and Great Britain. During the Polish-French negotiations in May 1939, France made a commitment that a full offensive, with all the might of the French Army, would be launched on the fifteenth day after the start of the war.[1]

Germany attacked Poland on September 1, 1939. Great Britain, true to its alliance with Poland, declared war on Germany on September 3, and later that same day, so did France; but the immediate military support that was promised never came. In spite of being let down by the Allies, Poland fought the enemy till the very end of the war, having the Home Army in Poland and an army formed in exile under Allied Command. To keep Polish authorities at ease during the first days of September, the Soviet Ambassador to Poland, Nikolai Sharonov, expressed sympathy for the Polish cause and even talked about the possibility of material help from the Soviet Union.[2] Ambassador Sharonov left Poland on September 11, 1939 under the pretext of inadequate communication with Moscow. On September 17, 1939 the Soviet Union, fulfilling the secret protocol of the Molotov-Ribbentrop Pact[3], attacked Poland without declaring war. The Polish Commander in Chief, Edward Śmigły-Rydz, considering the situation hopeless, ordered the Polish Army not to fight the Soviets, but at the same time not to allow themselves to be disarmed, and to withdraw to the neutral countries, mainly Romania and Hungary, and finally to France where the Polish Army could continue to fight Germany on the Western front.

The order of the Polish Commander in Chief, Śmigły-Rydz, caused tremendous confusion in the still bravely fighting Polish Army, and in many cases this order never reached the frontline. In the meantime, the Soviet Army, actively helping Germany to

---

[1] *Polskie Siły Zbrojne w drugiej wojnie światowej* (Polish Armed Forces During the Second World War), London, *Istitut Historiczny im Gen. Sikorskiego* (Historical Institute of Gen. Sikorski), 1951, Vol. 1, p. 99.

[2] *Katyń Dokumenty Zbrodni* (Katyn Documents of Crime), Trio, Warszawa, 1995, Vol. 1, p. 9.

[3] Andrew, Christopher & Gordievsky, Oleg, *KGB The Inside Story*, Hodder & Stoughton, London, 1990, p. 198. The Nazi-Soviet Non-Aggression Pact was signed on 23 August. A secret protocol provided that, in the event of a 'territorial and political rearrangement', Russia was to gain control of Eastern Poland, Estonia, Latvia, Finland and Bessarabia (in Romania).

destroy the remaining Polish resistance, took as prisoners of war 15,000 Polish Army and police officers, and also 250,000 privates and noncommissioned officers. The Soviets declared Poland a "non-existent anomaly" of the Versailles Treaty and proceeded to destroy everything that was Polish in the "conquered" Eastern Territories. The Soviets deported entire Polish families, particularly those of the military, to forced settlements in the vast expanses of Soviet Siberia and Kazakhstan. Men were generally separated from their families and sent to concentration camps in Northern Russia, while women and children were sent to other camps to fend for themselves under very trying circumstances.

Polish officers were placed in three camps: Kozelsk, Ostashkov, and Starobelsk (see map). In April 1940, while the Soviet Union was at peace with the rest of the world, the Russians executed in cold blood practically all of the captured Polish officers. Those from the camp of Kozelsk were killed at the Katyn Forest; those from Ostashkov at Kalinin (presently Tver); and those from Starobelsk at Kharkov; all killed in Soviet territory.

On June 22, 1941, Germany attacked the Soviet Union and German panzer columns swiftly moved deep into Russian territory. Immediately, the British Government and the exiled Polish Government in London, both at war against Nazi Germany, started negotiating with Stalin on how to engage in battle against a common enemy. Consequently, Stalin abandoned his cooperation with Hitler in the joint suppression of all things Polish, and now turned to the Poles for a common front against Germany, in cooperation with the Polish leader in exile, General Władysław Sikorski. Diplomatic relations between the Polish Government in exile and the Soviet Union were established on July 30, and a military convention was signed on August 12, 1941. The USSR agreed to allow the formation of a Polish Army in Russia, to grant amnesty to all Polish internees (for crimes never committed), and to annul the provisions of the Nazi-Soviet Pact regarding Poland.

When the Polish Army started forming in Russia from the ex-inmates of concentration camps, the question arose as to the whereabouts of the Polish officers. It appeared the Polish Army was missing 10,000 army and 5000 police officers. When confronted with the question of their whereabouts, Stalin replied that he had released all of them. The Polish Army was formed 10,000 army officers short, and was transferred to the British Command in the Middle East to take part in the North African and Italian campaigns.

In April 1943, the Germans discovered the graves at Katyn, about 15 km from Smolensk. They managed to unearth 4143 victims, identifying 2815 of them (67.9%)[4], and announced to the world this hideous Soviet crime. Since then, the term "Katyn Massacre" has been applied to the executions at all three camps. The Soviets immediately and brazenly countered by accusing the Germans of this very same crime. The Soviets claimed that the advancing German Army had taken over the Polish POW camp, abandoned by the Soviets, and then murdered the officers in the fall of 1941.

General Sikorski applied to the International Red Cross in Bern, Switzerland, to investigate this massacre. Stalin's immediate reaction was outrage, and he threatened to break diplomatic relations with the Polish Government in exile. Churchill and

---

[4] *Zbrodnia Katyńska w Świetle Dokumentów,* (The Crime of Katyn in the Light of Documents). Gryf, London 1989, pg. 111.

Roosevelt feared that the Alliance with Stalin might be strained because of this situation. In April 1943, even though Germany had already suffered defeat at Stalingrad, it was still a formidable force with which to reckon.

Thus, Prime Minister Winston Churchill and President Franklin Roosevelt, with full knowledge of who really committed the Katyn Massacre,[5] were apologizing to Stalin for the "mistake" Sikorski made of being concerned about the murder of his (Allied) Army officers. In spite of the efforts of Churchill[6] and Roosevelt[7], Stalin broke off diplomatic relations with the Polish Government in exile on April 25, 1943.

After World War II, there was a special conference of the four victorious powers, France, Great Britain, United States, and the USSR, meeting in London between June 26 and August 8, 1945. They decided on methods of procedure for the prosecution and trial of the major European war criminals. The Agreement and the Charter of the International Military Tribunal was established and became the document for the upcoming Nuremberg trials. The Charter laid down the crimes that the Tribunal was to try under the headings: "Crimes Against Peace", "War Crimes" and "Crimes Against Humanity."

Dr. Natalia S. Lebedeva, Russian archivist and historian, points out in her book on "Katyn" that the leaders of the Soviet Union understood they were guilty on all three counts. Therefore, during the negotiations in London, when working on the Charter of the International Military Tribunal, the representative of the USSR stubbornly demanded to add to the above mentioned Charter an amendment that the culpability for the crimes be limited only to the European **Axis Powers**. After intense negotiations, it became apparent that the Agreement was in danger and American Justice Robert Jackson went to Potsdam to consult with the American President [Harry S. Truman]. Eventually, both sides agreed that Article VI would state that the Tribunal was called to judge and punish the main war criminals of the European Axis Powers,[8] effectively giving the Soviets the reprieve they desired.

The Soviet Prosecution, headed by General R. A. Rudenko,[9] with outrageous impudence, brought charges at Nuremberg against the Germans for committing the Katyn massacre, and accused specifically Colonel Ahrens of executing the Polish Army officers. However, to the consternation of the Tribunal, Colonel Ahrens voluntarily appeared and testified at the trials. In spite of the efforts of the Soviet prosecution, the German officer's testimony cleared the Germans of the Soviet accusations.

'When Dr. Hans Laternser, the counsel for the German General Staff and High Command of the German Armed Forces, asked, "May I have the question put to the Prosecution, who is to be made responsible for the Katyn case?" the President of the Court, Lord Justice Lawrence, said, "I do not propose to answer questions of that sort."'[10]

---

[5] Kimbal, Warren, *Churchill and Roosevelt, The Complete Correspondence*, 1984, pp.192-193.

[6] Ibid., Message from Prime Minister to Premier Stalin, 25 April 1943, pp.193-195.

[7] Ibid., Message sent by President to Premier Stalin, 26 April 1943, pp.197-198.

[8] Lebedeva, Natalia S., *Katyń - zbrodnia przeciwko ludzkości* (Katyn - Crime Against Humanity), Dom Wydawniczy Bellona, Warszawa. 1998, pp. 21-22.

[9] Already in Ancient Rome it was recognized that *"Nemo iudex in causa sua."* (No one can be a judge in his own case.)

[10] Zawodny, Janusz K., *Death in the Forest – The Story of the Katyn Forest Massacre*, University of Notre Dame Press, Notre Dame, Indiana, 1962, p. 70.

As a result, the truth about the massacre of this large number of Allied officers was effectively denied for the next half-century.

It is of great historical significance that the International Military Tribunal at Nuremberg elected to ignore this case completely in its findings, and thus the official judgment of who actually murdered a large portion of the Allied Army Officer Corps was not established until the Soviet news agency TASS on April 14, 1990, announced to the world that it was, in fact, the Soviets who murdered the Polish officers.

What is most disturbing about the Katyn massacre is that it was covered up by the very institutions that were especially designed to uncover this sort of crime, to wit:

1) The International Military Tribunal at Nuremberg
2) The Free Press (lying by omission)
3) The Western Allies
4) Much of academia, particularly historians, who failed to properly research the history of the Second World War in Eastern Europe.

Louis FitzGibbon in his book *The Katyn Cover-up* states,
> "At conferences with the Soviets the Western Allies abandoned the lofty principles of the Atlantic Charter and abandoned Poland .... 'It was decided' – wrote Churchill – 'that the issue [of Katyn] should be avoided'." [11]

Then Mr. FitzGibbon continues,
> "But how does one avoid an issue, that affects the conscience of the entire civilized world, as it affects the very conception of law and justice, which are supposed to be the very basis of our civilization...." [12]

This book is the day-by-day account of Polish Army officer, Lieutenant Stanisław Swianiewicz, who was brought to the railway station at Gniezdovo, three kilometers from the executions, and then summarily recalled to Moscow for further interrogation, thereby being spared the execution to which he was now a circumstantial witness. Dr. Swianiewicz was not summoned to the Nuremberg Trials, so that he could truthfully testify at this crucial stage as to the identity of who really perpetrated this heinous crime. For posterity, he does this in this book titled, *In the Shadow of Katyn*.

Witold S. Swianiewicz [Translator, son of Stanisław]

---

[11] Churchill, Winston, *The Second World War*, Cassell & Co., Ltd., 1951, vol. IV, p. 681. "In the trials of Germans at Nuremberg for war crimes the murder of the Poles at Katyn was mentioned in the indictment of Goering and others, who laid the White Book of the German investigation before the court. It was decided by the victorious Governments concerned that the issue should be avoided, and the crime of Katyn was never probed in detail. The Soviet Government did not take the opportunity of clearing themselves of the horrible and widely believed accusation against them and of fastening the guilt conclusively upon the German Government, some of whose principal figures were in the dock on trial for their lives. In the final judgment of the International Tribunal at Nuremberg Katyn is not mentioned in the section dealing with the treatment of prisoners of war by Nazi Germany. Everyone is therefore entitled to form his own opinion, and there is certainly no lack of material in the many books that have been published by the Polish leaders still in exile from their country, and in particular those written by Mr. Mikołajczyk, the former Polish Prime Minister, who joined the first Polish Government after the war, and by General Anders."

[12] FitzGibbon, Louis - *"The Katyn Cover-up"*, London, Tom Stacey Ltd., 1972, p.55.

Stanisław Swianiewicz: 1899-1997

The ancestry of Dr. Swianiewicz is believed to be of Scottish descent and had as its original name: Swan. In the 17th century, Swans settled in the Grand Duchy of Lithuania. Dr. Stanisław Swianiewicz was born in 1899 in Dvinsk, a town belonging then to Imperial Russia, which is now called Daugavpils, a part of Latvia.

Stanisław was primarily a scholar and practically his whole life was connected with various universities. The interruptions in his academic career were the two wars: the Polish-Soviet War (1919-1920), and the Second World War (1939-1945).

In his childhood he attended Russian schools. In 1915, when the German Army approached Dvinsk, the family was evacuated to Orel (Central Russia). During the October Revolution (1917-18), Stanisław studied at the Faculty of Law and Social Sciences at the University of Moscow. As a high school student, he had come under the influence of Marxism, but the tragic realities of the Revolution and Civil War soon dampened this conviction. The terms of the Brest-Litovsk Treaty (signed between Imperial Germany and the Soviets on March 3, 1918) allowed people, who were originally from German occupied territories, to return home. In the summer of 1918, the family of Stanisław again lived in Dvinsk, which was now occupied by Germans.

After the Armistice of November 11, 1918, the Soviets began to occupy Dvinsk once more. Stanisław then became a leader of one of the cells of the clandestine Polish Military Organization.[13] Witnessing many executions performed by the Cheka,[14] his disillusionment with the Soviet system of government was further reinforced. When his cell was discovered in May of 1919, he escaped to the Polish Army, south of Dvinsk, and volunteered to become a soldier in that Army. While still in the army, he enrolled at the Stefan Batory University in Wilno (Vilnius, currently the capital of Lithuania) and attended the lectures during his leaves in the army.

When the Soviets began the invasion of Europe in 1920, he participated in the battle of Warsaw[15] as a corporal in the machine gun platoon. He received a military decoration, *Krzyż Niepodległości,* for his work in the Polish Military Organization behind the enemy lines.

Until World War II, Dr. Swianiewicz was connected with the Stefan Batory University in Wilno. He returned to this university as a student in 1921, and he received the Master of Law degree in 1924. He lectured in economics and after completing his doctoral thesis on Georges Sorel in 1927, achieved his "habilitation degree" in 1931, for which he had published his first book, *Lenin jako Ekonomista*

---

[13] Polish Military Organization [Polska Organizacja Wojskowa, POW]. The clandestine military order formed by Piłsudski in 1914; it spread throughout Poland and helped disarm Germans and Austrians in 1918. Also, it ran Piłsudski's intelligence and special operations network behind the Russian lines, and continued to function in secret during the 1919-1920 Polish-Soviet War.

[14] Cheka: All Russian Extraordinary Commission for Combating Counter-Revolution and Sabotage, (1917-1922), the first Soviet Secret Police.

[15] The Battle of Warsaw also known as "Miracle on the Vistula" fought in August 1920 between Bolshevik armies advancing on Europe and newly formed Polish Army is best described by Lord D'Abernon, who was in Warsaw in 1920, in his book titled, "*The Eighteenth Decisive Battle of World History*". Lord D'Abernon suggests that the Battle of Warsaw could be compared to The Battle of Tours where Charles Martel, in 732, stopped advancing Arab armies from Spain and thus saved Europe from Moslem domination.

(Lenin as an Economist). He was promoted to Chair in Economics in the Faculty of Law and Social Sciences. As a result of research, mainly in Germany, he also published a book on the economic system of Hitlerite Germany. Concurrently with his position at the university, Professor Swianiewicz was Head of the Economic Section of the Polish Institute for Eastern European Research, in Wilno.

When the Second World War was imminent, Dr. Swianiewicz was inducted as a lieutenant into the Polish Army, and fought for four weeks against Germany until the Soviet Army captured him. The author miraculously escaped death twice from the execution squads of the NKVD.[16] First at Katyn, where the murders of the Polish officers were already in progress, unknown to him and the other officers still waiting in the transport train. A written order from Beria had Lieutenant Swianiewicz whisked away from there and had him sent to Moscow for interrogation on the "accusation of spying," after which he was sentenced to eight years of GULAG.[17]

Based on the Polish-Soviet agreement of July 1941, he was finally released from the GULAG in the spring of 1942. It became apparent that Lt. Swianiewicz was the first Polish officer set free (and as it was found out later, the only one), who had been in one of the transports that had mysteriously disappeared from Kozelsk. Realizing that Lt. Swianiewicz might be able to give valuable information about the missing officers, the Polish Embassy delegate immediately put him under guarded protection from possible NKVD "jokes," before Lt. Swianiewicz traveled to Kuybyshev where the Polish Embassy was located and awaiting his report. The second miraculous escape from death was accomplished by outsmarting the NKVD, who slowly but surely were closing in on him again in Kuybyshev.

In the summer of 1942, he managed to arrive safely at the Polish Consulate in Tehrān. There he joined the Polish Army, which was moving in the Middle East under British Command. While still attached to the Army, the Polish Government in exile appointed him as head of the Polish Research Bureau in the Middle East.

In the spring of 1944, Dr. Swianiewicz was called to the Polish Government in exile in London, and he sailed to Liverpool in a British convoy through the U-boat infested areas in the Atlantic Ocean. After his arrival in England, he was put in charge of the Eastern Section of the Ministry which was preparing material for the expected Peace Conference that was to take place after the termination of hostilities.

When the recognition of the Polish Government in exile was withdrawn, he returned to his economic studies. Always foremost a scholar, Professor Swianiewicz served in various positions. In 1948 he became Head of the Depatrment of Economics and Commerce at the Polish University College, London, preparing Polish ex-

---

[16] NKVD – forerunner of KGB. The Soviet Secret Police evolved over the years under various names: in 1917, it started as Cheka, then GPU, OGPU, NKVD, NKGB, GUGB, MVB, KGB.

[17] The acronym GULAG, (*Glavnoe Upravlenye Lagerey*, or Chief Administration of Hard Labor Camps), one of the most horrific types of forced labor camps.

servicemen for the degrees of the University of London, and, afterwards in 1954, he was elected to a Senior Simon Research Fellowship of the University of Manchester where he was engaged in the research of underdeveloped countries. Later, he became an economics advisor to the Government of Indonesia under the auspices of UNESCO, and lectured economics at Gadjah Mada University in Jogjakarta.

On his return to London in 1958, he was elected to a Fellowship of International Studies at the London School of Economics, where he was engaged in the study of various problems connected with the industrialization of the Soviet Union. Already having had scholarly discussions on Soviet economy with the Soviet elite with whom he was imprisoned in the Lubyanka Prison, and having had the exceptional opportunity of acquiring "practical experience" of Soviet economy in the GULAG – fortunately denied to most western scholars – his expertise in Sovietology became unsurpassed. These studies found expression in his book, *Forced Labour and Economic Development*, published in 1965 by Oxford University Press under the auspices of the Royal Institute of International Affairs. In this connection, it should be mentioned what *The Economist* wrote about the author in 1965, after his book, *Forced Labour and Economic Development*, was published.

"Professor Swianiewicz was the last Polish officer to leave Katyn before the massacre. As one of the world's first Sovietologists he was interesting to his Soviet captors. He was interrogated, sentenced to forced labour and released under Polish amnesty. It is a remarkable coincidence indeed that this quintessential experience should have been undergone by an intelligent and open mind, adequately trained in Economics, yet of wide culture and steely objectivity." [18]

Doctor Swianiewicz came to Canada in 1963 to lecture as Professor of Economics at Saint Mary's University, Halifax, and, with an interruption of two years' lecturing at the University of Notre Dame, Indiana, stayed there until his retirement. Saint Mary's University awarded him the status of Professor Emeritus in Economics in 1973, and during the convocation ceremony in May of 1982, he became the recipient of an honorary degree of Doctor of Laws.

In October 1975, the Sakharov Hearings on the violation of human rights in Russia had been organized in Copenhagen. Dr. Swianiewicz was invited to give evidence on the Katyn massacre. Two weeks before the hearings, Professor Swianiewicz was attacked in Shepherds Bush, London, England, and was left unconscious on the pavement. Nothing was stolen from him and the police recorded the incident as an "injury in the street," but it was widely believed that the attack was part of a Russian attempt to 'silence' him before he went to Copenhagen to testify at the Sakharov Hearings. Dr. Swianiewicz recovered from the attack and proceeded to Copenhagen to testify as requested.

In 1976, the Institut Littéraire in Paris published a volume of his memoirs in Polish under the title, *W Cieniu Katynia* (In the Shadow of Katyn), for which the Polish

---

[18] *The Economist,* London, September 4, 1965.

Association of Writers Abroad awarded him the prize for the best Polish book published abroad in 1976.

After World War II, Dr. Swianiewicz lived mainly in England. He was unable to join his family in Poland because of the Soviet Communist system there, and his family was not free to leave Poland. In 1949, his eldest son, Witold, successfully escaped from Stalinist Poland to join him in England. In 1957, after 18 years of forced separation, Stanisław's wife, Olimpia, finally was given permission to leave Poland and they were reunited on the romantic island of Java.

Dr. Swianiewicz was a great admirer of Wagner's operas and enjoyed classical music. His favorite poet was Lermontov, a poet of Scottish origin, and he loved horseback riding and skiing. In 1990, at the age of 90, he visited Poland, after an absence of 51 years, where he was acknowledged for his participation in the Polish-Soviet War of 1919-1920, and awarded the *Krzyż Komandorski*.

He died in Chislehurst, England in 1997, and was buried in Halifax beside his wife, Olimpia.

-1917-

Student **Stanislaw Swianiewicz** in uniform of High School, Orel, Russia.

-1919-

Olimpia Zambrzvcka at 17. This photograph was taken in Minsk (Belarus) a few days before she crossed the Polish-Soviet front line as a clandestine messenger for the (PMO or) Polish Military Organization operating behind the Soviet lines during the 1919-1920 Polish-Soviet War,

-1926-

St Ann Church in Wilno (Vilnius) where Olimpia and Stanislaw were married in September of 1925.

-1930-
- Lieutenant Swianiewicz -
(fifth from right)
during military maneuvers

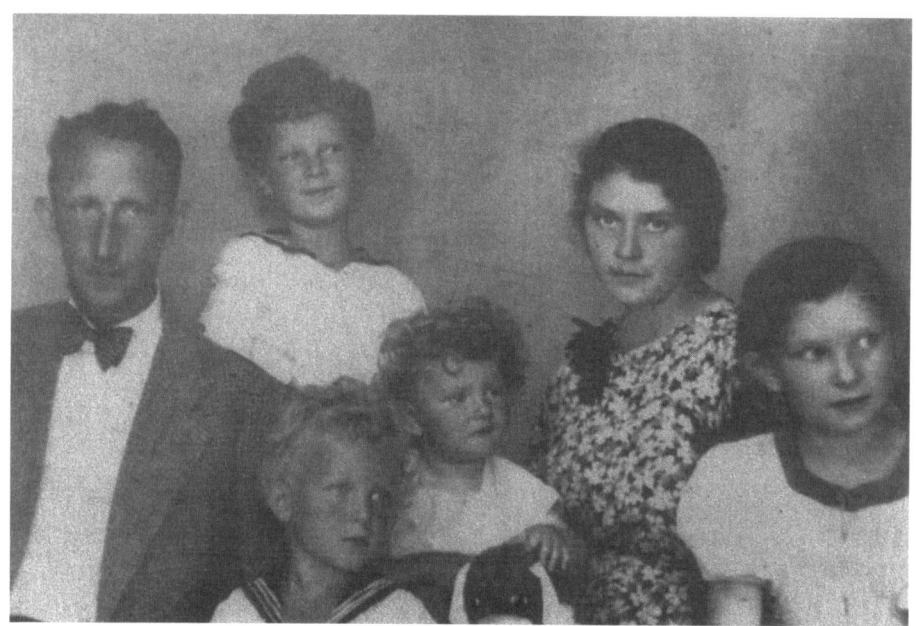

-1937-
The Swianiewicz Family

-1942 -

September, Tehran, Persia (Iran). After leaving the USSR, Stanislaw and General Wolikowski, Chief of the Polish military mission in the USSR, discussing the puzzling question about the fate of the missing Polish officers. The author witnessed the disembarkation of about 300 prisoners from Kozelsk when they were taken from the train at Gniezdovo station, 15km west of Smolensk.

-1943-

Lieutenant Swianiewicz in the service of the Polish Army under British command in Egypt.

-1956-

Dr. Swianiewicz with his wife (center, middle row), entered the service of UNESCO, and was sent as an expert in economics to Indonesia where he became professor of economics at Gadja Mada University in Jogjakarta, Java. Olimpia was finally allowed by the Communist regime to leave Poland and join him here after a forced separation of 18 years. Here honored at banquet.

-1962-

Professor Swianiewicz

-1970-

Stanislaw Swianiewicz with wife Olimpia and son Jerzy, during a visit with Witold, Maria, and their children, in Calgary, Alberta, Canada,

Author's Foreword

The following sketches are concerned with my experiences as one who participated in the Polish campaign of 1939; then, as a prisoner in Kozelsk, in Lubyanka, in Butyrki, in the Soviet concentration camps, and after my release, as a resident of the Polish Embassy of Kuybyshev and as a person who happened to come into contact with the key problems of the Polish Government in London, during the last stages of the Second World War.

Right at the beginning, I must make a statement: I did not witness the Katyn massacre, as was written in some American publications. I am the one surviving Polish officer from Kozelsk, who was taken to the railway station near Smolensk. There I was separated from the transport and sent initially to Smolensk, and then to the Lubyanka Prison in Moscow. I am the only one who was sent to the place of execution and came back, so I can shed some light on how the hierarchy of the NKVD organized the execution.

That stay in the vicinity of the Katyn Forest was an encumbrance on my whole life thereafter. From 1943, when the truth about Katyn became obvious, I have felt that since I – of the more than 4000 Kozelsk officers – was providentially the only one saved from execution and the one who reached the world of free people, I am burdened with certain responsibilities.

What those responsibilities are has not been quite clear to me. After the war, I returned to my profession as a university teacher and researcher in the field of economics. To be able to communicate well in the English language required all my attention. This kept me separated from the main currents of Polish life in immigration and from life in Poland. It seems to me that I have paid my debt to my fellow prisoners in the GULAG by publishing, in 1965, the book *Forced Labour and Economic Development*,[1] which had worldwide reverberations in social science publications.

I have not written very much about the case of Katyn, not counting the number of excerpts of my memoirs which found their way into *Zbrodnia Katyńska w Świetle Dokumentów* [The Crime of Katyn in the Light of Documents].[2] Now, after years of wandering through the universities of England, Indonesia, Canada, and the United States, I have decided in retirement to collect various sketches that I wrote in the last 25 years and to connect them into one logical entity. I hope it will be helpful to some future historians.

These memoirs are very personal, in the sense that I am writing not only about the events which I witnessed, and people whom I met, but also about how I appraised those events and those people at that time. Sometimes in those appraisals, particularly when it pertains to political and military events, I made mistakes. Sometimes I pronounced judgments that in light of today's events seem to be false, but in 1939 and 1941, they appeared to have logical substance. I do not deny that I see many things

---

[1] Swianiewicz, S., *Forced Labour and Economic Development*, Oxford University Press, London, 1965.
[2] Gryf, London, 1948.

differently today from how I perceived them about thirty years ago. But I would like to portray myself as I was in those years.

Before 1939, the chimera of a future Polish-German war tortured me for many years. However, I never considered that war as unavoidable. Because I did consider that war preventable, I think that my experiences will have a better historical perspective if I start by writing about the people and events which left certain impressions on me during my academic journeys to Germany, and my conversations at German universities and academic institutions.

Chapter I

THE APPROACHING STORM

The Polish-German Problem

The summer of 1939 was full of rumors about the upcoming war with the Germans. I was very much against this war, and I was hoping that at the last moment some kind of compromise would be found.

I belonged to the generation that fought for independence. Even before World War I, while a student of the Russian school, I was a member of one of the Polish underground groups. In the final stages of that war, I belonged to the Polish Military Organization. In 1919 and 1920, I served in the army as a volunteer. We were the first generation that achieved independence, while the previous four generations knew only defeat; however, they left us a great treasure of spiritual culture.

Poland, which rose up as a result of the 1918-20's battles,[1] did not quite correspond to my ideals, because I dreamt not about a nationalistic country, but about a multicultural commonwealth. The acquired independence through fighting, which I considered as a good and great treasure, should not now be lightheartedly risked by engaging in another war which, in any case in the first stages, had to bring us defeat. Therefore, I thought that it was necessary to make every effort to avoid war.

From the time when Hitler started intensive rearmament in 1934, and particularly after 1936, when the German military occupied the Rhine district, making it less likely that France would come to our rescue, I was convinced that our chances to repulse any German attacks were very slight. Since the year 1939, when Hitler placed a garrison in Slovakia, our borders with Germany were in such a configuration that we were in a military vise-grip.

A second element to consider was the difference in our industrial potential. If by some miracle we could manage to protect our central industrial district, our production of steel – and that means our ability to produce the necessary weapons to fight – still could not be compared with that of the German Reich. I was relatively well informed about the German military industrial potential because I had written a book – not only as a library study but after my journeys to Königsberg [Kaliningrad], Berlin, Kiel, and Hamburg – under the title, *Polityka Gospodarcza Niemiec Hitlerowskich* (Economic Policy of Hitler's Germany), which was published by the magazine *Polityka* in 1938.

The third element in my thoughts was my conviction that if we were to engage in a war against Germany, it would mean that Russia would occupy our Eastern

---

[1] The author refers mainly to the Polish-Soviet War, which started in February of 1919, as an undeclared war. While defeated Germany was withdrawing its troops from Russia, the Poles came in contact with Bolshevik Armies. This war culminated in a dramatic action in 1920 when the Soviets started a major offensive to conquer the whole of Europe and were crushingly defeated near Warsaw on August 15, 1920, by the Polish Army. A peace treaty was signed between Poland and the Soviet Union on March 18, 1921, in Riga, Latvia.

1

IN THE SHADOW OF KATYN

Territories. Obviously, I could not foresee in which period of the war that would happen and under what pretenses the Soviet Union would enter these territories; as an enemy or as a "friend", as an ally of Germany or, perhaps, as an ally of the West. That, of course, would depend on the circumstances. I did not have any doubts that the entrance of Russia into our Eastern Territories would mean the end of Polish influence over the region and an end of Polish properties. I had nothing against the idea of transferring those territories to an independent Ukraine or Byelorussia, if those countries would rise up, but I did not see any point in giving these territories to Russia.

I was not for maintaining large Polish estates in the Eastern Territories. On the other hand, I realized that medium-sized Polish estates often accumulated great treasures of art and culture, including small libraries, which were proof of the richness of thought, and a longing for the spirit of past generations. I did not doubt the necessity of changing the economic system and, in particular, agrarian reform, but I wanted this to occur in small steps that would not infringe upon the achievements of civilization, which Lithuanian and Ruthenian[2] nobility created under the influence of Polish culture. I considered that those treasures were an important factor in national movements: Byelorussian, Ukrainian, and Lithuanian, to which, in my understanding, the future of the eastern part of the Polish-Lithuanian Commonwealth belonged.

I felt that the entrance of Soviets in those territories would destroy those centers of traditional culture and would destroy the free development of the Ukrainians and Byelorussians. A group of my friends who were associated with the Wilno daily newspaper, *Kurier Wileński* [Wilno Messenger], also supported this idea of free development. This fear of the Eastern Collossus [USSR] should have dictated great cautiousness in our Western policy.

My conviction at that time, that our conflict with Germany would be a catastrophe, was not based on sentiment but on cool reasoning. There were some other people (not too many) whose trends of thought were the same. Most notable among these were: Stanisław Mackiewicz, editor of *Słowo* in Wilno; Adolf Bocheński, a young publisher of *Polityka*; Wacław Zbyszewski, who at that time occasionally visited Wilno; and, of course, Władysław Studnicki, who for many years advocated a treaty with Germany. People who reasoned this way did not have any real influence on our foreign policy and did not comprise a large group.

To have an agreement implies compromise. German tendencies, supported by all German parties, meant return of the Polish Corridor,[3] and this would be looked upon favorably by left-wingers in the West, not excluding France.

In 1928 and 1929, I spent quite a bit of time in Breslau [presently Wrocław],

---

[2] Ruthenians – the forebears of modern Byelorussians and Ukrainians – not to be confused with Great Russians [Muscovites]

[3] Polish Corridor – The piece of northern land next to the Baltic Sea which ran between Pomerania and East Prussia and separated the latter province from the main body of Germany. It was awarded to Poland by the Treaty of Versailles and was Polish territory between June 1919 and September 1939, and after World War II. This territory was historically Polish (i.e., before the partition of Poland in 1795 by Prussia, Russia and Austria) and was inhabited by the Polish majority. No provision of the Treaty of Versailles caused so much animosity and resentment as this arrangement ... also it could be said that it was one of the official reasons, if not the reason, the Second World War started. Also it should be noted that this requirement accorded with President Wilson's 13th point for giving Poland "A free and secure access to the sea."

THE APPROACHING STORM

where in the *Osteuropa Institut* I wrote my book about Lenin as an economist. I also tried to develop a model for a proposed Institute of Eastern Europe in Wilno. I often met the Polish Consul, Mr. Radowski, who did not have an easy life there because of the general hostilities. I was well received in the home of Mr. and Mrs. Radowski, and I often spent whole evenings with them. It was there that I learned about the many problems that Polish consuls had in Germany because of the lack of clear regulations about German transit of people and goods through the territory of Poland to Eastern Prussia. Mr. Radowski was of the opinion that it would be in Poland's best interests to create a situation of transit where Germany would not feel the existence of the Polish Corridor.

There, for the first time, I heard the concept of giving the Germans the right to build an extraterritorial railway and an extraterritorial highway through the Polish Corridor. As far as I could understand at that time, it was a Polish proposal that would satisfy the interests of both sides. It does not mean that Mr. Radowski decisively supported this project, but he considered it as a subject worthy of deeper consideration. As far as I was concerned, I came back from my journey to Wrocław with the conviction that we had to look for ways of settling our differences with the Germans.

After the war, in London I met Stefan Tyszkiewicz, an ex-initiator and chairman of the Polish Highway League. He told me that in the middle of 1930, a project to build a highway in the form of a bridge over the Polish Corridor had been in existence and Polish engineers had designed it. Tyszkiewicz informed Fritz Todt, the inventor and builder of German autobahns, about this project, and Todt became very enthusiastic about it. This project was to be financed mainly by Germany, but it would create enormous possibilities of employing at least several thousands of unemployed Polish workers. It would be an extension into Poland of the German operation, *Arbeitsbeschaffung*, [To Provide Work] in which Todt had played an important part. From the Polish military point of view, the project did not present any great danger because in the case of war, by pressing a button, one could blow up the bridge, which would have had mined pillars. Tyszkiewicz thought, as did Consul Radowski, that everything should have been done so that the Germans would not feel the existence of the Polish Corridor separating Eastern Prussia from the Reich. However, when Tyszkiewicz presented this project to the Vice-Minister of Communications, Piasecki, he rejected it outright, simply for emotional reasons.

In 1934, Marshal Józef Piłsudski[4] surprised the whole world by signing a Pact of Non-Aggression with Hitler for the next ten years. I considered this a high class act of diplomacy to our benefit. This pact was established while negotiations were proceeding to create the so-called "Pact of Four" (France, England, Italy and Germany) which, in actual fact, would have exacerbated Hitler's appetite at the expense of Poland. By signing the Non-Aggression Pact with Germany, Marshal Piłsudski, for all practical purposes, thwarted the "Pact of Four". Besides that, our pact of non-aggression meant reversing the order of German demands. During the times of the Weimar Republic, the

---

[4] Piłsudski, Józef (1867-1935), Polish Marshal, statesman, and the first president (1918-1922). This Polish patriot spent his life fighting for the independence of Poland. Piłsudski was not a nationalist. His vision for Eastern Europe was based on the Jagiellonian tradition of the old Polish-Lithuanian Commonwealth. He achieved independence for Poland in 1918. Józef Piłsudski defeated the Soviet march on Europe in 1920, but his dream of a Commonwealth of independent nations (Belarus, Lithuania, Poland and Ukraine) failed.

IN THE SHADOW OF KATYN

Germans had put the liquidation of the Polish Corridor as a first priority as was mentioned before. As a further step, they were demanding the removal of any barriers of unification with Austria; incorporation of Czech Territories, which were inhabited by a German majority; the abolition of the military constraints of the Treaty of Versailles; and the regaining of their colonies.

The pact of non-aggression did not mean that the Germans were giving up their demands for the Polish Corridor, but it gave a period of ten years to work out some reasonable compromise and influence public opinion in both countries to accept that compromise. Not long after that, as we all know, Marshal Piłsudski died.

Tactics of the Ministry of Foreign Affairs

In the middle of the thirties, Stanisław Mackiewicz and I occasionally went horseback riding in the areas surrounding Wilno. After trotting and galloping, we would slow to a walking pace. Mackiewicz would express his anxiety that our Ministry of Foreign Affairs was doing nothing to prepare some kind of solution to prevent a possible armed conflict with Germany. Mackiewicz was ready to go into far reaching concessions in the case of Gdańsk. From my perspective, I would repeat the concept which was given to me some time ago by Consul Radowski. I considered that this concept could give us a good compromise with the Germans. Mackiewicz maintained that the policy of our Foreign Ministry, as directed by Józef Beck,[5] was full of contradictions that could not be logically explained. In Poland and abroad, Beck's policy was considered as being pro-German. In the international arena, and particularly at the League of Nations, his moves facilitated the German political games. Meanwhile, whenever attempts were made in Polish society to discuss with the Germans ways that would not compromise our differences – and they would try to obtain adjustments – our Ministry of Foreign Affairs stopped those attempts. According to Mackiewicz, the Polish-German relations were loaded with emotions. If we were going to avoid a catastrophe, it was necessary to exercise great tact in making Poles and Germans understand each other's views and to calmly discuss them. The Ministry of Foreign Affairs was cooperating with the Germans in the sphere of highly skilled diplomacy, but it was against fraternization on the level of ordinary citizens.

I was soon to find out the truth of Mackiewicz's accusations. In the spring of 1936 (or perhaps it was 1935), I received a telephone call from the Dean of the University of Wilno, Professor Witold Staniewicz, who said that he had received word through the Ministry of Foreign Affairs that an excursion, consisting of 40 students of the University of Königsberg [Kaliningrad], would be coming to Wilno shortly, under the leadership of a Professor of Economics, Teodor Oberländer. The Dean added that he was not going to be present in Wilno during the time of that excursion, and he asked me to look after the guests and represent the University of Wilno for the professors and instructors who would be members of that excursion. He told me that as an ex-Minister of Marshal Piłsudski, he would not like to bind himself with various declarations that could be interpreted in different ways. He also told me that the administration of the university was going to look after the housing and transportation of the guests.

---

[5] Beck, Józef – Polish Foreign Minister (1932-1939).

THE APPROACHING STORM

I was somewhat surprised by this assignment because I thought that my rank was not sufficiently high enough to represent the university. I was not formally a full professor, but only a lecturer substituting for a full professor who had left to become the Polish Minister of Treasury. However, because of my specialty, I was a counterpart of Professor Oberländer in Königsberg. I had to my credit several major printed publications, and German publishers had favorably reviewed one of them. Among the professors of Wilno I was considered young and inexperienced, but Oberländer, who was appointed a professor after Hitler had come to power, was even younger than I.

I took considerable pains to see to it that Wilno would make the best impression on our guests. We showed them the historical richness of the Grand Duchy of Lithuania; we took them to Troki;[6] we showered them with publications from the Institute of Eastern Europe; we gave them comfortable lodgings at the university residences; and we gave them contacts with the students of the University of Wilno and with students of the School of Political Science, which was functioning in conjunction with the Institute of Eastern Europe. I invited the older members of the expedition to a private dinner at my home in Antokol, where my wife created a comfortable atmosphere. From the appetites of our guests, I came to the conclusion that the talents of our Byelorussian cook were highly appreciated.

I took them also to the cemetery of German soldiers from the First World War. In the administration of the province of Wilno there was a special division which looked after the war cemeteries. The cemetery of Zakret, which was surrounded from all sides by a forest, was very well kept. Above each grave there was a cross with a small plaque on which there was written the first and last name, also the rank and military unit to which the dead belonged. There were several hundreds of those graves. Our guests lined up in military fashion, and at a given signal they saluted the graves in Hitlerite fashion, raising their right hands; we as Polish guides took off our hats. Some of our guests were obviously moved and took lots of photographs. At this point, we demonstrated discreetly to our guests that Poles are chivalrous people, who knew how to respect the soldiers against whom the Polish Military Organization had fought in the last stages of the First World War.

Professor Oberländer emphasized that he had belonged to the Nazi Party even before he was nominated professor. I, on the other hand, stressed my skeptical attitude to all nationalistic extremes and my attachment to the ideals that had guided us in our fights for independence in the last century. But both of us were in agreement that, since Hitler and Marshal Piłsudski signed the Pact of Non-Aggression, our duty was to try not only to understand our respective positions, but also to transfer this sort of attitude toward our students. We were far away from pronouncing principles of abstract pacifism, but it did not mean that we should be fighting. Therefore, as economists of the two most eastern universities in our countries, we could consider the possibilities of economic cooperation in the framework of our geographic region. Professor Oberländer was preparing a book about agrarian overpopulation in Poland. As for me, I was under the influence of Keynesian economics; I was collecting data on how Schacht was financing the liquidation of unemployment. We both agreed that the economists of Königsberg and Wilno must maintain contact with each other.

---

[6] Troki. Presently Trakai. A town by the lake with an island where Witold, Grand Duke of Lithuania, built a big castle and it is now an historical monument.

IN THE SHADOW OF KATYN

At the beginning of the next academic year, I received a letter from the University of Königsberg inviting me to visit Königsberg together with my students. The possibility of visiting historical places in Eastern Prussia was also mentioned. Before answering the letter, I went to Warsaw to ascertain the attitude of the Minister of Foreign Affairs to this initiative. I talked to several high-ranking civil servants in the western section of the Ministry. I was told that the Ministry of Foreign Affairs would not object to my keeping contact with the University of Königsberg, but they categorically pronounced themselves against the excursion of the students. As far as I could understand, the upper echelon of the Ministry of Foreign Affairs wanted to avoid this kind of "fraternization" between Polish and German students. I was of the opposite opinion. I considered that the greater danger in Polish-German relations was not at the high-ranking level but within the hostilities of the common people on both sides, and it was there that we should have been looking for a thaw in relations. There was something in the policy of Minister Beck that I could not understand, but I found a certain comfort in hoping that he did, even though I did not know all the elements of this political game.

My impressions from Germany

I went to Königsberg after all, at my own expense. My main purpose was to become acquainted with the work of the *Institut für Osteuropeische Wirtschaft* [East-European Economic Institute], the head of which was Professor Oberländer. This stay in Königsberg, which lasted about one week, was a very interesting seminar-like experience for me on Polish-German problems as they presented themselves at that moment. During this time, I stayed in the private apartment of our consul, which was situated near the consulate. He was a rather middle-aged gentleman of about fifty, who before the First World War had been a lawyer in Gdańsk. Then he went to America and spent some time as a secretary for Ignace Paderewski.[7] He organized a supper and invited several employees from the consulate. From them I learned about the rather spontaneous emigration of young Germans from East Prussia to western and southern parts of Germany. East Prussia to a certain extent was losing its population. The German Government tried to arrest this process in the form of cheap investment credits for this province. The Polish Consul asked me if I could find out what the real purpose of the *Institut für Osteuropeische Wirtschaft* was because, in spite of all his contacts, he had not been able to do so. Today, living in Canada, I cannot remember his name.

---

[7] Paderewski, Ignace Jan (1860-1941), famous Polish pianist, composer and statesman.

He made his first public appearance in Vienna in 1887, in Paris in 1889, and in London in 1890. His brilliant playing created a furor that went to extravagant lengths and his triumphs were repeated in America in 1891. When World War I broke out in 1914, he dedicated himself heart and soul to his country's service. Subsequently he arrived in the United States giving numerous concerts and championing the cause of Poland. It is assumed that under his influence President Woodrow Wilson alluded to a "united, independent and autonomous Poland" (on Jan. 21, 1917). After the victory of the Allies, Paderewski returned to Poland. On January 17, 1919, he succeeded in forming a coalition government of which he became Prime Minister as well as Minister of Foreign Affairs, simultaneously obtaining for Poland official recognition by various powers and then regulating its international position. In view of some violent opposition he resigned his office on November 27, 1919.

At the onset of World War II, he became President of the new Polish Parliament in exile in France. In December of 1940 he went to the United States, and on June 29, 1941, he died in New York City.

THE APPROACHING STORM

My host organized three receptions for me. The first of them was rather official and included several professors of economics and the pro-rector of the university, who explained to me that the chancellor was called away for military exercises, which in itself characterized the psychology of the rebirth of German militarism. The university professors, who because of their ages had not taken part in the First World War, and therefore did not have military ranks, were called up for exercises, after which they were given the rank of noncommissioned officers. The second reception was a dinner at Professor Oberländer's place where I met his young and charming wife. The third, a supper at the home of Assistant Professor Peter Hans Seraphim, had a family atmosphere. Among those who were present were not only the parents of the host, whose father had been editor of a German magazine for many years in Mitawa in Latvia before the First World War, but also a few other Germans from the old Russian Baltic provinces. They were mostly elderly gentlemen who emphasized that during the old days there was a certain amount of brotherly feeling between Poles and Germans in the Baltic Provinces under Russian rule. Because I was born in old Polish Livonia,[8] we easily found names of common acquaintances that belonged to families who were friends with my mother before the First World War.

Hitler came to Königsberg during my stay there, which provided a chance for me to observe him from close up. My first reaction, which was the same one I had when I visited Breslau and was exposed to Hitlerites there, appealed to my sense of humor. However, it soon changed into an overwhelming fear while watching this spectacle of enthusiastic crowds. It was an example of mass psychopathology. The fact that this mass madness was happening in a nation of great technical and organizing talents, with hard-working people, awakened in me a sad premonition of the future of Europe.

After acquainting myself very superficially with the function of the institute, my conclusion was that a considerable part of its undertaking was devoted to the economics of transport through the Polish Corridor, even though the hosts were not inclined to inform me about the details of their work. I was under the impression that they were working on statistics for some future negotiations for the final settlement of a conflict with Poland (or arguments in settling this matter forcibly). I was pondering whether at home somebody was doing similar studies. If we were to conduct negotiations about the eventual easing of transportation through the corridor, our delegates would need to be armed with appropriate statistics. These negotiations would have to take place because of the nature of our pact of non-aggression with Germany.

I came back from Königsberg on the secondary railway line, Grajewo-Białystok, as the straight railway line Wilno-Kaunas-Königsberg could not be used because of the closed Lithuanian frontier. During my journey, I was thinking about the future of that old geographic region, consisting of East Prussia, Lithuania, and the Polish districts of Grodno and Wilno. It seemed to me that the history and geography would logically compel one to bind those districts into a common economic program. At the same time the differences of economic dynamics were extremely large. In East Prussia I observed a building boom. In Poland there was stagnation and torpor. It seemed to indicate that in the next decade, or perhaps the next few years, time was working against us. On the other hand, we had dynamic population growth, while in East Prussia, in spite of

---

[8] Polish Livonia, presently Latvia

artificially created investment dynamism, the population was diminishing. Logic would indicate that our "hungry people" could flood that desert as a result of some cataclysm whose nature and character no one was able to predict. I was of the opinion that we should try to avoid this cataclysm, primarily to maintain our newly won independence. Secondly, as thousands of other fathers with small children, I wanted to be able to see them grow before a new catastrophe started.

At the beginning of 1937, I received several months' leave from the University of Wilno, and again I went to Germany: this time to Berlin, Kiel, and Hamburg. It did not create a great interruption in my lecturing back in Poland because after my departure, there was a wave of anti-Semitic disturbances. Propagators of this movement demanded from the rector that he institute a regulation that the Jewish students sit on the left side of the lecture halls, leaving the right side free for the members of the ruling nation. The character of this demand illustrates the moral and intellectual level to which political thinking of the Polish young intelligentsia had descended in those years prior to the Second World War.

The purpose of my new journey to Germany was to study the unorthodox methods by which Hjalmar Schacht, Chairman of the Reichsbank – an old and experienced banker, who had little to do with Hitler's ill-inspired mysticism – was able to finance production and liquidate unemployment after Hitler came to power. In 1936, a new book by Keynes,[9] *The General Theory of Employment, Capital and Money*, came out with much fanfare. It gave a theoretical illustration of the financial policy of Schacht. Within a few months there were two translations of that book in Germany. In one of them Keynes himself wrote an introduction, which reaffirmed my impressions.

At the Institute of Kiel, I was accepted with open arms because of the very good references I received from the University of Königsberg. I was told immediately that if I needed materials concerning the policy of Schacht from the *Geheim Archiv*, they would be made accessible to me.

Right from the beginning, I became absorbed in the discussions about this epochal book of Keynes, even though I had great difficulties in grasping some of the mysteries of his theoretical reasoning. In Germany, departures from the methods of classical economics had a rather noisy character and could not always be taken seriously. Some professors of economics lost their positions over this. During my stay in Kiel, the lecturers of that institute organized a *Bierabend* during which they staged a Court to judge *homo economicus*, meaning a psychological type of person who had classical economics as the theoretical basis for his reasoning. This poor man, who once upon a time failed students during examinations, was condemned to death in effigy and his head was cut off during the noisy applause. The result of my studies in Kiel was my book, *Polityka Gospodarcza Niemiec Hitlerowskich* [The Economic Policy of Hitler's Germany], published in 1938 by *Polityka*, whose editor was Jerzy Giedroyc.

In Kiel, I found a room in the apartment of a retired naval engineer. He lived with his daughter, who in the old days would be regarded as an old spinster. The second daughter was a well-known singer in the Hamburg Opera. Her mother was also in Hamburg to chaperone her and so, because of that, there was extra room in the apartment. They took in two tenants: first, a captain in the newly formed naval aviation,

---

[9] Keynes, John Maynard (1883-1946). Famous British economist who revolutionized economic theories.

THE APPROACHING STORM

and the second, myself. Our rooms were adjacent.

Our landlady came about 8 o'clock every evening to bring coffee to my neighbor and a pot of tea for me, and she would stay for about half an hour in our rooms to express her philosophy. The subject was always the same: how to break away from Christian tradition in our way of thinking and behaving. Our landlady was a great admirer of Matilda Ludendorff, wife of General Ludendorff, who during the First World War was Hindenburg's chief of staff, and who in the twenties supported the Hitlerite movement. As a Doctor of Philosophy, Matilda Ludendorff wrote a book propagating the rebirth of the old German pagan religion. Christianity was looked upon in that philosophy as a product of the Jewish spirit. I called this landlady a "bigoted pagan".

My landlord, on the other hand, told me with understandable nostalgia about the old and happy days when, in the present library of the *Institut für Weltwirtschaft*, there was a magnificent club of the old Imperial Navy. In the house there was a considerable private library which was freely available to me. One day I took a hardcover volume of *Buddenbrocken* by Thomas Mann. When my landlord noticed that I was reading that book, he warned me that it would be better to leave it because it was *ein schmutziges Buch* (a dirty book). Thomas Mann, of course, was on the Hitlerite index.

Such was the atmosphere in Kiel, but in Hamburg it was different. Hitler was generally less popular there since the communists apparently had a considerable influence among the dockworkers. In Hamburg I witnessed a very characteristic scene. A German traveler came to a hotel with a suitcase in his hand and started with the usual Hitlerite greeting *"Heil Hitler."* A fat doorman in coattails replied with that great dignity of a sober-minded man, *"Guten Morgen,"* and then began to consider whether there was a free room.

Several times I asked the economists who were publishing research work at that time how they perceived the nonsense of Hitler's anti-Semitism, which did not exist in Italian Fascism. I had the impression that they were rather embarrassed, because deep in their souls they considered it as nonsense or, at least, a great exaggeration. They would say something about Jewish influence in banking and in free trade, and they would quote the studies of Werner Sombart.[10] My general impression was that they considered that we had to come to some agreement with that aberration as a part of a system which, after all, in spite of the prediction of the orthodox economist, was increasing production and liquidating unemployment. Those who were joining the Hitlerite party did not show much enthusiasm for the basic point of Hitler's ideology, which was anti-Semitism. It was difficult to imagine at that time that the outcome would be the gas chambers.

One of the conversations I had in Kiel made an impression on my mind. I spent several hours talking to the leader of the *Hitlerjugend* in the district of Schleswig-Holstein. He recently returned from France and spoke with great contempt about Frenchmen, whom he considered to be morally disintegrating as a nation and lacking any will to play a major role in Europe. It was difficult, to a certain extent, not to agree with him. It was the beginning of 1937, the year before the French, without firing a shot, allowed Hitler to take over the Rhineland, to which Germany had no right, in part

---

[10] Sombart, Werner (1863-1941). German economist, author of widely read history of capitalism. The most controversial aspect of his study is the role he assigns Jews as the chief creators of Capitalism. He is generally considered an apologist for German Nazism.

because of the Treaty of Versailles but also because of the agreement signed by Gustav Stresemann in Locarno in 1925.[11]

It would be considerably more difficult to help Poland and Czechoslovakia in case of a German attack on those countries. It was rather characteristic of the mentality of young Hitlerites that this gift from the French, which in fact saved Hitler, was looked upon with contempt rather than with admiration. The paralysis of the French will toward German rearmament played a great role in convincing the Germans that any resistance of Western powers against the conquest of Europe by Hitler was very unlikely.

It is interesting that several times I met with the opinion expressed by Hitlerites that there were only two nations that they would like to have on their side in the process of rearranging the world along their mode. Those nations were Poland and Yugoslavia, because they both had strong military traditions. At that time, the relations between Poland and Germany looked better than German relations with some other countries. Even when it came to Italy, there was the question of *Anschluss* (joining with Austria) to which Hitler gave priority over German-Polish borders and about which the Italians were experiencing great angst. Marshal Piłsudski was extremely popular in Germany. It was remembered that at the beginning of the First World War the Polish Legion commanded by Piłsudski fought against Russia on the side of the central powers (Germany and Austria); they repeated the compliments about the positive values of the old German Army, apparently given by Piłsudski in Geneva at the League of Nations . It had caused a certain amount of consternation to Mr. Stresemann[12] whose method was to avoid any mention of German militarism.

Just before I left Germany, I was invited for a *Bierabend*. It was given by the Rector of the University of Berlin on the occasion of a lecture about Polish agrarian policy delivered by Professor Witold Staniewicz. During this reception, which included the Polish Ambassador in Germany, Mr. Lipski, I sat next to a major of the German Air Force, who appeared to be a veteran of the First World War. I asked whether he was particularly interested in agrarian problems. His answer was that he represented the Air Force Ministry (Mr. Goering) and that they were conducting intensive studies about the landscape of Eastern Europe. I began to feel very uneasy. Several years afterwards, during the Polish-German War in September of 1939, when I was marching through the town of Garwolin, mercilessly destroyed by the German Air Force, I remembered my conversation with my neighbor at the reception in Berlin.

The striking characteristic of Germany at that time was seeing so many people in uniform, not only the military, but also those of various party formations. At the railway station, you could see a great number of middle-aged men – some with their fat beer-bellies augmented by the brown Hitlerite shirts – who were going for some kind of

---

[11] Pact of Locarno: a series of agreements made in 1925 whereby Germany, Belgium, France, Great Britain and Italy mutually guaranteed the peace of Western Europe, and Germany undertook to arbitrate disputes with Belgium, France, Czechoslovakia and Poland. The Treaties were initiated in Locarno, Switzerland, on October 16 and signed in London on December 1. The Pact was significant because it marked a break from the atmosphere of World War I, and former enemies committed to a peaceful policy amongst themselves. The Pact was in a sense a substitute for the Geneva protocol negotiated by the League of Nations in 1924 but never ratified.

[12] Stresemann, Gustav (1878-1929) German statesman; Foreign Minister from 1923-1929. Signed Pact of Locarno (1925).

THE APPROACHING STORM

exercises. One of my colleagues, a Jew from Wilno who for several years lived in Vienna, told me that in his understanding the particular pleasure of an average German was to march in file and obey orders without any ambition to lead. It was some kind of perverted drive to change human beings into obedient machines. A Russian had to be pushed into the file, while a German jumped into it of his own volition. Hitler satisfied the masses of average Germans with that perverted drive. What I am writing about concerned mainly Prussians, for as far as southern and western Germans were concerned, I had fewer observations. In that respect, the methods of Frederick the Great must have left an impression on the German mentality for many generations. In the postwar German Democratic Republic, the tradition of Prussian drills, parades and mass gymnastic exercises, et cetera, still persisted.

Some sociologists, for example, Aleksander Hertz, who came regularly to Wilno to deliver lectures at the School of Political Science and often spent evenings at my home, maintained that psychologically the present situation in Germany must lead to a war. Stanisław Mackiewicz, who often traveled to Germany and talked to people from many walks of life there, had the impression that Hitler wanted some small war to disarm the psychological situation and to create a belief that the spilling of German blood sanctified this present power of Germany. On the other hand, the average German did not want war and was afraid of it because the memories of all the shortages, which the German population was exposed to during the First World War, were still very much alive.

I left Germany in 1937 with the conviction that Germany, living in hysterical tension, could give the world many surprises, but that war, and particularly a war on Polish-German borders, did not seem to me to be unavoidable. The surprises, I felt, could arise mainly as a result of a specific system, coming from a national socialist revolution. Hitler created what Jerzy Sorel called a social myth; that is, the transformation of political and social values which hypnotized the most active members of society and also did cause a mobilization of the forces of production. The question of whether this picture was real or not, moral or immoral, was not the subject of my economic studies. The main thrust of my book, which I published after this journey, was directed toward the fact of creating the mobilization of the forces of production by means of that myth. I was engaged in this topic more theoretically in my doctoral thesis, concerning the psychological basis of production as understood by Sorel. Obviously I was interested in what kind of consequences the German experience could have on the economy of the world. In the matter of politics, in which I was interested rather marginally, I considered the possibility of a German-Polish War rather diminished after Hitler came to power. Hitler had broken with the spirit of Rapallo[13] – the quiet German-Soviet military cooperation connected in great measure with the treaty signed in the Italian seaport, Rapallo, during the international economic conference in Genoa in April 1922. Hitler's priorities were as follows: independence for German rearmament, *Anschluss* and Sudetenland, and also ideological war against

---

[13] Treaty of Rapallo signed April 16, 1922. During the conference of Genoa, which was designed to consider the economic relations of the participating powers with Soviet Russia, the Soviet delegates showed no desire to resume relations with the Allied and Associated powers, but to the consternation of the latter signed an agreement with Germany after secret negotiations. The main result of the Rapallo Treaty, secret at the time, was that Germany was able to produce in Russia new prototypes of arms, e.g. tanks, forbidden by the Treaty of Versailles.

communism. Therefore, he automatically put on the back burner the question of Polish-German borders.

Consequently, I was in agreement with Stanisław Mackiewicz, that the first half of the thirties was the most proper time to start some kind of voluntary attempt to obtain an agreement about a transit through the corridor and about the status of Gdańsk, in order to remove causes of possible conflicts in the future. Hitler was still too weak to talk with us from a position of strength, and that gave us a stronger negotiating position.

We have to remember that Hitler made German society hysterical. The question of emotions played a great role. Our press and particularly the so-called Red press read by the masses were extremely anti-German and caused an increase in tension. If the Polish Government intended to conduct negotiations, as one could conclude from the Pact of Non-Aggression, then it should have at least temporarily introduced some discreet censorship of the press. In the meantime, the government seemed to be pleased that the spontaneous anti-German feeling came from the rank and file, embracing small shopkeepers, workers, and academic youth. This attitude of the government was completely incomprehensible to me.

After returning from Germany and for the rest of 1938, all my free time from university engagements was dedicated to working on my book about the economic policy of Hitlerite Germany. From the French press, which occasionally came into my hands, I deduced that an opinion was formed in the West that in case of war against Germany, the real help could only come from Russia, and that Poland, as an ally of France, should allow passage of the Soviet Army through her territory. Some of the Polish Francophiles seemed to support that idea. The atmosphere of the eighteenth century, when the Russian Army would march at will through the territory of the Polish Republic, seemed to be reborn. I was convinced that Marshal Śmigły-Rydz[14] would never agree to that. But in this case, we would have to do everything we could in order to remove the possibility of military conflict with Germany. However, we had to remember that during the Kościuszko Insurrection,[15] the Polish-Prussian Alliance did not produce the expected results.

The threat of the partition of Poland seemed to appear in the distance. There were two basic roads that could lead to the partition of Poland. The first would be a military alliance between Germany and Russia. This had been favored by some Prussian generals during the spirit of Rapallo, with General von Seeckt, creator of the German Reichswehr after the First World War, in the lead. The second would be an alliance between Russia and the Western powers against Germany. In the first case the Soviets would march into Poland as enemies, in the second case as allies. In both cases

---

[14] Śmigły-Rydz (1886 -1941). A soldier who distinguished himself in the Polish-Soviet War of 1919-1920. He became Commander in Chief of Polish Armed Forces after the death of Marshal Piłsudski (1935). In 1939, after Soviets invaded Poland, he issued the fateful order to the Polish Army not to fight the Soviets but to withdraw to France through neutral Romania and Hungary in order to join the French Army and continue to fight against Germany. He himself crossed into Romanian internment. Later he extricated himself from Romania, went back to German occupied Poland, and died there.

[15] Kościuszko, Tadeusz (1746 -1817). In 1776 Kościuszko entered the army of the United States as a volunteer and brilliantly distinguished himself. George Washington promoted him to the rank of a colonel of artillery and made him his adjutant. Upon his return to Poland, Kościuszko took charge of a Polish uprising against Russians (1794). After an initial success at Racławice he confronted superior Russian forces. Kościuszko had gone through great pains to avoid provoking Austria or Prussia. Nevertheless, Prussian troops had joined the Russians and Kościuszko's forces were readily defeated.

the final result would be exactly the same. The task of our diplomats would require intelligence, intuition and genius. I was under the impression that neither Śmigły-Rydz nor Beck realized the burden of responsibility that fell upon them. They were running away from reality, hiding behind a smokescreen of Poland's invincibility. My guess was that Beck sincerely believed that in this manner he was executing the will of Marshal Piłsudski.

I was inclined to believe we should seek a solution in some kind of an alliance of countries in Middle Europe, where naturally Germany, as the most populated and richest country, should have played first fiddle. This view of mine was, to a certain extent, a reflection of the opinion which I had heard from Władysław Studnicki during my student years. However, at the same time I realized that Germany, as long as it was subjected to Hitlerite psychology, could not fulfill that role. In the concrete situation of the years 1937-1938, my concept could have only a purely theoretical meaning.

Stanisław Mackiewicz had seen the situation somewhat differently. He considered that some sort of stability in Europe could be achieved by creating an axis, Paris-Berlin-Warsaw, and that our diplomacy after the Pact of Non-Aggression with Germany should have moved in that direction in spite of ideological differences which had divided Hitlerite Germany and France of the Third Republic.

Expansion without Resistance

In 1938, changes in the international situation were occurring at a galloping pace. In March came *Anschluss* (German occupation of Austria), which Italy could not counteract because of its engagement in the Abyssinian [Ethiopian] adventure. Mussolini had to put a good face on it. Intervention by France and England was out of the question due to the paralysis of will that spread throughout French foreign policy and military command. When I spent two months in Vienna in 1935, I was convinced of Hitler's systematic preparation to penetrate various Austrian walks of life, but I never imagined that everything would go so smoothly.

In September, the question of Sudetenland exploded. In Munich, there was a meeting with Hitler and the Prime Ministers of the great European powers, to which the party most interested in the outcome – the Czechs – were not invited. France, who had a treaty of mutual support with Czechoslovakia, blatantly broke that treaty by agreeing to transfer Sudetenland to Germany. The British parliament accepted the Munich agreement with enthusiasm.

Our policy at that time gave a duplicitous impression. At the time when Czechoslovakia was obviously falling apart, the move to regain Zaolzie[16] was justified. However, we could have done it in a way that would have been less humiliating to the Czechs, even if we had our own accounts to settle with them for their horrible and abhorrent behavior in 1920, when Poland was bleeding in its fight against the Bolshevik hordes which Lenin had sent to conquer the whole of Europe.[17] During the Sudetenland

---

[16] Zaolzie, a piece of land contested by Poles and Czechs.
[17] During the Polish-Soviet War of 1920, when the Soviet Army was preparing to take Warsaw ... under the slogan by Marshal Tukhachevsky's order of the day: "Over Poland's dead body lies the way to worldwide conflagration", Czechs were cooperating with him by stopping transports of armaments from the West to Poland. Notwithstanding, Poland defeated the Bolsheviks in the battle known as "Miracle on

crisis, the policy of our foreign ministry gave the impression that we had some secret understanding with the Germans. Today, we know that this kind of understanding did not exist.

As far as Sudetenland was concerned, I listened to a speech given by Hitler on the radio in which he announced to the whole world that Sudetenland was his last territorial demand in Europe. That gave the impression that the territorial conflict between Poland and Germany, which was postponed by the pact of non-aggression to the year of 1944, could be settled.

In March of 1939, new events took place which gave me more of a shock than the *Anschluss* and Sudetenland incidents. The main event was the occupation of the whole Czech country by Hitler, in spite of his glorified assurances – given a few months earlier – that Sudetenland was his last territorial demand in Europe. The second one was the speech given by Stalin during the Party Congress that I immediately interpreted as a discreet offer in the direction of Hitler. I began to suspect that there might be some subtle connection between those two.

After receiving the news that the Germans were already marching toward Prague, I telephoned Prof. Witold Staniewicz to ask him how he saw the situation. He told me that in his understanding, this was an initial move by the Germans for some big military action; however, it was not clear yet in which direction this action would go. I completely agreed with him. By occupying the Czech country, the Germans became masters of all of Middle and Southern Europe. Because of their well-known industrial plants in Skoda, the Czechs had a large center of military production and had become one of the best-armed nations in Europe. Furthermore, the Czechs kept an arsenal for the so-called "Little Entente", to which, besides Czechoslovakia, Romania and Yugoslavia belonged. This Little Entente, even though it was directed mainly against Hungary, presented an important link in a system of agreements, which France had organized after the First World War, to stop the possibility of the rebirth of German militarism. Now this entire arsenal had fallen into German hands.

In my book about Hitlerite economic policy, I provided much information about the German economic penetration of the Balkans and the Near East. Now to that economic domination, a strategic military position had been added. The time had passed in which – as I thought, justifiably or not – we could negotiate with the Germans on the basis of equality. The occupation of the Czech country by Hitler also had other repercussions, which he probably did not expect. It caused a breakthrough in English public opinion, which then considered that war with Germany was inevitable and that the Treaty of Munich had been a huge mistake of French and English diplomacy.

Almost simultaneously with the march of Hitler into Prague, came the speech given by Stalin at the 18th Congress of the Communist Party of the Soviet Union. In that speech, in addition to all kinds of "anti-fascist" declarations, Stalin said that capitalist countries intended to push Hitler into incursions against the Soviet Union, and he expressed the hope that it would not happen because there really was no reason for conflict between Berlin and Moscow. All of that looked like some kind of proposition. I could not imagine that Stalin would make such a speech if some behind the scene contacts had not been activated. "The Spirit of Rapallo" – which had seemed to be stamped out and buried with the execution of Marshal Tukhachevsky and a number of

---

the Vistula River" and Europe was saved.

THE APPROACHING STORM

Soviet Generals in 1937 – was being reborn again.

Soon after, in April, came a pronouncement from Prime Minister Chamberlain that Great Britain was ready to help Poland, Romania, and Greece, if these countries were to be attacked by Germany and were to demonstrate the will to defend their independence and borders. For the moment, I had the impression that our negotiating position [Poland's] with Germany had been strengthened. I had read Hitler's book, *Mein Kampf*, in which he considered that Imperial Germany had made a great mistake having been drawn into military conflict with the British Empire during the First World War. But if the danger of war were to be taken seriously and if Poland were to negotiate with Germany, it had to be prepared to make some compromises. However, only a government that is based on a broad coalition of leading political parties could accept responsibility for such a compromise. Regretfully, Poland at that time had a semi-dictatorial government of prominent politicians from the Legion,[18] even though it did not have the complete approval of the whole Legion. This government was supported on the one hand by the army and on the other by the administrative apparatus that organized the elections to the legislative bodies. In reality, as often happens with such governing systems, they are dependent on public opinion and are incapable of making unpopular decisions. Any kind of compromise with Germany, however small and unimportant, would have been extremely unpopular at all levels of Polish opinion. In 1939, the main Polish political parties and influential lobbies were extremely anti-German: Endecks,[19] socialists, the national radical youths, Jews, communistically inclined radicals, the Catholic clergy, et cetera.

I maintain however that if, in the spring of 1939, a "coalition government" had come into being, then the representatives of the Endecks and socialists – if they had been given all the facts concerning power relations in Middle and Eastern Europe – would have had enough sense of responsibility to consider limited compromises with Germany, before it immersed the whole country into war and unavoidable foreign occupation. The creation of such a government should have been the responsibility of President Mościcki. However, President Mościcki appeared to be completely under the influence of the clique of advisors of Marshal Śmigły-Rydz.

At the beginning of 1939, when news started to spread that there was tacit German pressure concerning Gdańsk and an autobahn through Pomerania, I expressed my opinion in favor of a coalition government to Mackiewicz; but his attitude was rather negative. Mackiewicz was a very sober and logical critic, but he tended to lose his drive and ability to reason when it was necessary to put forward positive concepts. Now I regret that at that time I did not publish an article defending this concept. I have no illusions that it would have influenced Polish opinion, but today I would have left some kind of document for historians who are researching those days. The whole Polish nation, in all strata of society, was ready for extreme sacrifices. It was, however, advisable that those who would have undertaken those dramatic decisions would have represented the broadest spectrum of political opinion.

---

[18] The reference to Legion means the Polish military formation, which fought on the side of Austria during the First World War.

[19] Endecks: A Polish political party [National Democracy].

IN THE SHADOW OF KATYN
Doom over Poland

Foreign Minister Beck went to London to sign the military agreement with England. Coincidentally, I learned about Beck's negotiations in London during the same radio newscast that also brought the news of the suicide of Walery Sławek. I do not think that those two facts – that is, the signing of the military agreement with England and the suicide of Walery Sławek – were somehow interrelated, but in my memory they became interwoven into one picture of the harbinger of the coming cataclysm. This does not mean that I was against the alliance with Britain – quite the contrary – at that time, I considered that the alliance with Britain should be exploited. But the suicide of Sławek during the same days created in me a completely irrational feeling of some kind of doom hanging over us.

Walery Sławek, a true knight and an old fighter from the P.P.S. [Polish Socialist Party] whose whole life was dedicated to the service of the idea of rebuilding the grandeur of the old independent state, closest friend of Marshal Piłsudski (Sławek believed him to be a genius), twice Prime Minister and, after the new constitution, generally considered to be a candidate for President, shot himself in his apartment in Warsaw, leaving only a letter for President Mościcki in a sealed envelope. That letter, as far as I know, was never published. I never heard that Sławek had any objections toward foreign policy. He had, as far as I knew, full confidence in Minister Beck. The reason for this step was probably related to internal policy. Why he would choose to end his life on the day that one of the most important events in the life of reborn Poland was happening in London – the signing of the Military Agreement with Great Britain – I am at a loss to explain.

According to people who were close to Sławek, he had some kind of vision of the approaching cataclysm. It appears that Marshal Piłsudski, before his death, left Sławek some instructions on how to possibly avoid the dangers that were hanging over Poland. Apparently, Sławek had a guilt complex about the fact that he could not turn these events around and therefore he committed suicide.

Personally, I found this interpretation convincing since it reaffirmed my own impression of Sławek. Besides occasional meetings, I happened to have had a very interesting conversation with him in the first half of the thirties and thereby discovered his mode of thinking. It was at a supper given in a private home in which, besides the host, six people took part: the then present Prime Minister Janusz Jędrzejewicz; two former Prime Ministers, Walery Sławek and Aleksander Prystor; my friend Seweryn Wysłouch (then assistant professor of history and law at the University of Wilno); and Henryk Dembiński, known leader of the radical wing of Wilno youth who was already at that time strongly inclined toward communism. We spent more than four hours in a very free exchange of viewpoints concerning very important subjects.

The principal question hanging over that select group was this: What direction should Poland take? The external situation at that time was not threatening, but the constitutional matters were not solved. The normal selection of the governing elite through the system of parliamentary elections was skewed, and that worried Sławek. He maintained that the main task of the system, established after May 1926, was to give Poland a new constitution, so that when Marshal Piłsudski would be gone, the internal matters of Poland would be regulated by laws derived from that constitution. He

THE APPROACHING STORM

considered that political parties were unimportant because the judicial system would regulate Polish life after Marshal Piłsudski. Sławek repeated that several times: "*Poland will be ruled by the law*." The reason why I considered this sort of thinking as Utopian was that you must educate people to respect the law.

Meanwhile the system, for which Sławek was to a certain extent responsible, made the administration accustomed to bending the law in order to obtain electoral results that would ensure an easy passing of the new constitution. Expectation that the political parties must disappear was also Utopian because no one, especially Marshal Piłsudski, wanted to create a totalitarian system. A new constitution would not mean removal of political parties, but a new framework for their activities. Besides all that, all three distinguished participants who belonged to the governing body posed the question that troubled them most in the conversation: To what kind of young team should the Polish government apparatus be transferred? Coming out of that evening, I had the impression that the system of government, after May 1926, was leading us into a blind alley, and I thought that Sławek, consciously or unconsciously, also had that same feeling.

Sławek was the most reliable executor of various moves of Józef Piłsudski during the time when he wanted to rebuild the old Commonwealth as a federation. Beck became the Minister of Foreign Affairs when Piłsudski had already resigned himself to the idea of a nationalist Poland but still wanted to negotiate a position of world power. In 1919, I witnessed several officers, among them Marian Zyndram Kosciałkowski and Eugeniusz Olejniczakowski, who were engaged in composing a few sentences on a present for Captain Walery Sławek. These were the words: "To commemorate our common work on building a Great Lithuania." Soon afterwards, Piłsudski delegated Colonel Sławek to negotiate an agreement with Petlura.[20] I do not believe that Sławek shared anti-German emotionalism with most of the Poles. He seemed to like to get into discussions with Władysław Studnicki on the subject of Polish-German relations, and even as a Prime Minister, he found time to write personal letters on this subject. One of those letters Studnicki even read to me.

A few days after the tragic news of Sławek's death, in a crowd following Sławek's coffin through the streets of Warsaw, I found myself walking beside Professor Stefan Ehrenkreutz, who hosted that memorable supper with Sławek. My impression was that I was taking part in some kind of mysterious event. Some scenes from the drama of Wyspiański[21] went through my mind. I could not help feeling some kind of fate was hanging over Poland. The signing of the military agreement with England could fulfill the role of catalyst. It might have turned away the threatening cataclysm or it might have accelerated it. And here came into play the logic of a Greek tragedy.

As a response to our military agreement with England, Hitler announced that he was breaking off the Pact of Non-Aggression with Poland. Stalin, in the meantime, removed from the office of commissar for foreign affairs, Maksim Litvinov, a Jew, who was considered to be an advocate of an agreement with Western democracies, and he appointed in his place Molotov, a typical party bureaucrat, who was undoubtedly a Russian. Molotov was close to Stalin personally and was much better suited to deal with Germany. The world had moved even so much closer to the full resurrection of

---

[20] Petlura. A Ukrainian Ataman who fought against the Bolsheviks on the side of Piłsudski.
[21] Wyspiański, Stanisław (1869-1907). Painter, illustrator, poet, and dramatist.

IN THE SHADOW OF KATYN

the spirit of Rapallo.

Immediately, after breaking off the Pact of Non-Aggression, the German press became very anti-Polish. In the first place, they pointed out the injustice done to German minorities in Poland in exactly the same way as it had been done a year ago toward Czechoslovakia. Most of the Polish press became even more anti-German. They began to talk of the necessity of liquidating East Prussia. I even heard this opinion expressed by a high official in the Ministry of Foreign Affairs. Tourist excursions began to arrive from Germany to Gdańsk [Danzig], apparently consisting only of petty officers dressed in civilian clothes. They were the cadres preparing for some kind of a *Putsch*. In response to this, Poland started sending "corresponding units of tourists." At any time this could have erupted into a conflict between those tourists.

There was a lot of talk about the activities of the so-called German Fifth Column. In Wilno, where there were no large German settlements, I could not observe any kind of anti-government activities, and I am not sure if they could be noticed in other parts of the country. A total of 800,000 Germans lived within the boundaries of the Polish State. Many of them, if not the majority, were very impressed with the military and economic power of Germany after Hitler's ascendancy as leader. The assumption that they were capable of forming an organization for gathering intelligence or preparing acts of diversion in case of war was quite logical. After the Non-Aggression Pact, these Germans had been manifesting their loyalty toward the Polish State. In case of war in the East, one would have been able to count completely on their loyalty, as German settlers demonstrated in Central Poland in 1920. But after the breaking of the Non-Aggression Pact by Hitler, they were becoming an element that had to be watched very carefully. Those were the realities of the population structure of the Polish State, which every sensible Polish politician should have taken into account. The activities of German settlers, who were citizens of the Polish State, should have been watched very carefully, but inciting one part of the population against the other did not make much sense. Furthermore, any excesses could have led to an increase in tension.

The news of the concentration of German forces on the Polish border caused more anxiety. The Germans seemed to be doing it quite openly, so that people near the border and the travelers coming from the West could observe it without difficulty. It is hard to imagine that the German Chiefs of Staff would have decided on the high cost connected with this concentration of forces and weaponry without actually planning to use it.

Moods in Poland

The threat of war did not create any great anxiety in Polish society at large. It was assumed that it was not a real threat. All the time, one could hear the expression "a war of nerves." It was believed that Germany would decide not to go to war because the West would intervene. In Poland there was a general belief in the might of France, whereas in Germany it was believed that France was demoralized and incapable of any military effort. People were not aware of our desperate need for anti-aircraft defenses. Some people were hoarding food due to the experiences of the First World War, but this did not cause any great upsets in the market. The greater part of our society did not completely realize the difference between our military potential and that of Germany,

THE APPROACHING STORM

and consequently some Poles took on a very "cocky" mood.

To be truthful, there were a few who realized the disparity in military capabilities, but they did not expect total war. You would hear expressions of the sentiment that Hitler did not want the complete destruction of the Polish State, whose military and administrative apparatus could be useful to him to further realize his plans in the East. According to this point of view, it was assumed that he would want to achieve certain limited objectives. For example, taking over Gdańsk and the district of Pomerania in order to compel us to negotiate, with the Germans talking to us from a position of strength so they could impose their conditions on us. It would mean that Hitler would treat Poland the same way as Bismarck treated Austria during the war of 1866. It would have been logical if Hitler were actually getting ready for a military campaign against Russia. Then, our eastern borders would have given him convenient bases to launch an attack on Moscow and also launch an attack on the Ukrainian breadbasket and the Soviet industrial centers in the South. To support this idea, that Hitler had some plans toward Poland, was the fact that his demand of Gdańsk and the autobahn across the district of Pomerania [the Corridor] looked rather moderate in comparison to what was said in the Weimar Republic about solving the Polish problem.

On the other hand, the thaw in the Soviet-German propaganda war, which came after Stalin's speech at the 18th Party Congress, brought new elements into the situation which were difficult to evaluate at that time. People close to Trotsky[22], and there were many of them among the Jewish youth, were talking about a possible agreement between Hitler and Stalin to undertake common action against the British Empire. It seemed to me that no one in Europe wanted a war to erupt. I was hoping that at the last moment something would occur which could reverse the catastrophe. The Soviet Union was obviously interested in stimulating capitalist countries to attack each other. It would be consistent with the teachings of Lenin that the Soviets would not want to be directly involved in a war against one of the great powers.

In July 1939, before going on holidays, I went to S. Mackiewicz to ask him how he saw the situation. He was shocked concerning the general optimism of victory in a military conflict with Germany, should it occur. He had spent an evening in the milieu of one of the Polish political factions in Warsaw, where he heard an opinion that we were experiencing a singular historical opportunity to have Germany crushed; therefore, it would be a great mistake if our diplomats tried to appease the conflict with Germany. Beck, who was one of the most unpopular ministers of all the governments established after the 1926 *Putsch*, was now being considered almost a national hero.

Mackiewicz and I pondered over the upcoming waves of pro-Russian sympathies. Whenever one would ask the question, "In case of a war with Germany, would the Soviets attack us?"

The standard answer was, "Russia is big and does not need any additional territories." Politicians, journalists, high-ranking military, and university professors

---

[22] Trotsky, Leon, né Lev Bronstein, (1879-1940), leader of the Bolshevik revolution. He played a part hardly less important than that of Lenin in organizing the Bolshevik Revolution in 1917 and he became People's Commissar of Foreign Affairs in the new Soviet Government. Later on, Chicherin replaced him and Trotsky took over the Commissariat of War. After Lenin's death (1924), his influence declined, and he was ousted from the party by Stalin and exiled. He continued to agitate as an exile and was sentenced to death in his absence by a Soviet Court in 1937. He found asylum in Mexico, but in August 1940, a suspected Soviet agent assassinated him, supposedly on orders from Stalin.

said this; these were the people who really should have known the history of Poland and its partitions. This statement that the Soviets were not interested in our Eastern Territories, I heard as late as June 1939 from one of our most promising political economists, an agricultural expert who was well acquainted with Soviet Russia, but did not know the history of that country. Władysław Studnicki, more or less at the same time, heard this statement from Professor Kutrzeba, Chairman of the Polish Academy of Sciences and from Stanisław Estreicher, leader of the Stańczyk group of Kraków [Cracow].[23] Mackiewicz told me about his recent stay with the Radziwiłłs [prominent members of Polish aristocracy] at Nieśwież. They all expected Soviet help in the event of war against Germany. He told me particularly about one of the priests with whom he had a long conversation, and who was especially optimistic about the cooperation of Soviet Russia in case of military conflict with Germany. Two years later, when I was in a Soviet labor camp, I read an extremely interesting and well-written book about the conquests of Genghis Khan. That book described that in the periods immediately preceding the conquests of certain territories, they sent harbingers who would talk discreetly to the population at large about the benefits which would be brought by the incoming Tartar hordes.

Genghis Khan had an excellent, organized apparatus of quiet propaganda, which weakened the will of the victims to resist being conquered. In 1939, among the Poles, the Germans were doing everything to increase the will to resist, while the Russians were doing everything to weaken it. Why this subversive pro-Soviet propaganda had such success is not easy to explain. You must remember that this was the period immediately after the great show-trials and the great purges when countless thousands of people were sent to labor camps of which Poles had been generally aware. The mentality of Polish society immediately preceding the war of 1939 could be a subject of very interesting sociological and psychological studies.

Amidst Polish society, against these currents of patriotism, cockiness, readiness for all kinds of sacrifices, yet completely without any understanding of reality, one person stood out who, as has happened numerous times in Polish history, was a man of small build and inquisitive mind, of generous heart and extreme courage: Władysław Studnicki. In June of 1939, he published a book about the coming Second World War in which he fairly accurately foresaw the future event.[24] The book was confiscated before it had a chance to appear on the shelves of the bookstores.

In the summer of 1939, I spent my vacation in a small section of my father-in-law's estate that belonged to my sister-in-law. It was right on the Soviet border where the railway line Minsk/Mołodeczno crossed the international border. The Polish border corps had taken possession of part of the house, and the closest neighbor was a collective farm that occupied some lands of that estate, which were left behind on the other side of the border.[25] Barricades of barbed wire and constant military sentries separated us from that neighborhood on both sides. People from the Soviet side were frightened, and nobody had the courage to approach the barbed wire in order to

---

[23] A conservative group formed in the 19th century in Kraków. They criticized Polish uprisings against the occupiers as impractical in prevailing circumstances.

[24] Studnicki, Władysław, *Irrwege in Polen*, published by Göttinger Arbeitskreis, August 1951.

[25] In 1921, after the peace treaty was signed between Poland and the Soviets, the Polish-Soviet border was settled. As a result, about fifty hectares of the estate were left on the Soviet side.

THE APPROACHING STORM

exchange a few words with us. So it was a very quiet corner because communication with Polish centers was not easy. The railway in that part did not function and the nearest town, Radoszkowicze, was eight kilometers away. There was no telephone and no radio receiver on the estate. During the period of hay cutting and harvest, hardly anybody went to the little town; therefore, newspapers arrived several days late. Among the green hillocks and fast running streams, it was a calm, charming sort of Shangri-la. That year the crops were excellent, and I thought about what Adam Mickiewicz wrote in *Pan Tadeusz* [his most important work], about the year 1812,[26] in more or less the same vicinity.

For the feast of the Assumption of Holy Mary, we used to go to the fair in Plebania, twenty kilometers away, which was not far from the town of Krasny. I noticed certain improvements in the village's standard of living because many boys from the village arrived on bicycles. A few days later, the Polish border guards with the help of the local girls organized a play, illustrating the heroism and the inventiveness of the local youth in discovering Soviet diversionary tactics.

After a few days of glorious unwinding, tranquillity, and happiness because of a good harvest, I was overcome by anxiety. It looked like the calm before the storm. I decided to go to Wilno to find out what was really happening in the world. I made arrangements with my wife that the next day she should wait by the telephone in the closest post-office, which was in Radoszkowicze.

Before I left, I had a conversation with a very charming lady. She came from Volhynia,[27] a person with a higher agricultural education, who was well liked for her extreme kindness and tactfulness. I said to her, "It seems to me that the threat of war is imminent."

She answered, "Obviously, the war must come."

I asked her, "Why 'must'?"

"Because the Germans behave in such a way that they have to be brought to some kind of order," she replied.

"Are you really imagining that our regiments from Łuck, Lida, and Mołodeczno will march to Berlin to punish unruly Germans and then, full of glory, return to their original station?"

The answer was, "Obviously!" This meant that any other result – of a conflict with the powerful Third Reich – my sympathetic conversationalist could not imagine.

The place where my family was staying was 150 kilometers away from Wilno, but the journey to Wilno took almost a whole day. First, one had to travel ten kilometers by horse to the railway station called Olechnowicze, the last station on the railway line between Wilno-Minsk. Then, one had to travel by train to Mołodeczno where one had to wait for the connecting train from Stara Wilejka. Therefore, I arrived in Wilno when it was already evening. While I was traveling by droshky through the Wilno back streets, so dear to my heart and beautified by the orange rays of the setting sun, I pondered what kind of fate awaited those endearing town walls.

---

[26] Polish poet Mickiewicz wrote about the year 1812. "The year which peasants called 'a year of bountiful crops' and soldiers called 'a year of war'."

[27] The district of Volhynia [Polish name "Wołyń"] was part of Poland in 1939, presently part of Ukraine.

IN THE SHADOW OF KATYN

After arriving at my home in Antokol,[28] I left my luggage and immediately took the bus to the newspaper offices of *Słowo*. Stanisław Mackiewicz[29] was sitting in his editor's office, deeply moved. News of the Ribbentrop-Molotov Pact had just arrived. He did not need to explain to me what it meant. We both realized that the drama of our times had begun. After a while, quite in agreement, we analyzed the situation; Mackiewicz decided to ring up the press department of the Foreign Ministry in Warsaw and asked for their reaction to the news. The answer came. The Foreign Ministry maintained that the security of Poland from the East was not diminished by this Pact because we had a Pact of Non-Aggression with the Soviet Union, concluded in 1932 and again recently confirmed in 1938. Mackiewicz ridiculed the other party on the line without any restraint, accusing them of not realizing the seriousness of the situation. He decided to call London, where in anticipation of coming events *Słowo* had sent a special correspondent in the person of Wacław Zbyszewski. Eventually, we got a connection with him. Zbyszewski answered that he was too moved by the recent events that happened so suddenly in the international arrangements that he was, for the moment, speechless. It was clear that he was seeing everything in the bleakness of despair. It seemed to me that I completely understood his psychological state.

At about eleven o'clock at night, I went to the publishing house of *Kurier Wileński* which was, to a certain extent, the competitor of *Słowo*, where I belonged to the group of editors. At the entrance I met a lady, well acquainted with the editors of the newspaper, a student of fine arts, a talented painter and mother of two children. Happiness was beaming from her face; her big black eyes were sparkling with elation. I asked her, "What makes you so happy?"

She grabbed me by the hand, "You mean, you don't know? Hitler made an ass of himself." I felt my eyes popping out of my head from astonishment, and I was simply overcome by fear. To my mind came the saying of Zagłoba that human stupidity, just like God's mercy, does not have any limits.[30] My sympathetic conversationalist, visibly shaken, asked me, "Am I talking nonsense?"

I tried to explain to her that this "manner of behavior" had already been attempted by Prussian generals in 1921, and that it will be little joy to us what people will think of Hitler's inconsequential policies when, in a few days' time, Soviet tanks were going to move through our towns and villages.

---

[28] Antokol, presently Antakalas (a district of Vilnius).

[29] Mackiewicz, Stanisław, editor of a newspaper in Wilno, not to be confused with the earlier mentioned Adam Mickiewicz – the well-known Polish poet of the 19th century.

[30] Zagłoba. A well-known fictional comedian in Polish literature by Sienkiewicz.

Chapter II

MOBILIZATION

The next morning, as previously arranged, I phoned Radoszkowicze. I told my wife that she should take the children that same day and move away from the Soviet border to Wilno. I met them at the railway station late in the evening. I had a very difficult night and I was bothered by nightmares. I dreamed, among other things, that I was somewhere in Latvia (the place where I was active 20 years ago in the secret military organization) on a small railway station surrounded from all sides by Soviet troops, and at any moment the Soviet *Czerezwyczajka* [1] [Cheka] would start to arrest all the people at the station.

I woke up with a tight feeling in my chest. The sun's rays were coming through the shutters in our small house in Antokol, where the style of life and furniture were of the Wilno tradition. My wife was sleeping near me with a serene expression on her face. Birds were chirping in the surrounding garden. Again the ominous political news came to my mind, but I tried at the same time to convince myself that nothing horrific had happened as yet. The morning looked exactly the same as many other summer mornings in this house in which, through the many years, I found so much contentment, joy and happiness, and so much rest after various escapades behind the borders of my "country" which was the county of Wilno.

When I switched on the radio during breakfast, instead of the normal broadcast, I heard some ciphered codes being given. They were most likely mobilization orders; however, officially the mobilization was not yet declared. When I went out on the street, I learned there was no bus service because all transportation had been requisitioned for the transfer of troops. Therefore, we had to walk to the center of the town. On my way I saw many freshly and urgently mobilized junior officers driving in droshkies who were going to their regiments. When toward midday I phoned home, my wife informed me that I had received a draft card ordering me to immediately report to my regiment for active military service. To a certain extent it was a surprise to me. I was almost 40 years old. The last time I was on military exercises was in 1931, eight years earlier, when I finished a commanding officer's course. I was not familiar with the tactical changes in the small units that had to be implemented because of technical changes in the armies of our main neighbors. I was never trained in how to fight tanks. I had no idea of how to use anti-tank rifles, which apparently had to be assigned to each company. I did not know how to operate a movable radio station, even though each regiment had to be equipped with this. I had four children of which they must have been aware from my files. I did not represent the type of officer who needed to be inducted at the beginning of mobilization; however, I had a certain amount of frontline experience from the years of 1919-1920. I had expected that if war were actually going to break out, I would be called up during some later stage of its development.

I immediately returned home, changed into my uniform, and packed the most necessary things in my rucksack and small suitcase. I attached my handgun, leaving my

---

[1] The first Soviet secret police created by Lenin and run by Dzerzhinsky (a Polish nobleman), the forerunner of present KGB.

IN THE SHADOW OF KATYN

saber at home, considering that this item, necessary in times of peace whenever I was reporting to the regiment's commander, must be completely useless in a real war.

I prayed for a while with my wife and children. Then, I told them that if war really came, I wondered whose fate would be more difficult: mine, fighting in the frontlines; or theirs, in a town that had experienced both German and Bolshevik occupation during my youth.

Afterwards, I went to the center of town where my father lived, being retired from the railroad service. My morning depression had disappeared. Saying goodbye to my father, I had the feeling that I was entering into a world of great adventure. I felt anxious, but also felt the joyful excitement that one feels when in a spring sun one is skiing in mountains prone to avalanches. It occurred to me that if the adventure were to really happen, then I had seen my father for the last time.

Next, I went to the chapel of *Ostra Brama* [Aušros Vartai],[2] which was on the highway leading to Nowa Wilejka [Naujoji Vilnia], where my regiment was stationed. After a short prayer, I left the chapel deciding to stop the first military vehicle going in that direction. Just then, a motorcycle with a sidecar appeared, driven by the rather obese Captain Nowicki, from the 13th Cavalry Regiment. He was temporarily assigned to the staff of the 19th Infantry Division to which my regiment belonged, and delivered me in less than half an hour to the headquarters of my regimental command.

At the headquarters the sergeant, who was accepting the incoming, called-up reserves, looked into the files and brought out my card where it was written that I should immediately accept the command of the Supply Company and conduct its mobilization. A sealed envelope was also handed to me, which contained detailed instructions for my activities during the next thirty hours. Only after perusing the instructions did I fully realize what an animal the Supply Company was.

I had to look after the supplies for all kinds of extra units attached to the regiment, which were more numerous than what we had in 1920. These included sections of accompanying artillery, sections of anti-aircraft guns, outfits of scouts consisting of cavalrymen, cyclists and motorcyclists, platoons of pioneers, and a communications platoon. For all these units I had different responsibilities, and it was not always possible to intervene in all of their cases.

In the field I had to command the Regimental Supply Company, which was not an attractive function in a war with an enemy having definite air superiority. Furthermore, neither our regiment nor our division had any anti-aircraft guns, which should have been supplied to us. Only afterward, I found out that anti-aircraft guns of Polish production, which I had seen myself in the autumn of 1938 when I accompanied Vice-Premier Kwiatkowski while visiting the Polish central industrial district, were exported to England. On the outbreak of the war, the Polish fighting units, towns, and railway junctions were to feel the tremendous shortage of anti-aircraft artillery.

My company was situated in a village about three kilometers from Nowa Wilejka. In the next few days and nights, I often galloped to the regimental command to conduct various organizational matters. I was in excellent physical condition and this gallop gave me real joy. I began to forget all about my pessimistic analyses of the general situation. I was visited once by a commanding officer of a scout company, whom I had often met before when skiing in the hills between Wilno and Nowa

---

[2] A famous chapel in Wilno, situated in a sharp corner of the old defense wall around the town.

MOBILIZATION

Wilejka. When he told me that he recently acquired the news that we were going to march through Lithuania in order to attack East Prussia, and that the Lithuanian Government had agreed to let us through, I was inclined to believe him, instead of thinking the information was journalistic spinning. Generally, my psychological attitude had turned around. Some kind of trust was awakened in me to everything that was coming as an order from above. I did not have time to ponder over the mistakes of the government; however, I was irritated by the shortcomings in our mobilization. I was giving in to a general enthusiasm and a belief in our final victory. But... if we could not win the military campaign in confrontation with the German Reich, it would still be necessary to manifest the will of the Polish Nation to defend its independence. As far as this was concerned, all of the people in my surroundings, beginning with the conscripts coming from far away villages all the way to the regimental command, our attitude could not have been better.

The human resources that were arriving had great enthusiasm to work and to fight, but I had my doubts whether they were sufficiently prepared to confront tank and air attacks. Even though I had to command the Supply Company, recollection of the 1920 situation came to mind when supply company soldiers were forced to attack, as in the famous battle near Wkra, on August 15 of that year. The horses arriving through mobilization were not in too bad a condition, but the carts coming through the same route were in desperate shape. It was a surprise to me that in our mobilization warehouses we did not have a sufficient number of military carts, the production of which did not require foreign currency.

After a few days our departure time was established, and the whole town knew approximately when that was to occur. During that appointed late evening, when I was conducting my company's boarding on the train, among the crowds of people I noticed my wife and our two older children on the sidewalk. To board the troops took several hours. The wife of one of the noncommissioned officers took my children so they could sleep at her home, promising that she would bring them back at four o'clock in the morning when the train was apparently scheduled to leave. My wife stayed all the time by the railway station looking from afar at our activities. Close to three o'clock in the morning, we were told that the transport would leave in a few minutes. I jumped out for a while to embrace my wife. By no stretch of the imagination could one have predicted that our next meeting would take place eighteen years later at the airport in Jakarta, where I would be staying as a British citizen in the service of the United Nations. The great adventure or the chain of unimaginable adventures had begun.

To my surprise the train moved not west, in the direction of Wilno, but southeast in the direction of Mołodeczno. My first impression was that we were going to protect our eastern border. That was a task for which our division was especially trained. In 1930, when on military maneuvers, I had heard that the 19th Division of Infantry was a protective division; that is, a division that was to be used to protect the boundaries of the country so that mobilization of the main forces could be conducted. It would also be politically logical.

To leave our eastern border without any protection except a thin thread of borderline watchtowers would be equivalent to inviting Russia to enter our territories after some internal agitation, initiated by Soviet agents. If, however, the Soviets were forced to conduct a few days of heavy fighting with the Polish defense division, Stalin

IN THE SHADOW OF KATYN

would have surely hesitated, as an attack on Poland in those conditions would too obviously break the non-aggression pact, which was well known all over the world. It cannot be said, as it would appear from the telephone conversation of Stanisław Mackiewicz, that the non-aggression pact had no meaning. It certainly had if it were supported by the will of defense. In my opinion, we did not have to fight for immediate victory, but for honor and to emphasize our will to maintain independence in this war that had started to ignite. We had to manifest this will in an easterly as well as in a westerly direction.

During our journey, I did not go to the stuffy railway carriages of the second class, destined for officers; in fact, with several noncommissioned officers from my company, we arranged our sleeping quarters in the carts standing on railway lorries. The soldiers were adept at arranging blankets for us. It was a warm but very dark August night, as it usually is at the end of summer in the Wilno surroundings. The sky was full of stars. I was very tired and fell asleep almost immediately. Upon awakening, I saw that it was already well after sunrise. Everywhere on our way through the Oszmiana and Mołodeczno districts, numerous groups of peasants cheered us on. On the stopovers, women brought milk and fruit and did not want to receive any payment. Enthusiasm, which took hold over the whole of Poland, spread also into the eastern provinces inhabited by people speaking mostly Byelorussian.

In Mołodeczno, the locomotive moved from the front to the tail of the train, and shortly we moved in a southwesterly direction toward Lida. My assumption that we were moving to protect our eastern border proved to be wrong. In peacetime the 19th Infantry Division, that means the old Lithuanian-Byelorussian Division, was located in the triangle Nowa Wilejka (85th Infantry Regiment), Mołodeczno (86th Infantry Regiment), and Lida (77th Infantry Regiment). Now, we simply went around the triangle. Probably the line from Wilno-Grodno was clogged by transports of the First Division of Legionnaires, which were stationed in Wilno and most likely were also moving west.

In Lida, I found out that in our transport there was not only the command of our regiment, but also the command of a whole division and at least part of the division's supplies. On the railway platform, I met Colonel Tadeusz Pełczyński, who recently had become commanding officer of the 19th Infantry Division. We were well acquainted. He was somewhat surprised to see me in the uniform of lieutenant in one of his regiments. He invited me to the command carriage where he introduced me to General Kwaciszewski, who was known in the army as a great expert on heavy machine guns. From various conversations that I had at this time, I found out that we were moving west, and if the war started, our division would be attached to the supreme commander.

Shortly after, we moved in the direction of Baranowicze toward Warsaw. I returned to my cart on the lorry where I stretched myself comfortably with a book in my hand. In the eastern railway station in Warsaw, there were many ladies with baskets full of sandwiches and jugs of tea, coffee, and cocoa. Unfortunately, our transport stopped for only a few minutes and we moved further beyond the Vistula River in a southwesterly direction. I do not remember the exact name of the station where we disembarked. From there we marched a long time during the night. I only remember that after sunrise, we bivouacked in a large field on the outskirts of the town of Łowicz. On one side of the field there was a wall above which there was a towering, sturdily

MOBILIZATION

built church. I had a great desire to visit this town, famous for its handicrafts, but at any moment we were expecting further marching orders.

Colonel Pełczyński appeared among us. To his question about what I was doing, I answered jokingly that I was studying the problems of war economy from the bottom, and I was thinking mainly of the inadequate state of our carts and harnesses in the infantry supply units. In my understanding, pre-war Poland could afford to have better equipment. In this way, we engaged in a conversation about my studies of the economic policies of Nazi Germany, and especially the way in which the German rearmament was financed. Colonel Pełczyński, former Chief of Polish Intelligence, had been very much interested in my studies. We did not know at that time that there was someone else who was equally quite curious about my studies and had been carefully observing my moves in Germany. It was the Soviet Intelligence, as I found out a year later when I was an inmate of the Lubyanka Prison in Moscow.

Shortly after, the order to march was given. After several hours of rest and a bountiful breakfast, we moved forward in a tranquil atmosphere. The war had not yet begun. It was the 31st of August 1939. I do not remember the names of the places where we stopped for the night. The platoon of accompanying artillery and my company settled themselves in the buildings close to a big brewery. At night, a fire started in the large neighboring barn where a freshly cut crop was stored. Six horses died in the fire, the complete team of horses of one of the units of the accompanying artillery. We considered it a bad omen. It could be assumed that this fire was caused by sabotage, in other words, the work of the Fifth Column.

After sunrise, we observed several bombers flying west in close formation. It seemed as if they were German bombers returning from their mission; however, we did not know yet that the war had started. Some of us had encouraging thoughts, that it was our echelon flying toward the enemy territory. Shortly, I was called to the regimental command. The aide-de-camp informed me that a while ago he received a telegram that German panzer columns had crossed the Polish border. He communicated the order of the regimental commander that all the carts and horses should be camouflaged and that the people should not be on the streets without reason. The war had become a fact.

Chapter III

FROM PIOTRKÓW TO KATYN

Piotrków Trybunalski

For the next few days, we marched at night in a southerly direction. During the day, the sky was crisscrossed with white lines left by German observation planes flying at high altitudes. Some moves we had to make during the daytime; therefore, we needed to be very careful that the carts and people were well camouflaged. The German Air Force observed us, but did not attack.

On the fourth of September, we found ourselves in the woods surrounding Piotrków Trybunalski from the south and northeast. Our command expected that our first contact with the enemy would occur in this region. General Kwaciszewski arrived at one point and had a rather long conference with our Regimental Commander, Lieutenant Colonel Kruk-Śmigła. Several other officers and I stood outside the building awaiting the outcome. Then, the regimental commander gave a briefing to the three battalion commanders and to me as the commander of supplies. I believe that it was the fifth of September. Today, after so many years and without a map, I do not remember all the details.

The general disposition was that the regiment had to form a defense line on the outskirts of the forest northeast from Piotrków: the Second and Third Battalion on the first line and the First Battalion in reserve. I was ordered to keep my supply unit a little bit further to the east among the dense bushes. In the forest clearings there were stations of the 19th unit of light artillery (that means this unit of field artillery was attached to our regiment). Our section of accompanying artillery, under the command of Lieutenant Andrzejkowicz, was also being prepared for action. As far as I understood, our task was to prevent any attempts of the enemy to surround Piotrków from the north. The 77th Infantry Regiment and the Cavalry Brigade from Wilno (consisting of three regiments: the 4th, 13th, and 23rd) represented the reserve for this group with the intention of striking the enemy columns from the side, moving from the south.

September the 5th of 1939, turned out to be a rather difficult day in my short and unexpected function as an officer actively engaged during the September campaign. The enemy had knowledge that some of our units were hidden in this forest, which was north of Piotrków. Several times the air force bombarded the forest, making lots of noise, but little damage was done. The small fighters that were diving over the forest were more of a nuisance, chasing even single people with machine guns if they showed themselves in the clearings on forest lanes. I had to discontinue using the horse as a means of travel, because it was easier to spot a mounted person from above than one on foot. I was going down a narrow forest lane from the regimental command to my company when, suddenly, I noticed a German fighter overhead. I dove into the nearby bushes when a series of bullets sprayed from his machine guns. Luckily, none of them hit me. The situation created problems of sending food to those units whose provisions were part of my duties.

FROM PIOTRKÓW TO KATYN

By evening, we could hear sporadic gunfire coming from the south. It looked as if the enemy attacked Piotrków from the south and the 86th and 77th Infantry Regiments were defending it. From my perspective the situation eased a little because low flying enemy aircraft stopped bothering us; apparently, they were being used for different tasks. There was no difficulty in sending dinner to the units that were stationed and waiting for action. Enemy tanks were breaking into our territory, and artillery stationed close to my position opened fire, which meant that the Second and Third Battalions of our regiment had taken up the defense. My telephone connection with the regimental command stayed intact.

By sunset, soldiers from the 86th Infantry Regiment, who had survived the fight over Piotrków, started arriving. Some were wounded. They were coming in small groups, and, from their rather confused stories, it became clear that the ability of our infantry to counter a massive tank attack – overrunning our hastily made field fortifications – was almost nonexistent. The only weapon that our infantrymen could use was a hand grenade; many were using it with almost suicidal determination. The only force that could have stopped this avalanche of tanks would have been a strong artillery barrier. Individual artillery units of the 19th Regiment of light artillery, attached to various regiments, could not provide this barrier. The battle of Piotrków Trybunalski was undoubtedly very heroic and, as such, must be noted in the annals of the Polish Army. I could not determine whether or not the German infantry entered Piotrków behind the tanks.

After sunset, I heard the rumbling of tanks and the buzzing of engines east of the place where my company was located. There was no doubt that some motorized units were moving on the Piotrków-Wolborz Highway, a distance of about one half a kilometer from where I was stationed. We began to hear more distant noises of tank units that were moving on the western parts of the forest. Therefore, the woods in which we were located were being surrounded. I reported this by telephone to the commander of the regiment. His answer was that he was well aware of the situation and that he had already ordered the company of Captain Bychowiec, which consisted of part of our reserve, to secure our location from the northeast; that is, from the side of Wolborz. Furthermore, he instructed me to set up an observation post at the eastern edge of the forest to observe the highway. Obviously, a strike into the tank column moving toward Wolborz could have caused great confusion among the Germans, but in order to do that we needed to have had loads of anti-tank weaponry and artillery which should have been previously aimed onto the highway. Our reserve battalion, which was located one half a kilometer from me, would have been powerless.

About three o'clock in the morning, I received a telephone call from the commander of the regiment during which he told me that he had decided to break through the ring surrounding us, before sunrise, and that the point of exit for this operation was going to be the position of my supply carts. He ordered me to reorganize my company into a fighting company, using all the available arms we had on our supply carts. The carts, with all the other provisions, would have to be abandoned. At the same time, he told me that the telephone lines would be wound-up and that he, with the rest of the units, would be marching to our position.

Soon Lieutenant Wacław Urbanowicz arrived, an experienced professional officer, who in peacetime was commander of the Supply Company, but now belonged

IN THE SHADOW OF KATYN

to the regimental staff. He had with him a unit of about 15 men and the office carriage, on which there were the Regimental Colors. Soon after, the First Battalion arrived under the command of Captain Pawłowski; then, the Scout Company under the command of Captain Wiścicki; and finally, the platoon of pioneers under the command of Lieutenant Rekść with other elements of the 19th Division of light artillery. Lieutenant Urbanowicz told me that Lt. Colonel Kruk-Śmigła went to the position of the Second Battalion and was going to bring it to the assembly point.

Lt. Urbanowicz also informed us that General Kwaciszewski, during the inspection of the units of the 19th Infantry Division that had been spread out over a wide area, had fallen into German hands. It is very likely that he was the first officer of this division, who, in the process of this unusual war, became a German prisoner of war. The first officer of the regiment who was killed in action was Lt. Andrzejkowicz, commander of the section of the accompanying artillery that had conducted firing from a rather exposed observation post. The fate of Colonel Pełczyński was not clear; however, it was rumored that, somewhere, somehow, he had been surrounded by a German patrol. His accompanying soldier, who brought the colonel's horse to the place of assembly, was not able to say anything about Col. Pełczyński's fate.

We waited for almost two hours for the arrival of the other regimental units and Lt. Colonel Kruk-Śmigła. After sunrise, in complete daylight, Captain Pawłowski took command of everybody assembled and gave the order to march along the route previously ordered by Lt. Colonel Kruk-Śmigła. The platoon sent to take over the village, which was positioned northeast of our route, reported that the village was completely free of any German units. We crossed the highway Piotrków-Wolborz without any difficulty. We did not see a single German tank; the sky showed no sign of any German planes. It was only afterwards that we found out that Lt. Colonel Kruk-Śmigła had fallen into German hands.

The situation appeared to be as follows: In the evening of the fifth of September, and during the following night, the powerful German tank formations had broken through our almost archaic defense system and marched northeast in the direction of Skierniewice and Warsaw, without particularly worrying about the Polish units which were left in the district of Piotrków. The opportunity of acting against German supply lines was still open to us, but we were all bound by the orders spelling out the direction of retreat from this trap. The higher officer who could ignore the routine of the general staff and create an independent action was Col. Tadeusz Pełczyński, who was somewhere in these woods but without any communication with our large units.

We marched toward the east and crossed the Pilica River without major difficulties; afterwards, all of us hastened off during the entire night to Spała, to where the divisional headquarters had been transferred. At Spała, the Chief of Staff, Lt. Col. Tadeusz Rudnicki, gave us the orders to proceed toward Maciejowice and cross the Vistula River in that vicinity. Only Captain Pawłowski and his battalion, along with some light artillery guns belonging to the 19th Division of light artillery, managed to reach Maciejowice and marched over the bridge before it was burned. The other units were forced to cross the river at different points.

After crossing the Vistula River, we found out in Garwolin, ravaged by the German Air Force, that the military commander there was Major Nowakowski, originally commander of the Third Battalion of our regiment. Lt. Urbanowicz and I

FROM PIOTRKÓW TO KATYN

reported to him. He ordered that Lt. Urbanowicz, with two noncommissioned officers, should take the Regimental Colors to Lida where, apparently, the staff of our regiment was stationed. The remainder of men and I were to stay here to be at his disposition. He announced at the same time that he was given command of the regiment. He relocated me in the forest near Garwolin and ordered me to form regular companies from incoming men. There I formed two companies. Garwolin had sufficient military equipment and supplies; so, very soon we had everything we needed.

After two days, however, I received an order from Major Nowakowski to march toward Lublin in order to join with other units of the division which, according to him, were also moving in that direction. We caught up with these units which were already on the other side of Lublin on the fifteenth of September, and I reported to Lt. Col. Rudnicki.

"It is good that you managed to reach us," said Lt. Col. Rudnicki. "The division, organizing itself from the remnants of the 77th and 85th Infantry Regiments, is going to form one combined regiment. There are also remnants of the 86th Infantry Regiment here with Col. Peszek. We are going to fight. Tomorrow you report to Colonel Nowosielski." And he showed me on a map the place where I should report at sunrise.

Long marches on horseback followed. Comfortably rocking in the saddle, I pondered over the conclusions that I had drawn from the experiences of Piotrków. Those experiences completely confirmed my pre-war convictions that neither technically nor organizationally were we prepared to face the German tank and air power. Therefore, the people who were making decisions in 1939, which means, Beck [Minister of Foreign Affairs], Śmigły-Rydz [Commander in Chief], and Mościcki [President of Poland], should have made a maximal effort to avoid this war if they wanted to save the Polish Republic, which was built as the result of the First World War and as a result of the sacrifices which the Polish Nation endured during the war of 1919-1920. Our friendship with England should have been treated as a very strong trump card, which could have helped us to achieve a reasonable compromise with the Germans, but should not have been waved as a red flag, which brought Hitler into a state of frenzy.

The other conclusion that I came to was that, once we could not avoid the war, we should have at least exploited that tremendous fighting spirit that engulfed our soldiers, even though the most heroic stand of the old-fashioned infantry was incapable of resisting the massive attack of armored columns. The experiences of the 86th Regiment on the outskirts of Piotrków confirmed this. If, however, we had treated our war with Germany as partisan warfare, we could have caused a considerable amount of grief for the enemy. Remnants of our division lost much energy and time realigning, marching to the forest of Spała, traversing the Vistula River, and then again marching on the crowded roads to Lublin and Chełm. If we had stayed in the forest of Piotrków, the Germans would have had to concentrate a considerable amount of infantry in order to dislodge us from there. A similar state of affairs was probably happening to other units.

In order to conduct partisan warfare, one requires a previously prepared army. Well-camouflaged storehouses for food rations and ammunitions should have been prepared beforehand. We should have had two separate philosophies of field action: one, in case of war in the East; and the other, in case of war against Germany. It seemed to me that the Germans valued the Polish partisan activities very highly. More or less one year before the war, Stanisław Mackiewicz told me that *Frankfurter Zeitung* ran a special edition dedicated to the description of various European Armies. Therein, the technical backwardness of the Polish Army was emphasized, but at the same time they pointed out that the ability of that army to fight partisan warfare could not be treated lightly. That was probably the main reason why Hitler attached such great importance to Soviet help. The Germans required the massive Soviet cavalry in order to annihilate partisan warfare at the very beginning, which could have been ignited in the territories of the Vistula River. This task was completed faithfully by the Soviet Union in September and October of 1939.

Later on, in 1941, when I was already a prisoner in a Soviet concentration camp in the Far North, I read of the appeal by Stalin for partisan action because the Germans had attacked the Soviets. I concluded that Soviet experts had probably carefully studied our experiences in the September [1939] campaign. I remember also the opinion of Field Marshal Alanbrooke, that Stalin had an extraordinary intuition in the area of great strategy, which General George Marshall and Eisenhower lacked.

In a similar manner, the Polish Foreign Affairs Minister Beck, who made hollow gestures of power and our high level commanders, trained in great strategies and tactics, forgot that we would be dealing with an enemy who was considerably stronger. Therefore, our methods of operation should have been adjusted accordingly.

Reorganization of the Division

Earlier it was described how, during the 16th of September in a small place east of Chełm, we succeeded in rejoining the remnants of the 19th Division of Infantry which previously had gone in an easterly direction. I also mentioned a conversation with the chief of divisional staff, Lt. Col. Tadeusz Rudnicki, who ordered me to report the next day to Lt. Col. Gustaw Nowosielski, recently appointed commander of the combined regiment of the 19th Infantry Division.

The next morning, even before the sun threw its first rays on the treetops, I arrived at the prescribed place. Behind the village in a forest clearing stood the commander of the newly formed regiment, surrounded by a small group of officers. I observed the known faces of my colleagues from the forest of Piotrków (where our regiment, the 85th Regiment of Wilno riflemen which, under the command of Lt. Col. Kruk-Śmigła, tried in the first days of September to counter the German armored columns): Captain Pawłowski, commander of the First Battalion of the 85th Infantry Regiment; Captain Kowszyk, quartermaster of the regiment; and Captain Bychowiec.

The colonel was a strapping and well-built man in a long field coat, exhibiting the typical four cornered soldiers' cap received from mobilization stores without the mark of his rank. He appeared to me extremely handsome. His face portrayed manly features, yet with a mysterious longing in his eyes. That face seemed to be known to me as if I had seen it somewhere before. After a while, I remembered. It was in the old Russia toward the end of the other war. A secret organization of Polish boys operated from a high school in Orel, a town south of Moscow, where they dreamed about a military fight to gain independence, and they saved cards portraying Polish Legionnaires fighting against Imperial Russia on the side of Austria. One of the

FROM PIOTRKÓW TO KATYN

legionnaires in these pictures resembled Lt. Col. Nowosielski; he had that similar mysterious longing in his eyes. I imagined him to be carrying the volumes of Słowacki[1] in his backpack. Later on, I found out that Lt. Col. Nowosielski actually was a legionnaire. Oh, how the ladies must have admired him, I thought.

After a while, I reported to him, "Sir, Lt. S. from the 85th Regiment of Wilno Riflemen, by order of the divisional commander, I report: two officers, nine NCOs, four machine guns, 37 bayonets, six mounted scouts, and four supply carts."

The colonel received the report and subsequently he ordered, "Send the NCOs attached to the supply carts to the supply company, the mounted scouts to the troop of scouts, and the rest should report to the commander of the Second Battalion. As for you personally – I would like to contemplate for a while how to use you." At that moment, the quartermaster of a newly formed regiment, Captain Kowszyk, whom I knew from the maneuvers of the 19th Infantry Division during the reserve officers' exercise in 1930, approached the colonel and started whispering something in his ear. I guessed that he was referring to me. The colonel looked at me, and then he said again, "Lieutenant, I would like to keep you with the regimental command; I need an intelligence officer." I saluted back.

A few hours after that, the units of the newly formed regiment were assembled in the forest cutting trees to build an anti-tank barricade. The enemy armored columns were advancing about four kilometers from us. Intelligence concerning them was strange. Their concentration in this region seemed to be east of us, on the right side of the Bug River. Something very strange was happening in Volhynia and in the vicinity of Włodzimierz. But it was difficult to establish what it was. We did not have a radio, and in the disorganization of the first day of the existence of the new formation, it was impossible to organize radio contact. There was no communication; we were cut off from any knowledge of the general situation, and we had to act on our own. At night, the regiment moved east in the direction of Dorohusk in order to cut off German communication lines through the Bug River.

Dorohusk near the Bug River (September 18, 1939)

The battle started near the river on the 18th of September, and it lasted the whole day. We lost many people – a serious loss – but we stopped the Germans from crossing the Bug River from east to west. At the beginning of the battle, the colonel sent me with various orders to the reserve units and to the flanks. The duties of an intelligence officer are not only to collect information about the enemy, but also information about the strength of our own units. It was relatively easy to find out what was happening at the rear of our units. The command of our division was stationed there, and Lt. Col. T. Rudnicki was taking care of everything. It was more difficult to assess the situation on the flanks, and it was difficult to find out about the actual quality of our units and the possibility of cooperation with them. A similar situation existed in the commands of other units.

We had to find out information about ourselves. Sometimes this caused some unpleasant incidents. For example, once I was informed that a German "spy" wearing the uniform of a Polish major was milling around among our soldiers. The sergeant

---

[1] Juliusz Słowacki was a famous Polish poet, 1809-1849.

IN THE SHADOW OF KATYN

who reported this to me exhibited great urgency to deal with the "spy" right on the spot. I went immediately and met the authentic Polish major from the group of Col. Künstler (later on, a prisoner of Kozelsk). They were holding the positions opposite the railway bridge and blew it up, making it impossible for the enemy to cross to the left bank of the Bug River. The major was sent to liaison with us. He also wanted to personally find out what our fighting capacity was.

After a few hours, I returned to the regimental command. There was calm and order as it should be in a well-organized unit serving on the frontline: The carts and horses were well-camouflaged; unnecessary people were not milling about the village; telephone operators and observers were calmly going about conducting their business; the chief of the regimental office was preparing his daily report; and liaison personnel were slumbering under the wall protecting them from bullets. Along the river there was the staccato of machine guns. German artillery, not very intensively but systematically, was firing at the village and the crossroads at our rear.

At the regimental command, from all of the officers, only the second adjutant was present. "Where is the colonel?" I asked him.

"Who knows?" he answered. "He went with Lt. Sielicki to visit the position of the individual machine guns. Currently, he is with one of the platoons .... He pretends to be a hero ... you know." The adjutant was clearly irritated. "His place is here, by the telephones; the reports are coming here, and thus from here you have to issue commands, but he considers that his first priority is to give a good example to the soldiers."

I recollected how, in the year 1919, I had come in contact with the Fifth Infantry Regiment of the legion. There was a habit that the officers, to give an example of courage, always stood in a resolute position in the frontlines. Losses were tremendous, but the authority of the officers in battle was beyond reproach. The colonel is probably from the same school, I thought. There was nothing else for me to do but wait.

In the meantime, the rain of bullets began to intensify. I sat down on the porch of the hut where thick beams protected me from being hit. I observed the stupid hens that were chasing the buzz of some invisible bugs falling on the ground. In the mild autumn air cobwebs were flying. All around there was the aura of a calm and sunny September day. Lazy and warm thoughts started to overwhelm me. I remembered that tomorrow was going to be the anniversary of my wedding day, and slowly, reality and dreams began to mix in my slumber, which mesmerized me.

I was jolted from my reverie by the return of the colonel. The colonel looked tired after those jumps from trench to trench under the fire of enemy artillery and machine guns. I reported to him all the information I had collected. The colonel listened carefully and thanked me; then he sat down on an old tree-log that was lying in the yard and he looked intensely at the map. The enemy fire got weaker and bullets stopped falling into the yard. I took the binoculars, climbed onto higher ground, which was just behind the house, and started observing the enemy. I began to think of the strange tactics of this war. I was intrigued by the relative emptiness to the west of us, and the enemy's move away from the district of Volhynia.[2]

Suddenly, the colonel called me. I quickly stepped down from the small hill. "Sit down, lieutenant," he said. I sat down by him on the log. "Lieutenant, why did

---

[2] Volhynia was east of us; therefore, it was strange that the Germans were moving from east to west.

FROM PIOTRKÓW TO KATYN

you get up there? It won't help anybody with anything." He said this in a scolding, quiet, and tired voice, not looking at me, and again he started examining the map. I did not say anything. I did not know what to answer. I only looked at him with surprise. It was said by my regimental commander, who had just returned from the inspection of his units under extreme enemy fire.

A few moments later, the report from Captain Pawłowski came that the enemy was preparing for the crossing of the river. The battle intensified again. The captain of the 19th Regiment of light artillery, who was commanding our two guns, was performing miracles until one of the barrels of the anti-tank guns overheated and expanded. After a few hours the crisis was over. The barrage of fire got weaker and weaker as evening approached. The colonel decided to take advantage of the lull in fighting in order to feed people, replenish the ammunition to the rather inaccessible points, and to improve the trenches and camouflage. The regimental command was moved to a specially dug trench opposite the wall surrounding the small Greek Orthodox Church. Not far away, at the crossroads, there was a field hospital, which was very busy this day. Behind the building, in which it was situated, an officer's leg, which the doctor had decided had to be amputated immediately, was lying there, thrown out in a hurry. Village dogs were ferociously licking blood from the leg.

Behind the wall in the churchyard, several soldiers were digging a grave for Second Lt. Król. I had met him the same day in the morning, in the same yard, when the colonel sent me to investigate the situation in the reserve units. When I approached the platoon's location under the wall on horseback, a skinny and tall commander got up, approached me and introduced himself very politely, "I am Second Lieutenant Król." After a few hours, when the situation became critical in a section defended by one of the companies, the colonel sent me with the order for the platoon of Second Lieutenant Król to fill up the gap. When I approached them in the same place as before, the same tall shape of the commander got up, and he introduced himself again, "I am Second Lieutenant Król."

I looked at him. He appeared to me to be extremely sympathetic and distracted. I pondered briefly what his profession might have been as a civilian. There was no time for conversation. I related to him the colonel's order and, in a few words, I explained the situation. Second Lieutenant Król bravely fulfilled his task. The opening had been plugged, and the other platoon, which under German fire had started falling back, returned to its former position. But, Second Lt. Król paid for this with his life. Several soldiers brought his body to the same place, where before he was standing in reserve, and now, in the old cemetery near the Greek Orthodox Church, they were digging his grave. Second Lieutenant Król was lying stretched out with his face turned toward the evening sky. He looked just as solemn as when he twice introduced himself to me. The sergeant recited a short prayer from the prayer book while soldiers were standing with their caps off. The setting sun's last rays were touching the face of the fallen man. I made the sign of the cross and quietly said the prayer for the dead. Soldiers laid him in the shallow grave and started to cover his body with earth.

I suddenly felt a raving hunger. From the nearby field I dug out some sugar beets, cleaned them with my penknife and began eating them. The colonel, by the telephone in the trenches, started giving orders to Captain Pawłowski. Kitchen orderlies brought us tasty soup with a huge portion of meat. The colonel came out from the trench and sat near me. We were experiencing relief from tension after a day of devout work. "Eh, lieutenant, lieutenant … how much has one to suffer before one dies?" joked the colonel.

Both sides of the river, the west in Polish hands, and the east in German hands, became calm.

The day of dramatic news (September 19, 1939)

The next day was a day of dramatic news. It started with an unusual calmness. The Germans were standing on the opposite bank but did not engage in any activities. It looked as if they were preparing themselves for something unusual, or they were awaiting support. Even enemy aircraft – which the previous day were successfully chased away by our only anti-aircraft gun – were not appearing at all now. Shortly before noon, our artillery observer, looking from a tree with the regimental command nearby, suddenly reported that crowds of people were coming out of the forests from behind the German positions and were moving toward the river. They were not armed. After a while, a new report announced that the crowd was increasing and that they were moving toward the German positions. Without warning, the observer with a piercing voice superseding any imaginable terror cried out, "They are in our uniforms ... they are ours ... unarmed ... the Germans let them through ... oh, they are passing by the German tanks!"

With the speed of lightning, the news spread through our units; from our well-camouflaged defense posts, from our firing lines, from our ammunition dumps, and from our food storage, people started coming out. The whole regiment with bated breath was looking at the enemy positions. On the opposite side of the river, more Polish soldiers were appearing, looking for a way to cross the river. Shortly, the first messengers of the dramatic news were among us. They all were saying the same thing, "Russia is coming, the Bolsheviks are occupying Mołodeczno and Łuck." In detail, they described what happened to them. "We were defending Włodzimierz Wołyński and the Germans received a good beating from us; it did not appear as if they were capable of taking Włodzimierz. Unexpectedly, on the morning of the 17th of September, General Sawicki, who was our commander, collected the whole division and said that Russia had attacked our country, and that in these circumstances further fighting would be impossible. The general, with tears in his eyes, said that privates are to be released and are allowed to go home, but he ordered the officers to go by car to the Romanian border."

More and more representatives of that crowd were coming to our side; dozens of them were milling around our soldiers. On the river there was complete chaos. On the side of Volhynia there were the Germans, on the side of the Lublin district there was our regiment, ready to engage in a new fight; and through German positions and our positions there was the retreating division from Włodzimierz Wołyński, unarmed and without officers. I was afraid that the Germans would take advantage of this situation and cross the river, which on the previous day, we stopped them from doing. The Germans stood gloomily but splendidly in their large helmets and gray uniforms. For the moment, it appeared to me that in their attitude there was some kind of respect for our tragedy. Probably, they were considering the fate of our unit as sealed, and it was

FROM PIOTRKÓW TO KATYN

not worth their while to take any casualties, for which they would have to cross the river.

I was summoned to see the colonel. He was enraged. The order to dissolve the divisions and send soldiers home, he considered as a completely inexplicable deed. "Lieutenant," he was saying to me, "how can one dissolve units who have the weapons and are ready to fight? That what happened at Włodzimierz is terrible!" The fact that among us was a commander who dispensed soldiers from fighting shocked him more than the attack by Bolsheviks, about which we knew very little but could only guess.

"The greatest danger for us at the present moment is not from the Germans," continued the colonel, "but from the retreating crowds, who are mixing with our soldiers. This has to be stopped immediately. Take a special task force, set up posts and indicate the route through which these crowds can pass: no discussions, no talks, absolutely no mixing with our privates. Do you understand? We must maintain the morale of our regiment." I saluted and went to implement the order. In the meantime the colonel wrote an order which was read to all the units of the regiment. The colonel declared in it that the events that happened at Włodzimierz did not diminish our obligations as soldiers in any way. Warsaw and Lwów were fighting and our duty was to ease their fight by engaging the enemy. The war was not over and the Polish Nation was going to conduct it until final victory.

After one hour, the situation was under control. The stream of uniformed crowds had formed into a narrow river. On the firing lines of our regiment, calm and order descended. I was walking from unit to unit, looking into the faces of the soldiers, getting into conversation with noncommissioned officers. I did not notice any doubts. Not one of them wavered. The colonel should be extremely pleased that the psychological moment was won and discipline was not broken; we were ready for a further fight.

The result of successfully overcoming this crisis was rather unexpected. By the road, groups of our armed soldiers were gathering, and they were forcing the passers-by having better coats, shoes, and scarves received from mobilization magazines, to exchange them for theirs. The passers-by acquiesced without protest. This spectacle I found somehow very painful and humiliating. But one must admit that there was some justifiable soldiers' logic in it. "Sir," a corporal explained to me as he pointed out one of the soldiers of Włodzimierz, after I had shamed him for this practice, "he, with his excellent requisitioned coat, is going under the duvet with his 'broad', but I'm going to fight. He is going to relax with her and I'm going to rot in the forest. It's only right that he should have the worst coat and me the better one." I reported to the colonel these incidents that were multiplying. The colonel ordered these practices stopped, except for the taking of bicycles, which we needed for completing the bicycle platoon.

After some time, the colonel came out from the hut and went to the crossroads behind the village where the sentry was standing, requisitioning bicycles. I approached him, and we stood in silence looking at the stream of soldiers moving over the road cutting through the river terraces. I had a feeling that something was happening between us. I looked at the colonel; our eyes met and, at that moment, from the colonel's lips came a whisper that resembled a cry of agony, "Lieutenant ... Poland is dying." With a move that chased away a nasty fly, he wiped away a tear slowly streaming down his cheek. Controversial and wild thoughts were vibrating through my mind. I understood that much could be said, but those few expressions that condensed our inner truths, I could not find. I did not say a word. We remained standing in silence.

After the sunset, our regiment moved in a southerly direction to Dubienka. Meanwhile, a few mounted scouts and I moved at night to look for the divisional headquarters, which was also moving somewhere in a southerly direction. At the divisional command, a robust cavalry officer, Captain Nowicki, well known and popular in Wilno, communicated to all of us the most painful news given by Radio Moscow that the Red Army had taken Wilno. "But lieutenant, keep your spirits up; we have to hold on," added the cavalry officer, giving me an encouraging tap on the shoulder.

For the next few days we were on the move all the time. German aircraft were circling over us as before, but they did not fire at us. Instead they were throwing lots of leaflets. The text of a typical leaflet was as follows, "Soldiers, Russia moved against you. Your President, your Commander in Chief, and your Government ran away to Romania. You fulfilled your duty bravely, but the war is now over. Any resistance from your side will be a senseless continuation of blood spilling. You have to lay down your arms." I was riding along, looking into the soldiers' faces as they marched. Not even one of them was bending down to pick up the leaflets. Their faces were gray, solemn, and stubborn – real Lithuanians. At the head of the column with a forward guard, the colonel rode in a pensive mood as if he were meditating and in his eyes there was a yearning-like stare.

The battle near Tomaszów Lubelski (September 23, 1939)

A few days later, there was a battle near Tomaszów Lubelski. We initiated this battle, causing losses to the enemy and taking prisoners. As far as I know, it was ordered by the commander of our army (so-called reserve army), General Dąb-Biernacki, whose staff, at this time, was moving among the army units marching south between the Bug and San rivers. I think that Gen. Dąb-Biernacki considered taking Tomaszów as necessary in order to move the units, operating between the Bug and San rivers, closer to the Hungarian border. In this battle we were under the command of General Wołkowicki who was receiving orders from General Przedrzymirski. We did not take Tomaszów, in spite of making a considerable dent in German lines.

Before the evening, when the sun was setting behind the rooftops of the nearby village, an operational order came in. Glancing at it, I found out that we had to march in a northwesterly direction and that concentration should start on the 24th of September, near Suchowola. At that moment, a messenger from the Fourth Company came with the report that German couriers had arrived at their company, proposing that we should surrender immediately; otherwise, they promised complete destruction of our units in the next few hours. The colonel sent me to stop any talk with the Germans and to regulate the situation in the area of the Fourth Company – eventually, depending on the situation, offering the German messengers the option of being sent to the divisional command. In the meantime, the colonel gave the order that as soon as dusk came, various companies should start regrouping themselves into marching columns.

After fulfilling my duties, I tried to catch up with the departed regiment. It was completely dark. I was neither sure of the road along which I was running, nor of the direction; all I knew was that somewhere nearby the German units were also moving. At a certain moment, I rather felt but did not see a moving mass. I had bumped into my horse being led by a soldier at the end of the moving column of Capt. Pawłowski's battalion. I tightened the girth, mounted the horse and trotted in darkness to give my report to the colonel. Some time later, the column stopped; we were in the yard of an estate completely deserted by its inhabitants, and in the stable the bellowing cattle had been left without care. A further march along the road was impossible; in front of us were the Germans. The colonel and Capt. Bychowiec, with flashlights and compass, were bent over the map trying to find out which direction would give us a chance to move out of this maze. The battalion, in a few parallel columns, went across a field dotted with small hillocks.

Suddenly, a German flare lit up the sky over us. It became as clear as daylight, every smallest blade of grass under our feet was visible, and everything around us became more clearly visible than under normal sunlight. Soon a second and a third flare lit up. "The Germans see us," I said to myself, "soon artillery fire will start." But the Germans did not exhibit any further activities. After three-quarters of an hour, we were on the road on which our supply carts were stretched out. The colonel again had all his units under his command, disciplined and ready for further action. It was the night of the 23rd to 24th of September.

Concentration near Suchowola (September 24, 1939)

A small unit of mounted scouts and I arrived at the prescribed place of concentration a few hours before the rest of the regiment. On the way I passed moving reminders of the 10th Division of Infantry and also – as far as I remember – the 43rd Regiment of Infantry. I also discovered that units of the 41st Division under the command of General Piekarski were nearby, and a little bit further to the south were the remnants of the First Division of the Legion.

It was very early in the morning and still gray, but it was rather a long time before sunrise. I moved along the road where there were plenty of signs of the previous fighting. In the poor visibility of pre-dawn, I saw skeletons of blown up German tanks and conquered German cars, pushed off the road by our marching columns. One of the soldiers directed my attention to a demolished German plane, evidently shot down by us. When sidestepping from the road, my horse jumped violently away to avoid stomping on a German corpse. It was a young boy lying on his back with out-stretched arms. His congealed eyes, with an expression of surprise, were looking into the gray sky of the coming morning. General Władysław Anders had broken through here.

All at once, a few kilometers in front of us, extremely intense artillery fire started. I could not make out the source of the firing. Whose was it ... the Germans' or ours? I moved in the direction of white clouds coming from the exploding missiles, hoping to find someone who could give me a reasonable explanation as to what was actually happening here.

The firing stopped as suddenly as it had begun. It became strangely empty around me. I trotted across the field in the direction from where the sounds of battle had been coming. From behind the hillock came a group of about a dozen people with a machine gun. I approached them and, from the emblems on their collars, I recognized the Fourth Regiment of Uhlans belonging to the Third Cavalry Brigade. They were ours – men from Wilno! They looked extremely exhausted; they were on foot, and they had probably been through some very difficult experiences. I introduced myself.

"Lieutenant," said a cavalry officer, "Anders has broken through, but the Germans closed the ring after him again. We are cut off." We exchanged information. Our regiments will be too late, I thought. Had we been here earlier, we could have joined Anders' action and widened the passage.

It was already after sunrise when our regiment arrived. I submitted a detailed report to the colonel of all the elements of the situation that I had collected. We stood facing the morning sun on the edge of a hill gently sloping toward the east. In front of us there was an expansive view. To the left, between various trees, units of our regiment were taking up residence for several hours of rest. Steaming field kitchens were issuing morning soup; horses were being fed. Not far from the aforementioned trees, stood the hut in which the severely wounded Lieutenant Szamota from the 13th Uhlans Regiment was in the throes of death. About a kilometer from us, from beyond a range of hills, the red globe of the sun had just risen. The hills were cut by several ribbons of large and small roads and through them chains of military and civilian carts were moving down. Last week, the same carts were running away toward the east; now, under pressure of the oncoming Bolsheviks, they were moving west. From here they made the impression of snakes, helplessly twisting in the grip of mortal danger pressing in on them from both sides. There was a slight fog, giving the rays of the sun a reddish-orange hue; I considered it a bad omen.

I did not feel tired after the emotional happenings of the last twenty-four hours, but instead I was somehow strangely elated. My imagination was extremely active. From the morning mist, images of the past started emerging. I felt as though suddenly I was in an opera hall setting, where the stormy sounds from an orchestra were reverberating. I felt myself hearing fragments of Wagner's melodies, which always had overwhelming effects upon me. The music from *Götterdämmerung* thundered around me. Shadows marched through the fog, carrying on their shields the body of Siegfried. I am losing my grip on reality, I thought.

My memory began to reconstruct an unforgettable picture. Through the field of Mokotow, in front of a coffin standing high on top of the gun carriage, went a silent funeral procession.[3] Black, stormy clouds, coming from the east, were in the background. From afar, I heard the sound of thunder. After the passing of the funeral procession and the transferring of the coffin onto the freight train, which started pulling out slowly, lightning suddenly zigzagged over the scene, and only then, heavy rain came pouring down. I was looking at this entire panorama, and I was thinking about that coffin and the lightning zigzagging over it. I felt some difficulty in defining the feelings of terror coming over me. Yes, it was as if I were listening to a powerful symphony reproducing the fight of some transcendental elements coming from some extra dimension outside our cosmos. I was thinking of the cycles of the rise and fall of nations. I began my conversation with the colonel again, which had started a few days earlier when, at the sight of the army division departing without arms from Włodzimierz Wołyński, he had whispered to me these words of torment, "Poland is dying."

---

[3] Description of Piłsudski's funeral (1935).

FROM PIOTRKÓW TO KATYN

"Sir," I said, "I don't think that we could say that Poland is dying. Irrespective of the outcome of this war, some kind of Polish State had to exist. But, what kind? That we cannot guess today. It seems to me that in the life of Poland an epoch is ending, to which you and I were emotionally attached: the epoch of Józef Piłsudski – and now a different one begins. It is difficult to foresee what will happen. One thing seems to me almost certain: Poland in its present form will not return to the east. I realize well enough what the Soviets mean to do in the eastern districts. They will destroy all the pillars on which Polish culture supported itself."

At that moment, I felt that I could not find the synthesis of thoughts vibrating through my mind, that my words sounded shallow in front of the deep pain which, a few days ago, found its expression in the tragic whisper of the colonel. I felt that we were witnesses to something real that was dying and moving away to the irrevocable past. But what? I could not formulate it. The colonel stood pondering silently. He did not reply at all to my remarks.

After a few hours, the regiment started marching again in a southwesterly direction toward the forests situated on the right bank of the Wieprz River opposite Krasnobród. I trotted alongside of the marching columns and I thought about my unfinished conversation with the colonel. I caught sight of the Lithuanian coat of arms, worn on the collar of our uniforms. It was also the coat of arms of our regiment – a knight on a horse in pursuit of the enemy. On our Regimental Colors we had the embroidered picture of the Madonna of *Ostra Brama* and, on the other side, the Lithuanian coat of arms. Now, I managed to grasp the synthesis of the chaotic thoughts that were vibrating through my mind. Poland was not dying, but the so dear to us tradition of the Grand Duchy of Lithuania in the life of Poland was disappearing. This tradition had given to reborn Poland the moral title to the eastern parts of the Commonwealth of both Nations.

Centuries ago, the genius of our great rulers created a superior power which was able to ward off the waves of destruction hitting them from the great plains in the East. The wisdom of the rulers of Kraków and the farsightedness of the dynasty of Jagiellons[4] strengthened this power, cementing and creating the Commonwealth. In our times, Józef Piłsudski attempted to resurrect this great achievement, but he suffered defeat. His ideas were destroyed by nationalism. When Piłsudski was dying, he was already a defeated giant. Now, in this gale of stormy weather, the last links connecting us with the epoch of great glory were going to be broken.

But – I disputed with myself – could it really be said that the tradition of the Grand Duchy of Lithuania was dying? It could be that the present war and the present onslaught coming from the East might create conditions for its resurrection. The geographic position represents elements of force. If the Ukrainians, Byelorussians and the Baltic Nations were going to preserve their individuality, then in this corridor of land between the Baltic Sea and the Carpathian Mountains some formation would have

---

[4] The Jagiellons (1385-1572). Jagiellonian Dynasty was started in 1385 by the marriage of Jadwiga (Hungarian princess and heiress to the Polish crown) and Jagiełło (Grand Duke of Lithuania). At that time the Lituanians controlled the land all the way to the Black Sea (present day Belarus and Ukraine). Thus the union of Poland and Lithuania created the most powerful Commonwealth of Nations in Eastern Europe. In the Battle of Grunwald (1410), Jagiello defeated the Order of Teutonic Knights and thus stopped its further expansion. The Jagiellonian Dynasty ended in 1572 with the death of Sigismund-August who left no heir.

to rise up. This formation would have to defend itself and would have to protect them all from drowning by the waves from the East. Could it be that this formation would achieve even greater glory and greater meaning than the old Duchy of Lithuania? Could it unite with Poland? Perhaps Polish peasants and workers would be able to find a common language with Lithuanian and Ukrainian peasants in the same way as much earlier the rulers of Kraków were able to find a common language with the Ruthenian masters. Perhaps this present onslaught from Moscow would erase all traces of Polish culture in the Eastern Territories and this might create more favorable circumstances that would not impede the future process of integration. Could it be that a new federation might be supported by a stronger and healthier foundation than that of the old Commonwealth? Perhaps, but the thread of life's traditions joining us directly with the past would be broken.

Tradition is not only political plans and brainwaves, but also is connected with the past through a life chain of concrete human beings who were brought up in the atmosphere of certain notions, mores, and ideals. Belonging to this tradition are the small estates with pillars in front; mahogany chesterfields; desks made of a special kind of birch-wood; those yellow papers of old documents written in the old Ruthenian language; those faithful eyes of our women, who when giving themselves also gave their souls; the charms locked up in the Wilno walls. The knight on a horse (Lithuanian coat of arms) on the colors of our regiment and on the collars of our uniforms was also one of the elements of that tradition.

All that would not be able to withstand a new Soviet onslaught in the same way as Polish settlements had been unable to resist it in the Soviet part of Beylorussia (Minsk-, Vitebsk-, Mogilev area), and in the Soviet Ukraine. All that was going to be spat upon, raped, and destroyed. The vessels that harbored that spirit were going to be destroyed. The spirit is not mortal, and it will rise up from its ashes, often finding a new form for its manifestation. It is possible that at some time in the future the spirit of the Grand Duchy of Lithuania and the joined Commonwealth will be reborn in some new form, but it is heartbreaking when one realizes that so many things dear to one's heart are sentenced to ruthless annihilation. Man is attached not only to the spirit but also to the form, and he is attached to the symbols that express this spirit.

I looked at the Lithuanian coat of arms on our uniforms, and I thought that perhaps our regiment was the last of the Polish units – before the coming of a new epoch – which was tied to this famous tradition of power created some time ago by the Lithuanian organizational genius. The colonel, who hailed from the district of Kraków, was probably the last commander of such a unit. I was touched when I looked at the slightly bent silhouette on the saddle, several paces from me.

Doubts and decisions

The next day, the 25th of September, there was constant fire exchange with the enemy. The Germans were attacking Krasnobród and trying to establish a bridgehead on the Wieprz River. We were taking over the forest opposite Krasnobród on the right-hand side of the river. Several of our companies in the forward position were trying to open the road, fiercely spraying the German positions with machine-gun fire. The Germans were replying in kind. One of our platoons received very heavy casualties.

FROM PIOTRKÓW TO KATYN

That whole day, because of the heavy German fire, it was impossible to send food to the forward placed companies, which caused great anxiety for the quartermaster, Captain Kowszyk. The German artillery was firing lazily into the forest, making much noise but causing very little damage. German planes did not show themselves at all that day, but there was a lot of small arms fire. Altogether, it reminded me of the well-known pictures from the war of 1919-1920.

This day, four anti-tank guns with a complete crew joined our unit. We had experienced the shortage of those guns on our previous operation. This gave us a certain amount of confidence when we looked at the not too numerous German tanks creeping on the other side of the Wieprz River. These were guns, as far as I remember, of the Cavalry Brigade from Nowogródek which, during the night from the 23rd to the 24th, did not succeed in breaking through with General Anders.

Generally, our armaments and supplies were improving every day. We were gaining more people than we were losing. People responsible for the supplies were quickly adjusting themselves to the condition of guerrilla warfare, kitchens were issuing fat soups with huge pieces of meat in them; bread was being baked regularly in spite of the fact that we were moving constantly. Among the general chaos, we represented a moving object of discipline and organization – the central figure of this military operation was our commander.

That same day, the 25th of September, right after sunset I fell into a deep anti-tank trench and painfully twisted my leg. With difficulty I managed to reach our supply carts, and to make things worse, I was getting strong shivers. The NCOs from the supply company, who mostly belonged to my home regiment and who, together with me, departed from Nowa Wilejka near Wilno, put me in a cart and covered me with a great number of blankets. I fell asleep immediately.

During my sleep, I had a feeling that we were again marching. I heard a mixed cacophony of excited voices and I felt clearly that the cart was moving, rolling, and jumping on the forestry lane. After a certain time, I felt that somebody was bending over me; in my delirium, I had the feeling of seeing the picture of a worried looking mother bending over a sick child. I opened my eyes. Hovering about me, I saw the face of the master corporal whose function was to be responsible for supplying forage for the regimental horses. "What are the Germans doing?" I asked almost automatically.

"The Germans are retreating from Krasnobród," answered the master corporal.

Again I fell asleep, and again I heard a cacophony of voices, and again I felt the movement of the cart. When I woke up, the sky was already gray; however, it was still some time before sunrise. To my great surprise, I found out that we were standing in the same place. Near the cart there was the same tree which I had noticed when I was falling asleep in the evening. The master corporal was issuing fodder for the horses. I crawled out of my comfortable warm hole, made up of masterfully arranged blankets, and I limped, supporting myself on a stick, in the direction of the regimental command.

The colonel was standing near the road, leading through the forest to Krasnobród, and as usual seemed to be in a pensive mood. "Where were you lieutenant?" he asked when he noticed my arrival.

"I was sleeping in the supply unit," I answered with a wry smile, which pleaded for leniency.

IN THE SHADOW OF KATYN

We stood in silence. After a while the colonel, with a quiet voice, looking somewhere to the side, asked, "What would you do now, lieutenant, if you were in my position?"

I looked at the colonel, "Do you see any chance, sir, of breaking through to Hungary with the arms in our hands?" I answered with a question. The colonel made a negative sign.

"In that case, sir, I would arrange a briefing of all the officers, present the situation to them and order them to destroy all the weaponry so it would not get into enemy hands, and I would direct the people in small groups toward Hungary. In my opinion, it would be best if they stayed clear of the territories already taken by the Soviets. I would think that it would be best to move to the San River, taking the direction toward Kraków district and Slovakia."

The colonel retorted with annoyance. "Dissolve an organized, capable fighting unit? Unacceptable!" He replied in a manner that excluded any possibility of further discussion on this subject.

We stood silently again. I felt my mind being stimulated as happens when new ideas begin to bud. "Sir," I said, "I think that it is time to stop firing at the Germans. The battles that we are conducting are not battles for victory, but for honor and to manifest the will of the Polish Nation to defend the remains of the Commonwealth. We have manifested sufficiently our will as far as the Germans are concerned. Now we have to manifest this will with respect to the Bolsheviks. It seems to me that we have to put up a fight against incoming Soviet units and perhaps in this way fulfill our part."

I felt that my idea was pleasing the colonel. He looked at me wistfully. "Yes," he said, "but...." He stopped in mid-sentence.

I understood immediately his concerns. "I know, sir," I said, "you are thinking about the alleged order of the commander in chief not to shoot at the Bolsheviks. I don't believe in the authenticity of that order. Can one imagine that Śmigły-Rydz, who in his time did not want to execute the order of Marshal Piłsudski to retreat from Kiev, would now be signing these kinds of orders? However...."

At that moment, I started feeling doubts creeping into my mind. Śmigły-Rydz, one of the most popular officers of the first brigade – an excellent high-ranking commander of the campaign in the years 1919-1920, artist, man of great personal charm, pseudo-god of women and soldiers – exhibited a lot of naïveté when, after the death of Marshal Piłsudski, he started to meddle in political life. I remembered how Stanisław Mackiewicz (a conversation with him facilitated the arrival at my own conclusions about the happenings in international politics) had in recent years begun to express himself less favorably about the level of political intelligence of Śmigły-Rydz. I started to imagine what was now happening in the quarters of our Supreme Commander which, apparently, were already situated outside our country.

Most likely, there were numerous French liaison officers milling around who obviously had instructions to counter anything that would cause conflict with Russia. It was difficult to imagine what effect it had on our command. If it were true, that such an order was issued while facing Soviet troops occupying Eastern districts, it would be tantamount to Poland renouncing its Eastern Territories. I did not believe that Marshal Śmigły-Rydz could have issued such an order, but staff officers were talking about this, and rumors were also circulating among the rank and file. Under the influence of those

FROM PIOTRKÓW TO KATYN

rumors, the self-confidence was waning even among those who considered this order an absolute impossibility.

I looked at the colonel. I had the impression that my answer disappointed him – he had expected something else from me – he wanted me to confirm hidden thoughts, and he did not find that confirmation in me. It was only afterwards, in Kozelsk, that we finished this discussion. The colonel was somehow disappointed with my idea of dispersing the regiment into small groups that could penetrate into Hungary. The colonel considered that an organized unit capable of fighting should stay an active unit, which under no circumstances should be destroyed. At that moment, we did not yet know all the elements of the situation, and we could hope that we could play a part as a center of resistance, attracting the remainders of other units to us.

He was tormented about which direction to move in order to get the best chance for survival and then take part in new encounters. The strongest concept among us was that we should try to reach the Hungarian border. General Wołkowicki was also of that opinion. He maintained that the general direction of the march must be to achieve the hills and forest areas starting south of the highway between Lwów and Przemyśl. The colonel thought differently; his eyes looked mainly toward the northwest. Over there, Warsaw was still fighting. The colonel was pondering the idea that if we took a northwesterly direction, we could engage in fights in that region.

The argument against this concept was that, moving in the direction of Warsaw, we would have to enter the open territories, while during this campaign we were used to forests for our operations, because they protected us from tanks and German aircraft. The argument for the colonel's idea was that we were not aware of any large enemy formations in that direction. We were under the impression that northwest of us there was open territory. If we entered it, then we could try to reach Warsaw by intensive night marches. It was a concept, as far as I know, similar to that which General Kleeberg was trying to realize when, withdrawing his units from Polesie, he moved west. General Kleeberg was too far north of us, and we did not have any contact with him. The colonel was suffering in his dilemma for having the responsibility of making the decisions. In conversation with me, he was looking for arguments to support his hidden thoughts. In the meantime, he received from me the same "Hungarian" concept, only in a different version as far as its implementation was concerned. And that was the disappointment I caused the colonel on that day, as I understood later on.

While we were debating, an ordinary supply cart arrived, from which General Wołkowicki emerged. He and the colonel immediately engaged in conversation with each other. After several minutes, the colonel approached me and said in a somewhat solemn tone, "We are marching south. We will try not to get engaged into the fight and we shall try to take advantage of the space between the retreating Germans and the approaching Soviet units, and in this way achieve the Hungarian border. I consider that there is a great possibility that we will be taken prisoner by the Bolsheviks. I understand lieutenant, that you are especially heavily burdened, because Bolsheviks might have something against you. Besides, you have different ideas. As your commander, I am giving you a free hand. You can go west or choose the road that you would consider most proper. I'm asking you, however, that you'll inform me of your decision."

I thanked the colonel, and I asked him to have a few minutes to think it over.

IN THE SHADOW OF KATYN

The farewell scene with my family flashed before my eyes. It was a month ago, on the 24th of August 1939, the day of mobilization. Inside the large garden in the district of Antokol was the small wooden house, where in the room with the old mahogany chesterfield hung the large cross, bought by my wife with the golden coins that were a wedding present given by her aunt, whom she considered a saint. On the chesterfield, in a row, our four children sat, the oldest eleven years old, the youngest five. The children's eyes looked at me with confidence. My wife was standing beside me. I was saying ... "The storm is coming, the end of which nobody is capable of foreseeing. It is not known who is going to be exposed to bigger trials ... I, in the frontline, or you here. Let's pray so God will give us grace to preserve our honor. Let us all kneel together and loudly say the litany of the Holy Virgin Mary."

I pondered whether it would be an honorable decision to take advantage of the colonel's offer and leave the unit? Legally, there is no doubt I would be correct, but would I not break the principles of trust to my colleagues in arms, which is such an important moral principle of war? I felt that if I did this, a shadow would hang over me, which I would have to keep explaining to myself, to other people, and perhaps even to my own children.

During that moment, when I was standing like that, a military cart arrived from which a lieutenant colonel of artillery of middle height with a small black beard jumped out. I recognized him immediately; however, I could not remember his name. At the end of 1938, I was invited by the then Polish Vice-Premier Kwiatkowski to take part in a government excursion to visit various shops in the central industrial district of Poland. This lieutenant colonel accompanied us as a representative of the military and conducted the tour through the factories, providing explanations. Holding a map in his hands, he now ran to Lt. Colonel Nowosielski and a few other officers standing around him and started talking quickly.

"Gentlemen, what are you waiting for? Do you gentlemen realize that the Bolsheviks are coming from the east? Within two hours they could be here! Have you made your decision, gentlemen?"

At that moment General Wołkowicki approached. "We are marching to Hungary," said the general. The newcomer was shaken with disbelief.

"No, general," he said, "that does not make any sense. We all have to be in our country and right here defend its independence. If necessary, we will go underground and in this fashion we will further organize our struggle."

A discussion developed. A group of several officers participated in the talks. At a certain moment the general got irritated. "Colonel," said the general, "are you organizing a rally here?" The artillery officer again started arguing. The general changed his tune. "Attention!" shouted the general. The artillery officer stood to attention. "Colonel," ordered the general, "You will immediately go where you were going." The artillery officer saluted, turned back, sat down on his cart beside the coachman and moved away.

We stood in silence. The arguments of the artillery officer were probably convincing to many, but at the same time all of us felt that the stand of General Wołkowicki expressed some kind of soldiers' truth. What kind? It is difficult to define. The truth of war, just as the truth of love and death, has an irrational character. At that moment, General Wołkowicki had full control over us, as in critical moments a

FROM PIOTRKÓW TO KATYN

commander, who is capable of decision and will, controls his subordinates.

Instantly, Lt. Col. Nowosielski approached me. "Lieutenant, your decision?" he asked.

"Sir, I am staying," I answered firmly.

The colonel did not look at me and moved his eyes sideways. After a while, he said, "We don't have much time to lose. You take a car and immediately make a road reconnaissance." He spread out a map and started explaining his objectives.

After ten minutes, I was in a Warsaw taxi, which somehow was requisitioned by our regiment. I crossed the bridge on the Wieprz River, getting ahead of our mounted scouts who were entering Krasnobród. The streets of the little town were empty in the early morning hour. Only in one place, almost in the middle of the street, an old Jew with sideburns and a long, ginger-gray beard, in yarmulke and gabardine, looked with distrust at the slowly passing car. Our eyes met. In his eyes I could see the serenity of a man whose life was on a different level, far removed from the warfare, and to whom our causes, our hopes, and our defeats were completely strange. I thought that all the soldiers – Polish, German, and Bolsheviks – who right now were disturbing his everyday routine, were equally far and strange to him. I stopped and asked him a few stereotyped questions that a scouting officer asks when he enters a territory from which enemy forces had retreated not long before. Momentarily, I moved again and turned left on the first larger road leading south, first ordering the mounted scouts in the direction that my car sped.

To the right, from the side or the direction of Józefów, from behind the treed hills, colored with the red and gold of a Polish autumn, you could hear strong artillery fire. There the Fourth Division of General Piekarski was fighting. Suddenly, the artillery fire ceased. Most likely, they are negotiating surrender, I thought. When arriving at the place that was my main purpose of investigation, I concluded that the Germans were there. Without any incident, I turned my car around and went back. At the crossroads, I met the mounted scout patrol which had been following me. I stopped them, took my report book from my map case, and sitting comfortably in the car's cushions, I wrote a report, which a mounted scout immediately took to the colonel. Next, I concentrated my attention on the road leading more to the east, closer to the Bolsheviks. A few hours later, our regiment was marching on that road to its destiny.

Soldiers

For the most part of the next day, the 27th of September, our regiment was stationed around an estate situated in the forests east of the San River, in the northern part of the Lwów district. That morning I went on horseback to investigate a place in a southwesterly direction of about five kilometers. On my way, I noticed infantrymen moving among the bushes and country lanes. I moved across the field in their direction. As I approached, their commander came out of the bushes. It was Capt. Majkowski from the 41st Infantry Regiment, who before the war commanded a company in the military academy in Ostrów Mazowiecki, or perhaps it was in Zambrów. He belonged to the units of General Przedrzymirski and General Piekarski, who the previous day, after a short fight, had capitulated. Captain Majkowski had decided not to obey the decision to surrender and was trying to reach the Hungarian border. His idea was to requisition carts and in that fashion move his small unit, composed of two incomplete platoons, to the Hungarian border through the side roads. I told him about our regiment and the colonel's decision that under no circumstances would he capitulate to Germany and his recent decision to march toward Hungary. I advised him that he should immediately report to the colonel, and Captain Majkowski did so. It was the last unit that strengthened the fighting potential of our regiment, which had constantly increased up to this point. Later on, as inmates of Kozelsk and having lots of time to ponder, we debated with Captain Majkowski what would have happened if he had not joined our regiment. If he could have realized his own concept, marching by the side lanes and more to the west, could he have possibly reached the Hungarian border?

That same day, several NCOs from the 85th Regiment of riflemen came to me. They had left Nowa Wilejka together with me and were also with me near Piotrków; then later, we arrived together under the command of Lt. Colonel Nowosielski. These NCOs informed me that they had a cart, which had been ready for several days now, with provisions for three weeks, good horses, comfortable seats and so on, and that there was a place reserved for me in this cart. According to them, on the road on which we were moving there was no perspective of further fighting, only captivity. So, they said, it was better now, while there was still time, to go back to the place where our regiment originated – to our families – and then we could look around and find out what action to take again.

I tried to convince them of the chances of reaching the Hungarian border and coming in contact with our Allies in the West [France] and taking further part in the fight as part of the Allied Armies. Their answer was that the soldiers did not understand this Hungarian concept; this was the officers' idea. The soldiers were afraid that the Hungarians would put us into camps. The lot of an officer in an internment camp is often bearable, but that of a private is extremely hard. Soldiers want to fight, but they want to fight in their own country. From the time when it became obvious that the strategy of command was to avoid in engaging ourselves in a fight in order to reach the Hungarian border, in the rank and file, one could notice a psychological breakdown. If the masses of soldiers were still a unified whole, it was because of the rumor that we were marching to join General Sosnkowski, who apparently was fighting somewhere near Lwów. General Sosnkowski was, at that moment, a legend that revived the hopes of our soldiers.

This conversation depressed me. I had the best opinion of the NCOs who came to see me. For two of them, I had promised that at the first opportunity I would recommend them for a decoration. One of them, Corporal Sadowski, was a veterinarian in the 85th Regiment of Wilno Riflemen. In the second week of September 1939, after our defeat near Piotrków, a small group, consisting of three officers and several privates under the command of Lieutenant Urbanowicz, was trying to cross from the forest of Spała to the other side of the Vistula River. While going through various side roads, we had wanted to reach the bridge near Maciejowice but found it burning. Going further north in the direction of Góra Kalwaria, we met up with the units of the 13th and 23rd Regiments of Cavalry, who were getting ready to go across the river, not far from where the mouth of the Pilica enters the Vistula. Not a single means of river transport had been found. The cavalrymen who were trying to swim to the other side were drowning. The river was gray, mysterious, and treacherous. Dusk was arriving. Corporal

FROM PIOTRKÓW TO KATYN

Sadowski suggested that if we built a small raft, he would try to cross the river on it and bring the boats. His reasoning was straightforward; the boats could not have evaporated – if there were no boats on this side of the river, there must be some on the other side. After a few hours, in the black September night, Corporal Sadowski, on a small, rolling, and unstable raft, cast off into darkness. At about three in the morning, he came back towing two boats. The Regimental Colors were saved.

With the sequential ferrying, we managed also to transport all our men. The cavalrymen decided to swim across with the horses. They were holding onto the horses' manes; most of them were successfully swimming through the best part of the river; close to the opposite side, however, they went into a strong current which was throwing them back into the middle of the river. The desperate screams of drowning men were mixed with the high pitched whinnying of frightened horses, and in the twilight of the coming dawn German planes drowned out all the noise with their machine gun fire. Corporal Sadowski went by himself in a small boat to the middle of the river and while approaching some of the Uhlans, he shouted, "Son of a bitch, let go of the mane and grab the tail!" The ones who listened to his advice, in most cases, managed to save themselves. I think that many Uhlans owe their lives to him.

The second of those soldiers was a master corporal whose duty was to supply fodder for the regimental horses. He was a soldier full of imaginative daring, simply born for partisan warfare. In the first days of September, near Piotrków, in the forest surrounded by Germans, he started criticizing the order of the regimental commander to retreat and abandon the supply carts, on which there were lots of valuable supplies. He replied that he did not see any need to leave the supply carts – we would always have time to do this later and we should at least try to take them out of this maze. Then, after the dramatic crossing of the Vistula River, he did not lose for a moment his daring imagination, and he started right away to catch the loosely, aimlessly running, saddled horses. Many Uhlans from the Thirteenth Regiment drowned while crossing the river, but eventually, the horses managed to reach the opposite bank. We lost almost all our horses because we were ferrying ourselves in the boats, brought by Corporal Sadowski, but we saved all our men. This master corporal, whose name I cannot remember after so many years, had tremendous presence of mind in this situation, for he immediately started rounding up the horses of the 13th Regiment. As a result of his action, we had not only infantry units with machine guns but also a small mounted detachment.

Then, there was a discussion among the soldiers of what should be done next. Most of them were inclined toward the idea that we should march further east toward Białystok and Lida, where our regiment was most likely reorganizing itself for further action. This master corporal abruptly stopped the discussion, maintaining that it was our duty to join the first fighting unit and, as soon as possible, go back to the battle. Even a few days ago, on the 25th of September, amidst this strange chaos which was around us when we were standing in the forest near Krasnobród, he galloped in on a foaming horse and reported to me that during his search for fodder for the horses, he saw just a few kilometers from there, a unit of anti-tank guns moving in an easterly direction, straight toward the jaws of the Bolsheviks. At the same time, observers sitting on top of the trees were reporting to Lt. Colonel Nowosielski that they spotted a unit of German tanks advancing on the other side of the Wieprz River. We sped together with the master corporal *en carrière* and after three quarters of an hour the

IN THE SHADOW OF KATYN

officer commanding the anti-tank guns reported and was at the disposition of Lt. Col. Nowosielski, in that way increasing considerably the fire power of the regiment.

And now these faithful companions of mine, whose bravery I had an opportunity to witness so many times, came with a proposal that while there was still time, we should desert the regiment. I understood that there was a psychological crisis in the rank and file. I reported this immediately to the colonel. The colonel, in my presence, went to inspect the units. In one place, where there was the highest concentration of bivouacking soldiers, he ordered them to assemble. He said that it came to his attention that some of them considered that the war was over and wanted to leave the regiment. The colonel relayed to them information from the radio in Warsaw that the city was still fighting, and mentioned General Sosnkowski, who was still engaged in action at nearby Lwów. We were going south, where we had excellent chances of joining with General Sosnkowski. Finally, he demanded that those who contemplated going home to step forward. There was silence in the ranks, nobody moved. For the moment the crisis was postponed.

More or less after one hour, I was informed that groups of soldiers were forming who had decided to leave the regiment and destroy their weapons. I reported this to the colonel. He did not say a word; he did not even look at me; his sad eyes askance as if through the walls of the room he could see some faraway worlds. I went outside. The sparsely treed pine forest in which the regiment was bivouacking looked like a market place. Soldiers were dividing themselves into groups of those who were going and those who were remaining with the colonel. Calculations were made of how much weaponry was necessary for those who were staying, and the remainder was going to be destroyed so it would not fall into the hands of the Bolsheviks. With hammers they were breaking down the bridges of the machine guns, and the rifles and handguns were going to be put in the fire. I understood that any amount of persuasion would be useless. Perhaps there was some healthy instinct in these soldiers' logic, I thought.

I approached a sergeant major who was an armorer of the 85th Infantry Regiment and who had left Nowa Wilejka with me in September of 1939. I knew he belonged to those that were leaving. "Sergeant," I said to him, "could you do me a favor? Would you choose a good cavalry rifle for me and, most importantly, one whose straps should be reasonably comfortable." So far I had only a handgun as a personal weapon. After a while the sergeant brought me a perfectly shining barrel. I took my blotter and started writing a letter to my family, which I intended to give to the departing soldiers.

In the meantime, fire was set to the stack, which was sprayed with kerosene. Flames spread immediately. Almost simultaneously, a strong wind started blowing, hurling burning pieces into the air. The packages of ammunition thrown onto the stack were exploding with a dry crackling sound. In the clearing it became quite hot. The slanting red rays of the setting sun were mixed with the flames of the burning stack, giving a mysterious color to the branches of the nearby trees. I had a feeling that the fire from the burning remnants of our regimental possessions was igniting the world around us, and at any moment everything would come crumbling down. I could not bear it any longer; something painful was tightening my throat; a veil appeared in front of my eyes, giving everything around me strange misty outlines. I quickly shook the

FROM PIOTRKÓW TO KATYN

hands of the departing comrades in arms and slowly walked in the direction of the mansion. Behind the fences of nearby buildings and behind the wide branches of the trees, figures of peasants were moving like shadows, waiting for the booty of the disintegrating military arm of the Polish Republic. On entering the mansion, I came upon General Wołkowicki, Lt. Colonel Nowosielski, and Lieutenant Sielicki in the company of a tall, gray-haired lady into whose hands they were giving the "treasure", and charging her with the task of safekeeping – which every Polish woman would accept with reverence – the Regimental Colors of the 77th Infantry Regiment.

Old Soldier

The estate was empty. In the dining room, the table had not yet been cleared after tea; a big calf's ham was lying on the meat platter – only just started – and nearby were home-made cakes. The last rays of the setting sun were falling on the table throwing a red orange hue on the white tablecloth. It seemed to me that in the neighboring room behind the shut door lay the body of a deceased person. I stood, supporting myself lightly on my rifle, and started ruminating. I was thinking about my years as a boy – an adolescent – as if it were only yesterday: the student conspiracy circle at the beginning of the last war, celebrating national festivities, dreaming about the Polish Army, the secret Polish Military Organization acting behind the enemy lines, days of elation and of realized dreams; but now everything again seemed to be falling apart. Were those twenty years only a short illusion?

At that moment, I felt that I was not alone. I turned around. Right behind me stood General Wołkowicki, a tall man with an upright bearing despite certain deformities of figure; he had a big red nose, typical of people who through their long lives pumped into their organisms more than one barrel of alcohol. It seemed to me that I had seen his silhouette before on an engraving portraying professional soldiers of old times.

"Lieutenant, you're a defeatist," said the general. I looked at him with the expression of a criminal caught red-handed. "Lieutenant," continued the general, "I went through the whole of Russia all the way to Vladivostok in order to get to the then Polish Army forming in France. We shall manage to break through into Hungary now."

"General," I replied, "trying to reach Hungary is not the point, but...." I stopped abruptly. I felt that if I finished my sentence, it really would sound defeatist.

Later on, when I was an inmate of the famous Lubyanka Prison in Moscow, from the prison library they gave me the well-publicized Russian historical book by Novikov-Priboy under the title *Tsushima*[5]. There is the following scene in that book. On the flagship of Admiral Nebogatov, leader of the squadron, a war council is taking place. The situation is desperate in face of the far superior Japanese forces. The first to speak is the youngest in rank, a midshipman, Wołkowicki. "Initiate the fight, then scuttle the ship," was his statement. The author sets the midshipman, Wołkowicki, as an example of military responsibility against the degenerate higher leadership of the Imperial Fleet. This junior naval officer, Wołkowicki, now was General Wołkowicki in command of us near Tomaszów Lubelski.

---

[5] General Wołkowicki, as a junior naval officer, took part in the battle of Tsushima where, in 1904, the Russian Imperial fleet surrendered to the Japanese.

IN THE SHADOW OF KATYN

General Wołkowicki's educational background was that of a naval officer. After the Japanese war, he finished the Russian Military Academy for higher staff officers. At the beginning of the First World War, he was assigned to the Black Sea Fleet, which was then commanded by the famous Admiral Kolchak. After the beginning of the Russian Revolution, he managed to get to France by way of the Far East and from there, with the army of General Haller, he came to Poland as a commander of an Infantry Battalion. In the last year before the war against Germany, General Wołkowicki was already in the process of going into retirement; however, he was called up to active duty as a commander of the reserves in the army of General Dąb-Biernacki. In the second half of September 1939, after the Bolsheviks' incursions, General Wołkowicki went to the front where he took command of our division.

When we were at Kozelsk, I once asked General Wołkowicki, "General, in the last days of September, you already knew that we could not avoid being taken prisoners. You could have led us in such a way that, eventually, the Germans rather than the Russians would have captured us. You, General, consciously took a road rather closer to the Bolsheviks than to the Germans. Why did you do that?"

General Wołkowicki answered, "If we had fallen into German hands, we would be locked up till the end of the war, and we would have no chances of further participating in the fighting. Here we have many possibilities. Obviously, they can execute all of us, but it shouldn't deter us; death is a normal risk of war. But there is also a possibility that we might come out of here before the end of the war and still take part in the fighting."

General Wołkowicki was undoubtedly a born soldier. He was the same in the face of defeat of the Tsarist Russian Fleet near Tsushima as in the face of defeat of newly reborn Poland. In September 1939, as a commander, he could still make great decisions and carry them out. There was a certain amount of steadfastness in the silhouette of that old soldier with all his virtues and vices.

Colonel Nowosielski was a much more complicated personality; he was not only an intelligent and well-educated staff officer, but he also had a touch of romanticism. In the meditating expression of his handsome and masculine face, in his soft voice when addressing his subordinates, there was an aura of mystery. He was a soldier who grew up under the influence of Piłsudski's personality. As a frontline commander, he represented undoubtedly the best traditions of Piłsudski's era, so much darkened in the eyes of the Polish Nation by the mistakes and inequities of Polish politicians who were ruling the country after Marshal Piłsudski's death.

When I came out of Russia in 1942, I heard many stories about the so-called "heroes of the Zaleszczyki Highway,"[6] those high-ranking officers who, in September of 1939, were running away to Romania, taking with them their belongings and, from our meager army supplies, removing motorized transport for their families, having even their mistresses accompany them. A high-ranking officer, undoubtedly, was not a popular person in the Polish Nation after 1939, and I doubt whether he is today. But so little has been said and is being said about those high-ranking officers who, in the second half of 1939, were trying to fight from the forests and whose behavior was in every respect exemplary. So little was done to bring out the truth of those who died in the battlefield, or were sunk into the abyss of Soviet and German concentration camps,

---

[6] Zaleszczyki, a town close to the border of Poland and Romania.

FROM PIOTRKÓW TO KATYN

or were fighting under pseudonyms in the Home Army.

When I hear about those who had the misfortune to take part in demoralizing spectacles, which apparently took place in September 1939, on the highways leading to Lithuania and Romania, my thoughts always go to my commanders. Among "these" there was not a single one whom their subordinates could accuse of any lack of soldierly valor. My colleagues who are lying in the Katyn graves knew nothing about the scenes on the Zaleszczyki Highway. This old retired general, who, already after the Soviet attack, appeared in the frontline in order to assume command over the army remnants who were not giving up the fight; and this taciturn, handsome colonel, inspecting the most forward positioned companies during the action in order to give an example to the rank and file; these officers will always be remembered as a symbol of that spirit which existed in the officers' corps.

Captivity

The day that I am describing saw the end of our tragic military episode. While General Wołkowicki and I were standing in the sunlit dining room of the manor house, Colonel Nowosielski was issuing orders to form a marching column. We started moving well after sunset. The colonel was riding at the head of the column; the commanders of two battalions were conducting the remnants of their units, behind which there was a string of carts. Altogether there were about 300 men. By now, it was not the same well-knit fighting unit which only two days ago was fighting near Krasnobród; these were the remnants, impregnated with one common desire – not to engage in a fight, but to slip through the corridor between withdrawing Germans and incoming Russians to the Hungarian border. The night was quite chilly; it was impossible to stay in the saddle because my feet were freezing. I dismounted, loosened the girth and led the horse by the bridle. Not far from me, in the darkness of the September night, some human shapes were also moving. I was listening to their conversation. They were reserve officers from Silesia. They were talking about Russia as our natural ally. One of them was relating to his colleague that he always felt sympathy toward Russia. The conversation permeated with the faith that they considered Russia as our friend, ready to come to our aid. I began to think to myself: There is more wisdom among the Byelorussian peasants and Wilno riffraff, who at dusk had destroyed their weapons so that it would not fall into the hands of Bolsheviks, than there is among these intellectuals from Silesia.

In the morning, in a small village situated among the forest, we stopped for a rest. As usual, the battalion commanders established sentries with machine guns for protection. General Wołkowicki, after a certain amount of hesitation, ordered the sentries to be removed but the kitchens and carts to be camouflaged in the bushes growing nearby. Our only chance to break through was not to advance by aggresion, but by marching over the side roads and not drawing any attention to our presence.

After an hour, more or less, the Soviet cavalry who flooded the village engulfed us. The Regimental Adjutant, Lt. Sielicki, who was sleeping near me on a bundle of straw, did not have time to put on his uniform and was taken to Kozelsk in only a short riding jacket. The privates were released, but the officers were taken to the divisional command, ten kilometers away. On the way, there was a pause during which we were completely cleaned out of our watches and other valuables.

We were arranged in a semi-circle in front of the divisional command. The commander of the division, young and extremely energetic, came out saluting and greeting us in broken Polish and continuing in Russian, "Good morning, Mr. Officers. So the Germans arranged for you actually a total war." Then, with a noticeable approval, he started talking about the strategy of the German attack, and particularly about the role of air power in destroying Polish communications.

Someone from our file interjected, "Today the Germans made war on us – tomorrow they do it to you."

"*Nu, nam, nje sdellayut,*" (They are not going to do it to us) replied the Soviet general. "*Ah vot,*" (See) he added, pointing out the revolver on his breast, which was supposed to mean that the Soviet Union was sufficiently armed to repulse any attacks.

Next, the Soviet commander asked who, from the prisoners, had the highest rank. Someone pointed out to him General Wołkowicki and Lt. Colonel Nowosielski. "You, General, you must know the old Tsarist Army?" he asked General Wołkowicki. Then, the Soviet commander approached Lt. Colonel Nowosielski with some lengthy questioning which I cannot remember; anyway, it would not make much difference because the colonel did not answer. He looked at the Soviet commander as if he did not see him, as if observing some visions in space. The Soviet commander, guessing that the colonel did not understand Russian, asked the bystanders to translate it. One of our officers interpreted it.

To that, the colonel in his usually calm voice without the slightest shade of affectation answered, "Tell him that I have not the slightest intention of answering any questions."

The Soviet commander waved his hands, "I am not insisting, I am not insisting. If he does not want to, he does not have to." He then explained that only at the higher levels, where he was sending us, were we going to be really investigated.

The conversation was ended. They started loading us into a truck, which had just arrived. One of my colleagues complained to the Soviet commander of the division that on the way here our watches were taken. The Soviet commander called the commander of the convoy and told him to return the watches. After a few minutes, they brought a whole pile of watches, among which each one of us was allowed to find his own property. One of the Soviet officers remarked that the commander of the convoy would most likely be shot. One of our officers turned to the Soviet general with the pronouncement that the prisoners did not have any complaints regarding the incident with the watches. "Well, our military field judges don't joke around," he answered.

On the way, our guards informed us that, most likely, we were going to be handed over to the NKVD, which certainly was going to treat us in a far worse manner than the frontline Soviet Army. When we were driving through Tarnopol, my colleagues pointed out to me two Polish officers being led on the sidewalk by a Russian convoy. They said that one of them was Colonel Obertyński, chief of staff of General Dąb-Biernacki, and the other was Major Bąkiewicz, chief of intelligence of that unit. Because I had lost my glasses, I was not in a position to recognize them. In Lwów, we were placed for a few hours in the Town Square, and then we were transported to the railway station and put on a train. It was a most psychologically difficult moment, when the train crossed from the Polish border into the Soviet Union.

FROM PIOTRKÓW TO KATYN

Near the station in Podwołoczyski, there were several zones separated by wire where, under the open sky, Polish prisoners were kept. Besides the soldiers, there were also a great number of policemen who had been segregated into a separate unit of prisoners. After two days, we were loaded into Russian wide-gauge cattle carriages, which were extremely dirty. From there to Kiev, we were transported very slowly. For the first time we came into contact with the conditions under which prisoners were transported through the wide spaces of Russia. Coldness and starvation, thin layers of sticky, stinking dirt covering the floor of the carriages, lack of water, and no possibility of releasing one's natural need, except on the floor. After a few days of such a journey, we were escorted to go for a meal in Kiev, which was prepared in the barracks of the workers' cafeteria, not far from the station. In a huge wooden hall, we sat down alongside of the long tables. Everybody received a plate and a piece of bread; for each group of six people a bowl of tasty Ukrainian borscht was provided. In the barracks there was perfect cleanliness; the plates were clean, and the people in white smocks who served us gave a pleasant impression. These were a few hours of psychological and physical relaxation after our sad journey.

When we were taken for the meal, we noticed many women along the railway lines and railway buildings who – it was obvious – came here especially to look at us. They were looking at us with compassionate looks, some were even crying. This reaction was unexpected to us, and was moving and strange at the same time. Only afterwards, having met many Ukrainians in prisons and camps, I understood it completely. Before 1939, in the capital of the Ukraine, there was a popular legend about the splendid military organization of the Polish State, and many people were living with the hope that one day the Polish Army would bring them liberty. Now those liberators-to-be were transported in cattle trucks in the same way as millions of Soviet prisoners. It was causing sadness and compassion and, at the same time, grievance against the liberators for disappointing their hopes. At a certain moment, one of those women, in a few jumps, dashed through the armed sentries, ran to Lt. Colonel Nowosielski and pushed into his hand a big, home-made, white bread roll, and ran away before the colonel even had a chance to say thank you. Why, in a crowd of marching prisoners, did she choose Lt. Colonel Nowosielski? Was it a coincidence? Or was she attracted by the mysterious expression in the face of that handsome officer?

Putyvl

From Kiev we were brought to the district of Putyvl in the Northern Ukraine. Putyvl is a very old town. Prince Igor, whose fight against the nomadic tribe of Polovtsy (Cumans) is described in the oldest monument of Russian literature, *Lay of Igor's Campaign*, was once the prince of Putyvl. When we were led out of the train, I was trying to recall the modern version of that poem, which described the desperation of Princess Jaroslavna:

> *It is not the call of the cuckoo you hear*
> > *in the dark of the night.*
> *But in Putyvl Jaroslavna is crying, all alone,*
> > *by the city walls.*

IN THE SHADOW OF KATYN

The picture of a sobbing princess sitting on the town walls yearning and asking the wind to bring her the news, which was to be the news of the catastrophe, was responding to what was painfully tormenting my soul.

Near Putyvl, we were placed in a village from which the population had been evicted. There were fields of beetroots around us. Our group was placed in a house consisting of two separate apartments: one a three-room and the other a two-room apartment. In the two-room apartment, they brought a group of captured Polish police officers; in the other three rooms, they placed more than a hundred officers. Among them was a close group of about thirty officers from our regiment. From the others, I remember primarily a few higher officers from the staff of General Dąb-Biernacki: Colonel Künstler, who was their commander of artillery; Lt. Colonel Tyszyński, who was commander of engineers; and Major Solski.

Captain Piotr Dunin-Borkowski, with whom I became closely acquainted, also belonged to the staff of General Dąb-Biernacki. Known as an officer who completed the higher military academy, he went into the reserves and farmed on his wife's estate near Grodno. Also he had been socially active. He was a chairman of one of the combatant organizations, I think, the Union of Reserve Officers for the district Wilno-Nowogródek. When called up before the war, he was attached to the staff of General Dąb-Biernacki. Tall and dark-haired, with gentle manners, he probably must have made quite an impression on his surroundings. When I looked at him, I tried to imagine him in civilian clothes; I always thought he would look very stylish in dress-coat.

He spoke to me about the misfortune that happened to him just before the war: the death of his little daughter. A relative of his, a nun, said at the time that with the approaching calamities the pure soul of that child could become a shield for the whole family. When tormented about the unknown fate of his family, Captain Borkowski thought about the soul of his child and about the strange words of the nun, which now in the present cataclysm that touched Poland assumed new meaning. I remember once we talked about the mode of life of the prisoners, but I do not exactly remember what was said. All I recall is this last sentence said to me with a profound expression on his face, "Listen, it is necessary to pray." In his words there was the deep conviction that around us there were sources of a force about which people, blind to the truth of its existence, knew nothing. Later on, during different transitions of my fate, I often remembered those words and that expression on his face with which they were said.

In Kozelsk, Captain Borkowski later became an educational advisor in his dormitory, organizing lectures for his neighbors. I was one of the lecturers whom he engaged for that purpose. It was at Kozelsk he received the news which gave him peace of mind that his wife with children succeeded in moving from Grodno, under Soviet occupation, to Kraków, under German occupation, which meant that they were out of reach of Soviet deportations. I do not know when he was sent from Kozelsk to Katyn. It had to have happened some time at the beginning of April 1940, because afterward, during the liquidation of the Kozelsk camp, I did not meet him. In the report of the International Commission, which examined the Katyn graves, Captain Piotr Dunin-Borkowski was listed under the number 2283. Major Adam Moszyński, in his list of the victims of Katyn, quotes him twice: once as Borkowski and a second time as Dunin-

FROM PIOTRKÓW TO KATYN

Borkowski.[7]

A great source of material for the International Commission was supplied by examining the remains of the aforementioned Major Adam Solski, because on him they found several pages of his diary, in which he described the most important happenings in the life of the prisoners. This diary became one of the sources for reconstructing the history of the Katyn murders. The fate of two other officers from the staff of General Dąb-Biernacki's army, Colonel Künstler and Lt. Colonel Tyszyński, were completely different. They managed to avoid the Katyn Forest because they were selected for the so-called "villa of bliss" near Moscow, where several officers, with whom Soviet authorities were expected to have a certain amount of cooperation, had been sent. Colonel Künstler was later sent to the camp of Grazovetz[8], and after that he was in the Polish Army in the Middle East. The fate of Lt. Col. Tyszyński, who was apparently also staying in the "villa of bliss", is unknown to me. Apparently, he was also in the Polish Army in the Middle East but he became a member of the retired officers (so-called Group II).

The separate group in Putyvl consisted of cavalry officers with Lt. Colonel Żelisławski as their commander, who – as far as I remember – was next in command to General Anders who led the cavalry brigade in Nowogródek. Besides the officers from General Anders' units, there was also a small group from the staff of the military academy in Grudziądz with Lt. Colonel Wania and cavalry Captain Wacław Stankiewicz, native of Wilno, ex-officer of the thirteenth unit, with whom I started a great friendship. In March of 1940, when we were in Kozelsk, Wacław confided in me that during this Easter period he would like very much to go to confession and receive the Holy Sacraments. I talked to my colleagues who were organizing secret religious meetings, and I communicated to him the prescribed time and place. I think that it was a most valuable service that God allowed me to render to a companion just before the Katyn drama.

There were also two officers in our room who later on belonged to the organizers of religious life in Kozelsk. They were: one-eyed captain of engineers, Antoniewicz, who before the war was the director of the river port in Modlin and, in 1939, commander of the Battalion of Engineers, a native of Grodno; and his friend, First Lieutenant Połujan, who before the war was district engineer in Oszmiana. Captain Antoniewicz had great missionary zeal. Faith and piety radiated from him; he had a strong need to awaken in others these values, which were part of his inner convictions. First Lieutenant Połujan was, it seems to me, completely under his influence. Both of them were undoubtedly excellent soldiers; as Lt. Colonel Nowosielski did, they had kept the units in battle readiness till the very end, and they too had tried to break through to Hungary, arms in hand. Later on, in Kozelsk, First Lieutenant Połujan belonged to those who eagerly agitated for the strongest possible resistance against any attempt to transfer us to the German authorities. It seemed to me

---

[7] Moszyński, A., *Lista Katyńska. Jency obózow Kozelsk - Ostashkov - Starobelsk zaginieni w Rosji Sowieckiej*, London 1949. (Katyn List. Prisoners of the camps Kozelsk - Ostashkov - Starobelsk perished in the Soviet Russia, Gryf, London 1949).

[8] Grazovets, a town in Northern Russia where the prisoners from the camps in Kozelsk, Starobelsk and Ostashkov, who were spared execution, were sent; in total 394 persons (less than 3% of the total prison population).

that he was organizing a unit that had some specific plan of breaking through to Syria to join the army of General Weygand or anywhere to the West. He maintained that our efforts should not be directed toward rejoining our families, which at that time was expected if we were to be transferred to the German authorities, but mainly to attempt to take part in further fighting. In Putyvl, Captain Antoniewicz and First Lieutenant Połujan were organizing small groups dedicated to saying the rosary together. It was the month of October when in all the Catholic churches of the world rosaries were being said every evening. Today, when I remember these two individuals who had an unbreakable friendship, I think about them as modern crusaders.

In Putyvl, I also met a young scholar, Doctor Godłowski, who just before the war was nominated as a Professor of Psychiatry at Stefan Batory University. Professor Rose, world-renowned expert in brain research, who for many years worked in Germany, occupied this chair previously. To make it possible for Professor Rose to continue his work – who as a Jew could not do so in Germany after the Nazis took over – the University of Wilno formed a special institute for brain research. This institute was given the assignment of studying the brain of Marshal Piłsudski, and it was carried out with great veneration by the Wilno medical center, which among its staff had many admirers of Józef Piłsudski. The sudden death of Professor Rose was a great blow for this center and to find a suitable replacement was considered a task of great responsibility. As a result, the 37-year-old lecturer of the Jagiellonian University of Kraków, Doctor Godłowski, was the accepted choice.

In the summer of 1939, Professor Godłowski, together with his family, came to Wilno to take up his duties for the 1939/40 academic year. When war broke out, he was called up into the army as a First Lieutenant-Doctor and attached to one of the border guards' battalions in Volhynia. The Russian troops took him from the train in which his battalion was being transported to take part in the fight against the Germans.

When in Putyvl, Professor Godłowski delivered a lecture on the problems connected with brain research. It was an inauguration of a series of lectures, which developed extensively later on in Kozelsk. General Wołkowicki, who had worried about the morale of the prisoners, initiated this.

It was October 1939, in other words, during the time when universities were starting the autumn sessions. If it were not for the war, then most probably during this time Dr. Godłowski, as a recently nominated professor, would have had his inaugural lecture, which according to the tradition of the University of Wilno would be a public one. It surely would have been a memorable event in the medical department. As a result of the turbulence in which all of us were swirling in this frantic dance of elements, Professor Godłowski inaugurated the lectures in the most incredible circumstances. He was of more than middle-height with a pale but healthy face, and in black well-polished boots, his silhouette gave a certain elegance of expression. He stood with his back against a low and wide Russian oven and was talking about his specialty. Behind the small windows of that hut we could see barbed wire and, beyond the Bolshevik sentry, the expansive view of large fields of beetroots. On the floor of the hut, unimaginably crowded, officers were sitting and listening to the lecture. "This is the one, who was in charge of the marshal's brain," whispered someone behind me to his neighbor.

I have seen Professor Godłowski many times in Kozelsk. He happened to be

FROM PIOTRKÓW TO KATYN

placed in the most unpleasant and coldest halls of the camp. I remember seeing him on his bunk in coat and boots, reading the English version of Churchill's memoirs from the First World War. Always very calm and composed, he was neither an optimist nor a pessimist, and he was not influenced by the changing waves of moods which oscillated in the Kozelsk environment, for everywhere where people are in constant confinement, they are going to be influenced by each other. He was a tactful man as is typical of a highly cultured person, and he understood people, as a doctor of sick souls should; after all, it was his profession. Emanating from him was this harmony and inner strength. I did not notice that he was especially friendly with anyone, but he was generally respected and I never heard a word of criticism directed toward him. I cannot remember the day when he departed for Katyn; it seems to me it was in one of the first transports.

From the other prisoners, whom I met in Putyvl, I also remember General Bohatyrewicz and Pastor Colonel Peszke, a chief chaplain of the Evangelic-Augsburg Church. General Bohatyrewicz was about 70 years old and had been retired for many years. The Bolsheviks found him in Druskienniki, where the old man had gone for a cure. During the war of 1919-1920, General Bohatyrewicz had been a commander of one of the Lithuanian-Byelorussian Regiments; I think it was the Infantry Regiment from Grodno, belonging to the Second Lithuanian-Byelorussian Division (later the 29th Infantry Division). The old man was suffering from numerous heart attacks, but he held himself very well, was constantly in good spirits, and attempted to make the impression of being very brisk.

Pastor Colonel Peszke was well respected and liked. He was transferred with us to Kozelsk where he shared the same fate as that of the Roman Catholic chaplains. Together with them, during Christmas Eve of 1939, he was sent in an unknown direction. Probably, together with the others he is lying in some grave, perhaps in the vicinity of Katyn. I would think that one could propose the hypothesis that the martyrdom of Katyn started on the first day of Christmas 1939, when probably most of the Roman Catholic military chaplains were shot (Prelate Wojtyniak, Father Skorel, Father Colonel Nowak, and others).

In Putyvl, our group of the 19th Infantry Division was in the same room, and we slept on the extremely crowded bare floor. It was impossible for anybody to lie on his back. If someone wanted to turn over, he had to forewarn his neighbors as this could only be executed as a joint maneuver. Colonel Nowosielski was lying beside me; my legs were pressing on General Wołkowicki, which was rather comfortable, but extremely embarrassing. The general was in good form and was telling us fragments of his rich past. In 1904, he was taken prisoner of war by the Japanese, and from there he tried to escape to Australia, but was caught when he was already on a ship, pretending to be the son of a rich English woman while not knowing the English language. The Japanese court sentenced him to two years of imprisonment. The then midshipman Wołkowicki spent only six weeks of that sentence. He was talking about the Japanese military prison where, as natural mores of that country, there were neither beds nor chairs. With a sense of humor, he was saying that right now his only material possessions were an extra pair of long underwear, which he was using as a pillow. I also had noticed that the general started rather systematically to donate his bread ration to some junior officers, explaining simultaneously that he actually did not feel hungry.

IN THE SHADOW OF KATYN

Lt. Col. Nowosielski was, as always, pensive and not inclined to conversation. Whenever he spoke about his life before the war, his voice became even more subdued and soft-spoken. He spoke about his wife, who died from tuberculosis not long before the war; about the sad days of being a widower; about his sister and about the nice group of close friends among whom he passed his life, and about the higher military academy. Most of the time, however, he was quiet. The officers all looked up to him. Here, in this poor hut, in prison and depravation, he was always our commander, not only because of his rank, but also as a choice from our hearts.

After some time, they gave us wooden boards and allowed us to build double bunks. Again, I got my place near Lt. Col. Nowosielski. On the other side of me, there was an officer cadet from Silesia, previously mentioned, who even though offered a chance to leave Putyvl, had decided to stay with us voluntarily in order to share the fate of his comrades in arms. We also had permission for morning exercises. They were conducted with great skill by one of the company commanders from our regiments, a professional officer, who might have been a graduate of the Institute of Physical Education. The strange thing about him was that he was neither from eastern Poland nor from Silesia, but it seems to me he was from the district of Mazovia (northern Poland). I cannot remember his name, but I vividly remember the expression on his face; he had a small, stocky body with efficient movements. He was a man with a great sense of humor; his jokes were uplifting to our misery here in Putyvl, as well as later on in Kozelsk. When he noticed depression or when he was a witness of constant gossip about our release, he used to say, "Yes, the most difficult is going to be the first three years; after that, we are going to get used to it and then it will be easier." At that time, the thought that this captivity might last so long seemed to be something so monstrous that no one would even let that thought penetrate his mind, and the listeners, as a rule, burst into laughter as if someone told a good joke. It so happened that those few from the Kozelsk camp who managed to avoid the Katyn massacre stayed in the Soviet Union for almost exactly three years.

Only after some time, we realized that we were not the only "zone" surrounded by barbed wire, but in many other places they had allocated groups of Polish prisoners: officers, privates, and police officers. The police officers from the neighboring "suite" were soon taken away and probably deported; in their place they brought a number of privates, almost exclusively from central Poland. They were selected from larger camps and grouped according to districts. The promise of Soviet political officers, that they were destined to be returned to their homeland, seemed quite probable. I think that many of my colleagues received that exchange of neighbors (that means, departure of police officers and arrival of military privates) with relief.

Twice I had the opportunity to observe our police officers in the Soviet Union: once in Podwołoczyski, and a second time in Putyvl. Both times I felt a rather negative impression of them. The break up of inner discipline happened faster with them than with other categories of prisoners. They often complained about the order of things before the war during independent Poland. Their attitude toward army officers was unfriendly, often even hostile. In Podwołoczyski, I heard a group of police officers shouting in our direction, "Your rule has ended!" One would have thought that the police officers were the most deprived category of citizens in independent Poland.

I was a witness when, in Putyvl, General Wołkowicki was compelled to react

FROM PIOTRKÓW TO KATYN

strongly to the behavior of the police officers and forewarned them that after the return to the homeland, he would make them suffer the consequences. I am writing these words with real sadness, because the lot of the police officers was certainly not less tragic than the lot of my colleagues murdered at Katyn. About the six thousand murdered in the camp of Ostashkov, in the Kalinin district, to which most of the police officers were sent, we know nothing. One has to admit that Polish society is quite a bit less interested in their case than in the case of Kozelsk and Starobelsk. I would hope other observations as to the behavior of police officers in the Soviet camps did not confirm my impression. When I think of this, I cannot resist the presumption that there must have been some serious flaw in the selection and training of our police officers' cadres.

The short contact with a group of privates, lasting only a few days, left us with a favorable impression. Never in my life had I the opportunity to come into close contact en masse either with peasants or with the ordinary worker from central Poland. Most of the time in the army I had to deal with the Polish-Byelorussian soldiers, who were psychologically very different from the people in central Poland. Only for a short time during 1919, did I serve in an artillery unit consisting mostly of the riffraff from Warsaw, but they were a specific element and it is difficult to consider them as a typical representation of the Polish people. Wrocław is the only town where I ever lived within the boundaries of present Poland. Therefore, several days mingling with privates returning from Russian prison camps was rather a revelation to me. The main feature, which struck me the most, was their definite feeling of superiority to everything that they had seen in Russia.

Among the officers there was extreme dedication to soldierly duty, one might even say, total devotion to this duty. Russia was the treacherous neighbor who, by an unexpected attack in the back, made it impossible for us to fulfill this duty. Just because of that, the feelings toward Russia could not be positive. Disorder, dirt, stink, and boorish behavior, which we observed, awakened contempt in us. But equally, many officers and in particular reserve officers, with a certain amount of interest and good faith, listened to what Russian political officers said, or watched propaganda films shown in the late evening in our courtyard. When our officers answered Russian political officers that they would like to see Russia as a Polish ally to fight Germany, they said that with great sincerity even though their feelings toward Russia were often ambivalent. All the observations which I made in Putyvl (and later on also in Kozelsk) confirmed the impressions I already had between the wars: that the Polish intelligentsia, being en masse extremely anti-German, was also potentially pro-Russian.

In the attitude of the privates, I did not notice this complexity of feelings. Their attitude was completely clear and simple. It was an attitude of complete rejection of everything they had seen in the Soviet Union and had heard from political officers. With a great sense of humor, they told the stories about various propositions of a voluntary stay in the Soviet Union, which were often made to them. This group was impregnated with some kind of instinct, which formed a psychological wall around them which Soviet propaganda could not penetrate. I also made another interesting observation: The attitude toward the Germans was obviously saturated with the realization that they were the enemy who invaded us, but the hatred toward this enemy was more moderated than that which prevailed among the intelligentsia. At that time, my previous observations about the potentially pro-Russian attitude among the Polish intelligentsia were reinforced. I began to form a thesis that if, some time in the future, Russia psychologically were to conquer Poland, it would do so through Polish intellectuals, but not by gaining the sympathy of the Polish masses. The news, at present emanating from Poland, seems to confirm this thesis.

Our relation with these new neighbors could not be better. They brought with them a certain amount of Russian money, which they exchanged with us at a favorable rate since they expected to return to Poland soon. Tailors, cobblers, and watchmakers started functioning immediately, performing various small repairs. They took with them many letters to be delivered in Poland. They were moved during the night in the last week of October. It was a special night in Putyvl. Near to our building there was a road through which they constantly marched units of our soldiers from different "zones" who were singing Polish military songs. When they passed near our building, they shouted, "Long live Polish officers!" Such were the Polish masses in Russian captivity.

After the privates had left, it was communicated to us that we were going to be transferred to a place where there was going to be a larger concentration of Polish prisoners. Shortly, there was a formal transfer of prisoners from the Red Army into the hands of the NKVD, which was connected with multiple checking of names, ranks and so on. In the last days of October, we were ordered to march to a larger railway station near which there was a large sugar plant. We found numerous groups of officers bivouacking there who had come from other nearby "zones" of internment. Among others I met there was Wacław Komarnicki, my elder colleague from the Department of Law and Social Studies at Stefan Batory University.

Kozelsk

In the first days of November, we were transferred from Putyvl to Kozelsk. We traveled first north toward Bryansk, and from there in a more easterly direction toward the region of Tula. We were moved again in a cattle train, but these did have two tiers of bunks to sleep in. Again, my place was near Lt. Col. Tyszyński and Col. Künstler. During that journey, I found out from Lt. Col. Tyszyński that the place called Plebania, in the district of Mołodeczno where we went for the church fair on the fifteenth of August, 1939, which I wrote about before, was the property of his family. We remembered a number of common acquaintances. We disembarked during the night, and afterwards we had to march for several kilometers. A considerable portion of the road was through the streets of a small town. We saw no one. The people living in the dirty, small houses were all asleep. We had to constantly walk around muddy puddles on the unpaved streets.

Our escorts, who had police dogs with them, were rather lax. With a certain amount of quick thinking and luck, one could probably have slipped out from the marching column, but the presence of police dogs made the chances of escape rather precarious. I contrast this fact of comparative liberal behavior toward the convoy with the extremely strict supervision during the liquidation of the Kozelsk camp, five months later, when the prisoners were taken to Katyn. During that liquidation, we were taken in trucks after a very strict personal search where all sharp instruments were confiscated. We did not travel through the town, but in a round about way, and the embarkation point was on the sidings, away from the railway station. An attempt was made that the transports moving in the direction of Smolensk were not to be observed by the local population. After arriving at Kozelsk in the beginning of November, everything was being done in a less strict manner.

The Kozelsk camp consisted of two main parts: the monastery and the so-called "Skit". The monastery, founded by the Puzyn princes, was known in pre-Revolutionary Russia as *"Optina Pustyn"* and played a considerable role in the history of the Greek Orthodox Church in the centuries before the revolution. Apparently, for a certain amount of time, Rasputin lived there and had during the reign of Nicholas II considerable influence on the administrative policy of the church, appointing bishops to the throne, et cetera.

The monastery, consisting of several buildings that were mostly constructed from bricks, also had a few churches, a wall, and a moat surrounding it. Probably in the olden days, it was a defense fortress built in the vicinity of the Muskovite Dominions and the Grand Duchy of Lithuania. The "Skit" was a place in the small forest where, in the old days, Eremite monks lived. With the passage of time, guesthouses for the pilgrims were built there. Mostly, they were wooden structures of medium or small dimensions. After the war, Professor Wiktor Sukiennicki recorded with great accuracy a description of the conditions in the Kozelsk camp and also its topography. I have seen this work only on typewritten pages, about twenty-five years ago. I do not know whether it was ever published.

The first twenty-four hours in Kozelsk I spent in the "Skit". I was assigned to one of the small wooden houses where I found a number of Polish cavalry officers whom I met before in Putyvl. There were also a few officers from the motorized units, who stood out because of their leather jackets. Also among them was Captain Kozieł-Poklewski, the owner of a fur-animal farm in the district of Wilejka. I had heard about him before the war because his wife worked as a secretary in the Theological Department of the Wilno University. We managed to start a fire with wooden boxes, found by chance, and in this small house I spent an extremely pleasant evening dedicated to recollecting the traditions of our cavalry, while stretched out on the floor on a bundle of straw. It felt as if I was injected with some narcotic. Then, for the first time in my life, I found out how much pleasurable soothing, and even happiness, a man can find in the days of defeat by reminiscing about the achievements of the past.

The next day, the casual division of inhabitants of the monastery and the "Skit" was cancelled. Concentrated in the monastery were those who before the war lived in the territories presently occupied by the Germans and in the Republic of Lithuania; that is, those who could not be considered Soviet citizens. On the other hand, those who lived in the eastern territories of the Polish Republic, whom the Soviet authorities considered to be their citizens, were placed in the "Skit". I was assigned to the monastery, not only because I was living in Wilno, which in 1939 was transferred to the Lithuanian Republic, but also because I gave false data when they were listing us. I slightly changed the sound of my name; I did not mention being a professor, but I stated that I was a civil servant in the Industrial Commercial Chamber in Warsaw. Soviet authorities found out my real identity only in March of 1940, just before the liquidation of the Kozelsk camp. Between the inhabitants of the monastery and the "Skit", the Soviets made a strict cordon. One could achieve a certain amount of communication only with the help of Russian workers, who worked in both parts of the camp, or by the fact that "Skit" inhabitants were brought, on some occasions, to the baths in the monastery and were able to pass on some information to us.

A number of my recollections of Kozelsk (November 1939 – April 1940) were printed in *Zbrodnia Katyńska*, a collective book, edited by Professor Zdzislaw Stahl, which was published for the first time in 1948, with a foreword by General Anders.[9] I would not like to repeat the same descriptions here, which generally would be known to those who have read this book. However, I would like to highlight some general conclusions from those descriptions.

Very soon after arriving in Kozelsk, it became obvious that it was mainly an interrogation camp. From the point of view of the Soviet security services (NKVD), under the leadership of the infamous Beria, its aim was to find out the characteristics of each prisoner and divide them into certain categories, which could possibly be used for the services of the Soviet State. The Soviet Union did not sign an international convention about the treatment of prisoners of war. It did not recognize any principles, as far as the individual person was concerned, but was guided only by the interest of its state, and also by its international aim, which in a sort of obscure way was described as a world revolution. The Kozelsk camp can be described as a kind of research study on the mentality and certain characteristics of a different breed of people whom, in 1939, the Soviet Union succeeded in obtaining through its pact with Hitler.

The head of the team conducting those studies was Kombryg Zarubin (Kombryg – a commanding general of a brigade), a high official of the NKVD, a cultured man, who spoke several languages and was very pleasant in conversation. He reminded me of the highly educated officers of the Tsarist military police, whom I happened to meet on social occasions in the peculiar conditions of my childhood. I wrote more about Zarubin in the aforementioned book, *Crime of Katyn*.[10] Working under him were interrogating officers, mostly ranking from lieutenant to major, whose aim, as far as I could understand, was to analyze the characteristics of individual prisoners. Those characteristics were based not only on the investigations at hand, but also on all kinds of accessible data. Information about the officers who had been living in the territories which became occupied by the Red Army was easily obtainable from there.

In addition to this, there were a number of NKVD men with the rank of NCO circulating in the camp, who visited some of the barracks and engaged prisoners in conversations on political topics. They were called *politruks*. Officially their duty was propaganda; that is, enlightening prisoners about the superiority of the Soviet system. Actually, they were not so much concerned about propaganda, as trying to find out the attitude among the prisoners en masse. One would assume that they had to send reports of these talks and discussions. The final decision of all these reports probably belonged to the Kombryg, who very often went to Moscow and probably also visited the camps in Starobelsk and Ostashkov.

His report, in all probability, was the basis for the final decision on Katyn, but it is not certain that he submitted the decision of the "final solution". The decision to

---

[9] *Zbrodnia Katyńska w świetle dokumentów*, wyd. III poszerzone, Gryf, London, 1962. ss. 18-30, 40-49 (*The Crime of Katyn, Facts and Documents*, Polish Cultural Foundation, London, 1965, pp. 21-23, pp. 45-54.

[10] *The Crime of Katyn, Facts and Documents, pp.* 31-33.

FROM PIOTRKÓW TO KATYN

separate certain individuals from the general scheme of the "final solution" probably also belonged to him. So it was, as I perceived, in my case. I think also in the case of Professor Wacław Komarnicki, exceptionally knowledgeable in constitutional and international law, and who had been conscripted as an officer of the judiciary corps. The Kombryg, right at the beginning of our internment at the Kozelsk camp, ordered that Professor Komarnicki, who in the army had the rank of second lieutenant, be transferred to the barracks assigned to colonels, where there were better living conditions. During the liquidation of the Kozelsk camp, Professor Komarnicki was sent to the Grazovetz prison camp and almost immediately after the signing of the Treaty of Sikorski-Maisky in 1941, went to London to become Justice Minister in the Government of General Sikorski. Professor Kormanicki actively supported that treaty. After arriving in London, Minister Komarnicki applied some pressure in our Ministry of Foreign Affairs and in the Soviet Embassy, to bring about my release from the concentration camp in the Far North, where I was still being kept imprisoned in spite of the treaty to release all Polish prisoners.

In Kozelsk the prisoners received the right to send letters to their families, but also they had to give their return address as "Gorky's Rest Home", in Kozelsk. It is conceivable that there was some kind of plan to establish a sanatorium in the post-monastery buildings, where the district had an extremely healthy climate. To call the place a "rest home" where, in the old church buildings, five tiers of bunks were constructed in order to squeeze into them hundreds of prisoners, could be another example of calculated deception that is so much a part of Soviet life.

Because of this return address, there were some amusing misunderstandings. I was told about one officer from Central Poland who received a letter from his wife full of bitter reproach that while he was loafing around in a rest home, she and her family were starving. In another case, a reserve officer from Lwów showed me a letter from his wife, who was pleading with him that he should use his undoubted influence with the Soviet authorities so that the local authorities in Lwów would not place unwanted tenants in her apartment. On the other hand, it has to be admitted that the conditions of physical care were better than in the Soviet prisons. Each prisoner received 800 grams of black bread every day, and for lunch and supper they were given soup and kasha [porridge]. In the soup one could sometimes fish out a small piece of meat or fish. It was not enough to assuage hunger, but it was enough to stay alive and even to keep one's body in reasonable condition. Those who volunteered for some work inside or outside the camp received additional rations.

As to the morale and attitude of the prisoners, I wrote more about it in the book, *The Crime of Katyn*.[11] With a few individual exceptions, everything was done to give each other moral support. There was a belief in a final victory with the help and goodwill of our Allies. Poles are generally inclined to rely on the help and good will of the faraway West. At the beginning of the nineteenth century, they believed in Napoleon I; they believed in Napoleon III during the January Insurrection [the revolt against Tsarist Russia, which started in January of 1863]; and during the Second World War, they believed in Churchill.

An uplifting factor among the prisoners was a well-developed religious life. In Kozelsk, we had a number of military chaplains. Because all of them were in uniforms,

---

[11] Ibid., p. 21.

it took some time for camp authorities to find out that they were not regular officers. Among the Roman Catholic chaplains, I remember Prelate Wojtyniak (assistant to the field bishop), Chaplain Nowak, Chaplain Ziółkowski, Chaplain Skorel, and Chaplain Kantak, professor of the seminary in Pińsk, who was the only civilian among the priests and was taken to Kozelsk by accident because he was in the company of several officers when the Soviet sentry arrested them.

Because all common prayers were strictly forbidden, the saying of mass had an air of the catacombs. The priests did say mass in various hidden corners of the Greek Orthodox churches or even in some sort of basement, where Holy Communion, made from wheat bread collected from the bread rations, was offered. In all the barracks the habit of evening prayer was maintained, which was done in a form of three minutes silence. When at 9 o'clock in the evening, from some dark corner or from the choir gallery of the church, changed into a prison barrack, an authoritative voice would announce, "I am ordering three minutes silence," all conversation died and all movement stopped. Everybody remained in the place where that announcement caught him. Confessions were heard mostly during the walks in the prison courtyards. If you noticed an officer, walking arm in arm with a priest, this was an indication that the Sacrament of Penance was being given. There were many times when people, who had not considered themselves to be good practicing Catholics before the war, now made confessions about their whole past life and accepted Holy Communion. Personally, I came across two such people.

On Christmas Eve of 1939, all the priests were arrested and sent away: Roman Catholic priests, Greek Orthodox priests and Protestant ministers. The only exception was Chaplain Major Ziółkowski, who had been put into solitary confinement when he had been caught saying mass. Most likely, they forgot about him when they received the order to hastily transfer all religious spiritual leaders living in the camp. One may assume that they were all murdered, with the exception of Chaplain Kantak, who was segregated during the journey, probably because he was a citizen of Gdańsk (free city of Danzig). He had the privilege of being treated as a German citizen because the Soviet Union at that time had a military treaty with Germany. Eventually, during the liquidation of Polish officers' prison camps in the spring of 1940, he was sent to Grazovetz – a prison camp near Vologda. They sent about 400 officers there, more or less 3% of the total population of officers' prison camps. The motive of sparing the lives of those 3% is not less mysterious than the decision to murder 97% of the Polish officers. The Polish officers and officer cadets who were taken from Lithuanian internment camps in the summer of 1940, during the occupation of Lithuania, were also sent to the Grazovetz prison camp.

The fact that the time to deal with the priests was chosen during the Christmas period had a symbolic meaning that created a very depressing atmosphere among the prisoners of Kozelsk. When later on in the Soviet concentration camp, I met Russian monks who maintained that Satan rules over Russia, and that the leading people in the Soviet hierarchy were the special servants of Satan, I did not treat it as nonsense. I remembered what well-known Russian philosophers, Fyodor Dostoyevsky, Vladimir Solovyev and Dmitri Merezhkovsky, had been thinking. I also remembered the conversations with Marian Zdziechowski, a friend of our family and a great expert in Russian religious psychology. To underscore this fact, it is significant that the

FROM PIOTRKÓW TO KATYN

liquidation of priests during the Christmas period of 1939 was not only happening in Kozelsk, but also in Starobelsk, as we learned from those who survived Starobelsk.[12] Therefore, it must have been the result of centralized decisions. There are no indications as to the place and manner of the probable execution of priests during the Christmas period of 1939. In any case, not one of the aforementioned clergy was among the remains which were exhumed by the International Commission in 1943.

The factor that played a great role in keeping up the morale of the prisoners was the reading of a daily news report, which became institutionalized in the camp. This happened in the evening in the huge Greek Orthodox Church, where it was read with a very loud voice from some dark corners of the huge choir gallery; so the camp police, among the several thousands of listeners, did not have an easy task trying to catch the editors and those who were reading the already edited information and articles. On March 19, 1940, the day of St. Joseph, the daily grapevine was changed into celebration, dedicated to the memory of Marshal Józef Piłsudski. It was one of the most moving celebrations that happened in my lifetime. The news on international affairs was based almost exclusively on the Soviet press, which was accessible to the inhabitants of the camp. The main editors of our daily newsletter were: Second Lieutenant Leonard Korowajczyk, whom I knew before the war as a student at the Wilno University, connected with Catholic left-wing organizations; and First Lieutenant Janusz Libicki, docent of the University of Poznan. Libicki and I, both economists, had similar views on some internal Polish matters. During the liquidation of the Kozelsk camp, when Libicki was called to join the departing transport, I carried part of his belongings up to the point where we were allowed to accompany the departing prisoners.

The composition of the Kozelsk camp oscillated to a certain extent because, from time to time, some individual prisoners were moved out, but also small groups from other camps and prisons were brought in. In 1939, a group of reserve officers in civilian clothes had come from Wilno. They said that the Soviet authorities, after taking the town, announced that Polish reserve officers had to register with the authorities. A certain number of officers did report; they registered their names and were left alone. One day, however, all those who had registered were arrested and sent to the Kozelsk camp. I do not remember their names, but one has to assume that they are all lying in the Katyn graves because I never met even one person from that group, either in the army or in the free world.

In the beginning of 1940, a group of about thirty people, mostly civilians, were brought to the Kozelsk camp and were placed in separate barracks. A solid barbed wire fence surrounded it, which was kept under surveillance by a guard, creating a special zone inside the camp area. The prisoners were absolutely forbidden to have any communication with the prisoners of this internal zone. From time to time, they took a small group of prisoners from this internal zone to the toilets, placed in the camp yard. So, if one wanted to make contact with one of those prisoners, one would have to hide oneself in the toilet area and wait patiently until the next group from the internal zone arrived. In this manner, I succeeded in coming into contact with two people from that forbidden barrack.

One of them was Colonel Korniłowicz, who in the Ministry of Defense was

---

[12] Ibid., p. 34-38.

IN THE SHADOW OF KATYN

connected with the educational services of the Army. I was better acquainted with his brother, Chaplain Korniłowicz, who was assigned to the establishment for blind people in Laski, near Warsaw, and he directed the well-known retreat house in the same place. He was the same priest who gave Marshal Piłsudski the last rites a few moments before his death in 1935. Occasionally, I used to meet still another brother who was the Director of the Institute of Social Studies in Warsaw. Colonel Korniłowicz was married to the daughter of Henryk Sienkiewicz (author of *Quo Vadis?*) and was associated with what could be called the intellectual hierarchy of the then Polish society at that time. He was the personification of Polish spiritual cultures, as it appeared to me in that strange, yet very cordial meeting. Colonel Korniłowicz took my hand in both of his and pressed it warmly for some time. He was arrested while driving in a staff car in the southern part of Poland and could not understand why the Soviet authorities treated him as an especially dangerous prisoner who had to be isolated from other military prisoners.

The other person from the district of Podole, whom I got to know from that group behind the barbed wire, was a landowner who gave me his name as Czajkowski. He appeared to be between thirty and forty years old. In answer to my question about why he was arrested, he replied that he belonged to the Promethean organization. Prometheism was a movement of the nations of the Caucasus regions that were oppressed by Russia. In this movement, as far as I know, a number of Ukrainians and Poles participated, and also, there were representatives of the nations of Central Asia. The NKVD treated people connected with Prometheism with extreme ruthlessness. Therefore, I was somewhat startled by Czajkowski's openness to an unknown person about his supposed connections with that organization. I asked him several questions about the fate of a few landowners I knew from the district of Podole, for which I received a satisfactory answer. This group, in the special zone behind the barbed wire, was kept in Kozelsk for about two weeks. Then, they were deported to an unknown destination. I doubt very much whether any of them stayed alive.

Sometime later, a second group, which consisted of civil servants and members of the judiciary corps, arrested in the district of Volhynia, was added to the prisoners of Kozelsk. From one of them who had been the head of the administration in the town of Łuck, as far as I can remember, I received information about my acquaintances from that area. One of my friends, a civil servant from the administration of the district, was arrested and he disappeared without a trace. These arrivals from Volhynia were kept at Kozelsk until the final dissolution of the camp and, most likely, they are all lying in the Katyn graves.

When the Kozelsk camp was already completely organized and the investigations by the NKVD to establish detailed files were in full progress, a third group arrived, consisting of junior officers from Starobelsk. I cannot exactly recall the number of arrivals. I was told about 200 people, but it seems to me that this number was exaggerated. From them we found out about the existence of the Starobelsk camp and the prisoners interned there. According to what these arriving officers were saying, there was a tendency to concentrate staff-officers at Starobelsk, and to send the younger officers to Kozelsk. I even heard about attempts to establish a liaison by correspondence with the Starobelsk camp.

The fact that some officers were transferred from Starobelsk to Kozelsk throws a certain light on the interpretation of various discoveries made when investigating the

FROM PIOTRKÓW TO KATYN

Katyn graves. It explains why a certain number of officers, who originally were in Starobelsk, were found in the Katyn graves. This number, however, could not be more than 2% of the Starobelsk population. From that, one cannot conclude – as it was done mistakenly by the Germans, and then by the Soviets – that the whole camp of Starobelsk is represented in the Katyn graves. Let us hope that the place where the murder of Starobelsk prisoners was committed will one day be properly explained by future historians.[13]

In March it became known that some decisions about the fate of the prisoners had already been made. The members of the administration and the *politruks* talked about it openly, but probably only very few of them knew what those decisions were. This news caused an understandable excitement among the prisoners.

At the beginning of March, certain events transpired which – as far as I can assess – played an extremely important part in my destiny. One day, Tadeusz Wirszyłło, my colleague from the university who had worked in the Justice Department, informed me that he was called before an investigating officer who, while making a file on him, asked him about professors from the University of Wilno who might be present in the Kozelsk camp. Wirszyłło named Komarnicki, Godłowski and me, not realizing that I had given false personal data. The investigating officer appeared to be stunned by the news of my presence in the camp.

After a few days, I was called to meet with Kombrig Zarubin. I was somewhat surprised, because only staff-officers were called for an interview with Kombrig; the exception being Professor Komarnicki. Kombrig received me very politely. He did not mention anything about his knowledge that I had given false data. He said, though, that he realized we belonged to two divergent philosophies of thought and our outlook on the world was completely different, but he would enjoy tremendously a discussion with a man of opposite views. Our conversation lasted for more than two hours. It was difficult to find out what interested him the most. He asked me about my journeys to Germany before the war and also about my contacts and acquaintances in the Polish Ministry of Foreign Affairs. Otherwise, he jumped from one topic to the next; he was investigating my intellectual acumen from various angles in a very intelligent manner. As for me, obviously, I avoided talking about my federalist sympathies and my allegiance to the concepts represented by Józef Piłsudski in 1919. I suspect that this conversation played a great part in my future destiny and in separating me from the "standard solution" applied to Polish officers.

Shortly after this strange interrogation, Kombrig left the camp and I did not see him any more. From the prisoners who were transferred later on to Grazovetz, I heard that he was still seen in Kozelsk in May of 1940, immediately before their transfer to Grazovetz. In the camp it was generally assumed that his longer absence was somehow connected with the liquidation of the Kozelsk camp. At the end of March 1940, a new person appeared, an NKVD colonel of enormous size who had a ruddy complexion. We saw him sometimes strolling through the monastery courtyards.

More or less a month later, on the 30th of April 1940, I saw him on a siding near the station, several kilometers west of Smolensk (probably it was the Gniezdovo station), as he supervised the transport of prisoners to the Katyn Forest.

---

[13] Today we know that prisoners from Starobelsk were executed in the NKVD cellars in Kharkov and were buried near the village of Piatikhatky.

IN THE SHADOW OF KATYN

Those two high officials of the NKVD played an essential role in the case of Katyn. Most likely, Kombrig Zarubin wrote the basic report, but it is not known whether he put forward definite suggestions. That paper should be in the archives of the NKVD, and it will be an important task for future historians to study this document when the archives of the NKVD are opened. I believe that moment in time is not too far off, even if I should not be here to see it. This tall colonel with the ruddy face was undoubtedly the organizational director for implementing the decision. Kombrig Zarubin represented the intellectual part of this murderous organization that was the NKVD; this new tall colonel was assigned to do the "dirty work."[14]

One of the most mysterious orders, immediately before the liquidation of the Kozelsk camp, was the general compulsory vaccination against typhus and cholera, apparently because of the intended journey. The question remains: What was the point of giving protective inoculation to people who had only a few weeks of life left, and during those few weeks, they were to be hermetically sealed off and separated from the inhabitants of the country? It meant the cost of about four and a half thousand vaccines and the engagement of health care personnel. After the first injections, most of the prisoners had high fevers, which disappeared rather quickly. Some time later, they received the second injections, which did not produce any painful results. The most logical supposition is that the camp administration did not know about the final decision of the fate of the prisoners and were applying automatically some existing rules for their transport. But during my further prison and concentration camp career, when I was relocated many times, I do not remember that we were given any protective injections before the traveling; we were merely chased to the bathhouses.

The most essential information concerning the liquidation of the Kozelsk camp was detailed in the book *The Crime of Katyn*.[15] The first transport departed, according to the best of my memory, on the third of April 1940, and the first officer who was taken was a colleague from our regiment, Captain Jerzy Bychowiec, commander of the first company of the 85th Regiment of Wilno Riflemen. From then on, during the whole month of April and in the beginning of May 1940, they regularly took about 300 people every few days, sometimes a little bit less. As far as I knew from the people that were in Starobelsk, the size of the transports in April and May was somehow less from there than from Kozelsk. Most likely, the difference in the efficiency was between the teams of executioners operating in Katyn and in that other unknown place, in the vicinity of Kharkov, where they were liquidating prisoners from Starobelsk.

During the liquidation of the Kozelsk camp, it became quite obvious that the highest central authorities decided the fate of each individual prisoner. In *The Crime of Katyn*,[16] I described how I overheard the reception of telephone orders from Moscow about the composition of each transport. From the prisoners who were employed in the office of the camp, we do know that these orders had a regular character. When a year and a half later, at the end of 1941 and the beginning of 1942, General Sikorski,

---

[14] Dr. Lebedeva, Natalia, S., *Katyń Zbrodnia Przeciwko Ludzkości* (Katyn Crime Against Humanity), Dom Wydawniczy Bellona, Warszawa, 1998 (Warsaw book publisher), p. 162. In her book Dr. Lebedeva describes the above mentioned colonel in the following way: "This tall colonel was Colonel Stepanov; he was not directing the whole operation but was only responsible for transportation of prisoners and safeguarding the place of execution. Special units of the NKVD conducted the execution ."

[15] *The Crime of Katyn, Facts and Documents,* Polish Cultural Foundation, London, 1965, pp. 49-54.

[16] Ibid., p. 52.

FROM PIOTRKÓW TO KATYN

Ambassador Kot, and General Anders asked the Soviet authorities for the list of prisoners, the Soviet authorities replied that they were not in possession of such lists.

Near Katyn

I was called to join the transport on April 29, 1940. When those prisoners who were secretly overhearing the telephone messages from Moscow informed me that I was going to leave the Kozelsk camp that day, I immediately ran to say goodbye to several people whom I considered my special friends. My farewell conversation with Lt. Col. Nowosielski, which happened a few days earlier, was covered in the book, *The Crime of Katyn*.[17] The farewell with Professor Komarnicki stands out in my mind. After we had kissed each other goodbye, and I was already walking away, he called out to me. When I turned around, he got up, approached me and with the thumb of his right hand made the sign of the cross on my forehead. It was a symbol of delivering me into God's hands. The expression on his face and his gesture moved me deeply. It was the beginning of those two extraordinary days in my life when I, by divine judgment, made the journey to the closest vicinity of Katyn, and then again journeyed from Katyn to the special prison in Smolensk.

When I was officially called to join the transport, I took my bag with my miserable belongings and reported to the indicated place. Our transfer to a new escort happened like a solemn ceremony. They were transferring not only persons, but also our personal files. The thing that struck me at that moment, even if I could not explain it, was the fact that my file was of a different color from the files of the other prisoners. Today, after so many years, I cannot remember the colors, but it seems to me that all the files were red, while mine was white.

Also strange in this situation were the brutal faces of our escorts, which made a contrast with the rather kindly manners from those privates to which we were accustomed in Putyvl and Kozelsk. The average Russian, for I met many of them in my childhood before the First World War, has (or rather had in pre-Revolutionary conditions) a kindly attitude toward his fellow man. My mother, who before my birth was for a certain time a teacher in an aristocratic Russian home in Central Russia, also always emphasized this. Now, one could feel quite clearly that for the members of that new escort, we were rather dead objects to be manipulated because we were not considered human beings. They conducted a personal search in a rather brutal but efficient manner and took all the sharp instruments. Then, under much stronger escort than that to which we were accustomed, they conducted us to the trucks, which were waiting for us in front of the camp gate.

I was under the impression that we were driven on a different road from the one we had marched over from Kozelsk station in the first days of November 1939. We were taken to the siding where six carriages of "stolypin" type were waiting for us. This name came from Piotr Stolypin, under whose Premier-ship that type of prison carriage was introduced. The characteristic feature of those carriages was that they did not have windows in the individual compartments, but often a very small opening near the ceiling; the doors to the compartments could be locked only from the outside, giving one the feeling of being in an iron cage. Windows were only on the side of the corridor

---

[17] Ibid., pp. 53-54.

IN THE SHADOW OF KATYN

where prison guards were on duty. As I already mentioned, this type of carriage was introduced during the Tsarist rule, immediately after the Revolution of 1905, but it became particularly popular during Soviet times. I was the son of a railway man and spent my early childhood near the railway, remembering well the time of Stolypin. I do not recall having seen these carriages then. From what I could observe during my three years' stay (1939-1942) in the Soviet Union, this carriage was a normal addition to most of the passenger trains. Many Poles discovered the interior of this vehicle.

The normal capacity was eight people in a sitting position, or four in a lying position if you raised the shelves. They packed fourteen people into our compartment, eight sitting and two on each raised shelf in such a manner that the head of one was at the legs of the other. On the very top shelves under the ceiling where there was space for hand luggage, they put two additional people, who had the privilege of being able to look outside through the opening near the ceiling. I had a sitting place. Across from me sat docent Tucholski. I did not know him well, but I knew from my colleagues that, shortly before the war, he had returned from England where he had been conducting research work at the University of Cambridge. Next to me was a bearded lieutenant who was also a chemical engineer, and in Poland he had been an employee of some foreign company. In one of the other compartments was First Lt. Leonard Korowajczyk, about whom I wrote earlier, as he was the chief-editor of the spoken messages in the Kozelsk camp.

Normally the prison trains in the Soviet Union moved very slowly. In the thirties, they built huge industries but relatively few railway lines. The railway lines were overloaded, and those trains that did not have priority were kept for hours on the sidings until there was a free line. Prison trains, obviously, did not have priority. In our case, however, we moved exceptionally fast. In the early morning sunrise we reached Smolensk. In our compartment, only I immediately knew this place because, through the small part of the corridor window, I recognized the familiar domes of the Greek Orthodox Churches. I traveled through this station many times during the First World War, in the period of 1915-1918. At that time, I was a student in a Russian mathematical lyceum in Orel, while my father had the position of director of the railway in a zone close to the frontline. Part of his territory was often under fire from German artillery that frequently destroyed the railway-tracks and my father had to use an armored train to inspect the tracks and bridges. Many times I used to travel from Orel to Dyneburg (presently Daugavpils), through Smolensk and Vitebsk, to visit my father.

After a short stay on the line some distance from the main platform, the train started moving again. From what we could perceive, the sun was rising, seen somewhere at the back of the train, which meant that we went in a westerly direction instead of going, as I first falsely concluded, in a northwesterly direction because that was the Orel-Riga railway line route, so well known to me from my childhood years. After traveling several kilometers, the train stopped. From outside we could hear the sound of movement of a large number of people, the sound of running motors and the abrupt voices of command. There was no window in our compartment; therefore, it was difficult to find out where we were and what was happening outside. From compartment to compartment they started giving the news that disembarkation had begun.

After about half an hour of waiting, a tall and red-faced colonel of the NKVD

FROM PIOTRKÓW TO KATYN

came to our compartment. I described him before. He called my name and said that I was to be separated from the transport. He ordered me to take my belongings and to follow him. This aroused great astonishment. Our experiences up till now were that whenever a prisoner was moved to another place, they would send a private to communicate that order [see next page].[18] A colonel of the NKVD was of tremendously high rank in the social hierarchy of the Soviet Union; it exhibited a far superior status than that of an ordinary army colonel. The presence of such a high rank underscored the importance the Soviet authorities attached to this transport – and, the urgency of separating me from it.

When I was walking behind the colonel through the corridor of the carriages, I overheard the conversation among the prisoners in the neighboring compartments that probably the Lithuanian Government demanded that I should be sent back there. Lithuania was at that time [April 1940] still formally an independent country, even though it had Soviet military bases. The supposition came to their minds that my separation from this transport was through the influence of Lithuania, because before the war I advocated the Polish-Lithuanian Federation. Immediately after gaining independence for Poland, this program was supported by the Polish Head of State, Józef Piłsudski. However, this program had very few followers in Poland and even less in Lithuania. Piłsudski attempted to accomplish this by trying a series of *coups d'état*, which did not succeed because of the absolute hostilities of Lithuanian nationalists and the opposition of Polish nationalists.

When we went outside, I was over-awed by the scent of spring blowing from the nearby fields and forests even while there were still some patches of snow. It was a most beautiful spring morning. High above us in the blue skies a lark was soaring. Nearby were the buildings of the station, but you could not see any employees of the railway. The locomotive had already left. Something was happening on the other side of the train, but what, I could not see. When we were walking between the railway tracks, side by side, the colonel turned toward me and asked, "Would you like to drink a 'little tea'?" I stress here the diminutive form. In Russian tea is *chai*; the diminutive of *chai* is *chaiok*. The colonel asked me whether I would like to drink *chaiok*? Nothing more pointed to the fact that this man might have been the head of the executioners engaged in murdering my colleagues in the nearby forest.

We stopped near an empty railway carriage from which the prisoners had already disembarked. The colonel ordered me to get in and find a spot in one of the compartments; he slammed the door, consisting of iron bars, and told a soldier, standing in the corridor, to guard me and to bring me *chaiok* – and went away. The soldier expressed a certain amount of doubt whether getting tea from somewhere could be arranged. He asked me whether I had sugar, and after some time he brought me a kettle of boiling water into which he put some tea. I took out sugar, bread and herring, given to us the previous day, and I ate breakfast, which – under the conditions of Soviet prison transport – could be called a bountiful meal.

Again, behind the wall, I heard the noise of the throbbing of an internal

---

[18] Even in 1976, the author of the original text did not have the benefit of these authentic documents, which verify his earliest suspicions and claims. Copies of the original documents began being released in the 1990s, but very slowly.

IN THE SHADOW OF KATYN

NKVD USSR
28 April 1940
No 03692
MOSCOW

FROM DEPUTY COMMANDER NKVD USSR
FOR THE MANAGEMENT OF PRISONER OF WAR
TO LIEUTENANT OF GOVERNMENT SECURITY –

Comrade KHOKHLOV

By the order of the People's Kommissar of Internal Affairs of the USSR comrade **BERIA**, please issue an order for the transfer to Moscow into the Internal prison of the NKVD USSR, to the disposition of the 2nd Department of GUGB*, prisoner of war SWIANIEWICZ Stanislaw, son of Stanislaw. Born in 1899 (file No-4287), who is kept in the camp of Kozelsk.

Please inform me about the day of transfer.

DEPUTY COMMANDER OF THE 1ST SPECIAL DEPARTMENT NKVD USSR
CAPTAIN OF GOVERNMENT SECURITY:

(GERTZOVSKI)
(signature)

* GUGB - Main Administration of State Security (The Soviet Security Service within the NKVD, 1934-43). *KGB The Inside Story*, Christopher Andrew & Oleg Gordievsky, Hodder & Stoughton, p. XIV.

[Note: This document was obtained from the library and archives in Warsaw courtesy of owner Jędrzej Tucholski, whose father was traveling in the same compartment with Lt. Swianiewicz in the train destined for Katyn.]

FROM PIOTRKÓW TO KATYN

combustion engine and some kind of commotion. The guard, standing in the corridor in front of my compartment, turned his back toward me and looked through the window, which was on the other side of the intriguing commotion and noises. Near the ceiling of my compartment, I noticed a small opening through which one could see what was happening outside. I tried to climb up onto the top luggage shelf, pretending that is where I wanted to stretch myself after a whole night's journey. To my surprise, the guard did not protest. Whenever he looked in the opposite direction through the window in the corridor, I put my face close to the opening near the ceiling. As to what I saw through that opening, I can only repeat what I already told and wrote about on several occasions.

In front of me I saw level ground, partly covered by growing grass, where under the open sky they probably used to store some goods destined for transport, most likely timber. To one side of that ground was a road at right angles to the railway tracks; to the other side there was undergrowth. NKVD soldiers densely cordoned off the ground with bayonets fixed. This was an innovation as far as our experiences to date were concerned. Even on the front, immediately after being taken prisoners of war, escorts did not have bayonets on their rifles. The bayonet in modern warfare is more of a symbolic rather than a real weapon. In various functions behind the frontline, the order to put the bayonet on the rifle signifies the performance of an important function. The question arose: Why did escorting unarmed prisoners, from whom even penknives were taken away, suddenly become such an important and dangerous task?

From the road, a bus entered the grounds; a passenger bus of rather small size compared with those buses to which we are accustomed in the western cities. The windows were whitewashed with lime. The capacity of the bus was about thirty persons and it had a rear entrance. Another question came to mind. What was the purpose of whitewashing the windows? The bus backed up to the adjacent coach so that the prisoners could step straight into it. NKVD soldiers stood on both sides with fixed bayonets. This was in addition to the grounds being densely cordoned off by NKVD soldiers. The bus drove off and returned after half an hour to take the next contingent. One could conclude that the place to which the prisoners were taken was not too far away. What was the purpose of such a complex transport procedure, instead of ordering the prisoners to march, as on previous occasions?

The NKVD colonel, who had picked me out from my group, stood in the middle of the area with his hands in the pockets of his large coat. It was the same colonel whom I used to see at Kozelsk while liquidation of the camp was in progress. It was obvious that he was directing the whole operation. I wondered what kind of operation it was. I must admit that at that moment, in the rays of this wonderful spring day, the thought of execution had not entered my mind. A rather large car in the shape of a black box without windows was standing not too far away; an NKVD captain, aged well above fifty, stood beside it.

After some time, which was difficult to estimate because I did not have a watch, but I believe it was already in the afternoon, a noncommissioned officer of the NKVD came and told me to collect my things and to follow him. He led me to that area which I had been looking at through the hole under the ceiling of my compartment cell. We stood in front of the black box, where the colonel – who separated me from my group –

was standing together with this older captain of the NKVD. Only then did I realize that this car, in the shape of a black box, was the famous *chorney voron* (black raven) that was used to transport prisoners through the streets of Moscow. I was handed over from the colonel to the captain. The captain ordered me to get into the black box, to be entered from the rear. There were two seats for the guards and, one step higher, there was a door leading into a narrow passage and, on each side, there were three small cells with doors. Six prisoners, who might not know anything about each other, could be taken into this motorized prison. While I was being locked up, I managed to notice that the captain took a place near the driver. The guards who took the seats at the back had rifles, but without bayonets. Undoubtedly, the use of the fixed bayonet had a significant meaning, but I could not even guess then the motive for it. I was told to take a place in one of the cells. There was a narrow hard bench on which one could sit down. After the doors were shut, I sat in absolute darkness. Next, the car started moving. I made the sign of the cross.

The thought struck my mind that I was going to be executed.

The Soviet Union had never signed any conventions concerning the treatment of prisoners of war. It would be logical to assume that they were going to execute a certain number of my fellow officers whom they suspected of engaging in some unfavorable activities against the Soviet Union. The rest of the people, against whom the NKVD could not possibly have any individual charges, were probably going to be "forcibly employed" in their massive investment programs [e.g. industry, research laboratories, forced labor camps], which Communist Russia was trying to realize. In particular, good use could be made of the specialists among our officers: engineers, medical doctors, and agronomists. In spite of the fact that I had expert knowledge on Russia, I could not logically analyze the decisions of the NKVD. I started praying in silence. Before my eyes appeared the triangle of *Ostra Brama* (that famous shrine in Wilno). After about half an hour, the car stopped. The hinges of a heavy gate screeched and the car entered a yard. A completely new period of my wartime experiences had commenced.

Chapter IV

FROM KATYN TO KUYBYSHEV

Internal NKVD prison in Smolensk (April 30 - May 5, 1940)

At the end of my last chapter, I described my stay of several hours on the 30th of April 1940 at the station near the Katyn Forest and the circumstances of my separation from the transport of Kozelsk officers. It was definitely a turning point in my experiences during the war years. Only when the colonel, with his butcher's face, transferred me into the hands of the grizzle-faced captain, did I realize that I had ceased to be a prisoner of war in the eyes of the Soviet administration, and I had become a political prisoner belonging to a completely different department of the NKVD. It took me an even longer time to realize that the main reason for their interest in me was not so much about my publications on the Soviet economy and my book, *Lenin as an Economist*, published in Polish, in 1930 by the Institute of Eastern Europe in Wilno, as about my journeys to Germany in the period of 1936-1937, which I described at the beginning of my memoirs. Apparently, some high level echelons of the NKVD surmised that I possessed secrets of some of the behind the scenes political machinations. It is paradoxical that while I, as was described in the first chapter, "Approaching Storm", adhered to and even tried in some ways to contribute to the idea of trying to thaw relations between Poland and Germany, the NKVD meanwhile suspected me of being a Polish spy in Germany.

After I heard the closing of the heavy gate, the door of my small cell opened and I was told to get out. We found ourselves in a large courtyard surrounded on all sides by walls. The car was standing in front of a multi-storied house, which did not look like a prison. Most of the windows did not have bars, except for iron bars in front of the basement windows. I was taken into this basement to a room that looked like some kind of an office. The captain sat by the desk, while two guards started searching me. They told me to undress and to take off my long cavalry boots made of yellow leather, which were searched thoroughly to make sure that I was not hiding anything in them. But, generally speaking, by Soviet standards the search was rather superficial; they did not look into my mouth, and they did not check for prohibited materials in my rectum, which was a normal ritual for Soviet personal search. In answer to my question, "Where am I?" the captain replied politely that I was in the "internal" prison of the NKVD in Smolensk.

After the search and after the captain administered his report, I was led into a cell. It was a large clean room but, obviously, rather gloomy. It had a concrete floor; light was coming in through the barred window, through which I could sometimes see the feet of people walking through the courtyard. Along the walls there were three layers of collapsible bunk beds, or rather boards on which to sleep.[1] I counted that the

---

[1] Solzhenitsyn in his well-known book *"First Circle"* describes this type of bed fixed to a wall as a typical arrangement in the Butyrki prison in Moscow. During my stay in Butyrki prison it was not so. In March 1941, after receiving my sentence, for some time I was held in a large so-called general cell of Butyrki Prison. There was a long rather primitive row of plank beds of the kind in concentration camp barracks.

IN THE SHADOW OF KATYN

normal capacity of the cell was that of thirty prisoners. I was told that I could choose from any of the beds and that the prison restrictions forbidding sleep during daytime were not going to be applied to me. I could sleep as much as I wanted. They also brought me a mattress and sheets. In the corner was a pile of blankets and pillows that I was allowed to use in the quantity that I preferred. In another corner there was a bucket into which one could perform one's natural functions, but I was also told that whenever I would call, the guard would take me to the toilet.

They brought me dinner: a portion of bread, sugar and tea; it was already evening. The captain told me that I could take advantage of the prison store if I possessed any money. I showed him what I had, which was not very much. For all that money he ordered sugar and butter for me, which were brought the next morning. He also asked whether I would like some books. I said, "I'd be very grateful for that."

During my stay here and also during my walks to the toilet, which was a fair distance from my cell, I got the impression that this "internal" prison in the cellars of the Smolensk NKVD was almost empty and that I was the only prisoner present. I was convinced of this because there was no prescribed time for the issuing of meals. During my stay of five days inside that institution, when the guard noticed through the small window in the door that I began to get up in the morning, he used to start to light the camp stove and to prepare tea for me. They also lit the camp stove to heat up the dinner, which was brought from outside. There was complete silence in my prison; one could not hear any voices or conversation, and only rarely did the steps of the guard patrolling the corridor break the silence.

Near the entrance to the prison cellar were several rows of lockers with a height, width, and depth corresponding more or less to the human size in standing position. In the doors of those lockers were small openings for ventilation. It was obvious to me that those lockers were destined for people. I imagined that they were instruments of some fine tortures.

I once asked the guard about the purpose of those lockers. He answered in a completely natural way without any embarrassment that they were used when the prison was full, and when they were conducting intensive interrogations. In my later stay in the Soviet Union, I had the opportunity to get better acquainted with this sort of object. On several occasions, I sat or rather stood in them. They do not represent, strictly speaking, instruments of torture, but they are used to lock up the prisoners for a short time in order to avoid unwanted meetings in the prison hallways or before the offices of the investigating officers. Only sometimes are they used as a mild sort of pressure for recalcitrant prisoners who refuse to cooperate during interrogation. They are not to be compared with those refined methods of torture that were at that time applied in the Lefortovo Prison in Moscow. But in those days when I was kept in the Smolensk NKVD Prison, these lockers were requisites of the past and, as far as I know, were not being used while I was there.

Today, from the perspective of thirty years, when I think about the Katyn drama, my experiences in the internal prison of the NKVD in Smolensk make it easier for me to see the basic paradox of this drama. The decision to commit the Katyn massacre was taken during the time when the Soviet Union was going through a period of internal

FROM KATYN TO KUYBYSHEV

respite after the purges committed by Yezhov[2]. During these purges by Yezhov, the top echelon of the commanders of the Red Army and also the prominent leaders of communism were annihilated – among them some of the leaders of the Polish Communist Party, who were called to the "proletarian fatherland" in order to be murdered there in such a treacherous way. Hundreds of thousands of innocent people, communists as well as noncommunists, were also exterminated.

During my stay in Smolensk, in that empty internal prison of the NKVD, the instruments of intensive interrogation, which had become requisites of the past, did attest to this period of comparative easing of its hold on the population of the Soviet Union. That the years 1939 through 1940 were a period of diminished oppression for the population and a certain amount of improvement in the standard of living, I heard more than once during my travels through Soviet prisons and camps in the year 1941-1942. Apparently, in that period there was no mention of people dying of starvation in the Soviet camps. The veterans of forced labor told me that in 1939, in some of the camps, bread was apparently not rationed but was simply lying on the table, and any inmate could cut as much bread as he wanted. In other words, the standard of living in the camps reached the level of Tsarist hard labor camps, which Dostoyevsky describes so well in his famous book, *Memoirs of the House of the Dead*.

This relaxation of oppression was connected with the appointment of Beria as the Commissar of the NKVD, replacing the depraved, fanatic Yezhov. Beria rationalized Stalinist terror. He removed a number of unnecessary cruelties, introduced the right to a twenty minute walk for the prisoners, permitted the availability of books to some of the prisoners, reinstated, to a certain extent, the personal safety of the managers of industry, and sent a special commission to investigate the high mortality rate in the camps; but he was absolutely ruthless where he could see certain bases for terror, cruelty, tortures, and deportations. Svetlana Alliluyeva, daughter of Stalin, writes in her memoirs that her mother, who committed suicide, demanded that Stalin stay away from Beria because of Beria's repulsive personality, to which Stalin replied that Beria is a good "Chekist" (Cheka – abbreviation of the former name of the Soviet Intelligence Agency, forerunner of the KGB). Undoubtedly, Stalin was right.

Equally, during the time of my fellow countryman, Dzerzhinsky, as well as during the time of the degenerate Yezhov, the Soviet Security Service was simply a madhouse overwhelmed by the paranoiac fear of bourgeois agents, spies and saboteurs. Beria tried to transform this agency into a rational system of terror and cruelty. He operated not only by using fear in the face of terror, but also by the relaxation of police pressure as a political instrument. Marx taught the dialectical approach to socialism. Beria, undoubtedly, was a master in applying dialectics to the policy of terror, murders and deportations.

We do not know whether Stalin, Beria or Merkulov [3] (see next pages) initiated

---

[2] Yezhov, chief of NKVD (forerunner of KGB), known as the most tyrannical chief of NKVD, came to power in 1937 after the liquidation of the former chief Yagoda. The next two years of Yezhov's rule are usually known in the West as "The Great Terror" and remembered in Russia as *Yezhovshchina*. Yezhov was dismissed from the NKVD in December of 1938 and eventually liquidated. After Yezhov, Lavrenti Beria became the chief of the NKVD and he too was executed after Stalin's death in 1953.

[3] The decision to execute Polish prisoners from the camp of Kozelsk, Ostashkov, and Starobelsk was taken March 5, 1940, at the meeting of USSR Peoples' Commissariat for Internal Affairs and signed by Stalin, Molotov, Voroshilov, Mikoyan, Kalinin and Kaganovich, after Beria's request.

IN THE SHADOW OF KATYN

TOP SECRET
5 March 1940

USSR
PEOPLE'S COMMISSARIAT
OF INTERNAL AFFAIRS

March 1940
no 794/5
Moscow

<u>To Comrade STALIN</u>

A large number of former officers of the Polish Army, employees of the Polish Police and intelligence services, members of Polish nationalist c[ounter]-r[evolutionary] parties, members of exposed c[ounter]-r[evolutionary] resistance groups, escapees and others, all of them sworn enemies of Soviet authority, full of hatred for the Soviet system, are now being kept in prisoner-of-war camps of the USSR NKVD and in prisons in the western districts of the Ukraine and Belarus.

The military- and police officers in the camps are attempting to continue their c[ounter]-r[evolutionary] activities and are carrying out anti-Soviet agitation. Each of them is waiting only for his release in order to start actively struggling against Soviet authority.

The organs of the NKVD in the western districts of the Ukraine and Belarus have uncovered a number of c[ounter]-r[evolutionary] rebel organizations. In all these c[ounter]-r[evolutionary] organizations the most active members were former officers of the Polish army, former police officers and former military policemen.

Among the detained escapees and violators of the state

- The four authentic signatures of J. STALIN, K. VOROSHILOV, W. MOLOTOV, A. MIKOYAN across this page are clearly visible.
- On the left margin is written: "For-Kalinin", "For Kaganovich". It is assumed that these names were added by the personal secretary of Stalin.

FROM KATYN TO KUYBYSHEV

borders a considerable number of people have been identified as belonging to c[ounter]-r[evolutionary] espionage and resistance organizations.

14,736 former officers, civil servants, landowners, police officers, military policemen, prison guards, settlers and intelligence agents are being held in prisoner-of-war camps - more than 97% are Poles. (This number does not include soldiers and non-commissioned officers.)

Included are:

Generals, colonels and lieutenant colonels	– 295
Majors and captains	– 2,080
Lieutenants, second lieutenants and ensigns	– 6,049
Officers and non-commissioned officers of police, Border guards and gendarmerie	– 1,030
Police constables, military police, prison guards And intelligence agents	– 5,138
Civil servants, land owners, priests and settlers	– 144

18,632 detained people are being kept in the western region of the Ukraine and Belarus (10,685 are Poles). They include:

Former officers	– 1,207
Former police intelligence and military police	– 5,141
Spies and saboteurs	– 347
Former land and, factory owner, civil servants	– 465
Members of various c[ounter]-r[evolutionary] and insurrectionary organizations and other c[ounter]- r[evolutionary] elements	– 5,345
Escapees	– 6,127

IN THE SHADOW OF KATYN

In view of the fact that all are hardened and uncompromising enemies of Soviet authority, the USSR NKVD considers it necessary:

I) To instruct the USSR NKVD that :

    1) The cases of the 14,700 former Polish officers, government officials, land owners, police officers, intelligence officers, military policemen, settlers and prison guards being held in prisoner-of-war camps,

    2) Together with the cases of 11,000 members of various c[ounter]-r[evolutionary] organizations of spies and saboteurs, former land owners, factory owners, former Polish officers, civil servants and escapees who have been arrested and are being held in the western districts of the Ukraine and Belarus -

– they should be tried before a special tribunal and apply to them the supreme penalty – to be shot.

II. Examination of the cases is to be carried out without summoning those detained and without bringing charges, the statements concerning the conclusion of the investigation and the final verdict should be as follows:

    a) As far as people being in the prisoner-of-war camps on the basis of information sent by the authority looking into cases of prisoners-of-war, the NKVD USSR.

FROM KATYN TO KUYBYSHEV

4.-

b) As far as people arrested - on the basis of information sent by NKVD of U[krainian]SSR and the NKVD of B[elarus]SSR.

III. The cases should be examined and the verdict pronounced by a three person tribunal consisting of Comrades Merkulov, Kobulov and Bashtakov.

(Head of the First Special Department of NKVD USSR).

PEOPLE'S COMMISSAR FOR THE INTERNAL AFFAIRS

of the Union S S R   (L. BERIA)

[SEAL]

- Authentic signatures of Beria, one to the right and one on the left margin.
- Of the three persons named for the tribunal, Beria was erased and Kobulov added in Stalin's handwriting with a blue pencil.
- Above Beria's signature on the left margin it says: exe[cute my order]
- The meaning of the numbers in the lower part of page: o[fficial record] 13/144, [dated]: 5 March '40.

the decision for the physical liquidation of Polish officers. But we do know that the decision was preceded by several months of intensive investigations of the prisoners of Kozelsk, Starobelsk and Ostashkov as was described in *The Crime of Katyn*. We also know that the process of murdering was centrally regulated from Moscow, as was mentioned in *The Crime of Katyn*, with the telephone orders from Moscow to the command of the Kozelsk camp. The Katyn decision was undertaken, not in the heat of battle or in the midst of political tensions, but with cold calculation during the period of that general relaxation, the results of which I was able to observe while I was held in the Smolensk NKVD Prison.

Since it was in the framework of rationalized terror and cruelties during the period of relaxation that the Katyn decision was undertaken, one might ask the fundamental question: What were the Soviet arguments that weighed on this decision?

Today in the Soviet Union, there is a strong movement to improve the image of Stalin.[4] It is assumed that by liquidating a number of prominent communists, military commanders, and administrators of industry, Stalin committed a major mistake. However, in general, Stalinism as a system of government was an expression of historical necessities, and many hard decisions by Stalin were in agreement with the interests of the Soviet State. They condemned the monstrosities of the liquidation of Kulaks; they recognized the groundlessness of the execution of Bukharin, the most prominent theoretician of Russian communism after Lenin; they exonerated, in a way, the murdered leaders of the Polish Communist Party. Sadly enough, neither Khrushchev nor Brezhnev rose to the occasion to condemn the Stalinist policy of the physical liquidation of the Polish prisoners of war. Is it still to be assumed that this policy is a correct expression of the policy of the Soviet State?[5]

Prison Commander

The day after I was brought to Smolensk was the celebration of the First of May. In the Soviet Union, there are two holiday periods which, according to the founding fathers of the Russian revolution, were intended to substitute for the traditional holidays of Christmas and Easter: "November holidays" and "May holidays." It was a day free from work, which put people in a mood for more open communications. The captain personally brought me the books he had promised earlier. One of them I read with great interest. It was a book about Soviet Polar expeditions and Soviet investments in the Far North.

The atmosphere of the holiday spirit, which penetrated even through the walls of the prison, made our conversation more animated. The captain told me that he was the commander of the Smolensk Prison and this position also made him an administrator of the internal prison of the NKVD, which is the institution for special purposes. In a long conversation he talked more about himself than he prodded me. I found out that he had come in contact with Poles because he was born near Grodno, a provincial town in Poland. He told me about the improvement of material conditions in the Soviet Union, the emphasis on education, and the wonderful care his granddaughter received in

---

[4] "Today" is 1976, the year of the first edition of this original Polish text.

[5] For 1976 the answer appears to be YES, because the official acknowledgement of Soviet guilt by TASS did not occur until April 14, 1990, considerably later.

FROM KATYN TO KUYBYSHEV

kindergarten, and that he could afford to give small shoes and a pretty dress to his granddaughter. It seemed to me that this granddaughter was his pride and joy.

Our conversation developed warm notes between us. Therefore, I asked him if he could tell me why I was separated from my colleagues, the other Polish officers with whom I was interned in the Kozelsk camp? His answer was that he could not tell me that, because he did not know as he was only commander of the prison. From the general circumstances of the case, as far as he could tell, he considered that I must be some kind of a "great man" because the Soviet government was interested in me, so obviously, I had to be treated differently from other Polish officers.

So I asked him whether this special interest that the government was taking in me was expressed by the fact of my arrest and subsequent imprisonment. The captain flounced and said, "You are not under arrest." Then he explained that he received an order to hold me for a certain time until further orders as to my fate would come from Moscow. What he was able to do in this situation, he did. He could not place me in a hotel because he did not have the means of guarding me there, nor did he have the funds for it in his budget. So he decided to place me into the internal prison of the NKVD where from time to time they used to place Soviet people of high rank, and in this way he made sure that I was comfortable. This explanation I accepted with a great dose of skepticism. But a week later when, during my first interrogation in the Lubyanka Prison in Moscow, the examining magistrate showed me a letter from the Chief Public Prosecutor of the Soviet Union containing an order to arrest me, I understood that from the point of view of the Soviet judiciary procedure, this captain was correct. I was not "under arrest" during his care in exactly the same way as my colleagues – who were being executed in the Katyn forest by the special gangs of the NKVD executioners at that same time – had not been "under arrest."

At the end of our conversation, I asked the captain where my colleagues had been transported. He answered that he was only commander of the prison, and that the matters concerning POWs were not part of his jurisdiction. I was not satisfied with his answer and did not give up probing. What was happening to my colleagues worried me as much as the uncertainty of my own fate. After the unprecedented brutal treatment of us all between Kozelsk and the station near Smolensk where we disembarked, it was obvious that my colleagues were not being transferred to the Allies or to the Germans, nor were they being sent home. In each of these cases we would have been treated better than we were up until that time. I also could not understand why the prisoners had not been told to march, as in prior circumstances, but were transported in small groups from the station to some nearby location by bus. Why were the windows in the bus whitewashed? It seemed as if they had tried to hide the presence of the Polish officers from the local population in the district of Smolensk. This did not happen during previous transports. In 1939, when we marched from the railway station in Kiev to the nearby barracks for food, crowds of people were standing on the sidewalks. Women would approach the prisoners, and they would hand them bread or sometimes they even gave money, in spite of the fierce screaming of the guards. Why was there suddenly this ultimate separation from the population in such an innate Russian territory?

Since I rejected the possibility of an immediate mass execution, I considered the transportation of the Kozelsk officers to some camp, where the conditions would be

IN THE SHADOW OF KATYN

much worse than in Kozelsk, to be the most probable explanation; however, such a solution would not sufficiently explain the telephone calls from Moscow, nor the brutality of the guards, nor the whitewashed windows of the transport bus. So I asked the captain whether my colleagues had gone to some new camp near Smolensk. The captain declined a straightforward answer. The next day, when he visited me again, I repeated the question. I managed to squeeze out of him a very general sentence that around Smolensk there are various kinds of camps; it did not transpire from this that my colleagues were actually in those camps.

A few hours after the above described conversation, on the first of May, the doors to my cell were opened and the captain, without crossing the threshold, handed me a large bowl of macaroni with generous amounts of butter and three meatballs, stressing at the same time that he would like me to appreciate this great holiday. The portion was so large that it was not possible to consume it during one sitting. The next day the guard had to start the camp stove twice to heat up the leftovers of that festivity for me.

Today, from the perspective of many years, when I ponder over those dark days, it seems to me that I understand the captain's psychology. He was probably a kind man, basically well disposed toward the world and people. However, his attitude toward me was not because of that. Undoubtedly, he was impressed by the uniqueness of my fate, of which I knew nothing at that time, but he was very well aware of my circumstances.

Some time ago I read a novel; I do not remember the title or the author. It was about a condemned man whose rope snapped when he was hanged, and then all those present, including the executioners, became his friends, pleading for his reprieve. In ancient Rome, during the bloody games, when one of the condemned men or gladiators miraculously managed to escape death, the crowd generally took his side and demanded pardon for his life. It is human and understandable. So it was with Ursus and Lydia in *Quo Vadis?* (by Sienkiewicz). Thus, from the point of view of those NKVD men, who were direct or indirect witnesses of the Katyn execution, my case was equivalent to that of the breaking of the noose of the condemned man. Not only the commander of the Smolensk prison, who most likely was a kind man, but also the colonel with the face of a butcher – who might not have been a butcher – was under this impression. That is why, on the morning of April 30, this colonel, who most likely was directing the whole operation, when he separated me from my colleagues who were going to be executed, asked me if I would like some tea.

In the history of Kozelsk and Katyn there is still one more example of this same phenomenon. The man, who most likely played an important role in preparing the Katyn decision – it is not known whether, in fact, he was its author – appeared among those whose lives were spared, and managed to show a great amount of politeness and a positive attitude. I am talking here about Kombrig Zarubin, who represented the highest authority in the Kozelsk camp, before the camp was liquidated. Professor Wacław Komarnicki, who left the Kozelsk camp with the last transport in June of 1940 for Grazovetz, told me that Kombrig Zarubin had appeared again shortly before that final liquidation of the camp. He had vanished before the start of the Katyn transports. He was again very polite and talkative. This last transport went not to Katyn but to Grazovetz where, as we do know, the conditions were quite reasonable.

The mentality of the executioners, the NKVD men and the Gestapo men, is not

FROM KATYN TO KUYBYSHEV

easy to penetrate. As far as the Soviet security service is concerned, it is especially difficult because these are the people primarily trained in the dialectic attitude toward life.

Transport to Moscow (5th to 6th of May, 1940)[6]

I stayed about five days in the internal prison of Smolensk's NKVD. On the evening of the fifth of May, when I was already starting to retire for the night, I was told to collect all my belongings because I was to be taken on a journey. A few minutes later I was taken into the office where I was received by a group of four guards who searched me rather superficially, mainly to assure themselves that I did not have any weapons on my person. The captain was not present at this ceremony. The last two days of my stay in Smolensk, I did not see him at all. I wondered whether he had lost interest in me, or perhaps he had received rather detailed instructions on how I should be treated.

When I was taken out, I thanked the guard for his care and friendly attitude toward me. He stood to attention, saluted me, and wished me a happy journey. He reminded me of the type of well-trained and good mannered noncommissioned officers of the Tsarist Army, of whom I met so many in my childhood.

With their fingers on the triggers, four guards took me into the yard, two of them in front of me and the other two at the rear. We were walking slowly, almost solemnly through the well-lit yard in the direction of a black car, probably the same one that brought me to Smolensk from the station in Gniezdovo. I was overwhelmed by the urge to laugh. I did not have any weapons on me, and I could not possibly attack my guards; we were in a well-lit yard closed off from all sides by walls; I could not possibly run away. Why all these precautions, drawn out revolvers and fingers on the trigger? I turned around and grinned to the one who was guarding me from the left, holding his gun ready to be discharged. He scolded me in a threatening way and told me to march and not turn around. Moments later, we were in the car. Again I was placed, as in Gniezdovo, in the small cell (or rather the small compartment of the prison car), while two NKVD guards placed themselves in the back seats with their guns drawn. The hinges of the opening gate screeched.

Within a few minutes we were at the railway station. We stopped at a small square surrounded by a fence near the main railway station buildings beyond which one could see a part of the platform. In the square, a close-knit group of very poorly dressed people was already waiting, surrounded by NKVD guards with rifles. Mostly they were men of middle age. Almost all of them had wretched, dirty bags tied with strings over their shoulders (so-called *kotomki* in Russian), in which, apparently, they were holding all their belongings. I noticed also several older women, wrapped in dark scarves, who reminded me of pre-Revolutionary pilgrims; beggars who used to wander over the huge stretches of Imperial Russia from monastery to monastery, through the Caucasus Mountains and Syria, and sometimes they even arrived at the tomb of Christ

---

[6] See copy of authentic order (next page) to send Stanisław Swianiewicz to Moscow.

IN THE SHADOW OF KATYN

TOP SECRET
personal delivery

USSR

Peoples Commissariat
For Internal Affairs

Administration
NKVD USSR
– of –
Smolensk District

Secretariat
3 May 1940
No. 708/1

COMMANDER OF THE DIVISION OF NKVD OF SMOLENSK
MAJOR Com.[rade] MEZHOV

Smolensk

With the first departing prison transport, send the arrested Stanislaw SWIANIEWICZ, son of Stanislaw, who is being held in the internal prison of the UNKVD to the disposition of the Commander – Senior Major of Government Security Com.[rade] FEDOTOV.

HEAD OF THE ADMINISTRATION OF THE NKVD OF THE DISTRICT
OF SMOLENSK CAPTAIN OF GOVERNMENT SECURITY.

(signature)
(KUPRIANOV)

in Palestine. There were also several teenagers with a bold and daring look in their eyes, probably arrested for so-called hooliganism. At a certain moment, an order was given, and this whole group squatted down on the ground. The commander of the convoy was checking the list of those destined for the transport, calling in turn the names of each one arrested. The sight of that group of beggars squatting on the ground and rising to the brutal orders of the soldiers, who were well fed and dressed in warm coats, made a perfect picture symbolizing the social realities of the Soviet Union.

The passenger train, behind which prison carriages were attached, rambled into the station, another symbol of Stalinist Russia. The carriages stopped directly opposite the square. They opened the gate of the fence that separated the platform; the arrested people were marched in file across the platform and entered a carriage. Then I was taken. As far as I could see, the arrested people were densely packed into compartments from which emanated a foul air. For me there was a reserved, separate compartment with a bench, so I could stretch myself comfortably. My guards were taking turns before the barred doors of my compartment. During the train ride, there were two guards in the hallway: One who was looking after me, and the other who was looking after all the rest of the compartments and, from time to time, taking to the toilets those who were screaming particularly loudly about it. The teenagers were behaving quite noisily, often arguing with the guards.

The train stopped frequently, and at some stations small groups of the arrested disembarked. I think that those were peasants who were staying illegally in towns and now were administratively sent back to their place of origin. Stalin, introducing compulsory collectivization of Russian villages, revived many practices from the times of villein service. In the eighteenth century and in the first half of the nineteenth century, it was a normal occurrence that the police caught wandering villein servants and sent them back to their place of assignment. After serfdom was abolished, and the peasants were given small plots in 1861, peasants still did not receive the right of free movement because responsibility for taxation and for paying off the acquired land belonged to the peasant commune (*Obshchina*). Therefore, the peasant who was going to earn some money in town, but wanted to keep his plot in the village, could not do it without the permission of the village commune. It was only after Stolypin[7] introduced a number of reforms that the peasants were freed from the bondage of belonging to the village commune. Collectivization caused the revival of those bonds. Even today [1976], the member of a collective farm cannot obtain permission to live in town if he does not receive the approval of his own village authorities. In Stalinist Russia, prison carriages were thus not only used to transport political prisoners, but also to regulate the movement of people between village and town.

During the journey, a certain event occurred which intrigued me immensely, but which I came to understand only after the Katyn graves were discovered. When we were entering the train, one of my guards met his friend, who was guarding those prison carriages that arrived at Smolensk. From the lively greeting, I guessed that the friends had not seen each other for a considerable time. That night, when my guard stood watch in front of my compartment, his friend came to him for a chat. I was lying down

---

[7] Stolypin, Tsarist Minister of Internal Affairs from 1906 to 1911. His decree dissolved the peasant communes and each peasant was given the right to receive his share of the common land in full ownership.

with my eyes closed and pretended that I was sleeping. The friends were whispering to each other. My guard was relating with great emotion some sensational story. I could grasp only broken words from which I understood that the story was about Polish prisoners. I clearly grasped only one sentence, "And this one is to be taken to Moscow to be shot." I did not attach great importance to the saying, even if I considered this solution to my case highly probable; how could the guard in the security system, where the principle of secrecy is so strictly observed, know the intentions of the higher authorities toward my person? I was highly intrigued as to why Polish prisoners were the objects of such a long conversation, and what in our affairs was of such interest to people of the lowest rank of the NKVD.

Many times during the next three years I remembered the impression this conversation of whispering NKVD privates left on me. Not until the spring of 1943, when the case of Katyn was revealed, did the puzzle seem to me to be solved. My guard, who most likely was involved in the transport of Kozelsk prisoners, and might have been taking part in the execution itself, was telling his friend about his impressions. His sentence, that they were taking me to be shot, was completely understandable. Since he knew all my colleagues were murdered in that manner, there was no reason to assume that my lot would be any different.

I fell asleep lullabied by the movement of the train and the whispering confidences of the guards, the meaning of which I could not grasp. When I woke up, it was already daylight. In the corridor there was a lot of movement. All my guards, who probably had been sleeping in some separate compartment, were already up. The train stopped, and after a few moments I was taken out. People, shoddily dressed and mostly with tired faces, passed by quickly, trying to look in a different direction. The guards drew their revolvers. The two, marching behind me, pointed them in my direction, holding their fingers on the triggers. We left the Moscow platform through some side passage, in the same way as in Smolensk.

Suddenly, I heard the voice of a boy shouting, "Kostia, Kostia, look, they are escorting a Trotskyite!"[8] Immediately, a group of small street urchins joined the convoy. The children probably did get quite a kick out of this, because they were seeing what a live "Trotskyite" looked like.

Again I was placed in a prison car which immediately started moving. After some time, the car stopped and again hinges screeched with the opening of a heavy gate. We drove into a yard. I was told to get out. We were in the courtyard of the famous Lubyanka Prison. I had no opportunity to view the Lubyanka Square that I knew so well from my student days of the year 1917-1918, and which, during the times of Stalin, was renamed Dzerzhinsky Square.

---

[8] During Stalin's time, the most serious charge was to be accused of being a Trotskyite. Everyone knew that it was impossible to walk out alive from the Soviet prison system after having been accused of "Trotskyite deviation."

FROM KATYN TO KUYBYSHEV
Lubyanka (May 6, 1940)

I was led into a room that looked like an office of any large institution: desks, male and female clerks, and counters separating "clients" from administrative personnel. They told me to give my personal data. I asked them straightforwardly whether I was in Lubyanka. They answered in the affirmative. Then I was directed to some kind of waiting room where I was allowed to sit down. After some time, the guard opened the door of a side-room and told me to enter. I found myself in a small room looking like the cage of an elevator. While waiting, I saw the opposite door being opened and a young woman in a white doctor's coat entered; she was rather short and unattractive looking, wearing large glasses, but with an expression on her face which seemed to me sympathetic. For a while we stood opposite each other in silence. She seemed to be rather embarrassed. Finally she said, "So, you have arrived." The sentence by itself did not mean anything, merely an affirmation of an obvious fact, but it could express many things depending on the intonation of how it was said. I was under the impression that I detected a certain note of kindness. After a while, she asked in a manner that seemed to me also friendly, "Well, how are you feeling?"

A little bit surprised by the tone of her voice, I answered, "I feel like a person feels when he is in prison."

She retorted, "That's not what I meant. Are you healthy or not?" Then she asked whether I had any venereal disease. After my negative answer, she wanted to say something else, but the door through which she had entered opened, which was, apparently, a sign that this conversation had to end – she immediately moved back. The door from my side opened, and I returned to the waiting room.

I pondered for a while what this episode meant. If it were meant to be a medical examination, it was not. Anyway, for a medical examination there was no need to leave us alone in the room. If that young lady had been instructed to extract some information from me that would be important for my case, then she was not given enough time for that. My impression was that this episode was an expression of a certain method. Probably they were trying to bewilder a prisoner at the beginning of his investigation by creating various surprises for him.

Then I was led to a photographic laboratory where they took a number of pictures of me from all possible sides and took my fingerprints. I was also taken for a bodily search, during which they took away from me all "metallic" objects: penknife, small coins, and my purse because it had metallic edges; and they cut off all the buttons that they considered metallic. All those things were placed in a separate little bag, which they promised they would return to me in the eventuality of my release or transfer to another prison. The guard, taking away my medallion of Our Lady of *Ostra Brama* (Shrine of Our Lady in Wilno), which my wife had put around my neck when I was going to the front, intimated to me that God does not exist. Nevertheless, after some hesitation, he agreed to add it to the list of my personal belongings. This medallion I still saw when eight months later I was transferred from the Lubyanka Prison to the Butyrki Prison, but was unable to reclaim it when I was being released from the GULAG in April of 1942. The NKVD man also wanted to pull out the sort of horseshoes from the soles of my very comfortable cavalry boots, in which my feet felt like being inside pillows. When I started protesting, he acknowledged my objection, but he then considered that my boots should be temporarily taken away from me, and while in prison, I would get something else for the time being. So, during my whole stay in the Lubyanka Prison, I was in cavalry uniform and in some sort of slippers from the prison warehouse. The boots were returned to me eight months later when I was being transferred from Lubyanka to Butyrki Prison. I had to sell them when I was in the GULAG because no leather can stand continuous exposure to deep snow. The buyer, who was working in the planning office in the GULAG, paid me with bread, so for several weeks I was able to stave off starvation.

The Soviet bodily search is not only restricted to clothes, but it also includes searching the intimate parts of the body in which prohibited objects can be hidden. For the first time, I was subjected to this necessary process of a complete Soviet search. Then I was sent to the showers, which in the Lubyanka are not only well, but one could even say, luxuriously arranged. Generally the baths of the two main Moscow prisons – Lubyanka and Butyrki – have a good reputation among the prisoners. After bathing, I was given clean undergarments made from heavy linen. A little later they brought my clothes, still hot from fresh disinfecting. Washed and refreshed, I was being led by two NKVD guards deep into the cellars of the Lubyanka.

Psychoanalysis in solitary confinement (6th to 8th of May, 1940)

We entered a rather narrow corridor resembling the passages of the lower decks of an ocean-going liner. On both sides were narrow doors, giving entrance to separate cells. The difference was that in the doors were small openings, like peepholes, called in Polish prison jargon "Judasses", so the guards could constantly monitor the behavior of the prisoners. They opened one of the doors and told me to enter. The inside of the cell resembled the cabin of a ship. It had a very low ceiling, a narrow bed covered with a gray blanket, a small pillow with a clean pillowcase, and beside the head of the bed, a small table. There was no room for walking around the cell; the prisoner could either sit or lie in bed. He was allowed to lie only on his back while holding his hands on top of the blanket. There was no window and a rather bright light bulb was shining day and night. I was wondering whether this was their famous way of torture by using a bright light, about which I had heard so much before the war. In the next cell was a Soviet prisoner who, apparently, had undergone a complete nervous breakdown. He was moaning loudly, maintaining he was innocent, and he repeated assurances of his loyalty to the regime; he did not accept food. From the distant cells in the corridor there came similar wailings. At first I thought these groans were enacted in order to dispirit recently arrested victims. Before the war, I had heard that those methods were sometimes used to extract statements from defendants in show trials. Shortly after, I came to the conclusion that this was not so. A representative from the prison administration came to my neighbor's cell and started calming him down, and with a soft voice he tried to talk him into eating, saying that one should not give in to desperation and that one should never lose hope.

Stretched out on my bed with eyes closed because of the bright light, I listened to the voices coming from behind the thin wall, and I pondered over the mentality of my neighbor. I knew enough about Russia to conduct this analysis. I imagined that he must have been some representative of the high-ranking Soviet administration. Russia,

FROM KATYN TO KUYBYSHEV

during Stalinist times, with the help of the enormous apparatus of party bureaucracy, became politically and economically centralized. During the several years of Stalinist rule before the war, many people, who were laboriously climbing the ladder of a bureaucratic career, managed to establish themselves into good positions and to provide for their families a reasonably good life. They represented this "new class" described in our times in the famous book on this topic by Djilas.[9] But the threat of accidental coincidences, quarrels, or denunciations always hung over the head of these people. This might result in their arrest, which could mean a complete ruin of everything they had managed to accomplish in life: civil death and perhaps also physical death. The Lubyanka Prison where they held many high-ranking representatives of the Soviet administration was for these people the symbol of catastrophe in their lives. The realization that one is in Lubyanka, and therefore belongs to the category of "enemies of the people", caused a shock revealing itself differently in each case. I imagined that in the next stage that shock would transfer itself into a readiness to sign any accusation that would be dictated to the prisoner.

Quite naturally during my pondering, I came to comparing my situation to that of the prisoner on the other side of the wall. This prisoner was a psychological slave whose total will to resist, if he ever had it, was broken. He was prepared to lick and kiss the hand that was going to hit him and, perhaps tomorrow, would lead him to his execution in the cellars of the Lubyanka. I, as a member of the fighting army, was imbued with the will to win. In August of 1939, when I was going to the front, I had to be prepared that it might be necessary to sacrifice my life. Should it happen now, when I found myself in Soviet hands, it would be part of that war which was still going on, and the outcome of which was not at all clear as yet. So, if the execution were to come, one had to accept it with a soldier's dignity. One would have to pray to maintain this attitude which we called honor. So I was a different kind of prisoner from that Soviet comrade of misfortune, moaning behind the wall.

My thoughts about that Soviet man in the next cell were the reflections of the impressions which I received from reading, before the war, the reports of the trials of Zinovyev, Kamenev, Radek, and Bukharin (in 1937-1938).[10] My proud conviction that I was a member of the fighting army was an expression of that spirit which had penetrated the Kozelsk camp. There were many things which separated me from most of my comrades in misery in Kozelsk when it came to my attitude toward the world, toward people, and the nature of that historical upheaval which caught us in its turmoil; but all of us were joined by the common conviction that we were part of an army imbued with the will to fight.

Today, from the perspective of time, when I recall my experiences in Kozelsk and then in the Soviet prisons and camps, I think that this attitude of Kozelsk prisoners,

---

[9] Djilas, M., *The New Class,* Frederic A. Praeger, Publishers, New York, Washington, 1957.

[10] Zinovyev, President of the Communist International. On August 25, 1936, convicted of high treason, he was shot.

Kamenev, old revolutionary who was executed on August 25, 1936, for alleged conspiracy.

Radek, old revolutionary who, in January 1937, was tried for plotting against the Soviet Union and was sentenced to ten years imprisonment.

Bukharin, the most important theoretician of Communism. In 1937 he was arrested and tried as a member of "The Rightist-Trotskyite Block", and sentenced to death. He was executed on March 14, 1938.

which manifested itself on every occasion, not excluding the conversations with the Soviet political officers, played an important role in formulating the decision of the Katyn massacre by the Soviet authorities. This attitude was so glaring that it had to find its expression in the reports which Kombrig Zarubin most likely sent to the highest authorities of the Soviet Security Services, and upon which they finally decided on the physical liquidation of the majority of prisoners in all three officers' camps.

With all that, there was something in my psychological state, something which I could not understand, something that was in contradiction with what I went through during the seven months of my stay in Kozelsk. I could not understand this calmness, this relaxed feeling which overwhelmed me when I stretched myself in that solitary confinement in the underground of Lubyanka. It was contrary to my rather nervous nature. I felt as if it were already after the crisis, and not prior to the great crucible of Soviet investigations and my eventual trial. I was accustomed to analyzing my psychological states and my attempts at controlling them. I developed this habit when I belonged to the Polish student underground circles in the Russian school during the First World War. I had read *The Development of the Will* by Payot. This clean room in my solitary confinement, this reasonably comfortable bed, this light shining into my face compelling me to constantly close my eyes, was giving me the ideal condition for self-analysis, necessary for taking some sort of a stand toward everything that was happening around me.

In Kozelsk, I did not belong to the optimists, who were expecting a fast release from the camp and even a speedy end to the war. I believed that one has to face reality, to see things as they really are. Our stand must be imbued with the will to fight, but I considered that to develop this stand one should not be taken in by illusions. Even if from time to time I gave lectures as, for example, on the anniversary of the November Insurrection,[11] and regular lectures in economics, I avoided in all those talks optimism for the immediate future.

My pessimistic attitude concerned the general situation, as well as my own. My opinion of the general situation corresponded with my pre-war views, about which I have already written. Before the war, I maintained that Poland was not capable of withstanding a German attack because of the fatal arrangement of our borders and our backwardness in weaponry. A Polish-German war would also lead to the Soviet occupation of the Eastern Territories and all the suffering connected with it. My reasoning, that the Polish-German conflict must lead to the Soviet occupation of the Eastern Territories, was based not only on the conviction of treachery of Soviet policy (which might have been true), but on the straightforward reasoning that Russia could not afford a powerful panzer might, created by Hitler, to be situated near Minsk, on the pathways leading to Moscow, replacing a poorly armed Poland which had to carry machine guns on peasant carts. I considered, on the other hand, that Poland of that time was capable of withstanding a Soviet attack if it had been supported by German industry. My assumption was that this was also the reasoning of the Soviet experts.

---

[11] From 1795 until end of WWI, Poland was partitioned between Russia, Prussia and Austria. The November Insurrection in 1830 was a revolt against the rule of Tsar Nicholas I by the army of the Congress Kingdom of Poland, who were subjects of the Tsar. The revolt developed into the Polish-Russian War. It lasted just about a year and eventually the Poles were defeated and Warsaw was taken in December 1831.

FROM KATYN TO KUYBYSHEV

From that it could have been concluded that reasonable relations with Germany would secure Poland on both sides from German as well as Soviet attacks.

According to my judgment, one of the main tasks of Polish policy between the wars should have been to regulate our relations with the Germans. I do not know whether, during the reign of Hitler, this understanding would have been possible without an agreement of a common campaign against the Soviet Union, to which Poles were not inclined. The prospect that behind our eastern border we were going to have a counter-revolutionary Russian satellite of Germany, instead of having Bolsheviks, would not appeal to any sensible man in Poland. My judgment was, however, that an attempt should have been made to regulate Polish-German relations without having to face this extreme dilemma. The pact of non-aggression in 1934 created favorable conditions in that direction. Polish-German relations were loaded with imponderables: offended Prussian pride; nonsensical vexations with which Poles were pestering Germans traveling through the corridor to Eastern Prussia; phraseology of extreme Polish nationalism, in which anti-Semitism was in conjunction with anti-Germanism – these were the factors aggravating the situation. One should have tried before all else to solve the problems of those sectors.

I wrote about all that before. However, in the last days of August 1939, when the mobilization had begun, my expectations of the approaching catastrophe disappeared. The absorbing functions, which were assigned to me in my regiment; the excellent spirit of younger officers and soldiers; the commanders who set a good example; the military operations at the beginning near the town of Piotrków and then near the Bug and Wieprz rivers; the satisfaction from my own physical competence which I demonstrated, spending four weeks in the saddle; all that had filled me with an irrational optimism that started to crumble in the last days of September. When I found myself as a prisoner of war in Soviet hands and again analyzed my thoughts, I came to the conclusion that the actual turn of events was worse than my pessimistic expectations. Most painful to me was the unavoidable destruction of our cultural values accumulated during the centuries in the Polish estates and granges, in Lithuania and Byelorussia. And the people, with whom I had been closely associated, were all from those areas.

While we were kept in the Kozelsk camp, I estimated that the Polish international situation looked positively dismal. When in 1914 the Polish legions marched to the front, the Polish Nation was becoming an independent factor in international politics. In 1920, the improvised Polish Army decided the fate of Europe for the next twenty years. In 1939, when the last organized Polish units gave up the fight, Polish politics was unable to change its course, and it lost its independence. That constant concern of being able to maneuver or act had been a characteristic of the leadership exercised by Piłsudski during the years of 1914 to 1935. His last great move was the pact of Non-Aggression with Germany. Beck tried to continue this policy, but he did not have the psychological insight and political acumen to deal with such a great international stratagem.

In the Kozelsk camp, we received Soviet newspapers and from them we knew about the key role General Sikorski played in the Polish Government in Paris. I did not know Sikorski personally, but I knew many people who had close contact with him. He contributed great services as one of the creators of the Polish military formations in

IN THE SHADOW OF KATYN

Galicia before the First World War, but the old legionnaires did not like him. People connected with the University of Kraków, professors and journalists, were elevating his abilities. I did not find anyone who questioned his talents. As far as his foreign policy was concerned, he represented a movement that saw the international role of Poland as a faithful satellite of France. During the First World War, he was considered to be a Germanophile; during the twenty years of independence between the wars, he emphasized his sympathies with France. In the summer of 1939, I found an article in the *London Sunday Times* at the library of the University of Wilno, where Sikorski rather unequivocally suggested an alliance of the West with Russia against Germany, and the use of Soviet armored columns in the area of Eastern-Prussia. Because I knew that in Poland very few people read the English newspapers, I informed several people about this article, among others, Stanisław Mackiewicz, who immediately reacted to it in his Wilno newspaper *Słowo*.

I never suspected Sikorski of having special sympathies with the Russian Empire, and even less with communism, but also I could not imagine him to be politically naïve. So, I considered his article as some sort of a game that I could not grasp. Now Sikorski was the Prime Minister of the Polish Government recognized by all free countries in the world, and for millions of Poles, whether they liked him or not, he was the symbol of an independent Polish State. I pondered on how he would exploit his position when the moments for making key decisions arrived. I was far from overestimating the influence the Polish Government could exert on the coming events, while it was outside the Polish Territory. I asked myself whether, during this historic upheaval, the Polish Nation was going to be capable of playing some role in the defense of its individuality, its own spiritual traditions, and its own interests.

My comrades in misery in the Kozelsk camp believed in the western coalition, and had underlined with pride the fact that they were coalition officers. I was more skeptical about this coalition. I did not think it possible that Hitler could win a war against the British Empire, which represented, at that time, the greatest potential on our globe. Just before the war, I had pointed this out in my lecture at the club *Polityka*, and in my articles in *Kurier Wileński*, a Wilno newspaper. I did already believe then that once that magnificent nation had to engage itself in a war against Germany, Hitler would be destroyed. In August of 1939, Stanisław Mackiewicz was of the same opinion, for I used to discuss my analysis of the international situation in conversations with him. Lying in my prison cell, I also thought that when the peace talks would come, we were only going to be an object of trade among the great powers. Why should Chamberlain and Churchill be more magnanimous toward us than Napoleon had been?

Some of my colleagues were expecting the Russian-German war and had often told this to the Soviet political officers. I did not believe in this possibility. I knew that the Soviets would not attack first. On the other hand, Hitler, after plunging himself against his initial intentions into a war against the British Empire, could not now decide on a war against the Soviet Union unless he became mentally deranged. It did occur to me that in that last case, the Prussian General Staff would stop him from doing so. I also believed that most likely after the defeat of Hitler, which could take years, there would come negotiations with his Soviet Ally, after which I did not expect anything good for us in Poland. The other possibility came to my mind that after the defeat of

FROM KATYN TO KUYBYSHEV

Hitler, the national socialists themselves might start a communist revolution in Germany, and again we would be taken between the pincers.

Obviously, I did not exclude the possibility of Soviet-German hostilities, for example, in the Balkans or in the Near East, and that the Soviets might start playing on both sides, which could give some favorable odds on our personal fate. In that case several thousands of Polish prisoners could become a bargaining chip in the Soviet hands, which they could sell according to the circumstances.

Under the rays of that shining lamp, thoughts were circulating through my mind. I was going over old discussions, controversies, and remembered journalistic articles. These were not new ideas. It was a repetition of the same analysis that I conducted in the Kozelsk camp, walking for hours between the alley-like rows of bunk beds in the old orthodox churches of that huge monastery. As previously in the Kozelsk camp, two different personalities were arguing within me: The officer of the Wilno regiment of riflemen, who wanted to be similar to his colleagues and was accepting the greater part of their reactions; and the scientific analyst used to investigating the social processes. The second mercilessly criticized the first. But in all this psychological turmoil there was something new. My mental perceptions were not born out of despondency, which had overwhelmed me in Kozelsk. Something was happening in my subconscious that was changing the character of my spontaneous reactions. As if on my forehead rested some charitable hand, whence descended upon me faith and confidence.

I felt within me some new psychological elements, even when I considered that my personal perspectives could not be promising. When I was contemplating our futures in Kozelsk, I did not anticipate that the Soviet authorities would order the mass execution of Polish prisoners of war a few months after they were taken prisoner and were relatively well-treated by the units of the Red Army. It did not seem to me that the rulers of Russia could move so far beyond the principles that were accepted in the civilized world. I expected that the Soviet authorities would most likely try to use the Polish officers in the realm of their professional competence, after carefully acquainting themselves with the human material that they found on their hands. They would try to hold them under some system of supervision and control, and treat them as some kind of second rate trump card in various future international negotiations. It was my opinion though, that the Soviet authorities would probably select a certain group of officers who either were especially antagonistic toward them or were considered to be dangerous – and those officers they would quietly liquidate, or in some cases would make big show trials out of them. But I imagined that it was always going to be done by maintaining some procedural norms and some semblance of legality.

It seemed to me that I was an obvious candidate from that group of people that was destined for liquidation. In my life I had many conflicts with the Soviet State. In 1918, I belonged to the Polish Military Organization in Russia; and in the first half of 1919, I was operating for the same organization against the Soviets in the territories of present Latvia. Then, as a young scientific worker at the Wilno University, I was involved in studying the problems of the Soviet economy. I was mainly instrumental in the creation of the Center of Soviet Studies attached to the Institute of Eastern Europe in Wilno, which was one of the first institutes of Sovietology in the world. My thesis, on which basis I qualified to be an assistant professor, was a book titled, *Lenin jako Ekonomista* (Lenin as an Economist), published in 1930. In 1934, I published an edition in book form dedicated to the Soviet economy, which included some of my work together with the contributions of my assistants and co-workers. Doing research for this, we did try to be very objective. We had considered that the things that were happening in the Soviet Union were of extremely historical significance for the rest of the world; therefore, research needed to be done.

I had been fascinated by the enormous research that went into the preparation of the Soviet's First Five-Year Plan. But in our work, there were various criticisms and remarks that Moscow might not have liked. In the beginning of the thirties, the Soviet authorities had liquidated for similar analyses a number of Soviet economists who had been considerable contributors to the First Five-Year Plan. Did not they execute Bukharin in 1938, the most distinct theoretician of communism after Lenin? Why then should they be especially lenient toward me, once they started to investigate my case?

However, in my understanding, the most important element that made me an undesirable person for the Soviet Union was my active participation in the group of Wilno Federalists. This group, which had some members who had been in close association with Marshal Piłsudski, considered that the rebuilding of an independent Poland after the First World War must be followed by rebuilding the independence of other nations. And in future, together with Poland, these nations would form a federation or some kind of commonwealth. That meant that the Ukraine, Byelorussia, and Lithuania, and the two other Baltic States, together with Poland, should create a great union embracing a better part of Middle Eastern Europe. As far as my personal opinion was concerned, I did not consider a federation with Poland as a necessary condition of this program. It was imperative, in my view, that the Ukraine, Byelorussia, and Lithuania became independent nations, irrespective of what sort of policy these countries might conduct after receiving complete independence. The Wilno Federalists were against the complete incorporation of the territories of historical Lithuania into Poland, but they considered that in the future those territories must belong to an independent Lithuania and Byelorussia. Poland, on the other hand, must maintain certain rights in the Wilno district where the Polish population represented the strongest linguistic group. The obvious aspiration of that program was to give full independence to the territories of the Ukraine and Byelorussia that had become incorporated into the Soviet Union as fictitious republics and were now centrally ruled from Moscow. This program had put the Wilno Federalists in direct conflict with Russian Imperialism, as well as with Polish Nationalism.

The program of the Wilno Federalists naturally gave the impression of being related to the position taken by the so-called "Prometheans." Prometheanism was a movement of the nations subjugated by Russia, which were trying to become liberated: Ukrainians, Georgians, Tartars, Caucasus Highlanders, and also Don Cossacks, who considered their union with Moscow as an historical mistake. In the Polish Army there were a certain number of "contract officers" who belonged to those nationalities, mostly Ukrainians from behind the Dnieper River. Soviet intelligence was extremely interested in this movement. I was told about cases of kidnapping and murders. I did not have close contact with "Promethean" organizations; they were very secretive and, as far as I know, their main bases were not in Poland but in Turkey. But I was interested in this movement because of my membership in the governing body of the Main Institute of Minorities in Warsaw whose chairman was Leon Wasilewski, father of the famous

FROM KATYN TO KUYBYSHEV

Wanda Wasilewska.[12] If these interests of mine were to be revealed, I most likely would be tortured in order to disclose various details about which I knew nothing, because my interests in this organization were mainly academic.

So, after all, there were many reasons why the Soviet authorities should give special attention to my person. While in the Kozelsk camp, I lived in constant fear they would start investigating me. Objectively speaking, there are few things that are fearful. What is fearful? — That, which creates fear in us. It was a mystery to me why I was so much afraid of Lubyanka while in Kozelsk, and now, when this for which I had been trembling had become a fact, I stopped being afraid. I knew that many Russians considered the Lubyanka as the gloomiest place in the Soviet Union; I heard the moans of desperate people via the walls.

During my meditations and analyses, I was lying on my back with my hands on top as was required by the regulations. I heard every few minutes the movement of the cover of the Judas hole, and I knew I was under the control of the watchful eye of the guard. Prisoners in solitary confinement cells are always kept under constant observation; I think they want to prevent these prisoners from committing suicide. The bright light of the light bulb was shining into my eyes, so I had to keep my eyelids closed all the time. The rays from the light bulb were passing through my eyelids and were spreading with all kinds of colors of the rainbow, creating a myriad of movements and changing patterns. Those patterns were reminding me of something, and suddenly, I realized why. Some time ago, I could not remember where or when, I saw a beautiful illustration as a delightful introduction to a poem by Pushkin, "Ruslan and Liudmila." I started repeating parts of this rhyme that I remembered from my teenage years in a Russian school. I give here parts of this poem; however, I was reciting it in Russian.

> A green oak, overhanging the Bay,
> Has draped around it a golden chain;
> Where every night and every day
> A learned cat wanders again and again.
> When he turns right, he sings a song;
> When he turns left, he tells a tale.
>
> Such magic: see a forest ghost glide among
> The trees, where a water nymph sits, so pale,
> And there beneath, the elusive beast makes tracks.
> On a hen's feet a hut is set,
> Ah, it's Baba Yaga's pad!
> There in forest and ravine, phantoms wail sad tunes,
> And when the flood of waves will tear
> At coastal sand and empty dunes,
> Thirty Knights will appear,
> Rising from water upon the sand,
> With their Sea Guardian close at hand.
> ....

---

[12] Wasilewska, Wanda – a well-known Polish Communist, chairman of the (communist) Union of Polish Patriots during WWII in Russia.

IN THE SHADOW OF KATYN

> ....
> There's Kashchey, the weight of gold making him bend.
> There's Russia's spirit... That is Russian scent!
> ....
> ....

I was repeating all those verses, again and again. My memory started to recall further parts of this poem, which had been hidden in the deepest corners of my mind. These words, sounding with so much more charm in Russian than in any translation, were intoxicating and separating me from the real world, but not so much as to make me unaware of what was happening around me. The moans behind the wall stopped. The political ponderings and analyses, and my gloomy anticipation concerning my fate began to fade away, like the fading of the light on the TV screen when the plug is pulled. I felt myself immersed in the world of fairy-tales, being half-asleep and being semi-conscious. At that time, it never occurred to me that I was not only under the charming influence of Pushkin's poetry, but also under the influence of narcotics, which, apparently, at that time were added to the food for prisoners locked up in the small cells in the underground of Lubyanka. Later on in life, I had only once a reminiscence of what I lived through under that shining light of the bulb. It was in 1945, in London, when quite accidentally I happened to view a film that consisted only of the play of lights and various patterns; it was called "Fantasia."

For how long I was in that state is difficult to say. It seems to me that the whole period of my being in this cell must have lasted slightly more than 48 hours. I did not have a watch and I did not see daylight. I completely lost the sense of time. From time to time, they brought me food which was quite bearable. I ate it fast; then they asked if I wanted a second helping. After consuming a second portion, I quickly fell down on the bed, sticking to the position prescribed by the regulations by lying on my back. I closed my eyes under the rays of that light bulb and immersed myself in a state of half sleep and half consciousness, as if being in the vapors of some kind of narcotic until, suddenly, I was brought back to reality by a short order, *"Sobirajtes"* [Pick yourself up]. I was led to another cell.

Only later on, when I had already become acquainted with the mores and style of investigations in Lubyanka, I found out that the underground place for new arrivals of prisoners is called *pryomnik* (acceptor). The prisoner was treated there with reasonable courtesy. There were no buckets and for every call one was led to the toilet. The food was better than in the average prison. There were no prescribed hours of rest. Recalcitrant prisoners were not taken for detention, but they were urged with persuasion. In *pryomnik* no books were given, but generally in the other sections of the Lubyanka prison, books were allowed at the time when I was there.

The main purpose of *pryomnik* is to bring the new prisoners to some kind of psychological balance, as much as is necessary for effective interrogation. Lubyanka is not a penitentiary but an investigating prison; that means, no prisoner is held there after the interrogation is completed. Theoretically there are no penitentiaries in the Soviet Union; however, during my time there existed so-called *politisolators* (political

FROM KATYN TO KUYBYSHEV

isolation cells) where extremely important prisoners were doing time so that they would not mix with the masses of GULAG dwellers. In 1939-1940, they kept in the *politisolators*, for example: Karol Radek (somewhere in the Ural Mountains) and Bela Kun (somewhere in the south of Russia); Yezhov, apparently, was held in Sukhanovka, one of the gloomiest interrogating prisons, forty kilometers from Moscow. Lubyanka, as an interrogative prison, had a special purpose: Only those prisoners in whose depositions the central authorities were especially interested were held there and only for as long as those interests were paramount. After that, the inmates were transferred to other prisons, mostly to the huge Butyrki Prison where usually the prisoner was held until his investigation was brought to a conclusion and sentence was given. According to the statistics of my Russian comrades in misery with whom I was sitting in common cells in Lubyanka, 600 inmates were kept there at that time, while at Butyrki – about 20,000.

Before the war, when I read the reports of Soviet show trials from the thirties, I obtained an impression of how a prisoner's investigation was conducted for this kind of stage production. I know this was true of the cases for which such trials were being prepared. But only very exceptional cases were destined for this kind of show trial; then every smallest detail had to be staged. The majority of investigations during my time in Lubyanka did not go before a tribunal, but were dealt with directly by the NKVD, a so-called "troika."[13] My impression, from my eight months' stay at Lubyanka, was that the main purpose of investigations in that prison was not to prove someone's guilt; but for the NKVD to orient itself on various moods and movements of opposition in the country, and on various foreign forces which could represent a danger to the Soviet State. They paid great attention to what was happening in industry; therefore, the majority of examining magistrates had a technical background. Apparently, the NKVD was preparing strictly confidential reports that became available only to the members of the Politburo when these reports gave a realistic appraisal of the situation in the country. In those circumstances, it was important to prepare a prisoner in such a way that he would tell the truth. The stay in *pryomnik* was the first stage of that preparation.

From what was told by those examining magistrates, who in the course of time found themselves among the prisoners, it became apparent that in 1937 during the purges of Yezhov, the NKVD entirely lost its ability to orient itself to what was happening in the country because the arrested people immediately began to declare themselves guilty of the most fantastic accusations. It created a psychological atmosphere in which the Security Services lost their ability to separate truth from fantasy. One could not orient oneself in relation to the shortcomings of industry because every arrested manager of Soviet enterprise, right from the beginning was pleading guilty to sabotage, and at the request of the NKVD wrote a professional paper, using technical terms, to prove his guilt. One of the prominent engineers who was with me in the same cell and was himself writing such a paper told me that, apparently, this state of affairs was the main reason why Yezhov was "removed" and Beria appointed in his place. Beria was trying to put some kind of order into this madhouse and decided that, at least in the beginning of the investigations, it was necessary to bring those frightened people to some state of stability, so one could talk sensibly with them. I

---
[13] Troika means three investigating magistrates.

concluded from the conversations with Russian prisoners who were at that time also inmates of Lubyanka, that at the beginning of their investigations, the interrogator as a rule explained to them that the Soviet Government was mainly interested in knowing the truth as far as anti-Soviet activities were concerned.

Permanent inhabitants of Lubyanka maintained that in *pryomnik* they were adding all kinds of calming drugs to the food, but it was not possible to prove it. Apparently, the average stay of a Soviet citizen in *pryomnik* was between four to six days. I was kept there for a little more than 48 hours. Probably, they came to the conclusion that I was of sufficiently stable equilibrium to be put before the examining magistrate. Did *pryomniks* exist in other prisons? I do not know. I have never heard about it. I was under the impression that this experiment took place only in Lubyanka.

Cell No. 41

When I received the order to leave solitary confinement, two guards, supporting me on both sides, escorted me through some hallways and up the stairs. The staircases were protected with iron nets. Apparently, they were introduced in this building a few years earlier after Boris Savinkov[14] committed suicide by jumping over the railing of the stairs. Next, we ascended in an elevator. When we got out, they told me to wait. One of the guards went to the corner of the corridor, making a rattling sound that was meant to be a warning that a prisoner was being escorted. In Soviet prisons, the principle that prisoners from different cells should not see each other in the hallways was maintained. After a while, a third guard came with a key; we walked through a much wider corridor than in *pryomnik*; and on both sides I saw numbered cells. Each door had a Judas window with an automatically controlled cover, used for finding out what was happening inside the cell. The guard with the key opened one of the doors; they told me to enter and the door was locked behind me. I was taken aback and became extremely intrigued. It came to my mind that if this was that terrible Lubyanka, then my first impression told me this was a rather cultural and decent place of seclusion.

I almost believed that I was in a theater, and that the curtain, just raised, allowed me to see the décor and the actors, and with anticipation I was awaiting the beginning of the action. It all reminded me of some stage production I had seen before. I found myself standing in a rectangular room of average size facing a large window; bars were not clearly visible, only a kind of green painted iron mesh on the outside of the window obscuring the view below, but not blocking the sunlight and the sky. Two beds stood against the walls on opposite sides; the fifth bed was under the window of the wall facing the door. In the middle there was a table with a few chairs. It amazed me that they had a relatively large number of books. On almost every bed there was at least one book, and several books were on the table and windowsill.

In the room there were four men without jackets because it was rather hot. Obviously, they were without ties because ties are not allowed in prison as they are

---

[14] Savinkov, Boris. The former Socialist Revolutionary terrorist, organizer of assassinations in pre-Revolutionary Russia. During the years immediately preceding 1914 he withdrew from the active membership of the Party, and after the February 1917 revolution he became Kerensky's able assistant. After the Bolshevik revolution he devoted himself to anti-Soviet activities. He was caught by Soviet secret service when re-entering Soviet Russia, brought to trial in Moscow and died in prison in 1925.

FROM KATYN TO KUYBYSHEV

considered tools with which to commit suicide. Their white shirts of heavy linen were spotlessly clean. I did not know that they had just returned from the showers to which, in Lubyanka, they were led every ten days. What particularly struck me was the silhouette of a tall, young man with an energetic face who, at the time when I entered, was pacing the room while reading a book. The whole scene gave the impression of my being in a student boarding school instead of being in a prison cell. It came to my mind that this was some kind of stage production to trick me into disclosing something that they thought I might know. Everything seemed to be so incredible.

The inmates of the cell showed me the free bed and quite naturally, they started inquiring how I got myself into this place. I replied with caution, trying at the same time to find out whether I was a complete novelty to them, or if perhaps they already knew something about me. All the time I suspected that it could be some sort of deception. Three of the four tenants showed considerable curiosity about my case, and were quite willing to talk about theirs. The tall blond happened to be a mechanical engineer specializing in tank design. The second inmate looked strikingly Semitic; I soon found out that he was a member of the Communist Party, that he was born in Bobruysk and that until recently had been a vice-commissar of finances in the Soviet Republic of Kazakhstan, from where he was taken to Lubyanka. The third one was somewhat older, about fifty, with graying hair, and he was also an engineer who specialized in shipbuilding and who, during the time of Tukhachevsky and Admiral Orlov – who were both executed in connection with the Tukhachevsky case – was the person responsible for planning the expansion of the Soviet Navy. The fourth person, looking rather ill, was observing me, but kept himself aloof and did not say anything. When I finally said something to him, he answered me in Polish, "We know each other." He was Bronisław Skalak from Lwów, known activist of the Polish Socialist Party. As a matter of fact, we met exactly 18 years earlier, at the first constitutional convention of the Polish Socialist Youth, between the 7th and 9th of May 1922. During this convention, I gave a lecture on minority programs.

I had been invited as a guest to that convention because I did not belong to any socialist organization in Poland even if, at that time, I sympathized with the Polish Socialist Party and voted for that party during the first elections to the Sejm [parliament]. I took part in that convention because the organizers decided that someone of the Wilno academic environment should prepare the debate on the minority questions. At that time there was no socialist organization at the Wilno University, but only a gathering of leftists (Filarets, and later the Association of Progressive Youth); so they approached this organization which delegated me to give this speech. At this gathering, I participated in the lively discussions, but did not join the Independent Union of Socialist Youth, although I kept contact with some people whom I met there. Others I would meet on various occasions; however, after this convention I never saw Skalak again and had completely forgotten about him.

Skalak told me that he recognized me immediately, but preferred to be reticent because we knew very little of each other and he was not sure if I would remember him. I think that my fluency in Russian rather surprised him. Afterwards we became very friendly. Skalak suffered from tuberculosis, which was, as it seemed to me, in a rather advanced stage. He was taken away from this cell about two months after my arrival. In the autumn of 1941, I visited him in the GULAG hospital in the Republic of Komi.

IN THE SHADOW OF KATYN

He did not seem to be in bad shape then; however, the GULAG doctor maintained that he was not ready for transportation. I saw him again in Tehrān in the autumn of 1942. He died in London shortly after the war.

After the first exchange of greetings with Skalak, and while we reminisced about our previous meeting of 18 years ago, supper was brought in, consisting of kasha, followed by a huge pot of tea-substitute. I was given my daily portion of bread and sugar, and also two sheets with a clean pillowcase. The commissar from Kazakhstan took out the butter and invited me to partake in this delicious repast, so unusual for Soviet prisoners. It became apparent that the tall blond man had quite a substantial supply of sugar. I was also informed that Lubyanka had its own interior store, which the prisoners could use under certain conditions. It was the 8th of May, my name day. I thought about this incredible coincidence that for my name day they had arranged a festivity for me in the most unbelievable place, in the most unbelievable circumstances, and by the most unbelievable people.

As I mentioned before, one of the things that caught my attention on entering the cell was the relatively large amount of books. There were about twenty books from various spheres of knowledge. The book that the tall blond man had left open on his bed when I was brought into the cell was a volume of poetry by Mayakovsky,[15] admired greatly by this professional engineer. This engineer was brought recently to Lubyanka, from the Lefortovo Prison where he was tortured and had admitted to some absurd accusations, which almost certainly carried the death penalty. This young man now found an escape from reality by reciting the rhymes of Mayakovsky. We discussed the topic for the next few days. He was not able to make me appreciate Mayakovsky, even though I am a great admirer of Russian poetry. Equally, young communists in the beginning of the twenties could not convince Lenin that Mayakovsky was better than Pushkin. During that same day, I received from one of my co-tenants the biography of Stanislavsky, founder of the famous artistic theater in Moscow. It was exceptionally interesting for me because as a student in Moscow in 1917-1918, I had some contacts with one of the group of actors directed by Stanislavsky. From the other books which came into my hands at the beginning of my stay, and which I read, I remember the masterpiece by the Italian General Douhet on the strategy of the air force. There were also a number of translations of French and English fiction. With a certain amount of surprise, I asked from where all these books came. It was explained to me that since the time of the removal of Yezhov when Beria replaced him, the prisoners in Lubyanka had access to the books from a very good prison library. This library was created shortly after the Revolution from books confiscated from the homes of the executed members of the bourgeoisie. Every prisoner had the right to six books for ten days. Books in foreign languages and political books were excluded. Marx and Lenin were excluded too, because that would be political material; the translation of the book by de Gaulle (who at that time was not yet a politician) about the strategy of armored war was circulating from cell to cell. I observed then that the average Soviet intellectual was more inclined to think in categories of great political and military strategy than the

---

[15] Mayakowski, (1893-1930) Poet and playwright. During the Russian Revolution (1917) he emerged as a propaganda mouthpiece of the Bolsheviks. Toward the end of his life he was severely castigated by more orthodox Soviet writers and critics for his unconventional opinion on art, and this appears to have contributed to his suicide.

FROM KATYN TO KUYBYSHEV

average intellectual in the West, and the average intellectual Pole.

I was destined to spend more than eight months in this cell to which they had led me on the 8th of May 1940. There were constant discussions about the books we were reading. Meanwhile, the Soviet-German cooperation had repercussions on world politics. It seemed to me that this had great influence on the fate of the incarcerated Polish citizens in the Lubyanka Prison.

The composition of my co-tenants was constantly changing; some were led in and others were taken away. Representatives from various professions and layers of social strata passed through my cell. There were many engineers and administrators of industry; three students who were the leaders of communist organizations at their institutions; one representative of the central administration who was a blue collar worker by origin, who impressed me by the level of his analysis of the international situation. There was at least one representative from each of the most important non-Slavic minorities: Georgians, Tartars, Armenians, Lithuanians, and Estonians. There was not a single peasant directly taken away from the plow (so many of whom I was to meet in the GULAG); however, only one blue-collar worker had been directly removed from his workbench. Lubyanka was a prison for the representatives of the middle and higher layers of Soviet society, and above all, for the representatives of that new class about whom Milovan Djilas wrote his book. Each prisoner talked about himself, about his case, his profession, and his worries. If I could retrieve from my memory at least part of the conversations with them, a book could be created representing the problems of that class in Soviet society during the Second World War.

Residency in that cell transferred me into a completely different world of interests, reactions, and notions from those by which we lived in Kozelsk. Not one of my co-tenants had heard about special camps for Polish officers; however, some of them who were arrested after September 1939, knew that the Red Army had seized a large number of the Polish military. To show any interest in the fate of those whom the NKVD grasped in their clutches was not part of the Soviet people's concern. Thus, whatever knowledge I had of the fate of those military men, my cellmates only heard from me. A continuation of the description of my experiences in cell No. 41 would be going beyond the boundary of the assignment that I gave myself writing these sketches.

I think that the essential supplement to the history of the nine days between the 30th of April and the 8th of May 1940 and my subsequent transfer to cell No. 41 must give a clarification of the reasons for my separation from my colleagues; those reasons being the charges brought against me by the Soviet prosecuting office.

IN THE SHADOW OF KATYN

My case

Only a few days after my arrival at cell no. 41, I was called for a night's investigation. This was repeated for the next eight months, but not on a regular basis. During this occasion, I experienced for the first time in the flesh the special way prisoners were led to the investigations. The prisoner is told to keep his hands folded behind him; the escort on the left holds a strong grip on the wrist of the right hand of the prisoner; the escort on the right grasps the left wrist. It produces strong pressure in the small of the back. Beforehand, a warning was given that they were going to escort a prisoner; then a signal would come that the passage was free, and from behind the corner of the corridor, or from the doors of one of the cells, the team of three intertwined people jumped out and ran through the long corridors of the Lubyanka Prison. Generally, when one crossed from the prison territory into the NKVD office area, the pace of the run slowed down. At first, I thought that this was some kind of ill treatment, and then I even thought that this was some kind of introduction to the tortures. Before long, I became accustomed to this style of escorting prisoners in Lubyanka.

During the transfer to my first investigation, a certain occurrence took place which, as I found out later, was due to my ignorance of the habits of the institution in which I was kept. Lubyanka is an easily accessible prison for the highest security authorities of the Soviet Union. In the same building (or rather in the same complex of buildings), there were the central offices of the security authorities (called in my time NKVD). Lavrenti Beria was holding office there while I was in Lubyanka.

During the transfer as described above, the prisoner had to write his signature in a big book, which was placed on a small table at the division between the prison and the NKVD offices. When they asked me to sign it, covering up the writing above the place I had to sign, I refused, pointing out that I cannot sign something if I do not know what it is. Therefore, they took me to the next corridor and placed me in the same kind of iron box, which I had seen ten days ago in the NKVD Prison in Smolensk. I heard guards telephoning, asking for instructions on what to do with me. As a result, I was taken to the area where my *sledovatyel* [shled-oh-váh-til – examining magistrate] had his office, without them obtaining my signature.

When I came back to my cell, my co-tenants explained to me that my stubbornness was based on misunderstanding. This signature of the prisoner is necessary for two reasons: first, as a confirmation of the period of time during which this person was absent from the prison, which had a certain meaning because of the fact that after the investigations, sometimes, prisoners came back in bad shape; second, because the investigators received special overtime pay for night work, which was calculated on the basis of those signatures; therefore, they always wrote the exact time of the signing. The guards could not show me what was immediately above my signature because I did not have the right to know the signatures of other prisoners. After those explanations, I did not make any more objections, and on all subsequent trips, I placed my signature without demur in that book located at the crossing of the Lubyanka Prison and the offices of the NKVD.

On the first night of the investigation, the order of the public prosecutor to arrest

FROM KATYN TO KUYBYSHEV

me was handed to me, and I was required to read it and acknowledge with a signature that I had read it. I convinced myself then that the head of the Smolensk Prison, in the conversation which I described previously, was correct: From the point of view of the Soviet judiciary procedure, I was not arrested yet when I was in the dungeons of the Smolensk NKVD. Next, they gave me a written document issued by the general public prosecutor of the Soviet Union, charging me on the basis of article 58, paragraph 6 (meaning espionage), and this document gave the order to start the investigation of this accusation. It was explained to me, at the same time, that I was no longer a prisoner of war but that I was an offender who had acted against the Soviet State; therefore, I was going to be treated with the total severity of the laws of the Soviet State. Appropriate passages from the Book of Statutes were given for me to read which prescribed the highest degree of punishment for this crime; that is, execution. At my protestations that I was not a Soviet citizen, and that all the things that I was accused of I could not possibly have committed on Soviet Territory, they answered that hostile deeds committed anywhere in the world against the Soviet Union are punishable by the Soviet State. As far as my Polish citizenship was concerned, there was no such thing today because the Polish State had ceased to exist.

It really was a depressing night. Even if all my previous analyses were pessimistic, somewhere deep in my soul was the hope that all this might end in some kind of investigation, after which I would be sent back to the prisoner of war camp. Now everything became less probable. The only bright spot in the situation was Skalak's presence in our cell. Even if we could not effectively help each other, we could give moral support to each other.

I did not realize, at that time, that this decision of the public prosecutor to charge me with crimes against the Soviet State saved me from the Katyn grave. There is a general regulation accepted all over the world that execution does not take place before completing the judiciary investigation and the subsequent sentencing. That is why the section in the central apparatus of the NKVD in Moscow, which in all probability was conducting the Katyn operation, upon receiving the instruction to charge me, had to separate me from the rest of the Kozelsk officers and had to send me to the disposition of the public prosecutor.

When I read the documents of the public prosecutor in the office of the examining magistrate, I did not try to remember the date when it was issued. At that time it seemed to me unimportant. Today, when I try to search my memory for all the details of the days between Kozelsk and Lubyanka, it seems to me that I have reason to believe that the order to separate me from the other Polish prisoners was given before the transport to which I belonged left Kozelsk, on the 29th of April 1940, and that the authorities of the Kozelsk camp knew about this order. While we were transferred to the new gang of guards, and while they transferred the files with the personal data of each prisoner and his identification cards, which were the size of library cards, I noticed that my card was also of a different color than that of the others.

The question arises: Why was I not sent straightaway to Moscow from Kozelsk, instead of being included in the transport destined for the execution, which moved in a different direction, to the west, toward Smolensk? The most probable hypothesis seems to me to be that in Smolensk there was a kind of distributive, central point for Polish prisoners. For example, a group of fourteen officers had been taken there from Kozelsk on the 8th of March 1940, three weeks before the general liquidation of the Kozelsk camp had begun. From that group Col. Stanisław Lubodziecki, ex-public prosecutor of the Polish Supreme Court, was transported to the prison in Kiev where charges had been brought against him which ended with sentencing him to hard labor. Other officers, among them Col. A. Starzewski, ex-Polish military attaché in Belgium, had disappeared without a trace. It is quite probable that they are lying in a separate grave in the area of the Katyn Forest.

The intervention of the public prosecutor charging me with a crime against the Soviet State was, as I can deduct from various circumstances, a direct reason for separating me from the category of prisoners of war destined for immediate physical liquidation. I was accused of a crime prescribed in the Soviet Book of Statutes. Therefore, I was at the disposition of the public prosecutor's authority and my further fate had to be regulated by the Soviet judiciary procedure. The question then arises: What were the "charges" brought against me? This "indictment" against me did not have an immediate connection with the Katyn drama; however, it could throw some light on the Soviet motivations for the manner in which they treated Polish prisoners.

The accusations brought against me can be condensed into two main points:

1) My alleged cooperation with the Polish Intelligence, which consisted of directing the studies of Soviet Economy at the Institute of Eastern Europe in Wilno, in the years immediately before the war.
2) My alleged cooperation with the Polish Intelligence during my journey to Germany, in the year 1937 and my writing of the book about the economic policy of Hitlerite Germany, in the year 1938.

There were several *sledovatyels* who were assigned to my case. My first examining magistrate, who investigated me in May 1940, stated that as far as my Soviet studies and my publications in that realm are concerned, he did not intend to make any special reproaches; even though in my writings there were many slanders against the Soviet Union. However, as proof of my repentance, and because of my crimes against the Soviet Union, he wanted me to disclose the names of the agents that the Polish Intelligence sent to Russia.

The demand was absurd. Could one imagine that any sensible head of an intelligence network would inform university professors or journalists about the names of its agents? This question, for some time, was repeated during every interrogation. Sometimes, it was in brutal form connected with pushing me to the wall, and sometimes in the form of gentle persuasion. The latter had a farcical character; for example, the examining magistrate was so moved by my moral downfall that he used to say, "Tell everything you know, clear your conscience, and you'll see, it will be lighter on your heart."

From my cell mates, I knew that this appeal to clear one's conscience was a standard trick of Soviet investigations which gave many of the Russian prisoners reason for mirth; however, for many others it created a psychological atmosphere for "confession." For me, this typical trick was a confirmation of my opinion, already formed before the war, that the Soviet penal procedure had the characteristics of the Inquisition. In the Middle Ages, the woman accused of having relations with the devil also had to clear her conscience through admission of guilt and show her repentance.

On one occasion, I lost control and said, "I was not a spy, and I never traveled to the Soviet Union. But if I were an agent of the Polish Intelligence there is no moral degradation connected with it. I would simply be serving my country in the same way as Soviet children are taught that they, by every which means, should serve their country." The *sledovatyel* was taken aback; he thought for a while; then he told me that perhaps I was correct. My cooperation with Polish Intelligence did not constitute a moral downfall, but in that case, they would have to shoot me because I was an unrepentant enemy of the Soviet Union, who could not be rehabilitated.

Shortly after, the *sledovatyel* announced that different methods would have to be applied to me in order to loosen my tongue. I knew this meant that I would be sent to Lefortovo Prison where tortures were being applied. But I also knew from my co-tenants, that since the time of Beria's accession to power, the investigating magistrate needed the permission of higher authorities to apply torture. The next time, when I was taken for questioning, they led me through a carpeted corridor on another floor of the NKVD offices into a splendidly furnished and carpeted room; behind the big bureau stood a tall, relatively young, lanky dignitary, and as far as I can remember in the uniform of a colonel of the NKVD. My *sledovatyel* was also present. He was holding a briefcase in his hand, most likely containing the documents of my case. They directed all the lights on me, and the *sledovatyel* sat down on the farther corner of the sofa. The tall dignitary conducted the investigation. I announced right from the start that I had no reason to hide anything. My activities were open: I had lectured at the university; I had published books and written articles; I had journeyed abroad and met with people; I had taken part in meetings and discussions; I was fascinated about what was happening in the Soviet Union, and people with obvious communist sympathies had visited me to whom I had lent books published in the Soviet Union. Therefore, the assumption of my *sledovatyel* that the Polish Intelligence would open its secret files to such a garrulous person was simply absurd.

"Do you, in the NKVD, really have such a low opinion of the organization of Polish Intelligence?" I asked.

The investigation changed into a lengthy conversation on different topics. This dignitary asked me intensively about the activities of the "Polish Military Organization." I explained to him that this was rather a question of history than a question of actual Polish problems between the wars. During this conversation, the question of Polish prisoners of war accidentally surfaced. I told him that I did not quite understand why I was selected from the prisoner of war camp. I was not a Soviet citizen and could not be tried by the Soviets for what I did before the war in Poland; therefore, according to my judgment, the general principles of treatment of prisoners of war had to be applied in my case. To that remark of mine, this dignitary, not paying attention to me, turned to the investigative magistrate and informed him that a camp for Polish officers existed in the Soviet Union, where the living conditions were actually fairly good. At that time, I thought that this was calculated to induce me to greater cooperation during the investigation. Today, I am inclined to suppose that he had Grazovetz in mind, of which the *sledovatyel* could not have known, but this dignitary did know. This was the only time during the investigations when anything came up that could be considered as information about the fate of my colleagues.

IN THE SHADOW OF KATYN

After this interlude with the dignitary, the investigation of my activities resumed with a more intelligent character. They ceased to demand the names of agents from me, but they maintained that I had given a survey of the economic and general situation of the Soviet Union to the Polish Intelligence and to the Ministry of Foreign Affairs. My reply to that was that neither I, personally, nor the Institute of Eastern Europe had done this and nobody had demanded it of us. I did not hide though that I would consider it quite logical to make such a survey. The Institute of Eastern Europe was partly financed from public resources. It would not be surprising therefore, that those institutions, that gave us a certain amount of help, might ask us to do some surveys for them. But we did not do it. I would not have had time for this because of my lectures in the theory of economics at the two faculties of the university; however, I refrained from informing my interrogator that I would have had no objections in principle to doing those surveys if it had been demanded of me. My general stand was: I was loyal to the Polish State, particularly when the Polish Nation was waging war for its existence; and I had the hope that the day might arrive that the Soviet Union was going to support us in this battle; however, frankly speaking, concerning this last possibility I was rather skeptical. But this corresponded to the general line accepted in the Kozelsk camp.

One day, the investigation became atypical by Soviet standards; making an about-face, the examining magistrate, instead of accusing me, began to pay me compliments. He asked me about my contacts with Japanese Intelligence. I knew from my co-tenants in my cell that accusation of cooperation with Japanese Intelligence was a standard trick of Soviet investigations. Against each one of my Russian cellmates, this accusation was brought forward at a certain time but later on retracted. Obviously I denied this cooperation. Then the *sledovatyel* asked me politely, "Why was the Japanese military attaché visiting you?"

At that moment, I remembered that in my office in the Institute of Eastern Europe I actually had visits from several Japanese officers who were interested in our studies of the Soviet economy. I answered, "The Institute of Eastern Europe in Wilno was not engaged in secret activities. Various people used to come who were interested in our work; communists came, to whom I made available various literature; Japanese officers also came, and they even sent gifts depicting Japanese life painted on silk. It did not mean, however, that I was co-operating with Japanese Intelligence."

To my great surprise the *sledovatyel* did not burst out with threats, but he answered politely, "I am not accusing you of co-operating with Japanese Intelligence but am only asking you about the contacts, which does not have the same meaning. We have enough evidence that points out that you personally, in spite of great pressure, did not become a recruit for the Japanese Intelligence. But I have to tell you, that your section of economic studies was working for Japanese Intelligence." I flounced and said abruptly that after all I did know what was happening in my institute. "Don't be so sure of yourself," said the *sledovatyel*, and then added that when I refused the cooperation with Japanese Intelligence, some of my coworkers and assistants undertook to do so behind my back and were sending regular reports to Japanese Intelligence about the situation of the Soviet economy. The *sledovatyel* ended this night's conversation with the statement, in a rather friendly tone, "Those Japs are insolent." Then he called for the guards to send me back to my cell.

FROM KATYN TO KUYBYSHEV

When I came back to my cell, I could not fall asleep for quite a while. I was searching my mind for all the details of the Japanese visits. The truth was as follows. A few years before the war, I think it was in 1936, a Japanese colonel whose name I cannot remember came to me. He was a Japanese military attaché in Warsaw and proposed that they, meaning the Japanese military and diplomatic representatives, were prepared to contribute to research work on the Soviet economy at the institute by adding an additional research worker who was to be under my supervision. I thanked him for the interest and positive appraisal of our activities, but I told him that I could not give him an answer without the consent of the administration of the institute. I consulted the chairman of the administration, Professor Ehrenkreutz, who later became rector of the University of Wilno, and I told him about my conversation with the Japanese military attaché. To both of us it became clear that this case crossed the boundaries of international scientific relations, and most probably this eventual research worker would be an officer of the Japanese General Staff, whom I would have to educate in the problems of Soviet economy. Professor Ehrenkreutz said that we could not undertake any decision without consulting with the proper authorities in Warsaw. On the first occasion when both of us were in Warsaw, we went to the Eastern Department of the Ministry of Foreign Affairs. The chief of that department, Mr. Kobylański, said to us that this case belonged to the jurisdiction of the General Staff, and he advised us to go there. In the offices of General Staff, Col. Englicht, deputy to the chief of Department II,[16] received us and also quite firmly dissuaded us from accepting the Japanese proposal. As far as I could understand, he was rather offended that the Japanese Intelligence, without consulting with the appropriate Polish authorities, was trying to position its people in Polish institutions. When, shortly after, a Japanese major, deputy to the military attaché reported to me, I communicated to him in the most polite form the negative answer, and I considered the case closed. It is possible that the Japanese were offended and treated this as my personal attitude toward them and, in addition to which, there were a number of people in Poland who saw in my interest in Soviet affairs some hidden sympathy toward the communist system. And probably this version came into the hands of Soviet Intelligence.

Several months later, when I had another conversation with Professor Ehrenkreutz, he mentioned that he again had visits from the Japanese, and that one of the scholarship holders working under me had agreed – with the knowledge of Department II – to make reports for the Japanese attaché on the situation of the Soviet economy on the basis of his private agreement with the Japanese, and that the institute was not to be involved. I accepted this information without much interest; I was at that time absorbed in writing a book about the economic policy of Hitlerite Germany, and I did not spend too much time on Soviet studies at the institute. After that, I had completely forgotten about the conversation with Professor Ehrenkreutz until the Soviet magistrate reminded me of that incident. It looked as if the bragging statement of Soviet Intelligence, "the NKVD knows everything" was correct. In this case, actually, they knew more things about me than I could remember myself.

During my investigation, I was under the impression that of the two accusations about which I was originally charged – spying against Russia, and alleged spying against Germany – the second was of more interest to my investigators than the first. I

---

[16] Polish Intelligence

maintained that collecting materials for my book about German economic policy was based on purely scientific relations, and that during my stay in Berlin and at the *Institut für Weltwirtschaft und Seeverkehr* in Kiel, I did nothing that I could not tell to my German colleagues. The *sledovatyel* answered that Soviet Intelligence found out that during that time I had maintained connections with Col. Pełczyński, who was then head of Department II in the Polish General Staff. I did not deny it, but I declared that the acquaintance was of a private nature, and it originated when Col. Pełczyński was commander of the Fifth Infantry Regiment of the Polish Legion, stationed in Wilno, while I was an assistant professor lecturing in economics at the University of Wilno. But, even if Col. Pełczyński were interested in my book, I would consider it quite natural in spite of the fact that it did not have any confidential information. Poland was insufficiently armed, so the study of the economic background of German rearmament was simply a necessity for the high-ranking officers of the Polish General Staff.

From all these investigations conducted in a rather polite fashion, I did get the impression that my book on economic policy of Hitlerite Germany created great interest in some higher Soviet circles, and that the *sledovatyels* were instructed to collect all the information pertaining to the personality of the author, as well as the circumstances connected with the creation of this work. Finally, the examining magistrate ordered that I should submit, in writing, how the Germans had financed their rearmament. After that time the investigation consisted of my being taken to the office of the *sledovatyel*, late in the evening, and there through the whole night, I wrote about the "economic model of German rearmament." It actually meant that I was writing in the Russian language an abbreviation of some of the chapters of my book.

The *sledovatyel*, in the meantime, was occupied with his other affairs. I had the impression that he generally had little interest in what I was writing on the subject of how Hitler and Schacht financed German rearmament. Apparently, there was someone in the Soviet apparatus who did study this, and for whom my work was necessary. It is possible that my book on the economic policy of Hitlerite Germany was the main point of interest in my person by Moscow, which had so intrigued the commander of the prison in Smolensk.

My prison companions

Before I start describing my "sojourn" in the GULAG camps, I would like to devote a certain amount of space to my prison companions, particularly those who made an impression on my memory.

Lubyanka was a prison for the Soviet elite. Besides the party dignitaries who lost favor with Stalin, also many high executives of Soviet industry, factory managers, and chief engineers came there for incarceration. During the ten years before the war, my studies were devoted to the economic transformation that was happening in Russia. In the thirties, large industry was expanding in record time. Obviously, I was interested in the psyche of the people who were entrusted with the key executive positions in this great process of change. The common prison cell gave me an exceptional opportunity to look closely at some of them and compare them with the type of capitalist entrepreneur analyzed by economic historians, mainly by Werner Sombart.

FROM KATYN TO KUYBYSHEV

I consider Miroshnikov, a tall, well-built man of about fifty, as the one who stands out most from the administrators of Soviet industry with whom I shared a cell. I think I can mention his name without great risk because, according to my calculations, he should be about eighty-five years old today [1976], assuming he is still alive. Before the Revolution, he belonged to the working class and was an old communist. During the Civil War of 1918-1920, he was a commander of a division and, for a certain time, he was a deputy commander to the future Marshal Voroshilov. After the end of the civil war, he was transferred to industry in an administrative position. For many years he occupied an executive position as an advisor to the Soviet Government. Then he became Chief of the Aluminum Industry for the whole of Russia. He maintained that in this sphere of production it was the biggest enterprise in the whole world, surpassing all other capitalist syndicates.

Already in the 1920's, Trotsky relished making comparisons between the building of industry and military action, and proposed projects of partial militarization of the work force. Miroshnikov, undoubtedly, belonged to that type of party activist; therefore, he was transferred from the military to industry. He was an ideological communist. It would never have occurred to him that, while serving the Party his whole life, he would err in some way. When talking about the Party or about the Soviet Government or about the international politics of the Soviet Union, he identified himself with them. He was always saying "we," and "our politics," et cetera.

He did not like to talk about his predicament. It seemed to me that he had been tortured. One thing he told me was that almost all of those who were implicated in the same case were already executed, but he had been placed in some camp in northern Siberia. Now, however, he was brought back to Moscow to give some depositions in the additional process connected with this same case. If he denounced other people in the process, it was in agreement with his communist conscience. Using him as an example, I thought that he corresponded to that type of character that Koestler[17] uses in his novels, one who was convinced by the *sledovatyel* that for the good of the party he should plead guilty to crimes that were never committed.

Miroshnikov was well acquainted with international politics, but in the matters dealing with foreign policy, he was very pragmatic. He did not like Hitler and labeled the whole Hitler movement as one without principles, but he did not have any objections to the alliance between Stalin and Hitler and the attack on Poland in 1939. He could not understand the mentality of Poles, who seemed to have believed that Russia would stay neutral in a German-Polish war. In his opinion and from his objective analysis, it appeared that the Polish State, which existed before 1939, could only have maintained itself in some form of cooperation with the German Reich. Only this could have saved the Eastern Territories of that country from the eventual occupation by the Soviet Union. This blue-collar worker had, undoubtedly, the mind of a statesman, and he could think objectively.

He had a very good knowledge of our September 1939 campaign, because previously he had been imprisoned in the same cell with Lt. Col. Wiśniowski (later a general and chief of staff of General Anders' Army). From Miroshnikov I found out that General Sosnkowski, who for a certain time stayed in Lwów, occupied by the

---

[17] Koestler, Arthur (1905-1983), writer and journalist. His masterpiece is the political novel *Darkness at Noon (1940)*.

IN THE SHADOW OF KATYN

Soviet Army, managed to escape to Hungary. Wiśniowski had been caught by the Soviets while he was organizing the escape for Gen. Sosnkowski. Later on, when I accidentally met Gen. Wiśniowski in 1943, he confirmed this information that I had received from Miroshnikov.

The other person of great caliber among my prison mates was, as already mentioned before, chief of long-range planning for the Russian Navy. He was a typical Russian intellectual though he had a German name, Tischbein. In 1914, when the First World War broke out, he was a student at the Petersburg Institute of Technology in the Department of Shipbuilding. He was drafted into the army and graduated from Artillery School, and he spent the rest of the war as a frontline artillery officer. After the Revolution, he went back to the Institute of Technology to finish his studies. He was a close associate of Admiral Orlov. Orlov was commander of the Baltic Fleet and then commander-in-chief of the entire Navy of the Soviet Union, who later was shot in connection with the case of Marshal Tukhachevsky. Tischbein was also somehow connected with Marshal Tukhachevsky, though he talked less about Tukhachevsky than about Orlov. When Tukhachevsky and Orlov were arrested, Tischbein understood that his days were also numbered, for he was demoted to shipbuilding engineer; then he was arrested and accused mainly of sabotage. For four months I sat in the same cell with him.

Tischbein was foremost a specialist. He was not too much interested in party zeal. Besides his function as a planner, he was also editor of the Naval Section of the Great Soviet Encyclopedia; he even organized lectures about the fleets of Phoenicia, Greece and Rome for us. In 1940, the Soviet Navy was not very powerful. It could not be compared with the navies of Great Britain, the United States, and even Germany. Tischbein assured me that if nothing extraordinary happened, then within several years the Soviet fleet was going to be a first rate fleet, and perhaps even the strongest navy in the world. Today, in the seventies, we are witnessing the realization of this prediction, or rather the realization of the calculations of a man who was making those plans.

When I met him, he had already been incarcerated for about two years. I asked him whether he had been tortured. He answered that no sophisticated tortures were applied to him. He was only beaten, but rather with *lubia* [kindness], that means in such a way as not to harm his body. Finally, he came to the conclusion that he ought to plead guilty to something. So, he pleaded guilty to organized sabotage, and I assume that he must have mentioned some names. Something in his testimony did not wash.

One night, when after the interrogation he was brought back to the cell, I noticed that he was in a state of bewilderment. He immediately asked me whether I happened to know what the word "poc" meant. Awakened from my sleep, I tried to recollect my thoughts to see if, in one of the languages known to me, I had heard this word. Finally, I answered him that I did not know. Then he told me what had happened. The investigation in his case had a specific character that night, because three officers questioned him. At one moment they asked him whether he knew what "poc" meant. He understood that probably it was some abbreviation and without hesitation he answered, *"Pravoy Organisatziniy Center"* [Right Wing Organizational Center] and was ready to admit that from them he received instructions as to his invented sabotage activities. Before he could make further testimony, the *sledovatyels* burst into

FROM KATYN TO KUYBYSHEV

unrestrained laughter. They gave him a slight beating; then they called the guards and told them to bring him back to his cell.

Another prison companion, commissar of finances in Kazakhstan, a Jew from Bobruysk in Byelorussia – who had also awakened and overheard our conversation – said that "poc" according to Jewish jargon in his district meant simply, female sexual organ. One should have seen the amazement expressed on the face of our famous planner, reflected by the feeble light of the bulb on the ceiling. Helplessly he opened his arms and said to me, "Things became so confused. I thought that it was Right Wing Organizational Center, and this appears to be simply c...."

Everything became quite clear. The *sledovatyels* wanted to find out to what degree Tischbein's testimony was credible. One of the investigators, a Jew, wanted – through the use of this vulgar word – to convey that Tischbein's testimony was without any value. In the meantime the accused, in his fervor to admit to crimes which he had not committed, submitted the kind of testimony which, in the context of the *sledovatyels'* intentions, appeared to be quite comical. The investigation, however, continued and Tischbein received an order to work on a report in which he should explain in technical terminology how he did his sabotage. This report was made and the examining authorities acknowledged that they had enough material to close the investigations.

One day, a defense lawyer was placed into our cell. In the Soviet Union there exists an association of defense lawyers, somehow similar to the ones in the Western world. In political investigations the role of defense lawyers is almost nil. Most of the time they accept as fact the extorted admission to uncommitted crimes from the accused. They utter a few sentences, whereby they ask the court to take into account the mitigating circumstances. But in the case of misappropriation of funds or simple theft, the defense lawyer could be a real help.

So this defense lawyer, after acquainting himself with Tischbein's case, advised him that he should now submit an application for the appointment of a commission of experts to analyze his submission. The verdict of the commission of experts would not have too much meaning if the internal courts of the NKVD, the so-called "troika", dealt with his case. But the "troikas" at that time had a limited jurisdiction, and they could give no more than eight years of GULAG. However, if the case were to be sent to a normal tribunal, which was required to act according to more strict procedural norms, then the verdict of the commission of experts would have some real meaning. Tischbein followed his advice and he sent an application for the appointment of a commission of experts. After several days, he was taken from our cell, and I heard no more about his fate.

Miroshnikov had told us about the progress of the September campaign in Poland from the news that he had received from Col. Wiśniowski, but Tischbein did give us some information about the fate of Hungarian communists arrested in Russia, probably because of some ripple effect of the Soviet-German Pact. He was in the same cell with a Hungarian medical doctor who had been employed as an expert laryngologist in the hospital in the Kremlin where he had been looking after many prominent and well-known Soviet dignitaries, including Stalin himself. In that way we found out that Bela Kun, the leader of the Hungarian Revolution in 1919, was still alive in 1940, and was incarcerated in one of the *politisolators* [political isolation cells] somewhere in the southern part of the Soviet Union. This information I relayed later to Matyas Rakosi[18] when I met him in the GULAG in North European Russia.

Of the distinguished Soviet managers and planners, with whom I happened to be in prison, I remember a manager of the Flour Mill Trust in the Soviet Far East, a chief engineer of the aircraft industry in Gorki, and a chief engineer of a large tractor factory near Kharkov. For a while, an Armenian designer of artillery stayed in our cell, who told us that even if he were to be sentenced to death, the sentence would never be carried out because the Soviet Union did not have anyone who could replace him in the area of his specialty.

One night near dawn the doors were opened, and the guards guided in a new prisoner and pointed out the empty bed next to me. The new arrival was in a long, excellent, leather coat and a well-cut suit. When he emptied his pockets of the things he was allowed to keep, it became obvious that he represented a high standard of living, rarely found in the Soviet Union. Through half-closed eyes, I observed him with great interest. Finally, I asked, "Obviously you must be an engineer?"

The answer was, "Oh yes, and in addition, unfortunately a chief one." This meant, he was a technical manager. Later on when we were better acquainted, he told me that according to his calculations the average time-span of holding that kind of a position in large Soviet conglomerates was approximately four years. During that time, generally, something would happen so that one would end up in prison and, eventually in GULAG. One had to live in constant nervous tension because of chronic shortages of supplies and all kinds of structural defects, but all these inconveniences and risks were worth taking because of a high standard of living and the satisfaction one gets from being in a position of power. My interlocutor had a four-room apartment with all the conveniences of a newly constructed house; there were numerous rewards and high bonuses attached to his salary, and he had a car at his disposal. His view of Poles and Poland was of a rather specific nature. He came from a Jewish family, who lived in a small Ukrainian town that had belonged to the family of Branicki. Before the First World War, as a small-town urchin, the sight of Countess Branicka coming out of her palace and entering her coach had fascinated him. Never in his life did he come in contact with the Polish peasant, industrial worker, or intellectual. So I told him quite a bit about present day Poland.

Of all my cellmates who did not belong to the category of industrial managers and planners, the one who impressed me most was that tall blond, whom I mentioned before when I described cell 41. He was also an engineer, but it was not connected with the essence of his case. He was accused of murdering the well-known Soviet actress, Zinaida Reich, wife of Meyerhold, director of the famous theater of that name. This theater had seceded from the world famous Moscow Theater directed by Stanislavsky. Meyerhold was arrested, apparently by order of Stalin, and he disappeared without a trace. Shortly after, his wife was murdered; generally it was presumed that the NKVD agents did it, and they were also conducting the investigation into her murder. My

---

[18] Rakosi, Matyas (1892-1971) Communist sent by Stalin to Gulag and in 1942 shared misery and food with author of these sketches. Rakosi was released from Gulag and after the war was instrumental in establishing Communism in Hungary, and became Prime Minister. In 1956, after Khrushchev denounced Stalin at a closed session of the 20th Party Congress in Moscow, and amid increasing expectations of sweeping reform and democratization, the hard-line leader of the Hungarian Socialist Workers' Party, Matyas Rakosi, was forced to resign in July 1956.

FROM KATYN TO KUYBYSHEV

cellmate was one of the accused in this case. Zinaida Reich, before she became the wife of Meyerhold, was one of the successive wives of the outstanding Soviet poet Yesiennin and had a daughter by him. This daughter was married to the brother of my cellmate; therefore, the connection with the Meyerhold family.

At the beginning my cellmate pleaded not guilty to this murder. Then he was taken to the Lefortovo Prison until, after being beaten for a long period of time, he pleaded guilty not only to the murder of this actress, but also to dispatching information about the construction of Soviet tanks to Polish- and Japanese Intelligence. Afterward, the examining magistrate instructed him to write all the details on how he committed this murder. The authorities seemed to be very pleased with his fiction. The accused was sent back to Lubyanka, which the prisoners called "Sanatorium" because no tortures were applied there, and sometimes they brought the more important prisoners from Lefortovo for a kind of rest from agony. So, he had come from Lefortovo a few days before I was led into cell 41.

In Lubyanka, when he had rested and slept sufficiently, he became desperate about admitting to uncommitted crimes, which would result in an unavoidable death penalty. So he decided to withdraw his admission of guilt and, simultaneously, he submitted a complaint to the chief prosecutor of the Soviet Union describing the tortures to which he was exposed at the Lefortovo Prison. After a few weeks, he was called to the offices of the NKVD where a high official told him that his application had been looked at by the higher branches of the NKVD with a positive result; that is, they believed his denial of murdering Zinaida Reich and his spying for Poland and Japan; but still there remained the case of anti-Soviet conversations in which he had happened to partake, and because of that he was going to be punished accordingly.

My companion in misery returned to our cell beaming with joy. The normal punishment for anti-Soviet conversations was three years. He expected to be sent to research laboratories that were administered by the NKVD. That was the first time I found out about the existence of those laboratories, which later on became the topic in Solzhenitsyn's work, *First Circle*. Among the prisoners, it was also rumored that the well-known Soviet airplane builder Tupolev, who also had been arrested, was working at that time in one of those laboratories.

After a few days, the rehabilitated murderer of the wife of Meyerhold was taken away from our cell. I do not know what happened to him after that, and whether he managed to get into the research laboratories, which he saw as a new start in life. When about a half year later I received my verdict, and was kept in a large cell in Butyrki Prison, there were quite a number of prisoners, mostly foreigners, waiting to be sent to the GULAG. I found out that several other prisoners had been incarcerated with those who were also accused of murdering Zinaida Reich. In the end, all of them had admitted to being guilty of this murder. Shortly after the war, I wrote a short story about this abject and absurd event in *Orzel Biały* ["White Eagle" - a Polish émigré publication] under the title, "Competition for the Best Murderer," suggesting the hypothesis that the one of the alleged murderers, who was able to write the best description on how he committed the murder, had been shot, and the others were sent to the camps. How it really was, is impossible to verify. I am not even absolutely certain that this actress actually had been murdered, even though fellow prisoners maintained that everywhere in Moscow they talked about this. The investigating prisons of the

IN THE SHADOW OF KATYN

NKVD, at the time of Stalin, belong to the world of miserable anecdotes, where the authorities themselves could not distinguish between the truth and the products of degenerated fantasies of the investigating officers, who by application of tortures could extract the most incredible admissions from their victims.

Butyrki and the end of the investigation

During Christmas 1940, I was transferred from Lubyanka to Butyrki, the other prison in Moscow. When I was placed in a small separate cell in the prison bus, I overheard words spoken in Polish from the neighboring cell. I began thinking: Polish prisoners are being unloaded from Lubyanka.

In the Butyrki prison, I was put in a tower where apparently during the reign of Catherine II (called "The Great"), Pugachov was held. Pugachov, leader of the rebellious peasants in the Volga district, had claimed to be Tsar Peter III, husband of the empress. Supposedly, her lovers had already murdered Catherine's husband, Tsar Peter III. One entered into my cell by a spiral, narrow, iron staircase; the outside wall was of a semi-circular shape. At the beginning there was with me only one prisoner, a civil servant from the Commissariat of Foreign Affairs, an expert on the Orient, fluent in the Persian and Arabic languages, and expert in the affairs of the Near East. His case seemed to be deadlocked. He was already incarcerated for two years in this tower and never called for investigations. I would not have even dreamt, at that time, that I also would become an expert in Near Eastern affairs without knowledge of the Persian and Arabic languages. However, exactly two years later, in January 1943, the Polish Émigré Government in London entrusted me with the organization of Polish research on the Middle East with Jerusalem as its headquarters.

Shortly after, the third tenant was led into our cell. It was a *sledovatyel* from some provincial unit of the NKVD, not far from Moscow, claiming to be a victim of some villainous intrigue. He told me in detail as to who made this harmful denunciation and what it was all about. His history could paint a picture of Soviet provincial life, but today I am unable to reconstruct all the mishaps of that complicated case. My cellmate swore that he had never tortured any prisoners, and he even did not know that tortures were being applied in the NKVD. After a few months, I met him again in a transfer camp in Kotlas. He was fairly decently dressed in a jacket with a fur collar; he was working again in his profession because he was supervising the camp's prison, and he was looking forward very optimistically to his GULAG camp career.

This small-time wretch from the NKVD brought me news that deeply moved me. He previously sat in the same cell with General Anders and knew many details of his lot. I was led back into the ambiance of Kozelsk. In Kozelsk, I had my place in building No. 10, in the hall where the junior officers of cavalry were mostly placed. Anders was their hero, and his name was repeated all the time in the camp bunks. Almost all inmates of that hall belonged to those units of cavalry who, around the 20th of September 1939, found themselves in the region between the Bug and San rivers, and Gen. Anders took over command there with the intention of breaking through to Hungary. My war experiences connected me with them until I became a prisoner of war. In the morning of the 24th of September, I led a small unit of mounted scouts as a liaison officer of the advancing Infantry Brigade (77th and 85th Infantry Regiment) to

FROM KATYN TO KUYBYSHEV

Suchowola, in the region of Tomaszów Lubelski, when Anders' cavalry was breaking through the German ring which had closed them off from Hungary. Our brigade's intention was to enter the opening made by the cavalry. But when Anders with a part of his brigade had passed through, the ring closed again, separating him from the infantry and also from part of his staff and smaller units of cavalry. After being taken prisoners, Col. Żelisławski, second in command to Gen. Anders, became our Polish commanding officer in the camp near Putyvl in the Cernichov district. We all believed that Anders with his elite troops had reached the Hungarian border. We talked about it constantly. We had quite a shock when in Kozelsk, shortly before Christmas of 1939, we found out that Gen. Anders was also in Soviet hands, but we did not know the details.

Now, for the first time, I heard about the details. The imprisoned *sledovatyel* told me about the wound that Gen. Anders received near the Hungarian border when his unit was attacked by the Soviet Air Force. He informed me also about Anders' stay in the hospital in Lwów, that his family was allowed to nurse him, that he received permission to go into the German occupation but was later arrested in Brest-Litovsk. I was told also of the shock the general experienced when he learned about the defeat of France. Several times the *sledovatyel* mentioned the excellent footwear with the thick soles the general's wife apparently had given the general in Lwów. *"Charoshi muzhik"* [A fine man] – and with these words he finished his story about the general.

At Butyrki, when I was called for interrogation, I was told that another *sledovatyel* had taken over my case. He was a tall man with auburn hair, more than thirty years old, who during the interrogation behaved fairly decently, almost politely. He was, it seemed to me, an expert on Yugoslavia. In the room where I was being interrogated, almost the whole wall to the left of me was covered with ordnance maps of Yugoslavia on which many colored flags were placed. It probably represented part of the whole network of communist cells and other Soviet agents. Those maps fascinated me; I could not restrain myself from looking toward the left. It was in January-February, 1941, which means two or three months before the German attack on Yugoslavia. Those flags proved to me that Soviet agents actively were moving into the territory which the Germans and Italians had considered their own reserved sphere of influence. It was not difficult to suspect the possible consequences this state of affairs would have had on Soviet-German relations; however, I still did not believe that Hitler would decide to attack the Soviets, and that the German General Staff would permit it. Not able to contain myself any longer, I asked my *sledovatyel* what the present Soviet-German relations were. He answered that they were still good and friendly, but from the tone of his voice and from the smile on his face, which accompanied this answer, it became obvious that he did not give much credit to the durability of this friendship. My conviction of the complete improbability of a Soviet-German war began to crumble.

This new investigating magistrate also communicated to me that the authorities had decided to bring the investigation in my case to an end, and briefly informed me of the results of the investigation as he understood them. In his opinion, there were certain contradictions in my case that were difficult to explain. The material collected from various people who knew me before the war seemed to indicate that my attitude toward the Soviet Union was more positive than could be concluded from my behavior during the investigations. He told me that he himself talked about my case with many people, and it transpired that my attitude was not at all counter-revolutionary, that I was a democrat characterized by tolerance, and that I had an understanding of social problems. In the meantime, from the material collected during the investigation, it came out that I was not sincere; that I gave evasive answers; that I did not want to tell everything that I knew about various pre-war affairs in Poland; that I even tried to manifest my support of things that were reactionary in pre-war Poland; and that in my heart I was more in support of this than what the Soviet Union represents. In return I demanded that before my case was brought to an end, he show me the material collected during the investigations as this was my right according to Soviet judiciary procedure and was previously promised by this *sledovatyel*.

When, from the perspective of many years, I contemplate those investigations, I think that what the *sledovatyel* told me could have been quite sincere. It is true that before the war there were a certain number of people in Wilno who suspected me of having Soviet sympathies. It came from the attitude that I took in my publications, articles, and university lectures. I considered that the epoch of private initiative as the main engine of economic development had passed, and in our times in order to secure this development and avoid unemployment, great public undertakings were necessary, and the political system should be based on the ideals of collective action. These were my interests, having been conveyed in my publications, and it included my interest in the Soviet Union and in the economic system which Hitler and his associates had created in Germany. However, from the philosophical point of view, and of moral and political considerations, I equally rejected communism as well as nationalism; but my analyses of the development of a capitalist economy at that time were in some points similar to the communist theses.

At the end of the 1920s, I was very much connected with the youth movement, whose leader was a student of law, Henryk Dembiński. He propagated the principles of collective action in economic development based on Christian ideals. When the large wing of that movement, together with Dembiński, initiated a move toward the communist positions, I still maintained personal sympathies with many people from that group. I am sure that in Wilno there were certain communist sympathizers who considered that it was possible to converse with me and even to learn something. I am not surprised that agents of the NKVD, who conducted investigations in my case, had been collecting additional data about me from the people in whom they had confidence, and from whom they received a number of positive opinions.

On the other hand, I must admit that there was a certain amount of truth in what the examining magistrate said. During the interrogations, I had tried to hide my real attitude to pre-war problems of Polish life. The tactics that I applied during the investigation can be expressed in four basic points. First, I tried to avoid admitting to the things which, according the Soviet penal code, were considered an obvious crime. The Soviet penal procedure had in those days an "inquisitional" character, where admission of guilt and expression of contrition played a very important part. In the Soviet Union, there were two types of courts before which political prisoners were placed:

1) The secret courts of the NKVD, (so-called "troikas")
    in which the procedures were confidential.
2) The so-called "tribunals", whose procedures were
    similar to the courts in the rest of the world.

FROM KATYN TO KUYBYSHEV

The "troikas" judged on the principle of "revolutionary expediency" and the question of proving the actual crime was of secondary importance. On the other hand, the tribunals involved themselves in arguments with the prosecutor and – as my cellmates maintained – they sometimes rejected his conclusions. The *sledovatyel* who did not sufficiently prepare the case for the tribunal sometimes found himself in the GULAG. The case was considered well prepared when the accused not only admitted his guilt, but also brought certain additional elements that confirmed the indictment and implicated several other people. Such a confession was extorted by tortures, which had the nature of an inquisition. Torture was the rule during the time of Yezhov, but during the time of Beria, the investigating magistrate had to have special permission from the higher authorities before he could submit a prisoner to regular torture. From what I heard from my cellmates, one could conclude that if the prisoner did not admit his guilt when brought before a tribunal, he had a certain chance of coming off well. Therefore, it was very important not to give to the investigating magistrate this basic argument which, in the inquisitional procedure, is an admission of guilt.

It was extremely rare that an accused person who did not admit his guilt was put before the tribunal. These cases usually went to the internal courts of the NKVD. In the beginning years of Beria's regime, the maximum punishment which these courts could assign was eight years of GULAG. The cases that required more than eight years had to be placed before the "tribunals." Therefore, to maintain oneself in a position of not admitting any guilt, one would have a better chance for survival.

The second principle of my tactics during the investigation was to hide my connections with the Wilno Federalists. The Soviet policy is extremely sensitive to any attempted negotiations for cooperation among the nations incorporated into the Soviet Union or neighboring the Soviet Union, when that cooperation is not strictly controlled by the Soviets. However, this policy is quite tolerant to the expression of extreme nationalism, provided this nationalism stimulates antagonisms among neighboring nations. All the attempts to form a Balkan League or a Polish-Czech Federation were to the Soviets like a red flag to the bull, as we know from East-European experiences during the war and after the war. Anyone who attempted to foster closer ties between Poles and Ukrainians automatically became an enemy of the Soviet Union. The antagonism between Hungarians and Romanians or between Serbs and Bulgarians was like manna from heaven to the Soviet Empire. The Wilno Federalists, who propagated the idea of a growing understanding among the four nations living in the territories occupied by the old Grand-Duchy of Lithuania (that means Poles, Lithuanians, Byelorussians, and Jews), opposed the wanton ethnic policy of the Polish administration in the then Polish Eastern territories between the two wars. The Wilno Federalists were, from the Soviet point of view, an undesirable element that had to be subjected to some form of liquidation.

In the beginning of the 1920s, when the fate of Wilno was in the process of being decided, the fact that I was against incorporating this old capital of the Grand Duchy of Lithuania into the Polish State made me a highly suspicious type in the eyes of the Soviets. The program of the Federation of Nations consisted of giving independence to the Ukraine and Byelorussia, which would mean cutting off the Eastern Polish territories and, at the same time, pushing Russia further to the East. It would be better if they thought of me as a Polish nationalist who maintained that the country east of Poland was Russia. This strategy I already thought out in *pryomnik* where, in front of my closed eyes, I saw the glowing rainbow of the strong electrical glare of the overhanging light bulb.

The third tactical principle was to avoid anything that could give the impression that I was ready to cooperate in one form or another with the Soviet Union. In Kozelsk, I already came to the conclusion that one of the purposes of the very detailed investigation of each prisoner by the team of NKVD agents, led by Kombrig Zarubin, was not only to detect special enemies of the Soviet Union, but also to separate the people who could be useful to the Soviets either in the information services or in some other political activity. Personally, I was not any less afraid of that second distinction, than of the first. My impression was that in the personal attitude of Kombrig Zarubin toward the prisoners, he attached much more importance to the second aim than to the first. He had been interested mainly in those prisoners who had distinguished themselves on a higher level than the average person in pre-war life. He had directed his curiosity toward the staff officers, not so much toward the generals as toward the colonels and lieutenant colonels who had completed the higher military academies. Some of us had the impression that the individuality of Colonel Künstler was particularly highly rated by this Soviet investigator. By order of Kombrig Zarubin, one of the better buildings in the camp had been assigned to staff officers where each one received a separate bed with sheets.

When the tone of interrogation became polite and almost friendly, it was to me equally frightening as when it was boorish and brutal. Particularly when I began writing the summary of my book about the policy of Hitler's Germany, I had worried about what might come out of it. I tried to avert any possible proposition by constantly emphasizing my Polish patriotism and my loyalty toward the Polish State, which, the *sledovatyel* told me, did not exist. I was also extremely afraid that they might start to classify me as a Soviet citizen.

In underlining my loyalty toward the Polish State, I maintained the same line as most of the officers in Kozelsk did when confronted by Soviet political officers (*politrucks*) who came to the barracks and engaged in political discussions with the prisoners. Our officers maintained in these conversations that they were faithful to the Polish State independently of what political group was in government; that they were not impressed by the communist system and hoped that the time would come when Russia would be our ally against Hitler's onslaught. It seemed to me that this position was not only honest and honorable but also gave us the best chance of survival. I believed that our survival chances would be much smaller if the Soviet authorities considered us as their sworn enemies. To admit that one is faithful to his banners and to his oath of allegiance does not necessarily mean that one is a sworn enemy of the Soviet Union. On the other hand, an equally dangerous situation would be created if they began to look upon us as their "loyals".

During the interrogation, I tried to identify my position with that of the average imprisoned Kozelsk officer. Many times I demanded that, in my understanding, I had to be sent back to the POW camp in agreement with the existing international conventions. I assumed that the POW camp was the place from which one could get out into the wide world much easier than from behind the walls of Lubyanka and Butyrki. In that respect I was mistaken, even if I considered myself to be an expert on

FROM KATYN TO KUYBYSHEV

Russia. In this world of new morality – which had been created under the Stalinist system, and whose fundamentals of mass terror in 1918 had taken shape under the famous command of Lenin and Dzerzhinsky – the generally accepted principles of the civilized world as to the treatment of POWs had no existence.

Today, I ask myself the question: Did my investigating magistrates know about Katyn? They obviously knew that I came into the Soviet Union as a POW. I assume that as members of the NKVD apparatus, they knew something about the system of secret executions, but I do not think that they were totally informed about the lot of the majority of the Polish officers. It would be contrary to the principle of strict confidentiality that was exercised in carrying out the Katyn decision. When the Germans at Ponarai, near Wilno, organized the center for the execution of Jews, every peasant boy in the vicinity, every servant and kitchen maid knew about it. When our officers were unloaded near the station of Gniezdovo, I noticed not a single civilian, nor a single railway man. The station was like a ghost town; the territory was completely devoid of any possible observers; even the bus, which transported the prisoners, had whitewashed windows, and if a collective farm worker were to accidentally pass by, he would not recognize one single foreign military uniform.

When the people who occupied a high position in the Hitlerite administration maintain that they did not know about the extermination of Jews – I do not believe it, but if some NKVD official came with the assurance that he did not know about Katyn, I would be inclined to believe him. This secret was exceedingly well guarded.

The Verdict

From what the investigating magistrate told me at the end of the interrogation, I came to the conclusion that I was not going to be judged by the "tribunal" but by some other variation of the internal courts of the NKVD. At the end of February (1941), I was taken from Pugachov's tower so that the verdict could be announced to me. After crossing the prison courtyard, I was led into a cell where thirty people were already gathered, awaiting the decision on their fate. One by one they were called to the separate room where their verdict was pronounced. Mostly the verdicts were eight years of GULAG; however, there were a few cases when the punishment was five years. It did not matter very much, because we knew from the old-timers of Soviet prisons and GULAG dwellers, that the prisoner who succeeded in surviving to the end of his sentence usually got a letter from the internal courts of the NKVD, extending his stay in the GULAG for another five to eight years.

When I was called, a rather intelligent looking NKVD man communicated to me the standard eight years, including the time since my arrest; that is, from the time I left Kozelsk. He added that to fulfill my sentence I was going to be sent to the Ust-Wymsk complex of camps in the Republic of Komi, in the northeastern part of European Russia. He also communicated to me that if I were not satisfied with the sentence, I had the right to lodge a complaint to the Supreme Soviet. My answer was that I had no intention of taking advantage of this privilege, and I grinned. "Why are you laughing?" asked the official. My answer was that I was a foreigner, and that in the world a war was being waged and that my fate, if I managed to survive physically, would depend not on the number of years of my sentence, but on the possible change in the

IN THE SHADOW OF KATYN

international situation, which might bring me an early release and the right to leave the Soviet Union.

After the announcement of my verdict, I was taken to a large cell that was already occupied by more than sixty prisoners who had just received their verdicts. They were exclusively foreigners, to which they soon added several high-ranking Soviet officials originating from the ethnic minorities. The most numerous groups were Poles and Finns. Among the Poles: Col. Wacław Koc, ex-Chief of Staff in the district of Lublin; Dr. Stanisław Skrzypek, economist, assistant of Prof. Stanisław Grabski of the University of Lwów; and also Jan Adamus, a docent of the University of Wilno (later professor of the University of Łódź), at whose oral examination on his thesis presented to qualify him as an assistant professor, I acted as a secretary. The tribunal gave Col. Koc the death sentence, which was commuted to ten years of prison. Among the prisoners gathered, there were several representatives of European and Asian nations.

We were all intrigued by the presence of a real spy – a Japanese officer, who considered his mission in Russia as an act of sacrifice and was proud of it. He was not treated any worse than the imaginary spies, of whom there were many present in the cell. He told me that he was almost certain that soon he would be exchanged for Russian spies in Japan. His outlook on the future was much better than the prospect ahead of those fictitious spies.

My special interest was aroused by a man with higher education, a German communist and member of the Central Committee of the German Communist Party. A few years earlier, the party had sent him to Soviet Russia for the cure of tuberculosis. He spent considerable time in a sanitarium in the Crimea where he had excellent care. Then he lectured for some time at the University of Volga-Germans (a settlement of Germans in that part of Russia), in Saratov, I believe. When, during the great purge, they liquidated a number of old-Russian communists and started exterminating foreign communists who were present in Russia, he was arrested and spent almost a year in some damp dungeon near the Volga. Now he was waiting to be handed over to Nazi-Germans. I was very interested on his outlook of his future. He was quite disoriented and still dazed from his experiences in the dungeon. Generally, he tended to believe that his victorious fatherland, after defeating Poland, Norway, and France, would prove to be magnanimous and would forgive the prodigal son who had gone astray into the Marxist wilderness.

More than once, afterwards, I remembered his pitiful silhouette. His chances of survival were no better than ours, but his moral situation was much worse. We were members of a fighting army; he was battered and tortured by the representatives of the doctrine for which he had sacrificed his whole life, and by those under whose protection he submitted himself when he became seriously ill with tuberculosis. I was extremely interested in his analysis of the developing tendencies. An educated Marxist always starts his analysis from the existing forces and tendencies. I projected various concepts and I awaited his reaction.

In my understanding, Russian Communism was at that moment on a very interesting bent. Stalin and his nearest associates seemed not only to go into a political alliance with Hitler, but also in the direction of some kind of ideological synthesis; however, the rank and file of the party, according to what I could conclude from my conversations in the Moscow prisons, were still taking the position of distrust toward

Germany. The heads of German Communism were to be a gift that would cement the alliance of two totalitarian countries with world ambitions. As a basis of that friendship, there were certain brainwaves on how to transform the political map of the world. Hitler's ideas were known from *Mein Kampf*. However, when it came to Stalin's ideas, I remember a conversation which I had a few months before the war with Franciszek Ancewicz, a Lithuanian social democrat, who was an assistant to Prof. W. Sukiennicki in the Institute of Eastern Europe in Wilno. Ancewicz was carefully reading the world press and was quite interested in the political analyses that were coming from the Trotsky environment. He maintained that the farsighted aim of Stalin's policy was the division of the British Empire between Soviet Russia and the axis powers Berlin-Rome-Tokyo. Ancewicz maintained that this aim was logically connected with the systematic murder of old Bolsheviks and the ideologues of Marxist socialism in Soviet Russia. My German companion was by nature very careful not to make any definite stand, but I got the impression that he was psychologically ready to look for a compromise between International Marxism and Hitlerite Nationalism.

This evolution of Stalinism was interrupted by Hitler's attack in June of 1941. It created a situation where the "stock" of German Communists (and also of mid-European Communists) started to go up in value in Russia. Stalin had to return to the position of fighting against fascism and Hitlerism. Whether my German comrade managed to await this attack as a Soviet prisoner, or whether he was transferred before that into the hands of the Gestapo, I do not know.

Transport to the North

After receiving the sentence, I stayed in Butyrki Prison for about a week. From there I was taken first to a transfer camp in Kotlas and then to one of the camps situated in the tributary of the Wym River, in the Komi ASSR (Autonomous Soviet Socialistic Republic). The transfer took about three weeks and was very tiring. I was placed in a prison compartment, mostly with the members of the Central Committee of the Kazakhstan Communist Party. From them I found out that almost all the members of the Government of the Soviet Federal Republic of Kazakhstan were sentenced to the camps of forced labor for "nationalistic deviations". Among them, in the same compartment, was also the chief of the planning office of that republic, a Russian, born in Moscow, who was sent to Kazakhstan two years earlier as an expert in planning technology. He also received the verdict for the Kazakh's national deviations. In the neighboring compartment, there were mostly Azerbaijanis from the southern Caucasus, among them a lecturer in political economy from the Party School in Baku. A separate group was formed of Finnish military, mostly NCOs. They had been on some extended military patrol when the armistice between Finland and Russia was signed. They were taken prisoners by Soviets and they were not recognized as prisoners of war but were placed before the court for illegally crossing the border, for which they received five years of GULAG. After arriving in Komi, they could communicate with the local population, because the language of Komi is similar to the Finnish language, even though Komi is 800 kilometers away from the eastern border of Finland.

In the first part of my journey, I traveled with the commander of a division of the Red Army. He had been arrested quite recently, and he was well versed with the military operations in the West, about which I could find out very little when I was under investigation, because of the strict separation of the people from the outside world. He had thoroughly studied the operation of the British withdrawal from Dunkirk, and he maintained that the Germans would not be able to win the war. The conversations with him confirmed my opinion, which I had formulated while at Lubyanka, that the middle and lower echelon of the Soviet apparatus were anti-German, in contrast with the higher hierarchy.

Within this kaleidoscope of people in our transport, consisting mostly of non-Russians, there was a mixture of Moscow criminals, the so-called "Urki." They stole without any pity anything that was not guarded. Sometimes they applied open force when taking the meager bread rations from the political prisoners. In the camps they were considered to be a privileged element. Often they had positions in the administration of the camps. They were less careful than the other prisoners in expressing their political opinions, and sometimes they even dared to criticize Soviet leadership. While in the Kotlas barracks, I once heard one of the "Urki" trumpeting quite loudly to his bunk bed companions that Stalin poisoned his wife, Alliluyeva. They distinguished themselves in expressing extreme anti-Semitism, and they were particularly mean toward their prison companions who were of Jewish origin.

In Kotlas, due to the kindness of the doctor, I managed to get into the hospital for a few days, where I met an old Russian "Socialist Revolutionary",[19] Jefremov, who was a member of the Constituent Assembly dispersed by Lenin in November of 1917.* He had been an inmate of various Bolshevik prisons for about twenty years. His last place was in separate confinement (*politisolator*) somewhere in the Urals, where for a long time his companion in misery was Karol Radek.[20] As far as I could conclude from his talk, Radek was still alive and in reasonably good form at the end of 1940 (perhaps even at the beginning of 1941). Radek had the special privilege of being allowed to keep books in foreign languages in his cell, and he possessed small volumes of Mickiewicz' poetry from which he never parted, and he maintained that Mickiewicz was the greatest poet that the human race had ever produced.

My other comrade in the hospital represented at that time a fairly common belief that Soviet Russia was the creation of Satan or his servants. There are two versions of this kind of interpretation of Soviet reality. In one there are strong prevailing mystical elements, and in the other they are rather sociological. The first version is based on the conviction that Satan is actively intervening in the shaping of history. This belief manifested itself in the history of Russian culture at various intellectual levels; from illiterate peasants, who in the 17th century were seeking in the forest in the far north a shelter for themselves from the religious reforms of the Patriarch Nikon,[21] to the great

---

[19] Socialist Revolutionary Party, a clandestine party formed in 1900. In the post-revolutionary elections to the Constituent Assembly, the Socialist Revolutionaries (SRs) gained an absolute majority while the Bolsheviks won less than a quarter of the vote. When the Assembly met in January 1918, the Bolsheviks broke it up. * The author made a mistake. The Constituent Assembly was dispersed by Lenin in January of 1918.

[20] Radek, Karol – prominent Polish Communist.

[21] Nikon (1605-1681), 6th Patriarch of Moscow, Russian reformer and statesman. Patriarch Nikon came to the conclusion that the national religious traditions of the 16th century were antiquated and were based on ignorant distortion of ancient Greek originals of the book of service. Nikon insisted on his

FROM KATYN TO KUYBYSHEV

philosophers and thinkers, and writers like Fyodor Dostoyevsky, Vladimir Soloviev, and Dmitri Merezhkovsky. Peter the Great was considered by many contemporaries to be the embodiment of the anti-Christ. One must admit that the Soviet reality created exceptionally favorable conditions for the rebirth of this belief in satanic powers.

In my later experiences in the GULAG, I became familiar with the cases when some of the prisoners refused to go to work reasoning that any labor for the Soviet country would be like working for Satan. They were placed before the local courts, which as a rule pronounced the death sentence. Then the news of the execution was announced on a bulletin board near the guardhouse. I particularly remember the case when two Greek-Orthodox nuns made the same stand and were shot. As far as I understood, they believed that by this act of sacrifice, they were going to mobilize mystical forces, which would finally rescue their country from the evil vapors that had overpowered Russia.

The second interpretation of Soviet Satanism has a more rational character. It is based on the suspicion that somewhere in the central apparatus of Soviet Russia there are some conspiratorial groups who are admirers of Satan. They probably believe in the services they perform for the devil in the same manner that some of the witches in the Middle Ages believed that they had relations with the devil. To accept this interpretation, one does not have to believe in transcendental reality, but only to accept the fact that there are people who believe in Satan and want to perform services for him. Those groups were instrumental in creating a situation which led to a system of continuous mass murders: for instance, the cruel extermination of peasants during the collectivization; also just before the war in the period of Yezhov in 1937-1938, the murder of the most prominent military commanders of the Red Army and a considerable number of officers of lesser rank; and, the physical destruction of a great number of "old Bolsheviks" responsible for maintaining the doctrine and organizational framework of the party.

This kind of interpretation is not contrary to the Marxist method of analysis of social phenomena. A young student of mathematics who was accused of belonging to the Trotskyite organization told me about it, and he warned me at the same time that simple conversation about these possibilities could result in execution. It was at night and this student was obviously excited and terrified when he whispered these things to me. We were lying in adjacent beds, while our eyes were fixed on the "Judas" opening which was being opened from time to time. One of the other prisoners who was sleeping nearby could have overheard us; so I did not have the opportunity to ask him about several points which were not very clear to me in his narrative. Today, when we are faced with the problem of explaining the Katyn decision, the hypothesis of that "Trotskyite" should not be rejected out of hand. It is possible that Dostoyevsky's vision, when writing his famous novel, *The Devils*, was the vision of a prophet.

From Kotlas, we were transported to camps in the Republic of Komi in ordinary cattle carriages instead of the prescribed prison carriages. The supervision was less severe because we entered a region of taiga, where escape, particularly in winter, was physically impossible. Just before our departure, they added a couple of strange prisoners; the man, of middle age, was a deaf mute; the woman was a young girl of

---

corrections. A long struggle began between the faith of the Old Believers and Nikonianism, as the official church is now generally called.

IN THE SHADOW OF KATYN

North Mongolian type. She did not know Russian. The only thing that she could explain to us was that they were arrested in Estonia. When this deaf mute received his portion of bread, he placed it in front of him on the floor and stood while performing a long prayer before consuming it. The prisoners, not excluding the "Urki," looked at it with astonishment, but also with obvious sympathy. As far as I could understand, those Estonians were members of some sect, and they were arrested and sentenced for spreading religious beliefs. In the same carriage was a bearded peasant, who was also doing time for religious convictions, but he represented somehow a different type from my comrade whom I met in the hospital in Kotlas. After the arrival at our destination, when it was necessary to register ourselves in order to receive our ration of bread for the next day, this bearded peasant refused, justifying his action that it would be contrary to the Lord's prayer, which clearly orders us to ask for our daily bread for today – not for tomorrow. Somehow, I managed to arrange it for him without his participation, explaining to the authority that we were dealing with a deaf illiterate here.

During my journey in the cattle train, I managed to acquire some information which could be of interest to researchers of modern history of Russia. It pertains to the fate of Yezhov, ex-chief of the NKVD, who was responsible for the particular wave of arrests and murders in the years of 1937 and 1938. In this cattle train, in the bunk directly above me, a higher Soviet official traveled with me, who was head of a section in the Commissariat of River Transport. Yezhov, after being dismissed as chief of the NKVD, had been Commissar of the River Transport for several months and this official, obviously, must have been in contact with him. Shortly after Yezhov was arrested, they also arrested from the Commissariat of River Transport a number of officials who were Yezhov's subordinates. Before receiving his verdict, this Soviet official traveling with me was taken for a confrontation with the imprisoned Yezhov in some place not far from Moscow. One could assume it was the Sukhanovka Prison situated several kilometers from Moscow. This prison had the dreary reputation that every tortured prisoner there admitted his guilt, even those who had managed to resist it in the Lefortovo Prison. It must have happened some time in the second half of 1940.

According to my prison companion, Yezhov was in good physical form, dressed in the same tunic in which he discharged his tasks during the time of his wretched power; he wore the same leather belt, which meant that he was not subjected to the usual prison regulations. From the conversation, it could be deduced that Yezhov had been accused of organizing some secret group of his followers and had admitted his guilt. When Yezhov was asked whether my prison companion belonged to this group, Yezhov gave a negative answer, after which the conversation was abruptly finished. As a result, my prison companion was removed from the case for which Yezhov was being tried. Since a person who was recently confronted by Yezhov could not be given back his freedom, he received the standard eight years and was sent to the same system of camps as I was. At our destination, we were separated and I never saw him again.

Upon that arrival, the group to which I belonged was hastened on foot for about twenty kilometers; then we were held freezing in more than minus twenty degrees temperature for about half an hour in front of the camp's gate, beautified by the written slogans announcing: MORAL REBIRTH OF FALLEN PEOPLE THROUGH THE EDUCATIONAL VIRTUES OF WORK. During the twilight, after leading us inside the camp zone, we were taken into the dining hut, where behind the long tables we could sit on wooden benches.

FROM KATYN TO KUYBYSHEV

They gave us some swill in which, apparently, small pieces of fish were supposed to have been floating. The fact that it was a hot meal was in itself a blessing. Then, after supper, I went outside the hut and stood enchanted. The sky was iridescent with a glitter of soft, bluish silver rays, contracting and expanding or elongating and forming one big star covering the whole northern part of the sky, and again repeating this myriad of patterns. The brilliance of Aurora Borealis remained in my memory as the beginning of a new chapter in my strange experiences as a captured prisoner of war in Stalin's Russia.

My GULAG experiences

My stay in the camps lasted from the second half of March 1941, till the twentieth of April 1942, when I was released and started my journey south. This stay in camps is divided into two periods: First, until the so-called "Amnesty"[22] and release from the Ust-Wymsk camps, which happened in August 1941; second, from the end of August of 1941 till 1942, when I was sent back to the GULAG together with Lt. Adam Telmany, ex aide-de-camp to the command of "Zwiazk Walki Zbrojnej" (The Organization for Military Action) in Lwów, because we were excluded from the category of those who were destined to be released. Telmany was released in January of 1942; my release came in April after the interventions by Ambassador Kot (in Kuybyshev), and Ministers Wacław Komarnicki and Kajetan Morawski, who directly approached the Soviet Ambassador in London.

The first period was comparatively bearable; the second, that is, the winter in 1941-42, gruesome – famine, frost reaching -50 degrees C, stacks of frozen corpses thrown into the camp yard waiting for the doctor who had to write the death certificates. Avitaminosis was common, and Pellagra (deficiency of niacin) was the most threatening form. In January-March of 1942, it was a completely normal occurrence that during the morning reveille some of the prisoners could not get up because they were already dead. The highest percentage of mortality was among Ukrainians and Moldavians from Bessarabia and Bukovina. Caucasians, Finns, Chinese, and Russians, of whom comparatively there were not too many in the camp, showed a much stronger resistance.

In February of 1942, my physical state was totally desperate. My legs were covered with lesions due to frostbite. I moved with difficulty; there could not be any question of my going to work in the forest; my state in camp terminology was known as *dokhodiaga* [coming to an end], and I calculated I would last another three weeks. The camp doctor, Dr. Badjan, asked the administration of the camp for permission to put me into the hospital for some time: formally, as a sick man, but de facto, as a doctor's assistant. This request, to everybody's surprise, was granted readily by the commander of the camp. Dr. Badjan was a Romanian Jew, who during the First World War served as a lieutenant in the Austrian Army; then he studied at the University of Vienna. Before the Second World War, he practiced medicine at Chernivtsi. He was brought to

---

[22] After the German attack on the Soviet Union (June 1941) Stalin signed a military convention with General Sikorski's Polish Government-in-exile in London. This agreement granted amnesty to all Poles being held in the Soviet Camps in order to form the Polish Army in the USSR and help in the war effort against the Germans.

IN THE SHADOW OF KATYN

the GULAG at the beginning of 1941, together with the transport of Ukrainian peasants from Bessarabia and Bukovina. Dr. Badjan's request was motivated by the need to have an assistant who knew the Russian language and with whom he could communicate in the German language. Because of the large number of casualties in the hospital, they were behind in paper work, meaning the preparation of the necessary documents concerning patients and the preparation of death certificates. We prepared the documents in such a manner that Dr. Badjan dictated to me in German, and I wrote it in Russian. These two months as an assistant to the camp doctor allowed me to become acquainted with the problems of arctic medicine in the same way as later on, during my work for UNESCO, I came into contact with tropical medicine problems.

The readiness of the commander to transfer me to the hospital became clear after my release, when I became acquainted with various documents concerned with my case, which were shown to me in the Polish Embassy in Kuybyshev. At the beginning of 1942, the Polish Ambassador, Prof. Stanisław Kot received detailed information as to exactly where I was and about my disturbing health status from Polish Jews who had met me. Ambassador Kot, deciding that he had to act quickly to be able to save me, did not go through the regular channels as required by proper diplomatic procedure. Rather, he sent a telegram directly to the commander of the Ust-Wymsk camps where I was staying, demanding – according to the Polish-Soviet Pact – my immediate transport by air to Kuybyshev at the expense of the Polish Embassy. The administration of the camps could not release me without a decision from the higher authorities, but they considered they should keep me alive in order to avoid responsibility. That is why the request of the doctor that I be kept in the hospital with an increased ration of bread (one kilogram daily) was granted, and this saved me from the usual fate of the camp's *dokhodiaga* – meaning death from starvation and exhaustion.

The reaction of the camp commandant to the intervention of Ambassador Kot is understandable if one would take into consideration the general situation at that moment. The Soviet Union was waging a mortal war, and not many people in Russia believed in its successful outcome. The Germans were still near Moscow, even if their first impetus of advance was stalled in late 1941. The administrative apparatus, controlled with an iron fist by the NKVD, was performing with automatic precision – it seemed to me better than during the First World War – but also without belief in the final victory. Delegates of the Polish Embassy moved freely through the parts of the Soviet Union that were still unoccupied by Germans; they were establishing their offices and were storing canned food and clothes supplied by America; they were organizing boarding schools in which there were meetings for religious services and lectures. All that was disorienting the Soviet administration. Nobody knew to what extent the Polish-Soviet agreement gave privileges to the Polish Embassy and their representatives. Under these conditions, the official notification to the camp command, that the Polish Embassy was particularly interested in the fate of some prisoners who had not been released as yet, compelled the camp commander to at least take special care of this prisoner.

In this period of my stay in the camp, I did not have any news that could shed any light on the fate of my fellow prisoners of war, except for two events that should be noted. The first occurrence was the news about Polish military personnel, among whom there were many officers, who worked on the construction of the railway from Kotlas to

FROM KATYN TO KUYBYSHEV

Vorkuta in the summer of 1941. It seemed that they were part of the complex of camps called "Sievzeldorlag", assigned to building that railway. Apparently, there were several hundred of them. I knew this from the Russian prisoners who had the opportunity to talk with them. Personally, I twice saw the marching columns from far away, and judging from the shape of their coats, I noticed that officers had to be among them. Obviously, I could not come close because I was in a guarded convoy. After my release in 1942, I gave this information to the representatives of the Polish Embassy and the Polish military authorities: first in Kotlas, and then in Kirov. At that time, we came to the conclusion that those groups must have been released immediately after the announcement of amnesty; that is, at the end of the summer of 1941, probably before a representative of the Polish Embassy happened to arrive at the railway line Kirov-Kotlas-Vorkuta. The Polish military prisoners from that complex created some separate group, and we could not find out from where they were originally brought to that place.

The second event concerned the ex-Kozelsk prisoner, an officer cadet, Pawlukiewicz, whom I met in the fall of 1941, in the system of Ust-Wymsk camps, where he was working as an electrical technician. He was taken from Kozelsk before the liquidation of that camp had started. I found out that he had been imprisoned in Moscow for some time, after which he received the standard eight years of GULAG. He was a Russian living in Poland, and he had played a certain role in Russian students' organizations, while studying at Polish universities. According to the Soviet interpretation of the agreement with the Polish Government in London, they did not have to release him because the agreement concerned only Poles. Soviet authorities treated Polish Jews as Poles, but they refused the release of Ukrainians, Byelorussians, and Russians, in spite of their having Polish citizenship. In actual practice, however, many Ukrainians, Byelorussians, and even Russians slipped through to the army of General Anders, which was being organized in Soviet Asia.

NKVD as an Enterprise

As far as my camp experiences are concerned, a detailed description of them would be stepping beyond the boundaries of these sketches of my memoirs. Anyway, on the topic of organization of life and conditions in Soviet camps, considerable literature already exists, to which I have added some of my experiences. I should like to limit myself to only a few generalities, which – it seems to me – might have a certain meaning in the evaluation to the background of the Katyn drama.

First of all, as I have already shown in my book, *Forced Labour and Economic Development*, camps during Stalin's time played a considerable role in the Soviet investment policy. The profits from the camps covered a considerable amount of expenses connected with the increasing national expenditures, but most certainly, they covered almost completely the cost of maintaining the huge NKVD apparatus, which in Stalin's time expanded to one of the largest, and one could even risk stating "the" largest enterprise in the world. It conducted huge construction projects, mostly in the far regions of the Soviet Union; it built railroads, roads, and canals; it exploited forests on the huge stretches between the Finnish border and the Pacific Ocean; it owned coal mines and farms, and it possessed its own research institutes in the same manner as great monopolistic industrial concerns. The aggregate amount of the work force, free and enslaved, employed in the NKVD enterprises during the period when I was there as a slave, had to extend to more than 7 million people, and that was during the time when the NKVD was experiencing a great shortage of workers. The necessity to find new sources of that force was one of the factors of the huge wave of arrests in the years 1937-38; the so-called "Yezhov draft." The maximal exploitation of the workforce was then one of the main principles of the NKVD policy. That was my impression, which I brought out after being in the jaws of that institution for almost three years. I was told about numerous occasions when the NKVD, even without the formal reprieve of their death sentences, employed some specialists who had been given death sentences by the tribunals. Some of my cellmates in Lubyanka maintained that there were occasions when the NKVD announced the fulfillment of verdicts, but the "condemned to die" were taken away to work in laboratories and establishments of the NKVD under different names.

The productive potential of the Polish officers' camps was very large, thanks to the great number of specialists: engineers, technicians, agronomists, doctors and veterinarians. In Kozelsk alone, there were about three hundred doctors. All the time, during my stay in the camps, I thought that this potential was somewhere and in some way exploited by the Soviets. However, the NKVD preferred to destroy this potential, instead of using it in some economical, rational way. Those who were ruling Stalinist Russia considered other factors more important than economic effectiveness, and these tipped the scales toward the Katyn decision; that is, the massacre of Polish officers. Without a doubt, behind their decision stood a certain way of reasoning. Possibly, a future historian will be able to unravel what it was. Today, we have at our disposal only some hypotheses; there could be several of them. I do not think, however, that the knowledge of the Soviet system of forced labor could be helpful in explaining this decision.

Minorities

The second general characteristic of these segments of the Soviet system of camps with which I came in contact was the preponderance of non-Slavonic minorities of the Soviet Empire, and also Slavonic and non-Slavonic elements from the recently occupied territories in the West (meaning: the Baltic countries, Eastern Poland, Bessarabia and Bukovina), as well as a disproportionate number of foreigners. I had this impression when I was traveling from Moscow to Kotlas and Komi where, in our transport, there was a preponderance of Kazakhs, Tartars, Azerbaijanis and Finns. In the camp I met a great number of Polish Jews. In the years 1940-41, the Russians deported more than one million people from Eastern Poland, transporting them partly to the camps and partly to the so-called *Posholki* (distant settlements from which they were not allowed to leave). According to the estimate made by the Polish Embassy in Kuybyshev about 30% were Jews. At that time anti-Semitism was still officially disapproved of in the Soviet Union. Jews were deported, not because of racism, but as an "anti-class element" because they mainly engaged in middle trades which, according to Marxist terminology, meant unproductive work.

In the summer of 1941, before the German attack, they still brought to our system of camps large transports of Ukrainians and Moldavians from the recently

FROM KATYN TO KUYBYSHEV

occupied territories of Romania. In some *lagpunkts* (lagpunkts consisted of between 500 to 1,000 prisoners) they were an absolute majority. In the camp, I also found out that many Greeks were living in Russia, who had held tenaciously to their Greek citizenship, even if they had never been in Greece. They mainly lived close to the Black Sea and particularly in the Odessa district. I also met a certain number of Persians, originating from Soviet Azerbaijan. One has to remember that this Soviet province, to which the great oil industry center of Baku belongs, was taken away from Persia [present day Iran] in the first half of the 19th century.

The Chinese should be given a special mention. In pre-Revolutionary Russia, there were many Chinese who walked from house to house selling mainly silk and various brands of tea. They reached in their journeys as far as the Eastern Territories of the old Polish-Lithuanian Commonwealth. I remember from my childhood the times when, before the Chinese Revolution of the year 1912, the men wore long braids and the women wide slacks. During the October Revolution, the peddlers disappeared, but many Chinese went to serve in the Red Army as Soviet mercenaries, emphasizing often in their broken Russian their purely commercial attitude toward this service, "*sowiet plotit moja strejalet*" ("Soviet pay, I shoot"), but at the same time exhibiting excellent military qualities. Our participants of the 1919-20 campaigns must well remember the Chinese units on the opposite side as serious adversaries. In 1940, the action was started to transpose the residing Chinese of the Soviet Union to the GULAG. The NKVD was of the opinion that every Chinese person was a potential Japanese spy. Therefore, almost all of the thousands of Chinese residing in camps had the verdict – "suspected of spying." [In the Soviet Union, the NKVD could send anyone to the GULAG "on suspicion of spying."] I am inclined to assume that the NKVD was taking Chinese to the camps mainly because they were excellent workers.

After the outbreak of the Soviet-German war, in the camps they created special penal brigades consisting of spies and saboteurs. Naturally, they were mostly Chinese brigades. Because I was sentenced for "spying," I was also assigned to such a brigade. The brigade consisted of more than thirty people, among whom there were only six non-Chinese. The leader of the brigade came from the Far East, and he was Japanese. The others were European: two Germans, two Hungarians, and one Pole (author of these memoirs). One of the Hungarians had the name Varga and was related to the famous Soviet economist of the same name. The name of the second was Rakosi; he later became the Stalinist dictator of Hungary. I had more in common with him than with the other members of the brigade because of our interests and studies. Naturally, it created some affinity between us. At various times, he told me the fragments of his past: membership in the Government of Bela-Kun during the Revolution of 1919; leadership in the communist underground in the Carpathians; a position of vice-director of "Intourist" in the Soviet Union; and then, the position as President of the Soviet Academy of Architecture, even without having the formal qualifications for this last position. He was sentenced in the same way as the majority of the members of the brigade, for being "suspected of spying," but his term was only five years. He was looking rather optimistically toward his future in the Soviet Union. He confided in me that there was somebody in Moscow looking out for him so he could survive the camp experiences. And actually, a short time after our conversation, he was appointed to the safest and most comfortable position to which a prisoner could be assigned: manager of the canteen for the technical and administrative personnel of the camps. The food that was given to these personnel, even if they were also prisoners, was quite decent. The manager of this canteen must have had enough to eat, in spite of the famine that was all around us. In this position he did not forget about me, and he brought me some food secretly. One time there were real cutlets of meat. It was the first time since my stay in the Smolensk prison that I managed to receive such a luxury. The Hungarian émigrés, to whom I confided my experiences with Rakosi, maintained that I was probably the only human being who spoke about him in a positive light.

In that brigade, the results of the work of cutting the forest were not judged individually, but on the principle of the results of the whole group to which one belonged. The work consisted of cutting the trees, cleaning the branches, and sawing, depending on the usefulness of the material (building material, railway sleepers, pit props, pulpwood, and firewood). The norms required to obtain a full food ration were very high, and only a man with great skill or exceptional physical strength could do it. To be assigned to the brigade of felling trees was, in many cases, equivalent to the death sentence. In the group of Romanian-Bessarabians, which was sent to our camp in August 1941, there were about 250 people, mostly between thirty and forty years of age. In March 1942, when I was doing the prescribed by-the-rule statistics, I found out that in the period of seven months there were about seventy deaths in that group which was more than one-quarter of these people. People died mainly because, if the norm was not fulfilled, the food ration was decreased. Exposed to minus thirty degrees of freezing temperature, a starving man found it even more difficult to fulfill the norm and was dying because of malnutrition. The Chinese, however, who were often very small and looked weak, distinguished themselves in that, as a rule, they fulfilled the norm and obtained full food rations. Our Japanese brigade leader (foreman) realized very quickly my meager possibilities as a lumberjack and assigned me to the purely Chinese crew. The work was divided in such a way that I was used mostly for clearing the ground from snow (the layer of snow was sometimes as high as two meters), to clearing the branches from the trunks and sometimes cutting the smaller trees. In those conditions, it was difficult to calculate the individual input, but it was clear that my contribution to the common enterprise and to the good results of our section was less than proportional. My four Chinese comrades had not only to fulfill full norms of work but also to supplement my shortcomings, which were caused by my lesser experience. I never heard any complaints because of that. In all my later experiences with the Chinese, these camp impressions were affirmed: excellent workers, very conscientious, not demanding, quite hardened to discomfort and the experiences of fate, and with all that, very good and loyal friends.

The stay in the camps in 1941-42, compelled me to reassess my impressions which I brought out of Smolensk, that the Soviet Union was going through a period of relaxation after the purges of Yezhov. These impressions were probably true for the ethnographic Russian regions to which the district of Smolensk belonged. It was not true, however, for the territories inhabited by non-Russians, and particularly non-Slavonic nationalities, where the force of repression in Yezhov style was fully maintained. In 1940, the NKVD, looking for slave labor for their enterprises, had turned mainly to the recently acquired territories, in agreement with Hitler; that is, the territories of Eastern Poland, the Baltic countries, and also Bessarabia and Bukovina,

FROM KATYN TO KUYBYSHEV

taken from Romania and Hungary. In addition to the same system of camps where I was, transports came mainly from the Caucasus and in particular from Soviet Azerbaijan.

At that time, I was under the impression that Soviet Russia was transforming itself into a typical imperial country with the disposition of some relative tolerance toward the members of the ruling nation, but nevertheless ruthlessly exploiting the conquered nations and minorities. Today, from the present perspective, I consider my opinion, at that time, though correct, as a great simplification. The case of conquered nations in the Soviet Union has many aspects: historical, psychological, and ideological. The essence of the matter was extremely obscured by, apparently, liberal legislation and the system of hypocrisy, officially called the application of Marxist dialectics. Stalin himself contributed considerably to develop this system of hypocrisy when immediately after the October Revolution, he was nominated Commissar of Nationalities.

Several years later, when I was already outside the borders of the Soviet Union, the news started arriving about the deportation of whole national groups: Crimea Tartars, Chechens, Kara-kalpaks, Kabardians, Balkars, Kalmuks, and Volga-Germans. According to statistics by R. Conquest,[23] in the years 1943-44, they deported more than a million people, mostly to Central Siberia and to the Far Eastern regions. The generals of the NKVD, who directed this inhumane operation (for example, the famous Serov, butcher of Lithuania), received high decorations. Only after Khrushchev's speech at the 20th Party Congress were some of those deportations called off, and other deportees allowed to return to the place of their ancestors.

The question arises as to how to explain this deportation as sociological and psychological phenomena, for I do not think that the economic considerations played a major role. To extract from the economic apparatus, during famine caused by war, several thousands of people engaged in agrarian production and depositing them in uninhabited steppes was economic nonsense, as was the physical liquidation of so many highly qualified specialists among Polish prisoners of war.

The official explanation of deportation, that the members of those national groups were showing sympathies toward the Germans during the war, or were not sufficiently condemning their fellow countrymen, who voluntarily reported themselves to the services under the German command, is not convincing. As it appears from my camp experiences, the mass deportations from the Caucasus and Kazakhstan already started before the war when nobody could even dream about the voluntary formations of Caucasians attached to the German Army, while Ribbentrop and Molotov were conducting negotiations about Russia joining the Pact with Germany, Italy, and Japan. When it comes to the behavior of daring Caucasian mountaineers during the war, one should not be surprised that the brothers and cousins of those Chechens, Ingush, and Kara-Kalpaks with whom I was sharing GULAG bunks, started reporting themselves en masse as volunteers immediately after German military units appeared in the Northern Caucasus. It was a reaction to the deportations that were proceeding before the war and became most intensive in 1943-44.

I do not think that my theory, which I developed during my stay in the camps, that in the Soviet governing strata they had the mentality of imperial masters, gives sufficient explanation of those deportations. In this there was a manifestation of some

---

[23] Conquest, Robert, *Soviet Nationalities Policy in Practice*, New York, 1967, p. 104

kind of passionate drive to destroy their neighbors, which is a specific characteristic of Muskovites. Imperial nations conquered colonies in order to exploit them. Russia was conquering in order to absorb, deprive the national individuality, and destroy. This tendency to destroy exhibited itself with respect to the nations that voluntarily joined the union with Russia, originally attracted by the common religion, as for example, the Ukrainians or Georgians. The motto to absorb and destroy is imbued into the Russian thought. Pushkin wrote that all Slavic streams must dissolve into the Russian Sea. Lermontov (my favorite poet) and Leo Tolstoy – who as officers took part in subduing the Caucasian highlanders – could not rise to the occasion to condemn those imperial fights, even if both of them subscribed to the philosophy condemning war as a social phenomenon.

The first historical occurrence, known to me, of those cruel destructive tendencies was in the 15th century by Ivan III. The rich Republic of Novgorod, a member of the Hanseatic League, was destroyed, and the surviving population deported to the Volga region. It seems to me that these destructive tendencies are connected with the essence of imperial dynamics of Russian statehood; I am not sure, however, if they determine a feature of the Russian national character. One could give many examples when the most prominent representatives of that destructive policy were actually foreigners who, brought in by historical waves, directed Russian policy. Catherine II, who realized her project, the partition of Poland (1795), and who started a great colonial policy in the Ukraine, was German. In our century, Dzerzhinsky, who by his policy of oppression of Georgians caused even the indignation of Lenin, was a Pole. Stalin and Beria, most likely the authors of deportations of Caucasus nationalities, were both Georgians.

It is worth noting in the deportations which took place in 1943-44, that there was a tendency to destroy mainly those tribes who had put up an armed resistance against the conquest of the Caucasus by Russia in the 19th century. They were the people who were faithful to Islam, while the Christian nations and tribes, as well as Armenians and Ossets, and also partly Georgians in the 19th century took a pro-Russian position, or at least were wavering. Their decisive struggle against Russia, equally white as well as red, started only in the period when the Soviet Union was forming, as is so well described in the book by Richard Pipes[24] on this topic. This struggle was doomed to fail because of lack of support from the victorious coalition and the exceptionally shortsighted policy of Kemal's Turkey.

Because I am writing these memoirs with my thoughts on the Katyn tragedy, with which I came into contact so closely, the question arises: Is there any connection between Katyn and the deportation of nations? Both actions, that is, the Katyn massacre and the deportation of various minority groups, were happening during the same time span and occurred under the same Soviet leadership. The same executive apparatus of the NKVD conducted these two crimes. There is, however, between them a basic difference. After the famous speech by Khrushchev to the 20th Party Congress, the deportations were condemned and called off. There were even certain attempts to partly compensate for the previous wrongdoing. Katyn was not included in the registry of Stalin's "mistakes." Officially, the unacceptable fiction that Germans committed the

---

[24] Pipes, Richard. *The Formation of the Soviet Union*, Communism and Nationalism 1917-1923, Harvard University Press, Cambridge, Mass., 1964.

FROM KATYN TO KUYBYSHEV

Katyn massacre is still being maintained [book was written in 1976]. This accusation that was brought forward by the Soviet prosecutor during the Nuremberg trials, was not confirmed in the verdict. The question arises: Who murdered those prisoners? The answer, in the light of what we know about Katyn, does not seem to be in any doubt.

The Katyn model and the model of deportations were only two examples of the same coordinated action intended to clear the foreground for further expansion of Soviet Imperialism. It cannot be ruled out that in some actions the NKVD had applied both models. One has to remember that in the period of mass deportations many of the arrested disappeared without a sign of their whereabouts. In many cases the person could be traced to a certain point and then from there had vanished. In all likelihood every inhabitant of Eastern Poland or the Baltic States could give a number of such examples, to wit: The disappearance of the mayor of Wilno, Dr. Maliszewski; and Dr. Jakowicki, Professor of gynecology and ex-rector of the University of Wilno, who at the outbreak of the war was chairman of the Union of Legionnaires; the disappearance of civil servants from Łuck, of whom I remember only one name, my old university colleague, Bohdan Alexandrowicz.

Among the arrested and deported members of minorities was a separate category consisting of members of the local communist parties. As it transpired from the conversations of the Romanian communists whom I met in the GULAG, Soviet security authorities, after occupying Romanian provinces in 1940, were interested mainly in the local communist groups. As a rule, they arrested communists of Jewish origin because they suspected them of Trotskyite sympathies. Among the others, they made selections, isolating mainly those who distinguished themselves with independence of thought.

This specific nationalistic attitude manifested itself toward the foreign communists staying in the Soviet Union, and from what I have heard, most of them were behind bars on the eve of the German attack.

Doctors

Since I am writing about the camps, I should not forget to tell about another part of my experiences. I call it "flowers in the manure." It is a paradox that happens more than once in the conditions of great cataclysms of communal life as in war or revolution. When, many years ago, I read the novel by Remarque about the First World War – of rather anti-militaristic disposition and ridiculing all patriotic phraseology by means of which the German press and Prussian school were beautifying the soldier's life – I was struck by what he characterized as a most beautiful phenomenon of war: the spirit of comradeship and of personal fidelity which arises from belonging to the same fighting unit. To a certain extent, the impressions of my thirteen months frontline service in 1919-20 are in agreement with that book. The institution of war from the point of view of common sense is absurd; each war demoralizes its participants as well as the civilian population. But during each war there is a flowering of unquestioning moral values, like flowers growing in the desert.

This paradox, which is the basic paradox of human destiny, flourished in the most unexpected way in various aspects of camp life. Fyodor Dostoyevsky, more than any other writer I know, had an innate intuition of the entanglement of good and bad. To penetrate the atmosphere of the camps requires a genius like him. The Tsarist penal

IN THE SHADOW OF KATYN

servitude that he knew and described looked like a boarding school for good children in comparison with the Soviet GULAG.

However, among this dirt and manure sometimes flowers of human goodness bloomed. I am thinking of the phenomenon of common help and readiness to oblige among complete strangers. The moral atmosphere of camps was dreadful: famine, stench, and exploitation of human work exceeding the limit of human endurance. Those were the consequences of a system, which, in spite of socialistic theory, created a war of everybody against everybody where only by deceit, theft, and debasement a human being was able to survive. It's a sphere in which Satan was operating. On the other hand, there were people from the administrative apparatus and people from the camp surroundings, who tried to exploit every possible loophole in the instructions and regulations that were given by the authorities, to lighten the burden of at least some people, even though it was impossible to do so for the entire mass of prisoners. If I survived all the horrors of the Northern camps during the winter of 1941-42, it could only be possible because many times when it seemed to be a hopeless situation, somebody appeared most unexpectedly who stretched out a helping hand and created a situation where further struggle for survival was possible.

Foremost among those occurrences, which I call "flowers in the manure," were the camp doctors. The medical profession in Russia had an excellent tradition of a positive attitude to social work. In the second half of the 19th century, during the time of the movement of Narodniki,[25] the most ideal elements among the young Russian intelligentsia went into medicine. The memoirs of ex-political prisoners from the Tsarist's times often underline the positive role of a doctor. The Soviet doctors at my time, meaning more than thirty years ago, appeared to be faithful to this tradition. After all, they themselves were prisoners even though, in comparison to others, they lived in privileged conditions. They were supervised by the head of the medical services who generally was a "free" man, some kind of half-literate belonging to the party, or some kind of undereducated nurse. If, however, in the frame of this supervision, the doctor could lighten the fate of someone else, he did it even at the risk of exposing himself to repression.

Particularly one silhouette of such a humanitarian doctor stuck in my mind. I am thinking here about Dr. Orlov, widow of Admiral Orlov, commander of the Soviet fleet who was executed in connection with the case of Marshal Tukhachevsky. I wrote earlier about Admiral Orlov. Mrs. Orlov was sentenced in agreement with the so-called "Ladies' Clause"; that means, in agreement with the NKVD principle that the wives, sisters, and other female relatives of the executed, outstanding members of the party or administration, were sent to ten years of forced labor.

During my time in the Ust-Wymsk's camps, the sister of known Georgian communist, Abel Yenukidze, stayed there as a prisoner. Abel Yenukidze was past chief of the Council of Peoples' Commissars and ex-secretary of the Central Committee of the Party, who disappeared during the purges in the second half of the thirties. In the case of Marshal Tukhachevsky, the NKVD not only imprisoned his wife, but also his mother, sisters, underage daughter, and two of his ex-wives. The daughter of Tukhachevsky, as well as his sisters, survived the camps and participated in the solemn celebration after Tukhachevsky's exculpation, organized by the Frunzi Higher Military

---

[25] Narodniki - populists: a leading socialist group during the Tsarists' time.

FROM KATYN TO KUYBYSHEV

Academy in January 1963. Dr. Orlov, during a few conversations I had with her in March of 1942, appeared to be a typical social worker and doctor. That is how I always imagined Russian students who studied medicine or nursing, so they could go among the "common people." In looks and manners, she reminded me of a well-known medical doctor from Wilno, Dr. Skwarczyńka, a dedicated pediatrician.

I believe that in the Komi Autonomous Soviet Socialist Republic many camp prisoners who succeeded in surviving the winter of 1942 owed this to Dr. Orlov. I mentioned before the high mortality rate in the camps during this winter, and I partly compiled statistics for this while working as an assistant to the camp doctor. This high mortality started to worry the authorities who were responsible for fulfilling the plans. Apparently, Beria himself became interested in the catastrophic percentage of mortality in the northern camps. In the central administration of camps they coined the slogan: Let's rebuild the work force. Thus, the central authorities of the Ust-Wymsk camps, apparently aware of the individual qualities of some prisoners, appointed Dr. Orlov to tour the various camps and for her to find out the reasons for the high mortality and to suggest remedial actions. Owing to the outcry, visitations, and suggestions of Dr. Orlov, the rights of the doctors were extended in awarding normal food rations to a certain percentage of the prisoners, irrespective of the amount of work performed. The doctors always had this right, but only in exceptional cases and only with respect to those who could fulfill at least 30% of the assigned norm of work. Now it was applied to a wider range of prisoners. These acts of grace were introduced mainly as a means of improving the output of work. The doctors also seized this opportunity to save, from death by starvation, those who could not be transformed into fully and physically able workers. From my few and rather short talks with Dr. Orlov, I obtained the impression that her fervent wish was – as far as it was humanly possible – to save those thousands of people, thrown into the Northern camps for hard labor, from famine and ill-treatment. I witnessed the respect, bordering almost on worship, with which the female inmates met Dr. Orlov.

My impression about the humanitarian attitude of Russian doctors was already established by the stories I heard in Kozelsk from the Polish officers who had been in Soviet hospitals. In Kozelsk, there were a certain number of officers who had been wounded and ill when taken into captivity and had spent some time in the Kiev hospitals. All of them spoke with great respect of the doctors as well as of the Ukrainian and Russian hospital personnel. I am quite aware from what I write here about the Russian doctors that there must have been some exceptions. My impressions are based only on accidental experiences; however, they gave me the basis for intuitive insight as to the general psychology of some social and professional groups in the Soviet Union thirty years ago. I do know that the Soviet Security Authorities, as well as the Hitlerite Gestapo, managed to produce teams of doctors capable of all kinds of atrocities, but my first contact with a female doctor of the NKVD in the Lubyanka prison left me with a rather favorable impression.

It is more than thirty years since my experiences about which I am writing, but to what extent the system managed to demoralize and debase the medical profession during that time, as it does with everything that comes into its grips, I do not know. It seems to me that among the doctors – and most likely in other strata of Soviet society – there are some forces that resist those degrading influences, because the types of doctors, which Solzhenitsyn describes in his very realistic novels about the state of Russia in the fifties, are rather positive.

One who was rejoicing

In the most difficult period of my stay in the camps, during 1941-42, I found a considerable amount of moral support in conversations with an artist from Leningrad, who, as a reaction to all the misfortunes and the sufferings of a camp prisoner, was going through the process of religious rebirth and who, as far as I know, during his life of freedom had never been connected to any religion. His last name has slipped my memory. Anyway, it was almost never mentioned. In the camp, he was popularly known as "the painter", and some people addressed him according to the Russian custom by his Christian name and that of his father; hence they called him Nikolai Peotrovich. From the expression on his face, to the way he talked, to his posture and movements, there was something that immediately made him stand out among the hungry, dehumanized, and stupefied people. His age was very difficult to estimate; at one moment he looked 60, at another 30. He had white hair with a slight shade of yellow, the color of ripe rye; it could have become gray or maybe it was his natural color. His face was pale and gaunt looking, but its expression was youthful; so it could have been the face of an old or that of an extremely emaciated man. His eyes were pale-blue, like the northern sky; there was something elusive in them which meant that he looked not only at things externally, but also at the inner regions of self, into worlds not to be perceived by the senses. Later on, I found out that he was about sixty years old.

Before the First World War, he lived in Paris where his pictures were shown more than once. In 1913, he returned to Russia and established himself in pre-Revolutionary St. Petersburg. He had moved in aristocratic circles and had access to the court where he painted the portraits of great princes. For him the Revolution was not a personal catastrophe: the new regime was not destroying artists; on the contrary, there were attempts to pamper them. The Head of the Commissariat for Education and Culture was Lunacharsky, whom he knew well from the Paris coffeehouses: there were more orders than he could fulfill. In 1937, there came the terrible days when the leadership of the NKVD was taken over by the infamous Yezhov. Hundreds of thousands of people of all professions went to the camps, among them Nikolai Peotrovich. He was not accused of anything. He was not even investigated. One day the members of the NKVD appeared and announced that he, as a "socially dangerous" individual, was going to be sent for five years to the corrective labor camps.

Nikolai Peotrovich was sent to the camps that were engaged in logging in the Far North. Because of his age and heart condition, he received the status of invalid of the first category. According to the camp regulations, an invalid of the first category was exempt from going into the woods, but he could only be used for work inside the camp. This status of invalid had allowed Nikolai Peotrovich to survive more than three years before I met him.

According to the principle proclaimed by the NKVD, every prisoner should be employed in his professional specialty as far as circumstances allowed. They tried to

FROM KATYN TO KUYBYSHEV

give to Nikolai Peotrovich the job of painter. When it was necessary to paint the floor of the office of the commander of the camp, they sent Nikolai Peotrovich. When the roof on one of the administrative buildings was being covered with sheet metal and then it had to be painted, they would send for Nikolai Peotrovich. But his general function was to tar and lime the toilets. It was also considered a painter's job. In the meantime, between those artistic engagements, Nikolai Peotrovich was employed to assist with office work in the department of planning under the supervisor of the camp administration.

The light work was a blessing in the lot of Nikolai Peotrovich. The other blessing was that he possessed a quilt. It was an authentic quilt of the color red filled with cotton wool; the kind one often sees in middle class homes. It was now very dirty but still in reasonably good condition. Nikolai Peotrovich considered this the main reason that he was still alive. Outside, the northern winter was fierce; the temperature was often falling to minus 40 and even to minus 50 degrees Celsius. The hut in which we lived was not well provided; it had many unfilled cracks so that the wind very often played around the bunk beds. We had only one iron stove that warmed the place in a radius of about five meters, but beyond this area, it was cold. The quilt held the remainder of the warmth that otherwise escaped from the emaciated body of Nikolai Peotrovich. To keep this quilt in his possession was one of his main worries. It was not an easy task. So-called Urki – Russian professional criminals – mostly filled the hut in which we lived. They formed an organized group, who, in a quite ruthless manner, terrorized political prisoners. They snatched the meager rations of bread from the political prisoners almost openly, and kicked them out of the better spots of bunk beds. The quilt was a glaringly obvious object that could not be hidden easily. Nikolai Peotrovich's free moments were spent sitting on his treasure. But before he went out to work, he had to solve a very complicated task: to find a safe place for his quilt. This constant preoccupation to protect the invaluable quilt was the main reason for our closer acquaintance. At that time, I was relieved from going to work because of frostbitten legs. My legs were in a desperate state; I had to stay constantly in one place. So, I was the right man to guard the quilt. I readily agreed because in the same barrack was another person not fit for work; so, without a doubt, not even for a moment was the quilt going to be without protection.

It so happened that in the evening after returning from work, Nikolai Peotrovich reported to collect his treasured article, and we started a conversation. These conversations became moments of spiritual relaxation. New lights kindled my thoughts when I listened to his reasoning. I felt then that the world that surrounded us was perhaps the real world, but that is not the essence of the matter. Somewhere very close the truth exists and one should make a constant effort not to move away from it. Nikolai Peotrovich lectured me about his philosophy of life. His inexhaustible topic was the Sermon on the Mount.

"I am rejoicing Stanislaw Stanislawowicz," Nikolai Peotrovich said to me one evening, "I am constantly rejoicing."

"What are you rejoicing about?" I asked with surprise.

"Because, you see, it is written in the gospel...." Nikolai Peotrovich quoted in the Greek Orthodox Slavonic language the words of benediction, " 'Blessed are those who mourn, for they shall be comforted' – so, I am rejoicing." He continued to say,

IN THE SHADOW OF KATYN

"We are on the lowest level of poverty and degradation, so deep in the valley of tears, so from this only happiness can burst forth. They (when referring to the Soviet Regime, Nikolai Peotrovich always used to say "they") drum into the head of the whole of Russia the principles of material dialectics. The dialectics are not only laws for the material world but also for the spiritual world. Suffering somewhere at some stage must transfer itself into its own antithesis, which is happiness. But certain conditions must be observed: one must assume a certain attitude toward suffering and take a suitable stand. We cannot imagine, Stanislaw Stanislawowicz (referring to me), how much happiness is going to await us for what we are suffering in here." He continued with, "I am feeling this coming happiness and I am rejoicing and rejoicing more."

'Blessed are the poor in spirit, for theirs is the kingdom of heaven' was another topic of his meditations.

"What does poor in spirit mean?" asked Nikolai Peotrovich. "Do you think that those are the uneducated, the naïve, or perhaps those who cannot grasp complicated things? No, they are those who have accepted humility in their lives, who accept with happiness anything that life brings to them as a gift of providence. Spiritual poverty is not based on what one possesses or one does not possess, but on what the character of our desires is. You can be as poor as a church mouse, but in spirit you may not be poor. You can possess the entire world's goods, but be poor in spirit. You know, until now, I could not rid myself of certain desires, which I had as a young man. When I was still in Paris, I decided that I would go to America, and I wanted to establish my studio there, but the war interrupted it. Until now, I am still dreaming, and still have a hope that eventually I will go there. That means that I am still not poor in spirit. Now, what about the quilt; if I would be poor in spirit, I would not bother about its preservation. I think, however, that if I could get rid of those desires my happiness would be purer."

The second position of the philosophy of Nikolai Peotrovich was the conviction that life is beautiful. When he told me that for the first time, I reacted spontaneously, "Yes, but not here."

"Yes, in here too!" exclaimed Nikolai Peotrovich. "Go out of the hut and look how beautiful the iridescent rays of Aurora Borealis are. If one sees that, doesn't one feel as if this is one of the manifestations of absolute beauty? Is not life worth living and suffering, so one can look at such a wonder?"

Not only in the occurrences of nature, which are pleasing to the eye, did Nikolai Peotrovich see the beauty of life. The beauty, according to him, resides mainly in the reflections of the human soul, in relations between man and man, in the bonds that are being tied between the human souls. From some of the remarks of Nikolai Peotrovich, I knew that he was married twice and that both women were still alive at the time of his arrest. I do not know what caused the split with his first wife; I never asked him about it. I do not know who the guilty party was. But sometimes when he told me about past events in his life, he talked with the same degree of sentiment and gratefulness about both women. He was full of optimism and believed that he would still see them, but in any case, he believed that established bonds would find some continuation in what was going to connect the human souls in a future life.

The conversations with Nikolai Peotrovich gave me injections of faith in some deeper sense among all these gloomy things which one could see happening around us. We were in extreme penury and exhausted; our legs were covered with sores and

FROM KATYN TO KUYBYSHEV

immensely swollen; our bodies covered with ulcers; all around us, there was dirt, brutality, anger, and hate. During those conversations, I always had some strange feeling of expectation. As if in a moment some kind of curtain was going to be ripped open, and the brightness of truth that is shielded from the human mind and the secret of evil and suffering would become clear.

The conversations with Nikolai Peotrovich poured some optimism into me and rekindled in me a faith in man. But, at the same time, there was some innate desire in me to contradict him. Perhaps, I wanted to provoke him into new pronouncements and comfort myself with his unfaltering optimism. To his arguments about the beauty of life I answered, "Our life here is lice ridden and dirty; we suffer from famine and cold, but that is not the most repugnant side of it – it is the dehumanization of man, and the complete decline of human dignity. Take a look at the women in the camp. I spent a considerable amount of my life in the military; I took part in two wars, and I know a soldier's life well. But such profanities, such perverted conversations as they are conducting, I never heard before. Almost each one of them is ready to give herself to the camp's cook only for a smile, not only because she is hungry, but simply because the cook in the camp is an influential person. But among them, there are those who in the free world were mothers and wives; and for certain, they had some sense of a woman's dignity. And this attitude of the prisoners permeates to the weak and the ill; that beating of them, kicking them out of the better spots, and pushing them away from the stove. I remember some time in my early childhood how hens were pecking at an ill chicken trying to get close to them for some grains of food. Later, I saw terrible things; I saw the intestines coming from people who were still alive when grenades burst their bellies. But they were quickly taken away by the stretcher-bearers, and I would soon forget about those impressions. But the memory of this chicken gave me nightmares all my life. Today, I am reliving it in reality among people. And now, look, Nikolai Peotrovich, at those shapes that are closing in on us in order to overhear our conversation in the hope that something of that they can take to the NKVD official. Where is the beauty in that?"

Nikolai Peotrovich became pensive. After a moment, he fastened his blue eyes on me. "Stanislaw Stanislawowicz, you painted a true picture, but not completely. Adversities often liberate the evil that is hiding inside man, but they also liberate the hidden beauty of the human soul. This beauty acquires a particular brightness on a background of ugliness; only we, intensely concerned with our own suffering, fail to see it. It is all true, but where in your portrayal is a place for Nadezhda Alekseyevna; where is there a place for these sectarians; where for the old anarchist, who manages the baths... why have you forgotten about them?"

I was dumbstruck. Indeed, I did not take those people into account. Nadedzhda Alekseyevna was a relatively young woman of about thirty, who was working as an assistant accountant. I did not know her very well. I only knew that she left behind a husband and two children somewhere in the Ural Mountains at the time of her arrest. She was imprisoned because, apparently, at some time, somewhere, she said something jokingly about the cult of Stalin. Anyway, the case was not investigated. The NKVD, on the basis of an informer's denunciation, sentenced her as a "socially dangerous person" to five years of GULAG by a simple administrative decree. She was completely unlike other women in the camp. Hardly ever could one hear her talking;

IN THE SHADOW OF KATYN

most of the time she was silent. Generally, her big black eyes were lowered; however, at times when she looked at the person to whom she was talking, there came a breeze of some other world that was living in her soul. In her presence, swearing disappeared. She was definitely attractive, but very emaciated. It was difficult to imagine any man making a proposition to her, which was so often made almost publicly to the women in the camp. Her attitude was somehow different, even though she was as much a slave as any of us, deprived of any rights. There was some inner strength in her, which compelled others to respect her. She smiled brightly whenever she met Nikolai Peotrovich; those two understood each other.

The sectarians were called the two Baptists: one was old, about 60, and the other was young, about 25. They were ordinary Russian peasants, and they worked on the so-called general work in the forest, and never tried to evade it. Because they were used to hard labor since childhood, they managed it quite well and even managed to fulfill the prescribed norm, which gave them a more reasonable food ration. They were not the only prisoners in our camp who were imprisoned for having religious convictions; they were not the only Baptists. But others, more or less, fell into an atmosphere of anger and hate. Those two preserved their equanimity. They treated everybody with the same warm-heartedness. They helped everybody they could. Particularly very impressive was the younger, tall man, extremely strong physically, an excellent worker; he smiled very brightly whenever I had a chance to talk to him; his crystal soul shone through his eyes, so it would seem that the world around us was becoming brighter. He reminded me always of a picture of St. John, the apostle, which I saw in some gallery.

It is true that I did not take all these people into account in our conversation. I treated them as exceptions, which did not determine the truth of our camp life. I had been pondering where to place them in the general picture of camp life.

Nikolai Peotrovich seemed to have guessed my thoughts. "The real role of these kinds of people in our reality is greater than it seems to you," he said after a while. "You should understand that Russia is an exceptional country. It is a country in which Satan is revealing himself. I already notice your smile. Your smile is precisely the expression of your over rationalized civilization. But after all, you are a believer. We Russians always had a feeling of the reality of the devil in our past – and a believing Russian has this feeling today. And you, Stanislaw Stanislawowicz, you have been in Russia for so many years, don't you have a feeling that with his grotesque shape he punctures through the Russian reality?

But, Stanislaw Stanislawowicz, he is not going to win; he is going to be ruined exactly because there exist people like Nadezhda Alekseyevna; like our doctor; like the sectarians. Most of all he is afraid of the purity of human hearts. It does not matter what convictions those people have, or what they believe in. For example, I do not know if or how Nadezhda Alekseyevna believes, if in anything. The doctor seems to be a complete non-believer, while the anarchist believes in his own way, though it is difficult to understand him. It also does not matter if someone is without sin. We all, Stanislaw Stanislawowicz, are sinners. But in all those people there is some spark, some element of grace, some subconscious will not to lose this grace. In Russia, there are still many people with pure hearts, more than you know. On them the power of evil, which is ruling over them, is going to be shattered. I know it is going to happen and I am already living through the joys of victory.

FROM KATYN TO KUYBYSHEV

In the Russian language there is a combination of two words, which sounds strange when you translate it into any other language: *'svetloye pinyie'* ['enlightened singing']. It is like a choir of angels. It is the singing that in our Orthodox churches reverberates during the Night of Resurrection; it is the soft, joyful singing of the victory of bright spirits over the powers of evil. It seems to me already that sometimes I am hearing this singing. Very often I dream of the Orthodox Church; all the lights are shining; the Orthodox priests' chasubles are glittering with gold; and the harmonized choirs are singing. And I feel so well, such joy in my soul. I awaken and I rejoice, rejoice."

Several days after this conversation, the following incident happened. In the camp courtyard I saw Nikolai Peotrovich carrying his meal. He walked hunched over, wearing a torn cotton-filled jacket, and worn-out gaiters; he was moving with extreme care over the rough and icy road. In both hands he held a small bowl of soup with a 300-gram piece of wet black bread on top. Painted on his face was the expression of some strange, almost touching reverence with which he fixed his eyes on this piece of bread. This was a common occurrence in the camps during that terrible winter. The prisoners were becoming almost psychotic about bread. Often, before they consumed bread, they were kissing it, giving it tender names, and making the sign of the cross over it. This reverence seemed interestingly enough mainly applied to bread, but not so much to the other consumable items. There were even cases when the prisoners who received fish, willingly exchanged it for a piece of bread of lesser caloric value. Nikolai Peotrovich had submitted to this psychosis; he seemed in a trance judging by the way that he was gazing with such rapture at the bread.

At that very moment, another prisoner passed by, a professional criminal, a huge and strong fellow; in a lightening-like move, he grabbed the bread that was held by Nikolai Peotrovich. Nikolai Peotrovich lunged trying to defend his treasure, but the criminal pushed him, and Nikolai Peotrovich fell face down on the ground, the soup spilling over. In a few big leaps, the criminal ran behind the corner of a nearby hut.

I ran immediately to Nikolai Peotrovich. He was lying with his face down and did not move while he groaned softly. I started lifting him up. When he fell, Nikolai Peotrovich cut the skin over his right eye on a piece of sharp ice. From the wound blood was dripping on the snow and on my hands. From the eyes of Nikolai Peotrovich there came big tears. I took him under the arm and guided him toward the hut. After a moment, Nikolai Peotrovich realized who was leading him and also realized that he was crying. Through the veil of wet tears his pale blue eyes looked at me, "Stanislaw Stanislawowicz, don't you think that I am crying! Maybe really I am, but somehow it only looks like it. In reality I am rejoicing; everything is happening for the better, and the world is so beautiful...." I did not answer. I guided him into the hut to his place in the bunk and covered him with his invaluable quilt.

A few days later, I was taken to the hospital, and then there was my release from the camp. I never saw Nikolai Peotrovich again.

IN THE SHADOW OF KATYN

The Anarchist

He was more than 60 years old, which meant that during the outbreak of the Revolution, he was already a grown man of about forty. During his young days, he was an industrial worker in the textile industry. Today, I do not remember what his specialty was. Once upon a time, I managed to read an illegal pamphlet about the views of Prince Peter Kropotkin, a Russian anarchist, a distinguished geographer and explorer of Siberian geography, who became an apostle of anarchism, rejecting equally the imperial power as well as the dictatorship of the proletariat, and also Marxist dialectics. Because of that, even in the period before the First World War, he aroused the anger of Lenin, whom he must have met when they both were émigrés. Kropotkin went to live abroad after his bold escape from the fortress in Petro-Pavlovsk.

My fellow prisoner, who somehow had managed a personal contact with Kropotkin, adopted his ideals. He maintained with obstinacy that every organization, whether governmental, religious, or professional, corrupts human individuality and makes it more difficult for a man to fulfill his destiny. He believed in God and insisted that every human being not bound by social ties must find his or her own way to come to Him.

In the period before the Revolution, he was imprisoned many times for spreading these ideals. After serving his time, he used to go back to his profession and his propaganda. But not until Soviet times was he put behind bars permanently. He maintained that the Soviet regime created the most atrocious forms of repression, even worse than those we know had happened in ancient history. He did not hide his convictions and expressed them constantly and openly – interestingly, he suffered no ill consequences. He belonged to the category of people whose lives are guided by ideals.

He belonged to that class of camp veterans who were respected not only by the other camp prisoners but also by the camp administration. He was one of those who had survived the Gehenna of building the canal between the Baltic and the White Sea (the Beloye More Canal). During my time, there was a custom that for those who went through the hell of Beloye More Canal, an attempt was made to give them lighter work. My friend, the anarchist, became the caretaker of the so-called *sushshelka* (the disinfecting house). It was a constantly steaming dugout, built in the vicinity of the camp baths. It fulfilled a double function: to dry the clothes of those prisoners who worked in deep snow, and to use it as a disinfecting chamber. Every evening, from various barracks, they brought the wet clothes and footwear of the forest workers, and then in the morning before the reveille, the caretaker would return to the representatives of the barracks the items that were well dried. The disinfecting of clothes that were brought from the baths was a different matter. The heat generated by the stove of the *sushshelka* was not enough to destroy the lice, which after this operation seemed to have acquired a greater reproductive vigor. When the order came that the doctor must determine the cause of death of each prisoner, *sushshelka* received a third task: to thaw out the corpses before autopsy. The bodies of the dead were lying in heaps in the camp yards, frozen as hard as stone at -30 degree frost. When the doctor would order the autopsy, the bodies would be brought in a sleigh to the *sushshelka* and placed on the bottom of the disinfecting chamber to be thawed out. It required several hours, but sometimes the bodies lay there for several days. Entrance to the *sushshelka* by the

FROM KATYN TO KUYBYSHEV

prisoners was absolutely forbidden with the exception being the cases when one would bring a great amount of items to be dried or disinfected.

One day, my anarchist friend told me, that it seemed to him that his *sushshelka*, in some cases, performed healing functions. People are dying, not only from malnutrition and hard work, but also because of the bitterly cold winter from which there is no way to escape. In the disinfecting chamber, there was a considerable difference in temperature between the air near the ceiling and on the bottom where the warmth was rather pleasant. According to him, spending several hours in the lying position in the disinfecting chamber might help the dying organism to survive the arctic winter. When they brought the dead bodies for thawing out, he tried sometimes to smuggle into the chamber a person who was still alive and needed some warmth to extend his life.

I accepted his advice, and under his supervision I started coming for this special kind of medical treatment. When I was lying in the dark between the dead bodies, I felt how the pleasant warmth spread through my whole body. To sit up was impossible because one meter above the floor the air was already too hot. After several hours of this cure, when one walked out, the frost did not seem so terrible; the warmth absorbed in *sushshelka* still heated the bones. One day, two persons arrived to take the dead bodies for autopsy. They grabbed them by the legs and pulled them in such a way that the heads were bumping on the floor. I was lying very quietly hoping that perhaps they would miss me. One of the workers grabbed me by the legs and tried to pull, then I moved. "Look," he told his comrade, "this one has thawed out and starts moving." There was no surprise in his voice, and he was trying to pull me further. I kicked him with all my force. This incident did not cause any repercussions. I still enjoyed the benefits of *sushshelka*.

This medical treatment lasted for about two weeks, and then I was taken to the hospital. Those two weeks were probably the most critical period during my stay in the camp, when my organism was on the borderline of physical endurance. It is quite possible that this anarchist saved my life.

After two months' stay in the hospital, the order arrived for my immediate release in connection with the so-called "Amnesty" for Poles. I did not have time to say goodbye to my anarchist friend and to thank him for his companionship and care. After leaving the GULAG, I thought not only about the cruelty, brutality, and moral degradation, which I witnessed, but owing to him also about the kind people I met there.

Release from the camps

About the 20th of April 1942, the camp management received an order to send me to the central administration of the Ust-Wymsk camps to take care of the formalities connected with my release. The distance from the camp in which I was kept to the central administration was about 50 kilometers by rail. It was one of the most physically unpleasant journeys that I experienced during my stay in Soviet prisons and camps. It was late at night; a mixture of snow and rain was falling while a strong wind blew. The train in which I traveled was attached to an antique locomotive, most likely constructed in the previous century, and consisted of several open carriages on which some kind of cases stood. One of the carriages contained a small hut for the conductor and the guards. The guard told me to sit down between the cases, and he and a few other NKVD men gathered into the hut. To my remark that there was enough room for me in the hut too, he answered that it was inconceivable to place an inmate in the same spot with free people. For two hours, the mixture of snow and rain pelted my face, and my clothes, a cotton-filled jacket and trousers, were completely drenched.

The next day, I received my documents of release; in each one of them in front of my name they had added "citizen". The documents allowed me to travel to Kotlas, where supposedly a representative of the Polish Embassy was regulating further moves of Polish citizens released from the camps. I was issued a new jacket and better footwear, so I could more "appropriately" represent to the outside world the lifestyle in the Soviet camps. Since the regulations forbade entering the trains without a delousing certificate, I had to go to the camp's baths to perform this delousing ceremony. After washing myself, while I was waiting with a number of local prisoners in birthday suit for the return of our clothes from the disinfecting oven, right then the bathhouse was inspected by some high-ranking functionary of the NKVD who happened to know about me. In very strong words he scolded the manager of the bathhouse for the harm he had caused me for allowing my clothes – those of a free man – to be placed in a disinfecting oven together with those of prisoners. I found out then and there that lice that inhabit the clothes of a free man do enjoy a higher social status and could not be subject to the same liquidation treatment with the groups of lice that suck the blood of slaves. In this manner, in a period of less than twenty-four hours, I discovered the depth of utter humiliation to which, according to the new civilization created in Stalinist Russia, the slave was subjected; and also found out those honorable privileges that were given to the people who were apparently free.

When I arrived in Kotlas by train several days later, I noticed a military man in uniform on the railway platform who wore on his armband a strap that said "Poland". He was an officer of the Polish armed forces being formed in Russia, who had pertinent information for the occasionally arriving Polish citizens from the Northern camps. He tried to catch those who were to be sent to the military units stationed in Russian Central Asia under the command of General Anders. He sent me to the nearby barracks, which were assigned to the recently released (by Amnesty) Polish citizens, where they were supposed to give me provisions for the journey and issue the necessary documents for traveling. One of the first questions I asked him was, where the other Kozelsk prisoners, my friends and comrades of misery, were. I already imagined that they most likely had formed the main cadre of that army, about which I had learned from the occasional newspapers arriving in the camp. This officer told me that a great mystery surrounded Kozelsk, and that there was only a small group of Kozelsk prisoners in the camp at Grazovetz,[26] and no further information about the rest of them at all. Equally, the fate of the majority of officers of Starobelsk and Ostashkov remained unknown. Generally speaking we were short about 10,000 officers who had been taken prisoner by the Russians. He also told me that all the delegates of the army and the embassy had instructions to collect as much information as possible that might lead to some trace of them, for up till now nothing concrete was found. Finally, this

---

[26] Grazovetz, a town in Northern Russia where the prisoners from the camps of Kozelsk, Starobelsk and Ostashkov who were spared execution were sent, in total 394 persons (less than 3% of the total prison population).

FROM KATYN TO KUYBYSHEV

officer told me that perhaps it was luck that I was arrested and sent to Moscow because everyone had great doubts that they were still alive.

The barracks for Poles, who came from the North to Kotlas, were about 400 meters from the railway station. There were several rooms in which about 300 people were staying at that time. It was already evening, and they gave me some kind of soup and told me to find a bunk for sleeping. The next morning singing awakened me; they were religious songs coming from one of the neighboring rooms. I quickly dressed myself so I could take part in the service, but I managed to catch only the very end of Holy Mass. It was the first collective service in which I was able to take part since that clandestine Holy Mass in the catacomb-like conditions in the Kozelsk camp at the end of 1939.

In the administration of this transportation center in Kotlas where I asked for travel documents, so I could join the army, I was told that for some time there had been precise instructions regarding me, and that as soon as I appeared, they were to send me immediately to Kirov. There the main delegate of the embassy for Northern Russia would personally like to have a conversation with me and from there, eventually, I could join the army. They gave me documents and the next day I traveled to Kirov.

In Kirov, Otto Pehr, the main delegate of the embassy for North European Russia, a lawyer in Grudziądz [northern Poland] before the war and well-known socialist activist, received me with open arms. He told me right away that to get me out of the GULAG was one of his specific assignments in the Northern Soviet Union, that Ambassador Kot reminded him about this all the time at Kuybyshev, and that the Polish Government in London showed great interest in my case. He also told me that as far as he knew there had been discussions concerning me between the Polish Government and the Soviet Ambassador in London.

From what I know, the northern Polish delegation had quite a store of clothes and tins of food accumulated from America. Immediately on my behalf, Otto Pehr ordered the storekeeper to provide me with some decent clothes, underwear, a coat, footwear, et cetera, and he demanded that I should undress and dispose of all my rags. I thanked him very much for the clothes, but I was not about to get rid of my camp outfit. I considered the *telogreika* [body-warmer], jacket, cotton-filled trousers, and *valonki* (felt-boots) a convenient way to dress in the far north, blessed by centuries of experience of Mongols and other local folks. After all, we were still in the North. Besides, those items, so useful then, would represent a great memento in future times if I could manage to keep them. Otto Pehr, however, considered that several months of experience spent in pulling people out of the claws of Soviet slavery had taught him that the camp dwellers, as a rule, had a complex of great attachment to riches, which for the beggar in Soviet camps were his warm clothes. He insisted that he wanted to immediately break these complexes of the Soviet camp dweller which, according to him, existed within me. So, I had to give in. With a great amount of pain, I watched how the orderly disposed of my camp property. They also gave me a certain amount of American canned food, which I could combine with the rations to be given to me from the barracks that were under the administration of Polish delegates.

Very soon I realized that if all the outposts of the Polish Embassy were showing so much interest in me, it was not because they considered that saving my life was so important for Poland, but mainly because the news of my being in the Ust-Wymsk

IN THE SHADOW OF KATYN

camps meant that I was the first officer found from the missing transports which left Kozelsk during its liquidation between the third of April and the twelfth of June of 1940. From those transports only one had been found: The transport which left last in June of 1940, and which was directed to Pavlishchev-Bor and Grazovetz. It consisted of about 150 prisoners; the other transports were lost without a trace. From the time of signing the Polish-Soviet agreement in August of 1941, the search for traces of the missing transports was continuous. I, myself, was the first trace. Several Kozelsk officers were released from prisons because of "Amnesty," but not one of them had originally belonged to the normal liquidation transports; they had been arrested individually, before the liquidation of the camp. My case was really of an exceptional character. I had left in a normal liquidation transport on the 30th of April 1940; I was not in Grazovetz; but after the "Amnesty" for Poles, I was suddenly found in the camps of the Komi Autonomous Soviet Socialist Republic. The Polish authorities hoped to be able to cull some information from my experiences during April 1940 to April 1942, that could be used to solve the mystery about which Stalin, Molotov, Beria, and Merkulov equally responded in a highly enigmatic fashion when they were asked about those transports.

Naturally, the conversation generally focused on this agonizing mystery. I spoke to the delegate about my experiences and, three weeks later, I wrote about them in my statement to General Wolikowski, Chief of the Military Mission with the Soviet Government. After listening to my story, Pehr came to the conclusion that the mystery, instead of becoming clearer, became even more obscure. My observation, that at least part of the transports went from Kozelsk in a westerly direction and stopped near Smolensk, demanded new directions and methods of search. Pehr said, "You must tell everything as soon as possible to the ambassador." To my remark that my formal situation as an officer called to active service demanded I immediately report to the closest military unit, Pehr answered that he would mainly try to organize my transport to the embassy, which at that time was in Kuybyshev, near the Volga, to which the whole diplomatic corps from Moscow had been evacuated, and eventually, from there I would be able to go to the Polish Army in Central Asia.

"To organize this transport is not as simple as it might seem at the moment," continued Pehr. "We have conducted your case in such a way that they had to release you. The text of the Polish-Soviet agreement concerning the release of Polish citizens staying in Soviet prisons is abundantly clear. The NKVD couldn't possibly tell us that they could not find you because for some time we had correct and precise information about what was happening to you and where you were. Now, I am afraid that if we were to issue you the ordinary documents for travel to Kuybyshev or to the army, you simply would not arrive there. So, we have to organize the journey in such a way that we are sure you will. It will require time to extract the necessary documents from the local NKVD."

During my almost two weeks' stay in Kirov, when Pehr was preparing my journey to Kuybyshev "so I would arrive there," I came to the conclusion that he had great talents in dealing with the local Soviet authorities. One of the characteristics, which elevated his authority, was that his Russian was very poor and he spoke with a strong German accent. This special kind of authority of his was one of the paradoxes of Soviet reality. During the First World War, he had served as a reserve officer in the

FROM KATYN TO KUYBYSHEV

Austrian cavalry. He had distinct manners and a well-fitting dark blue suit, which gave him a certain style. The local Soviet high functionaries in Kirov decided that he was an *Americanyetz* [American] who had come to assist the Polish Embassy, and that because of the present treaty with the United States, he had to be treated with special respect. In fact, Pehr had escaped from the advancing Germans into the territory of Eastern Poland where he had been embraced by the Soviet invasion and was deported to some settlement in the Soviet Union from where, after arriving at the Polish Embassy, he went into the service of the exiled Polish Government in London.

He knew how to take advantage of that specific inferiority complex which characterized the representatives of the Soviet apparatus in respect to the West. It seemed to me that this complex was one of the elements of the Stalin era as in the same way the characteristic of that mentality gave way to an aversion to intellectuals who might criticize and ridicule everything. This complex expressed itself at various times in a paradoxical manner; for instance, the imprisonment of foreign communists who "in the proletarian fatherland" had looked for care and shelter as opposed to the privileges that were given in Lubyanka to arrested people from Central Europe in whom they had discovered high aristocratic connections. Lenin, Chicherin[27], Lunacharsky[28], and Trotsky did not suffer from those complexes, but this "new class" of Party bureaucrats, who projected absolute power to Stalin, was impregnated with distrust and some kind of conscious realization of their own inferiority.

Lenin had introduced "NEP" (New Economic Policy) and had offered concessions to foreign capitalists because he wanted to expose the Russian communists, through contact with them, to the more progressive methods of economic administration. The "new class" created instead a wall completely separating Russia, not only from the bourgeois strata of the West, but also from the revolutionary movements in the West. Those who during the time of NEP had experienced some Western contacts and those who had participated in the Spanish Civil War, including a considerable part of the foreign communists staying in Russia, were locked up and were even sent to the execution cellars. Therefore, when the war started and the fate of the Soviet Union depended on American supplies, the members of the local Soviet administration were disoriented and, to a certain extent, even overawed when doing business with the Western coalition, whose members were increasing in the USSR. Pehr took excellent advantage of this temporary disorientation of the Soviet apparatus

---

[27] Chicherin, Georghy Vasilevich (1872-1936) was well educated in Imperial Russia and entered the diplomatic service in the Archives Department of the Foreign Office. From 1897 onward he was gradually drawn into the revolutionary movement. He was well traveled abroad: Germany, England. In 1918 he returned to Russia and was appointed People's Commissar for Foreign Affairs. Chicherin conducted Russian policy continuously from 1918 to 1930.

[28] Lunacharsky, Anatoli Vasilevich (1875-1933) a Russian politician, author and dramatist, was born in Poltava of well-to-do parents. He joined the revolutionary movement when at college in Kiev, and afterward studied natural science and economics in Zurich. In 1903 Lunacharsky joined the Bolshevik wing of the Social Democratic Party. He was well traveled in France and Switzerland. In March 1917, he joined Lenin and Trotsky in Russia. During the November Revolution and during the Civil War, Lunacharsky was one of the ablest speakers of the party. He became People's Commissar for Public Instruction from 1917 to 1929. He also ensured the preservation of works of culture and art during the Civil War. He promoted mass instruction, while his special concern for the welfare of the theater furthered the development of the Russian stage.

of terror and dictatorship, so that he would be able to save a number of Polish citizens held in North-European Russia in the various corners of the Soviet system of slave labor.

Was the suspicion of Pehr – that the NKVD was trying to organize some sort of ambush in order to liquidate me – justifiable? I do not know. However, the journey was organized in such a way that it would be very difficult to do away with me "on the sly". First of all, I was not to travel by myself, but in the company of Pehr's representative who was carrying diplomatic mail and, on the way, was supposed to take care of me because of my supposedly bad state of health. Before the war, he had been employed in one of the offices in the district of Nowogródek, and he looked more like a professional boxer than a medic. We were supplied with the most formal travel documents, issued by the NKVD for our journey to Kuybyshev. The NKVD also gave us permission to buy tickets for the "soft carriage" [first class] from Kirov to Gorky [former Nizny Novgorod], and they had requested reservations by telegraph on the ship sailing on the Volga from Gorky to Kuybyshev and Astrakhan. We were also well supplied with food, e.g., pork. Besides that, the wife of my attendant had managed to bake an assortment of pastries for us from the supply of American flour; it all reminded me of the Easter holidays. Obviously, we still needed to go to the railway baths to go through the prescribed sanitation processes.

In Kirov, just before my departure, I observed the newly formed military units ready for departure to the frontline. Judging by the amount of people, it was an Infantry Brigade. Only the first platoon had rifles, the others were without armaments. They had no machine guns or anti-tank weaponry. The people whom I asked surreptitiously about it explained to me that the weaponry was sent to the frontline by separate NKVD transports. The "new class", whose interests were expressed by Stalinism (in spite of the fact that many of its representatives also went to the GULAG and execution chambers), had to their merit that they knew how to learn from past experiences. The great mistake of the Tsarist system during the First World War had been that, mobilizing almost eleven million, it had armed workers and peasants. The going expression of the Russian Army during the First World War was "armed peasantry." The February Revolution of 1917 was the work of generals and the upper class bourgeoisie, who had wanted to overthrow the system of autocracy in order to improve conditions for running a war more efficiently. But eight months later, the outcome of the October Revolution was decided by this armed peasantry, who had been promised peace and ownership of land by Lenin. The "new class" made sure that in the Second World War, weaponry was not going to fall into the hands of the masses for it to be used against the Soviet ruling elite. The head of this military apparatus was Beria, promoted during the war to the rank of marshal, even though he was not involved with military frontline operations.

At the station, after showing the NKVD permits, we bought our tickets without any difficulties. By the entrance to our carriages, the NKVD functionaries inspected once more the documents of each member. Everywhere was order and cleanliness. It made a positive contrast in comparison to the Russian railways in the First World War when, as a teenager, I often traveled through Russia. During the First World War, there was chaos in the movement of trains, and the carriages were unbearably packed with people. Now our train left punctually from Kirov, and we arrived punctually in Gorky.

FROM KATYN TO KUYBYSHEV

It was unthinkable for anyone to enter the soft carriage without a ticket, while during the times of Kerensky[29], the sight of an overindulged soldier placing his muddy boots on the seats of the red plush upholstery in the carriages of the first class had been a common occurrence. The Red Army soldiers, whom I saw in the train or in the streets of Gorky and Kuybyshev, spoke politely and behaved decently. The NKVD was ruling everything with an iron fist.

At the Gorky railway station, the representatives of some Polish institutions directed us to the local delegate of the Polish Embassy. In his office we were told that one of the cabins on the ship had already been reserved and that the ship was sailing in two days; in the meantime, we were to live in the office of the local embassy delegate. In about two hours after our arrival, we received a very courteous phone call from the local chief of the NKVD, who wanted to find out "how Mr. Professor is feeling." Because of such great interest in my person, I came to the conclusion that it would be ill advised to roam through the town, which for many reasons attracted me very much; so I stayed for the entire two days in the embassy office. In Gorky, we experienced several German air raids which did not seem very dangerous to me. The Russians undoubtedly had a lot of anti-aircraft artillery, which had been the Achilles' heel of our defenses in 1939. All in all those air raids did not seem any fiercer than the German air raids on Dyneburg [Daugavpils], for I had witnessed many of them in the years of 1915-1917. It meant that German air power was not as threatening to the Russian towns as I had imagined.

The ship in which we sailed was still from pre-Revolutionary times when rich people spent their vacations traveling in luxurious conditions through the tremendous waterways of the greatest river in Europe. We were assigned a large cabin with two extremely comfortable couches covered with leather. It was an exceptionally pleasant journey. The May sunshine poured its rays on the nearby bushes and treed areas on the shore while in the low lying areas there were still patches of snow; the radiance of the sun made the river sparkle, and the wind brought the scents of nature of the awakening spring. At the ports of call, I listened with delight to the characteristic rhythmic songs of the Volga dockworkers.

We enjoyed a great feeling of relaxation. It seemed to me that due to the foresight of Pehr, I was completely protected from any unofficial "jokes" of the NKVD. I did not have too many worries about my family. I had received news that they were seen in Wilno (Vilnius) shortly before the German attack [June 1941], so I had every reason to believe that they, thankfully, survived till the Russians were thrown out of town [three days later]. I did not think that the Germans provided any danger for them. Of course, there was always the threat of starvation, but they could always fall back on the small estate of my father-in-law, where at least there should be enough potatoes. All four of our children had spent their vacations in the atmosphere of the impoverished estate in Byelorussia. I could expect that in the same manor-house they would be able to survive the war storm now that the Russians were thrown out of there.

During those days of sailing, I went on the upper deck to enjoy the soft rays of the spring sun, drinking in the scent emanating from the nearby meadows, and thinking

---

[29] Kerensky, Alexander Fyodorovich (1881-1970). He was a Russian Socialist, who became Russian Prime Minister from July 25, 1917, until the outbreak of the Bolshevik Revolution. Vacillation and indecision marked his government with almost a complete breakdown of law and order.

about things close to my heart and things of a more general nature. What tormented me most was the anxiety about what might have happened to my colleagues from Kozelsk, and also from Starobelsk and Ostashkov (about whom we had a certain amount of information during our stay in Kozelsk). The painful elements attached to the historical problem of Poland-Russia occupied my mind.

Ten thousand Polish officers, many of whom had numerous connections in all parts of the world, did not represent the "needle" mysteriously lost in the turmoil of the war. One of these officers should be able to give some sign of life; after all, so much information about me reached the embassy in Kuybyshev. I excluded the possibility that in this country, where the NKVD was overseeing, reregistering, and controlling everything, the authorities did not know what happened to those officers. My observations of the liquidation of the Kozelsk camp had convinced me that the decision about the fate of each individual prisoner was centralized in Moscow. Most likely, each one of us had his own individual file in the central offices of the NKVD. The conclusion of that reasoning raised the possibility that the larger portion of my comrades in misery from Kozelsk might not be alive any longer. But also my emotions could not accept the idea of centralized mass murder. Everything that I went through in the Soviet Union, and about which I have written above, pointed away from the psychological possibility of such a solution. In Smolensk and Lubyanka, and even in the camps, I was better treated than I had expected to be, and I was taking that into account in my reasoning. If, however, they had been murdered – as was assumed by many people with whom I spoke – it would be a grave element of historical significance.

One day, the truth is going to be known; the moral shock that this will create will weigh heavily on a number of generations, not only between Poland and Russia, but also on the general outlook of the role Russia played in Eastern Europe and in the world. The mass terror that was propagated by Lenin and Dzerzhinsky was justified by the theory of class warfare. Here, if it were really a massacre calmly undertaken after more than a half year of deliberations, the argument of class struggle would not hold up. It would be an act of pure Russian Imperialism, where all the methods of extermination applied by the Tsarist Government to the Polish nation became a pale imitation in comparison.

During this comfortable journey relaxing in the sun's rays of warm spring that were reflecting from the waves of the Volga River, I tried to establish an historical perspective of my experiences of nearly three years (September 1939-May 1942). The fact that my colleagues from Kozelsk had mysteriously perished increased the inner turmoil of my feelings toward Russia. In general, my personal attitude toward Russia was the typical love and hate affair. I had finished school in Russia. I was an ardent lover of Russian poetry, and I believed in the artistic genius of that nation. I had Russian cousins and had felt comfortable in Russian circles, of which I became convinced anew during my stay in Lubyanka. In my life I knew many Russians who had distinguished themselves with extraordinary kindness and goodwill toward their fellow men. When I was a small boy, I heard from my mother and aunt a considerable amount of good things about their uncle's Russian wife who had died in the year when I was born and was, apparently, a woman of generous heart. Therefore, in the years of early childhood, I had become used to thinking about Russian women as basically kind and friendly human beings in whom one could confide. Later on in my school years and in the beginning of my university studies in Moscow, a serious minded Russian girl of my age had a great influence in formulating my interests and my attitude toward life. However, since the time when I started thinking politically; that is, from the beginning of the First World War, there was no room in my ideals for any Commonwealth arrangement between the old Polish Republic and Russia.

In my political attitudes, there was no rancor toward what was generally being called the East, as it happened to be among many Poles. Conversely, this East was close to my heart; I actually belong to it with my whole cultural background. I considered, however, that this East must be defended against destructive actions of Government organizations, which grew around Suzdalian Russia[30] and Moscow. While still in my very early youth, under the influence of historical novels by Dmitri Merezhkovsky,[31] I developed a conviction that together with the great creative values of the Russian spirit certain elements of absolute evil were lodged in the Russian statehood. My stay in the camps affirmed this conviction.

As for the history of Poland, I used to look at the part the Polish-Lithuanian Commonwealth played in the East. Still in the Russian school, I learned about the history of Poland in the secret student circles by way of self-study. I was fascinated by the history of the Grand Duchy of Lithuania and the Polish-Lithuanian Union; the Cossack and Tartar regiments in the service of the Commonwealth; the Ruthenian Greek-Orthodox churches ringing the bells to celebrate the victory over the Prince of Moscow, "enemy of the Greek-Orthodox Church"; the Jagiellons (a Polish-Lithuanian dynasty), who, when coming to Wilno, proclaimed their edicts in the Ruthenian language; and the religious tolerance during the Reformation. I was never sure whether Prince Janusz Radziwiłł,[32] whom Sienkiewicz censured in his trilogy novels, and Hetman (army head) Mazepa[33], who was criticized by Pushkin, were mistaken in seeking an alliance with Sweden. I thought that Poland of the 17th century should have developed close ties with Sweden; however, the basic line of Polish policy in the 20th century should have been seeking the support from the Germans.

This general attitude of mine transferred itself into a concrete political program which I formulated several times during my student years when, after the war of 1919-1920, I left the army. The main point of this program was to push Russia behind the river basins of Dvina and Dnieper and to create in the area between Russia and Germany something on the pattern of Switzerland – a multilingual country with a common defense and foreign policy. Warsaw did not necessarily have to be the center of this new creation, but in my concept it would have to play an important role in the

---

[30] Suzdalian Russia, a country north of Moscow around Jaroslavl, Rostov, and Suzdal, influenced by Viking settlements in the 7th Century.

[31] Merezhkovsky, Dmitri Sergeyevich (1865-1941), novelist, critic and poet, born in St. Petersburg, Russia. He studied at the university there, then became a writer, producing the historical trilogy *Khristos i Antikhrist* (Christ and Antichrist), and books on Tolstoy, Ibsen and Gogol. He opposed the revolution in 1917 and fled to Paris in 1919.

[32] In 1655, when the Swedish King Charles X invaded the Polish Republic, the Grand Hetman of Lithuania, Janusz Radziwiłł accepted a Swedish protectorate over the Grand Duchy of Lithuania

[33] When the Swedish King Charles XII invaded Russia, then Mazepa, hetman of the Cossacks, attached himself to Charles, and took part at the battle of Poltava (June 28, 1709) which ended in a Swedish defeat. Charles and Mazepa made their way as fugitives to Turkey.

IN THE SHADOW OF KATYN

education of the Ukrainian, Byelorussian, and Lithuanian intelligentsia, supplementing in this respect the role which Thomas Masaryk [founder-president of the Czechoslovakian Republic, 1918-35] had assigned for Czech Prague and, to a certain extent, competing with Prague. The condition for realizing this program had to be the regulation of relations between Poland and Germany. The Ukrainians, Byelorussians, and Lithuanians, even more so Latvians and Estonians, would not see any benefit in a closer relationship with Poland for as long as the threat of serious conflict with the Germans existed. However, an arrangement among these countries would make it possible to have a united defense against the pressure from Russia, provided they had the support of German industry.

Therefore, since the very beginning of the reborn Polish State after the First World War, I was a strong advocate of finding the means for an agreement with Germany. I was also a great admirer of Józef Piłsudski; it seemed to me that his Kiev expedition, his help given to Latvia in rebuilding its independence, his stubborn opposition to the peremptory incorporation of Wilno into Poland, and his careful attitude toward Germany were similar to my political views. In the year of 1920, there were strong possibilities of accomplishing this goal, but neither Poles nor other nations of this geographical region, not even the great powers who won the First World War, were psychologically or ideologically ready for this solution. Piłsudski was, as a matter of fact, alone with a small group of his adherents among whom none were excelling in individuality. Would the Second World War bring out these possibilities?

The Soviet Union was quite capable of defending Moscow, which was the center of the communication lines of that country. I, however, was in doubt whether it would be able to maintain the line of the lower Volga and the great centers of the oil industry. If all that were to be shattered, what would come next? I was convinced that the Germans eventually were going to be beaten; the difference in potential was too obvious. Did the Western Powers have some sensible program for Eastern Europe? Was there anyone in London or Washington who would be capable of working out such a program? It seemed to me that it would be very desirable if some strong Ukrainian group, actively cooperating with a Western coalition, would try to accustom Western opinion to the idea of an independent Ukrainian state. I tried to think in terms of the interests of the whole 16th century pertaining to the Polish-Lithuanian Commonwealth as some sort of integral part. Was there anyone in London who was thinking in the same terms? This I intended to find out in Kuybyshev where according to Pehr several of my pre-war friends were staying in the embassy.

Never in my life have I been an active politician; I did not belong to any of the political parties. In spite of my being an adherent of Piłsudski, though I was not uncritical, I never belonged to any of the political parties supporting him. However, I was very much interested in political ideas, and I contemplated what kind of concept of postwar Europe would be created in the great centers of world politics.

I was, after three years of prisons and camps, at the threshold of a new period in my life. My thoughts were running ahead, giving birth to many question marks, and then again were going back excavating from my memory shadows of people and things which, belonging to the irretrievable past, had been stimulating my dreams during stuffy nights in Soviet prisons. Russia, which made such an impression on me in my childhood and youth, was becoming a political and personal problem for me again. I

FROM KATYN TO KUYBYSHEV

thought about the family of my mother, of whom most members had died on the scaffold or in Siberian prisons for partaking in the Polish Insurrection, and others had mixed with Tsarist generals. I also thought of various friends of my parents, and about the tragic fate of many Russians among whom I had spent my childhood, and about the early years of my youth. With longing I returned to thinking of my family, about whom I expected to discover some news at the embassy.

In this mood of pensiveness, rather than excitement, I left this comfortable ship at the dock in Kuybyshev, the town that during the war was the second capital of the Soviet Union.

Chapter V

KUYBYSHEV

The Embassy

The embassy in Kuybyshev had more the character of a rescue operation than a diplomatic representation. Nobody knew exactly how many Polish citizens were deported between October 1939 and June 1941. According to approximate estimates, about 1.2 million had been placed into GULAG camps, prisons, and forced settlements. According to the agreement signed between the Polish Government in London and the Soviet Government in August 1941, all those people must be released, but only a few people could expect to leave the Soviet territory before the end of the war. Most of those required material and moral help. Thousands had come to obtain their Polish passports. Sometimes, it was difficult to know whether they were really Polish citizens, because there were cases when permanent inhabitants of the Soviet Union presented fake documents of Polish citizenship in order to obtain permission to leave the Socialist motherland at the first opportunity. News was coming in continuously that the Soviet authorities, in defiance of the clear wording of the agreement, continued to hold Polish citizens in various camps and forced settlements. Therefore, when I came to the embassy, the two most active departments were the Department of Social Care, managed by Stefan Gacki, and the Department of Intervention under the direction of Professor Sukiennicki. This last department was gathering evidence on all the deportees and was organizing intervention on behalf of those who needed to get special protection and assistance from the Polish State.

The political problems and particularly the basic question of future Polish-Russian relations had become of secondary importance among the members and residents of the embassy. The only man questioning Polish-Russian relations and continually returning to it in his discussions was Ksawery Pruszyński, who had arrived from London as a press attaché. At the embassy, we had only one member with diplomatic experience, namely Minister Henryk Sokolnicki, our ex-consul to Finland. Ambassador Kot understood his mission mainly as being a rescue operation, treating the political question as not being of a primary concern. All the time he emphasized that he did not have diplomatic experience, and that he did not have knowledge of Russia. He was an outstanding historian of culture, and he was particularly distressed by the news that was coming out of Poland about the policy of physical extermination conducted by the German forces of occupation against the Polish cultural strata. He considered that maximal effort should be given to save the members of this cultural elite who were also perishing in the GULAG camps, prisons, and forced Soviet settlements. He pulled from the far reaches of the Soviet Union literary men, artists, scientists, and journalists whom he was bringing to the embassy and tried to expedite them beyond the borders of the Soviet Union. After my arrival at the embassy in Kuybyshev, I found outstanding representatives of Polish literature: Wacław Grubiński, Władysław Broniewski, Wiktor Weintraub, Teodor Parnicki, and the before mentioned, Ksawery Pruszyński. From the university professors there were: Stanisław Kościałkowski (history), Skąpski

KUYBYSHEV

(chemistry), Wiktor Sukiennicki (professor of law, who, as I mentioned before, was conducting a very important function connected with the embassy affairs), and from the known pre-war journalists: Bernard Singer, and Roman Fajans. Besides that, there were several known social and cultural activists, who could not be classified with the above three categories; among them was an outstanding Wilno Jesuit, Father Kucharski.

Immediately, after arriving and settling down in a kind of boarding house that was attached to the embassy, I went to report to the chief of the military mission, General Wolikowski. Naturally, our conversation was about the mystery of Kozelsk. The general requested that I write a report about what I observed during the transport from Kozelsk to the internal NKVD prison in Smolensk. This report focused the attention of Polish authorities on the district of Smolensk where investigation of the region might throw some light on this tortuous mystery. It was a completely different geographical direction of search from where the staff of the Polish Army in Russia was occupying itself. Simultaneously, I sent copies of my report to the ambassador and the intervention department of the embassy. Prof. Sukiennicki seemed to be particularly surprised by the news that at least part of the Kozelsk prisoners were sent to the region of Smolensk. The particularly intriguing question was why the Soviet authorities, in spite of constant and one could even say insistent questioning from the Polish Embassy and the command of the Polish Army in Russia, never mentioned this region. In my report it was clear that the transports were not a matter of a local decision, but were very scrupulously and exactly regulated by the central authorities in Moscow. There was no doubt that all the data in connection with the transports were in possession of the central authorities of the NKVD.

A few days later the ambassador invited me for a lengthy conversation. I left with the impression that there was friction between the embassy and the military authorities, consisting of the command of the Polish Army organizing in Russian Central Asia and the military mission in Kuybyshev, which negatively influenced the coordination of efforts in the search for missing officers and policemen. I had the impression that Prof. Kot was rather unpleasantly surprised when I told him that I went to report to the military mission as my first step in Kuybyshev. He told me that he did not see why that had been necessary upon my arrival because the Government in London had plans for using my qualifications other than for the military. I explained to him that according to Polish law, an officer called to active military duty must report to the chief of the military mission according to the regulations which ordered any officer who managed to extract himself from captivity to immediately report to the nearest known military authorities. I told him simultaneously that I was ready to undertake any work that the legal Polish hierarchy would like to assign to me, but this had to be done formally with the military authorities to which I was going to be attached.

Furthermore, during our conversation, I came to the conclusion that the ambassador and Gen. Sikorski in London were somewhat surprised by the discussions which General Anders, on his own accord, was conducting with the British on the subject of transferring Polish units from Russian Central Asia to the British operational military command in the Middle East. The ambassador also complained to me that the army, under the instructions of the British, was doing intelligence work in the Soviet Union, and this could endanger our rescue operation which the embassy was conducting for the Polish population that had been deported to the Soviet Union. Knowing the

IN THE SHADOW OF KATYN

Soviet resentment of foreign intelligence and its traditional distrust of everything that was British, particularly if it was connected with Central Asia and the Near East, I thought the anxiety of the ambassador was well founded.

During several hours of conversation with Prof. Kot, he told me about many things that had happened in the Government in exile; first in Paris and then in London during the three years that I had spent in prisons and in the Soviet camps. In particular, Prof. Kot was outraged by the action of President Raczkiewicz, who had tried to separate the position of Supreme Commander from that of the Prime Minister of the Government in exile; General Sikorski held both these functions. From my conversation with Prof. Kot, I assumed that the friends of Sikorski persuaded the British to exert pressure on the President to abandon his concept. At that moment, I recollected my contemplation in Lubyanka Prison about the limited freedom of Polish politics as a result of the situation being created during the outburst of war. I was extremely grateful to Prof. Kot for his kindness and goodwill toward me; however, I thought the political camp he represented did not have the perception of dignity of the country that Marshal Piłsudski had portrayed.

Prof. Kot also told me about the opposition that had arisen in émigré circles because of the Polish-Russian agreement of 1941. This agreement, which General Sikorski had conducted of his own accord – without even consulting with the Foreign Minister, who at that time was August Zaleski – caused the release of tens of thousands of Poles who had been deported to Soviet camps and forced settlements, and allowed at least the partial rebuilding of the Polish Army. However, the question of the Polish-Russian border remained open. That meant that Stalin, even in those tragic days of August 1941 when hundreds of thousands of soldiers of the Red Army were surrendering without firing a shot at the advancing German panzer columns, did not abandon the advantages given to him when signing the pact with Hitler. In the same way as twenty years earlier the Russian General Denikin[1], who even in the most tragic moment for himself, did not want to abandon territorial gains caused by the partition of Poland. Many people in London and in Poland considered that the conditions of any agreement with Russia toward the further conduct of war must be clear: a Soviet renouncement of the Pact with Germans as far as the division of Poland was concerned, and the clear renunciation of any territorial gains the Soviets had acquired when they broke the Non-Aggression Pact with Poland in 1939. Because of the arbitrary behavior of General Sikorski in this matter, several ministers resigned from the Polish Government in exile in London. General Sosnkowski and August Zaleski resigned.

According to Prof. Kot, obtaining those agreements from Stalin at that moment was impossible; in the meantime, the case was urgent because of the fear that the majority of Polish prisoners would physically not be able to last another winter in the Soviet camps. Besides, this agreement provided a serious possibility of considerably rebuilding our Polish military forces, and it could become a tremendous trump card at

---

[1] Denikin, Anton I (1872-1947) was a Tsarist general, former Chief of Staff of the Imperial Russian Army and Commander of the White Russian Army in its fight against the Bolsheviks. Early in the fall of 1919, General Denikin commanding Don Cossacks and the elite Volunteer Army, equipped with British tanks, reached Orel, 250 miles south of Moscow. Then numerically superior Red forces counterattacked and drove him back, and in March 1920 the British evacuated the remnant of his army from Novorossiysk.

KUYBYSHEV

the end of the war. Ultimately, the shaping of the border was going to be decided by the relative amount of forces at the end of the war, not by some kind of agreement signed at the beginning. Therefore, for General Sikorski the priority was to rebuild the army, postponing the question of the border as being less essential, particularly because all the territory which the Soviets had claimed were under German occupation. Professor Kot was gathering signatures from the Polish ex-Soviet prisoners in support of General Sikorski's decisions. In the conversation concerning this matter, I declined to take a clear stand. Today, however, when I am looking at the question of the Polish-Soviet agreement in 1941, in the perspective of what we went through, I think that Sikorski and Kot, rather than their opponents, were correct.

During this conversation, I asked a question that today I consider to be characteristic of my state of mind when I left the prison. I asked Prof. Kot to what degree the news, which I had read in various publications imported by the embassy, that the Germans were organizing the massive extermination of Jews by gassing them was true, or was it only propaganda of the Allies. I have seen much cruel suffering caused by men to men in my life. As a teenager I saw the frontline of the First World War; I saw the Russian Revolution; I witnessed the massive executions by the *Czerezwyczajka* (Extraordinary Commission founded by Lenin in order to fight counter-Revolution: death squads). Several times I saw acts of thoughtless cruelty as a result of the chaos of the September campaign; recently I went through the Soviet prisons and camps where I had heard so many stories of the methods of torture applied by the NKVD. I knew, from the time when Beria replaced Yezhov, there was some kind of normalization of tortures in the Soviet Union, since their application by the investigating magistrate was subject to the approval of higher authorities. Immediately after the First World War, I had heard stories of how, in the dermatological hospital in Sawicz Street in Wilno, the Germans gassed several infected prostitutes; meaning that Germany already had a tradition of using this method. But I could not imagine that any country would systematically apply all the apparatus of the existing technology in such a vulgar way to exterminate whole ethnic groups, consisting of hundreds of thousands of people. I always thought that there are certain moral imperatives, the trespassing of which no organized country, even an organized totalitarian country, would dare to overstep. I believed that these imperatives were a fact, not a pious postulate. In reply to that, Prof. Kot showed me several confidential reports from Polish underground organizations and asked me to read them. I had no more doubts: German gas chambers were a reality.

This confirmation was of basic importance to my personal view of the war which was being waged at that time. I had always been an advocate of looking for an agreement with Germany, regardless of the system that was reigning there. It had also always been clear to me that if there were to be a war against Nazi Germany, it would be a ruthless war. During my pre-war journeys to Germany, I formed the opinion that the Hitlerite policy toward Poland was oscillating between two extreme concepts: alliance or extermination. I partook in many discussions on the consequences of this situation. But from the time of knowing gas chambers were constructed, it was the end of any political concepts; we were entering the world of ruthless moral imperatives. Hitler and his party represented an absolute evil, and they had to be broken because they were endangering the whole basis of human cooperation on this earth. The question of the interest of the Polish State, because of this basic fact, had to be put in second place:

IN THE SHADOW OF KATYN

Hitler had to be fought, even if the interest of the Polish State required compromise. In spite of everything I had seen in the Soviet Union, and in spite of other monstrosities of which I knew, but had not seen, it still did not seem to me that the Soviet system would allow similar methods. I doubted if my colleagues from Kozelsk were still alive, but it did not seem possible to me that they had been liquidated by the method of a massive plan of organized murder.

Some time after my conversation with Ambassador Kot, Father Kucharski communicated to me that Bishop Gawlina would like to talk to me, and he asked me for a private dinner in one of the corners of the embassy. I was surprised to find out that the temporary residents of the embassy included the field bishop of the Polish Army. He had been visiting Polish units in North Africa and in Russian Central Asia, and he was looking for occasions to meet with Poles freshly released from the Soviet camps. The fact that a Polish field bishop had been allowed to visit Polish divisions stationed in Kazakhstan was a glaring example of the chaos that had engulfed Stalin's country. Bishop Gawlina was obviously moved by the case of the missing officers, but he was also equally interested in the general problems of the camps and the conditions of morality under which prisoners were existing. I told him that contrary to what came out of the stories about German camps, I did not notice a conscious and intentional cruelty in the Soviet camps, and that the high mortality and the intolerable conditions of Soviet prisoners were the results of systems rather than that of the people, who under tremendous pressure were executing the instructions of the Central Authorities. I told him also that after Beria had replaced Yezhov, certain trends could be detected to preserve human life. The existence of these tendencies spoke against the assumption that our officers were simply murdered; but, on the other hand, it was difficult to imagine that some terrible catastrophe had taken the lives of all of them simultaneously in the three camps that were hundreds of kilometers apart.

The case of Ehrlich and Alter

Besides the mystery of the missing officers, there was another disturbing case that weighed heavily on the Polish Embassy. It was the case of Ehrlich and Alter, even though we did not know, at that time, about their execution. Henryk Ehrlich and Wiktor Alter were active socialists, who were two of the leaders of "Bund." "Bund" was the Jewish equivalent of the Polish Socialist Party; that is, their ideology was the same as that of the Second International[2] (A Socialist and Labor Party founded in 1889). Bund people did not adhere to the Zionist ideals and associated the future of the Jewish working class in Poland with the fate of the Polish State. Alter was a member of the committee of the Second International and was also an appointed member of the Polish National Council in London, which acted as a substitute for the Polish Parliament. Both of them fled to the East before the Hitlerite invasion and in this manner fell into Soviet hands. After their release, they made a number of contacts in Russia and abroad, and they developed some kind of action intended to consolidate communist and non-communist elements, which were decisively anti-Hitler. They founded in Russia a Jewish anti-fascist committee. The Soviet authorities seemed to have acquiesced in this

---

[2] Second International, the Labor and Socialist International. It organized in 1889, they opposed war, broke up when World War I began, and later revived and opposed Communism.

KUYBYSHEV

action. Ehrlich and Alter had at their disposal certain secretarial staff and transport, which meant they were surrounded from all sides by *agents provocateurs*.

From what they told me in the embassy, I had the impression that as socialists who believed in Marxist mythology, they imagined that because of the Fascist Hitlerite danger, the moment had come to liquidate the contention between the Second and Third International[3] (founded by Communists in 1919), and probably they expressed these opinions. If that actually was so, then they really were showing great naïveté, and completely misunderstood the mentality of the people who were ruling Russia. First of all, the spreading of this kind of ideology within Russia would undermine the whole basis of Stalin's dictatorship; however, under certain conditions it could be a commodity for export, but under no circumstances would it be allowed for internal consumption. Secondly, one has to remember the boundless contempt that the ruling circles of Stalinist Russia had for all kinds of Western-European humanitarians, equally of the socialist as well as of the bourgeois-democratic classes. I am underlining here the adjective Western-European, because as far as American "friends of the Soviet Union" were concerned, the attitude toward them was rather more complicated. Thirdly, one has to remember the increasing wave of anti-Semitism, which Stalin more or less discreetly endorsed. Such outstanding representatives of the Second International, who were Jews, portrayed in the Soviet Union a condition tantamount to being twice as undesirable.

One evening, Ehrlich and Alter, who, as many other members of the embassy, both had membership cards which allowed them into the diplomatic restaurant where one could dine well and rather inexpensively, went there for supper and never returned. After several days of searching, which did not produce any results, the local NKVD admitted that they had Ehrlich and Alter under lock and key. The international wheels were set into motion, among them Mrs. Eleanor Roosevelt herself, but they could not pull the outstanding Jewish socialists from the claws of the NKVD. This event caused a depressing atmosphere among the residents of the embassy, particularly among those who did not have diplomatic passports. It was understood that anybody could find himself right back where they had been rescued from by the agreement between General Sikorski and the Soviet Union.

I was also told in the embassy that when Prof. Kot, at one time, turned to the Vice-Commissar of Foreign Affairs, Andrei Vyshinsky – who, as Molotov's deputy, usually received foreign diplomats accredited to the Soviet Government – with the request to release Ehrlich and Alter, he answered, that it was impossible because they were German spies. Prof. Kot tried to argue, pointing out that they were socialist activists, known all over the world and, furthermore, they were Jews. Vyshinsky, taking Kot by surprise, answered that Trotsky had also been a socialist and a Jew, and proved to be a German spy. What kind of retort could an ambassador accredited to this Soviet Government give?

Vyshinsky was one of the most despicable figures in the Stalinist system. He was undoubtedly an intelligent man and learned lawyer, who wrote several books on various topics and played a significant part in Soviet higher education. Before the Revolution,

---

[3] Third International (or Communist International, also known as Comintern), organized to unite all Communists of the world; actively opposed to Second International; dissolved May 1943.

and also in the period after the Revolution, he was a member of the Menshevik[4] faction of the Russian Social Democracy. Apparently, he moved to the Bolsheviks after 1920. During Stalin's dictatorship, he played a considerable role as a chief prosecutor and as a main organizer of the famous Soviet show trials. He contributed considerably to the execution of a number of old Bolsheviks and friends of Lenin. He was the main chief prosecutor in the trials of Zinovyev, Kamenev, Bukharin, and others. He was one of the main executors of the policy which Leonard Schapiro, in his fundamental history of Soviet Communism, calls the struggle of Stalin against the Party. During the war (or perhaps immediately before the war), he went into the Foreign Service as a deputy of Molotov. Ehrlich and Alter represented the same direction of Socialist thought with which Vyshinsky was connected, at least since 1903, till the time he transferred himself to the Communists circa 1920. He must have known their names long before they found themselves in the Soviet Union. It is not impossible that he played some personal role in their liquidation. Kot once told me that he asked Vyshinsky about his Polish origin. Vyshinsky did not deny it, but he emphasized that he had no connection anymore with anything that is Polish.

      The case of Ehrlich and Alter had such an effect on me that now, as a free man and living in the embassy, I started to more ruthlessly evaluate the cruelty of the Soviet system than when I did this in the camps and prisons. This case also made me realize that the Soviets in decision matters care quite a bit less about world opinion than was generally assumed; even if they sometimes tried, in a disguised way, to influence that opinion. Ehrlich and Alter were condemned at the moment when the Soviet Union, after its unfortunate attempts to be friends with Hitler, was fighting a desperate war for its existence. In this war all the socialists in the world and all the Jews seemed to be natural allies. It was only the beginning of the war. The Soviet Union required material and technical help from the West, and it was not clear to what extent this help was going to be given. The Jewish anti-Fascist committee which Ehrlich and Alter attempted to create could have been very useful in enlarging this help. However, the Soviet authorities decided that to get rid of two socialist leaders was more important than all the international regards and considerations, even more than the urgent requirements of waging war. The case of Ehrlich and Alter put a new evaluation on the perspectives of the search for our missing officers. When in Kozelsk, I often heard the opinion that in the final analysis none of the extreme cruelties in the form of execution or sending us to heavy labor should be a threat; because even if the Soviets did not sign the Geneva Convention, with respect to the treatment of POWs, they would have to reckon with world opinion. If, in this dramatic moment, the Soviet authorities ignored the appeal of outstanding representatives of American public opinion, including Mrs. Eleanor Roosevelt, then why should they worry about the fate of Polish officers who definitely had less friends in the Western press and on the radio than the outstanding leaders of Jewish socialism. My optimism on the possibility that at least some of our officers could still be found had been based on the premise, which I had heard in the

---

[4] In the early 1900s, the Russian Social Democratic Labor Party split into two main groups. V.I. Lenin led one group that believed that a single, centralized party of professional revolutionaries should lead the revolution in Russia. The other group believed in a broader party open to anyone who believed in revolution. Lenin began calling his followers *Bolshevik* (majority), and his opponents *Menshevik* (minority).

KUYBYSHEV

prisons and camps, that the massive executions had been stopped as soon as Yezhov was removed as Commissar of the NKVD, and Beria was nominated in his place.

We do not know what the actual reasons were for the execution of Ehrlich and Alter, but we have to assume that it was a personal decision of Stalin. In agreement with what I have already written, the reasons for their execution were rather in the nature of infighting within the Party. This execution was a warning to all outstanding members of the Party, so they would not dare to come into contact with the circles belonging to the Second International or international Jewish organizations. At the same time, a gauntlet was thrown at the feet of the whole Western Democracy. They did not even bother to organize show-trials, as in the case of the outstanding representatives of the Party opposition, and even before that in the case of the outstanding representatives of the democratic movements of socialism (that is, Mensheviks and Social-Revolutionaries).

The treatment of this case was in the gloomy Stalinist style, and also was a warning of what the West might expect if the Soviet system came out of this war victorious. We, the embassy inhabitants, thought at that time that the way in which the case of Ehrlich and Alter was handled by the Soviet authorities must shake public opinion in England and in the United States. After having spent several years in camps and prisons, we did not realize at that time how little public opinion was inclined to react to Soviet crimes and misdeeds, and how callously the press, radio, and film industry lied to its readers and listeners about all these cases. Every action that might have been undertaken to stir up this opinion would have been fruitless.

In the embassy, among the people with whom I talked about Ehrlich and Alter, Bernard Singer, a known Polish-Jewish journalist, was particularly shaken. He used to write in Yiddish papers and in *Nasz Przegląd* [Our Review], a well-edited daily in the Polish language, representing the interest of the Jewish population and containing generally good information. Rumor had it that Singer was the best reporter in Poland. I used to meet him before the war. In the fall of 1938, we took part in a government excursion to the "Central Industrial District" (COP), the head of which was the Vice-Premier of Economy, Eugenius Kwiatkowski. The reason I was invited for this excursion was the interest that was created by my book, *Economic Policy of Hitlerite Germany*. For five days we toured various industrial establishments. When having our meals, I always tried to find a place near Singer, who had a great sense of humor and whose conversation was always interesting. He had connections with all the legal and illegal political movements, not excluding communists.

In Kuybyshev, I met my old friend Singer warm-heartedly. Shortly after my presence at the embassy, he received a painful blow: the news came that his son, who served with the Carpathian Brigade,[5] was killed in action in Tobruk. While crying, he read the letter from Jerzy Giedroyc in my presence. Giedroyc served in the same brigade and had been at the scene of the incident. Singer assured me many times that if he could ever manage to get to the West, he would try to create from the Ehrlich and Alter affair a new case similar to that of Sacco and Vanzetti, Italian anarchists

---

[5] The Carpathian Brigade was a military unit under British Command, which consisted of people who managed to escape from German occupation through the Carpathian Mountains via the then neutral Balkan States and joined the Polish Army in the West.

IN THE SHADOW OF KATYN

sentenced to death by the United States courts. When the execution of those verdicts took place, the whole world protested. Singer was so moved by this thought that he constantly dictated to the stenographers articles, even though they did not have a chance of being published. I believe that Kot sent them to our embassy in the United States.

Singer and I became quite close for the next few months after our meeting in Kuybyshev. In August of 1942, we accompanied Ambassador Kot from Kuybyshev to Persia; and then for a few weeks, we lived in the same hotel in Tehrān. Among us he was the most astute critic of Soviet relations, and he was the most successful of any of us in enlightening Kot as to the numerous misdeeds perpetrated by the Soviet system. When I met with Singer in Jerusalem in November 1942, he took me to Wiktor Weintraub, and we went to a small hotel in New Jerusalem that was run by an old Jewish woman from Eastern Poland, who used to boil water in a samovar. She gave us pastry, e.g. bagels, and she would make fish soup on Fridays and chicken soup, Jewish style, on Saturdays. Singer and I stayed there for several weeks. I took great delight in this mode of living as if I were back in Oszmiana or Święciany (small towns near Wilno). Later on, I managed to get a room in the convent of the Dominicans where there was the world famous Papal Biblical Institute, and I lived there for the next few months. At the beginning of 1943, because of Singer's connections in the Jewish Agency, he managed to obtain a car and a guide so we could visit a number of *kibbutzim* in the territories of what was then Palestine. We journeyed with Wiktor Weintraub and Prof. Sukiennicki for almost a whole week. We managed to visit all kinds of *kibbutzim*; some of them were inhabited entirely by communists who displayed many photographs of Trotsky. Singer was still unwavering in his intention to make Ehrlich and Alter's case one of the central themes of his writing and journalistic activities. Shortly after, he succeeded in going to London.

In May 1944, I found myself in London and did not have many occasions to meet with Singer. We moved in different Polish military and political émigré circles, and also in different British circles. It did not attract my attention if anything was written about the case of Ehrlich and Alter in the English or Polish press. I had the general impression that Singer had lost the energy and drive to push this case. I do not know if he made any attempts in this direction. Possibly he was under pressure of his close friend, Isaac Deutscher, a Polish Trotskyite, who immigrated to England before the war, and had a good position among the British press as a contributor to *The Observer*. During the war, Deutscher promoted in the British press the Soviet point of view concerning Eastern Europe. After the war, Singer wrote in a periodical being edited in England in the Polish language under the auspices of the Polish Communist Embassy.

When one day we met again, he asked me to his suite for supper with the condition, however, that I was not to ask any questions connected with the reasons for his transfer to the services of the communist government. He made the impression of a man being gripped by a vise and having his movements restricted. Of his old sense of humor, nothing was left. He was obviously ashamed of the about-face. In this respect, he was different from another friend I met in Kuybyshev, Ksawery Pruszyński, of whom I will write later, who went to the services of the Polish People's Republic with "flying banners", and the conviction that he was doing the right thing.

Today, in the work of Sovietologists and historians, we cannot find much about the case of Ehrlich and Alter. This case became drowned in the deluge of other problems and news.

The mystery of Leon Kozłowski

Before I arrived at the embassy in Kuybyshev, there was another unpleasant happening about which not too much was said; but it intrigued me tremendously then, and still puzzles me even more now. It was the "escape" of Leon Kozłowski in a westerly direction through the frontline when war was being waged. He had been a Professor of Archeology at the University of Lwów and a Chairman of the Council of Ministers of the Polish State. Was it really an "escape", or was he simply seized by the advancing German Army? I do not know. I was told that it was an escape, and his case was presented in this light in a communiqué on German radio.

If it were really an escape, then it was quite an achievement, particularly if one takes into account that he did not know the Russian language. I was also told that the Polish military authorities, functioning as the Polish Army in Russia, had investigated the case and condemned him to death in absentia.

According to another version, he went from the embassy in Kuybyshev to General Anders' Army to enlist as a volunteer. After the war, I was told by Prince Eugeniusz Lubomirski that he had been living with Leon Kozłowski in the same barracks in General Anders' Army before he disappeared from there.

The Russians had earlier deported Kozłowski, apparently from Lwów or from Eastern Central Poland. During the period of 1940-41, there were in the Russian prisons three ex-premiers of the Polish Republic: Leopold Skulski, Aleksander Prystor, and Leon Kozłowski. Prystor, according to the Soviet authorities, died in prison; we could not get any information on the whereabouts of Skulski. After the so-called amnesty, they released only Kozłowski. He stayed for some time at the embassy in Kuybyshev fulfilling various auxiliary functions. Then he reported to the Army.

I did not know Kozłowski personally, but I knew many people who did. All spoke about him as a man of great intelligence and perspicacity, but he was also of unstable disposition and had a disorderly personal lifestyle. He had apparently a great sense of humor and very often would express his political opinions in an amusing way. Several times I heard of his view, expressed in private conversations, that it was necessary to have closer relations with the Germans. He was also far from considering the Northeastern Territories of the reborn Polish Republic as an inseparable part of Poland. Franciszek Ancewicz[6] told me that when several Lithuanian journalists interviewed Kozłowski about his thoughts on the problems of Wilno, Kozłowski answered that it was an internal matter for Lithuanians to discuss and he, as a Pole, did not consider himself authorized to speak on this topic. So, he advised that this question should be directed to the Lithuanian members of the Polish Government, as for example, Marian Kościałkowski, or Aleksander Prystor; they both had held the office of Chairman of the Ministerial Council.

To escape to the German side, at a time when a Polish Army was being put together in Russia by the legal Polish authorities so they could fight the Germans, was undoubtedly an act of treason and should be treated accordingly. On the other hand, in

---

[6] Ancewicz, Franciszek – Lithuanian journalist.

IN THE SHADOW OF KATYN

the case of Kozłowski, it was not an act of political opportunism, but rather of considerable independence of thought and tremendous personal courage. This courage he also showed during the press conference which the Germans set up in Berlin shortly after his "escape". He criticized not only the Soviets but also the Germans, which caused the interruption of this conference. I imagine that in the Soviet prison, he must have gone through a certain process of self-analysis, as I did. What were his thoughts? That remains a mystery, which he most likely took with him to the grave. In Middle-Eastern Europe, there were many people who were tortured by the oscillations of choosing Hitlerite barbarism or the Soviet danger. An example of this is General Mihailovich, ex-Yugoslav war minister, and the leader of the anti-German partisans during the first years of the war, who was executed after the war when the communists came to power in Yugoslavia. These oscillations, which bothered many people in Eastern Europe, found their reflections in the controversial novel by Józef Mackiewicz,[7] *Nie trzeba głośno mówić* (One Should Not Speak Loudly).

While I am writing my memoirs, I should not forget to mention one person out of the very small number of Polish "Germanophiles", whom I met several times in 1943 and 1944: Adolf Bocheński. As a young man, he became a sensation early in the 1930s because he wrote a book about the position of Poland between Germany and Russia. Stanisław Mackiewicz considered this book as the most outstanding analysis of the international situation of Poland since the controversial thesis by Roman Dmowski,[8] and Władysław Studnicki[9] on the same topic, which was put forward even before the First World War. Bocheński had arrived at different conclusions from that of Dmowski. On the basis of cool and exhaustive — you might even say Machiavellian — analysis of all the elements of the situation, he came to the conclusion that the secure development of a reborn Polish State must be based on the mutual confidence of relations with Germany, and it must be friendly. As it seems, toward the end of his life, this book contributed to the basic revision of Dmowski's old views about the situation of Poland between Germany and Russia, as I had concluded from talks with Adam Heydel, who had stayed in personal contact with Dmowski.

Bocheński belonged to the generation which, though born before Polish independence, entered the political arena after Piłsudski's *coup d'état* of May 1926. Bocheński was the main theoretical brain behind the magazines, *Bunt Młodych* (Youth Revolt), and *Polityka* (Politics), which in the thirties exerted a considerable influence in Warsaw mainly because of the organizational talents of Jerzy Giedroyc. Personally, I did not belong to this club because their social conservative ideas were alien to me. However, I was very much attracted to their thesis of creating a flexible Polish foreign policy, and I admired their high intellectual level. There, I acquainted myself with Adolf Bocheński more closely, and quite often he came to see me in Wilno. During the war, Bocheński found himself in Paris where he completed military college in Coetquidan. He took part in the expedition to Narvik and in the battles near Tobruk, and several times he received military distinctions and received the *Virtuti Military*

---

[7] Mackiewicz, Józef – Polish writer.
[8] Dmowski, Roman – His view was that the principal threat to the survival of the Polish Nation lay in German Imperialism, and he looked for protection to Russia. In return for loyalty to the Tsar, he expected wide concessions. He enjoyed the support of Russian Liberals, and in the Duma (parliament) during 1907-1912 was working his way toward demands for Polish autonomy.
[9] Studnicki, Władysław – Polish Germanophile.

KUYBYSHEV

Cross (the highest Polish military decoration) for burning down the enemy's observation tower near Tobruk. This intellectual proved to be an excellent soldier, who was a shining example of personal courage for the whole brigade.

One day, late in the autumn of 1943, the three of us were sitting in a small coffeehouse in Jerusalem: Adolf Bocheński, Włodzimierz Hagemayer, who also served for some time in the Carpathian Brigade, and I. Bocheński started to develop his view on the political situation. Waging further war against Germany did not make political sense to him. At that time, Germany was clearly losing the war; consequently, the much more dangerous threat of the Soviets was increasing. According to Bocheński, the German Army – in spite of all the savagery of Hitler's policy toward the occupied nations – was fulfilling a positive role as a bulwark against the not less savage threat of the Soviets. This conversation took place when the truth about Katyn was already known in the Polish Army in the Near East, which was preparing for the Italian campaign. Hagemayer became irritated by Bocheński's point of view and said, "You know, if that is really what you believe, the solution for you is quite simple. We are not far from the Turkish border, you can easily manage to go there and establish some form of cooperation with the Germans."

Bocheński did not take offense and gave a serious response to Hagemayer's irony, "Your reasoning is quite logical, but, you know, there are those imponderables: regiment, banners, oath. Those are the things which weigh more for me than the political logic."

At that moment, I thought about Kozłowski. After all, he was also an old legionnaire. Piłsudski's legion was one of the most romantic episodes in Polish history. I cannot imagine that for Kozłowski those imponderables would not have played a role. But if they did, what were the arguments that outweighed a soldier's honor?

Shortly after the war, I heard that Kozłowski died during the bombing of Berlin in 1944 or 1945. However, Professor Szawłowski, lecturing in Political Science at the University of Calgary, in Canada, showed me a Polish paper *Życie Warszawy* [Warsaw Life] from the 23rd-24th of June 1974, where in the obituaries an announcement appeared of the death of Leon Kozłowski, which had occurred on the 11th of June of the same year, somewhere in the "foreign lands" with information about the funeral mass in the church of *St. Karol Boromeusz*. His sisters, family, students, and friends signed the obituary. From this announcement, we could not find out where Kozłowski spent his last thirty years, which made his fate even more mysterious.

IN THE SHADOW OF KATYN

The case of Rola-Janicki

The incident, which hampered the function of the embassy as a rescue mission, was the case of Rola-Janicki. He was one of the embassy delegates, who had been organizing care for the released camp dwellers and deportees in one of the far-away provinces of the Soviet Union, somewhere in Siberia. He had come to Russia from England, and he had possession of a diplomatic passport. He was an officer assigned to the Foreign Service, but I do not know if he was a professional or a reserve officer.

In June of 1942, he arrived for some official business in Kuybyshev, and on the same day, wanting to have some luxury, he went to the diplomatic restaurant where he left his briefcase. The local agents of the NKVD examined the contents of the briefcase, and apparently they found incriminating material and perceived him to be working for a foreign intelligence service. I do not know whether it was a purely military or industrial information. Knowing the tactics of the NKVD, they usually provided this sort of material in order to frame whomever they wished. No one in the embassy explained it this way. Nobody accused him of cooperating with the enemy. Everybody with whom I talked, at that time, made it clear that he was acting in a rather very nonchalant manner on some intermediate or direct instructions of the English Intelligence Service, meaning working for a country with whom we, as well as the Soviet Union, were in a military alliance.

The Soviets are very sensitive on the subject of foreign intelligence. Before the war there existed an almost paranoid suspicion of ubiquitous and omnipresent spies. I had come to the conclusion from talks with people accused of spying – of whom I met so many in prisons and camps – three intelligence services were considered particularly dangerous before the war: English, Japanese, and Polish. I myself received a sentence of eight years in GULAG for spying, and the only proof were my articles showing intricate knowledge of the workings of Soviet industry. The guaranteed verdict for spying during the war was the death sentence, but as Rola-Janicki possessed a diplomatic passport, he received an order to leave the Soviet Union within the next twenty-four hours.

Rola-Janicki spent the night before his deportation in the room where I stayed together with Wacław Grubiński, Prof. Stanisław Kościałkowski, and a few others whose names I have forgotten. Opposite my bed was the door, which was always open to the small room where Władysław Broniewski, Bernard Singer, and someone else were sleeping. In the bed to my left slept Wacław Grubiński, who with his Epicurean philosophy, with his friendly attitude to everyone, and with his discreet humor was an ideal companion through thick and thin. To my right was a free bed, where upon this evening a tall gentleman was lying, fully dressed with his nose in the pillow. He did not get up to introduce himself to me, and I do not know if he introduced himself to anyone else. The evening atmosphere was quite gloomy in our room. On the one hand, we were trying to respect the tragedy of that man; on the other hand, there was something very unpleasant in his disinclination to speak to us. I was very much interested to know how much material in that briefcase was authentic and how much was planted by the NKVD. He left our room without a single word. Apparently, he went by himself by train in the direction of the Persian border. Some people had doubts that he would ever

KUYBYSHEV

get there. But I was told that he had been seen in Iraq as a commander of one of our staging posts for the Polish Army on its way from Persia to Syria and Palestine.

The case of Rola-Janicki had tragic consequences, for it gave the Soviet authorities the ammunition to strike at the social services that our embassy had managed to build all over the Soviet Union. Prof. Kot felt extremely dejected and complained about the army. It seemed to me that the case of Rola-Janicki accelerated his removal from the embassy in Kuybyshev, as also the removal of General Wolikowski, chief of the military mission in Kuybyshev. In his place Lt. Col. Tadeusz Rudnicki, ex-chief of staff of the 19th Infantry Division, arrived as a military attaché, whom I previously had met on the day before the battle near Tomaszów Lubelski in the second half of September 1939. Lt. Col. Rudnicki, in the last moment of encirclement of the divisional staff by the Soviet units, managed to change into civilian dress and in this way avoided the lot of those officers in that division who had stayed with their units and today are lying in the Katyn grave.

I do not know all the details of the incidents with Rola-Janicki, or the type of information he was collecting. However, the general circumstances of this case seemed to me quite clear. In 1941, when a team was forming to go together with Prof. Kot from London to the Soviet Union, they looked for suitable people who could perform the function of district delegates of the embassy, and who could organize the care of the many thousands of Polish citizens who had been deported to far away provinces of that huge country. They had to be people in good physical and psychological condition, capable of withstanding difficulties and dangers connected with traveling through huge expanses, where they had to deal with famine, spreading epidemics, and chaotic communications. These kinds of people were only to be found in the army. Therefore, it was decided to transfer a number of officers to the Foreign Service, and they were given diplomatic passports.

It is natural to assume that British Intelligence Services asked them at the same time to perform certain observations about which Ambassador Kot probably knew nothing. There were no malevolent intentions with respect toward the Soviet Union. Good intelligence service was the tradition of the British Empire; it covered not only adversarial countries, but also their allies. It is difficult to plan military operations, not knowing the potential of your allies, even if you are in great sympathy with your partners. The English General Carton de Wiart, who had retired to the Pripyat Marshes in Eastern Poland because of the opportunity to hunt, had suddenly twenty people reporting to him at the outbreak of the war because the British Government had assigned him some official functions. These people were working for British Intelligence in Poland, even though Poland was an allied country and England went to war to defend Poland.

Those that make basic decisions concerning war and peace must have correct information on the potential and possibilities of their partners. This truth was not sufficiently understood by us, Poles. Before the war, many times I heard conversations on the topic that, apparently, neither our government nor the military authorities had any clear idea about the technical and psychological capabilities of France to give us any real help in case of war. In 1937, when I was in Germany collecting information for my book *Polityka Gospodarcza Niemiec Hitlerowskich* (Economic Policy of Hitlerite Germany), I heard the opinions of various leaders of Hitler youth that France

IN THE SHADOW OF KATYN

was not psychologically capable of fighting a war. Apparently, our military attaché in Paris, Col. Błeszyński, was interested more in the history of art than in the French Army. I saw Col. Błeszyński on the 15th of August 1920, at the moment when he conducted a disorganized but successful counter attack against the Bolshevik units on the Wkra River. There, under a hail of bullets, he was magnificent. Col. Błeszyński most certainly belonged to that common type of Legion officer who displayed great virtues on the battlefield, but aside from that, he was more interested in art, literature and philosophy than in the military profession. This romantic style was characteristic of the Piłsudski era.

It seemed to me that in 1939 the basic political decisions of our authorities were taken blindly without understanding those of Great Britain and what her possibilities for giving us effective help were during the first period of the war. Signing a treaty with England was a great achievement which might have facilitated various diplomatic moves in order to prevent the September catastrophe, but it would not help us prevent the catastrophe once the melody of guns had started. In the spring of 1939, Lloyd George delivered a great speech in parliament in which he depicted the military weakness of Poland and that of England in the context of the situation of 1939. From personal contacts, I became convinced that our high-ranking military had not been inclined to take into consideration the analysis of that old, sly fox. I am sure that the British military staff was aware of our military weaknesses, even though Polish society was still in high spirits. Why did we not get a substantial loan for rearmament, or why did we not get equipment? Conversely, we had to supply England with anti-aircraft guns, the production of which I witnessed in the Central Industrial District when I was there with Vice-Premier Kwiatkowski and which could have certainly lengthened our resistance during the September campaign. In the eyes of the British military staff, in case of a German attack, we were condemned even if the Soviet Union had maintained benevolent neutrality. Before the war, we most certainly had intelligence working in Germany and Russia, but we did not bother to get a clear picture of the potential of our allies. The British operated on a different principle; you need to have precise information about your friends as well as about your enemies.

During 1941-42, Great Britain was faced with the problem of sending aid to the Soviet Union. It was important to know how far this help would contribute in weakening the German momentum. The Poles wandering across Russia could have supplied one of the many channels of this intelligence. I do not know whether this case was ever presented to General Sikorski; consequently, Polish military authorities would not have been in a position to refuse this cooperation. We were part of the Allied Army; Great Britain entered the war in defense of Poland, and the British treasury funded the Polish Army.

Ambassador Kot, however, could have exercised his veto, particularly pertaining to his personnel occupied with social welfare. He went to Russia having two purposes: first, to give immediate support to the hundreds of thousands of deported Polish citizens; second, to create an atmosphere of friendship and common trust between the Government of General Sikorski and the Soviet Union. In Poland, no one had been upset when British agents traveled throughout our country. I myself, willingly and openly, had criticized the Polish policy toward ethnic people when Frank Severy, British General Consul in Warsaw, approached me on this subject during his visits to

KUYBYSHEV

Wilno. The Soviets, however, were especially sensitive toward foreigners who were looking for any kind of information, particularly, if they were on the scent of British Intelligence. The Russians traditionally considered the British Empire as their potential enemy. It was necessary to have a strong demarcation line between social welfare and the other functions of our embassy. Prof. Kot, before he left for Russia, should have demanded a solemn oath from those officers who were incorporated as part of his mission, that they would not collect any pure intelligence material under the protection of their diplomatic passports. But, of course, at that moment it was difficult to foresee everything – even if Kot had known Russia somewhat more and had a better idea of the requirements of war from the British point of view.

My contact with the Polish Intelligence Services, conducted by our officers arriving from London, was in August of 1942 – about two months after the incident of Rola-Janicki. Shortly after my arrival at Tehrān – having accompanied Ambassador Kot, mostly by way of the Volga River and Caspian Sea through the port in northern Persia, Pahlavi – I was contacted by a Polish captain, whose name I cannot recall, and was asked if I would like to have a conversation with him. He introduced himself as a chief of the agency of Polish Intelligence attached to the General Staff, directly controlled by London, but not connected with General Anders' Army (which at that moment was in the process of moving through Persia from Russian Central Asia to Iraq). I agreed willingly. I found out that this captain was mainly interested in the state of navigation on the Volga River between its mouth and Kuybyshev. Immediately, I realized the importance of this inquiry; I, myself, was interested in the economic potential of the Soviets and their logistics at this stage of conducting war. One has to remember that it was shortly before the battle of Stalingrad when the Germans were already approaching the Volga River. Unfortunately, I could not give this captain a clear view because I did not have a comparative yardstick: I did not know how this navigation looked before the war. This captain, however, had little interest in my general assessment and my pondering over this subject. He wanted to know how many oil tankers we had seen traveling up the Volga River. I had difficulty here with a definite answer; I had seen the tankers though I had never counted them. I even had difficulty in estimating how many tankers we saw in one day. Obviously, if I had known I was going to be asked about it, I would have been more observant and I would have been able to provide numbers. This conversation made me realize what kind of difficulty Rola-Janicki must have had. He probably had been ordered to collect definite data in some sphere. He must have been making notes and he must have kept them in his briefcase, which unfortunately fell into the hands of the NKVD.

The case of Rola-Janicki brought out the delicate situation of our émigré Government between England and our newly acquired ally – the Soviet Union. As a Commander in Chief, Sikorski, could not refuse to cooperate with British Intelligence in Eastern Europe; as a Prime Minister, sensitive to creating an atmosphere of mutual trust with the Soviet Union, he could – as far as the civilian personnel of the foreign service was concerned – exclude this cooperation. It proves how right President Raczkiewicz had been when he wanted to separate the office of Prime Minister from that of the Commander in Chief; however, Ambassador Kot expressed his indignation about this view during the conversation we had shortly before the case of Rola-Janicki exploded. General Sikorski undoubtedly tried to create an atmosphere of mutual trust with the

Soviet Union, but it was not possible as long as the case of the missing officers had not been solved. The incident with Rola-Janicki created an even more turbid atmosphere.

The case of Rola-Janicki – which in the first instance seemed an insignificant slip – had tragic consequences. In July and August of 1942, several of the embassy outpost employees in various parts of the Soviet Union were arrested; many of them perished in the prisons; most likely, they were shot. Irrefutably, the Soviet authorities had decided to restrict the actions of the Polish outposts anyway, but the case of Rola-Janicki gave them some semblance of justification and an excuse to apply drastic measures.

Ksawery Pruszyński

After my arrival at the embassy, my main source of critical information on the interrelations of military and political Polish exiles was Ksawery Pruszyński. He came to Kuybyshev from London together with Ambassador Kot as an embassy press attaché. He was an advocate of Sikorski and even more so of Kot. But his inborn literary talent and sense of humor made him also see their negative side. His stories were intertwined with anecdotes exposing the small-mindedness of human nature, in sharp contrast with the reality that one was taking part in a great historical drama.

I knew Ksawery for a number of years before the war, as he spent quite some time in Wilno as a regular contributor to the *Słowo* newspaper edited by Mackiewicz. Besides that, I used to meet him at the offices of *Polityka* in Warsaw. He was about ten years younger than I, which meant he belonged to the generation which had not been educated in schools that were run by the occupiers, and had been too young to take part in the fight for independence in 1918-1920. As far as I know, during his university studies he had belonged to the youth supporting power politics, a conservative organization with which I did not have any connections. Stanisław Mackiewicz tried to draw young conservative writing talents to his newspaper; e.g. Bocheński, Zbyszewski, and Pruszyński.

During the Spanish Civil War, Ksawery went to Spain as a correspondent for the Polish Press, and he found himself on the Republican side. His reports, written with great talent, were impregnated with sympathy for the will to fight and the resistance shown by the Spanish left, which had defended itself against the coup of the generals sympathizing with Italian Fascism. These reports had caused amazement among Ksawery's conservative friends in Poland. About that same time he made a journey to Palestine, together with émigrés from Poland, and again he produced a series of reports conveying that same kind of sympathy. These reports were edited later in books that gave him a certain amount of fame. He was considered a young literary talent, one that blossomed in independent Poland. His writings were in demand. Some Czech circles suggested to him that he should write about Czech topics, and in this manner he could enter the Czech literary field.

Ksawery was not drafted to the army in 1939. After the September defeat, he managed somehow to get to the West, completed the military college at Coetquidan in France in 1940, and as an officer cadet, who took part in the expedition to Narvik, was awarded with the military decoration *Krzyż Walecznych*. After the Sikorski-Maisky agreement in 1941, when Kot was assembling the embassy team who had to go to the

KUYBYSHEV

Soviet Union, he was able to obtain Pruszyński for the diplomatic corps. At Kuybyshev, Ksawery made numerous contacts in diplomatic circles and among foreign journalists, and he also attempted to ingratiate himself – as far as that was possible – into the Russian environment. His inclination to romance and the fascination that women held for him helped him accordingly.

The embassy published a paper destined for the army, which under the command of Gen. Anders was being formed in Russian Central Asia, and for the multitude of Polish citizens released under the so-called amnesty from the camps, prisons, and forced settlements in the Soviet Union. The press department of the embassy had a collection of journalists with literary talents that would have been the envy of any newspaper in pre-war Poland. I have already mentioned previously a number of literary men and outstanding journalists, whom I met at the embassy at the beginning of June 1942. At the head of this team was Ksawery because he was the one among the literary men who had come from London and had a diplomatic passport. All the other members of the press section were ex-camp inmates or deportees, whom Kot sheltered in the embassy, giving them employee status.

This accumulation of a large number of people, not formally belonging to the diplomatic corps, on the extra-territorial grounds of the embassy in Kuybyshev irritated the Soviet authorities. Kot, as long as it was possible, ignored Soviet grievances. He even dared to communicate directly – avoiding the formal channels through *Narkomindiel* (Soviet Ministry of Foreign Affairs) – to the local authorities at the place where it was necessary to extract a Polish citizen from the GULAG. Ksawery maintained that if the ambassador had been a professional diplomat, many of the people who owe Kot their lives would not have been saved.

In the summer of 1942, Ksawery became seriously ill with typhus. The day when I arrived at Kuybyshev was the day of crisis for Ksawery. Fortunately, the next day his health started to improve. During his illness, he had been nursed with great sacrifice by his distant cousin, Teresa Lipkowska, the sister of Gen. Sosnkowski's wife, and the daughter of the well-known Polish-Russian activist, Władysław Żukowski, who in pre-Revolutionary St. Petersburg played a considerable role in Russian industry. Teresa, more than anyone else, had become exposed to this illness.

Shortly afterwards, we started our long conversations. Ksawery told me in great detail everything that had been happening in émigré politics during the almost three years I had been in captivity. When Ksawery started to become stronger, we had our chats on the beautiful beach on the opposite side of the Volga River, a little north of the center of Kuybyshev (pre-Revolutionary Samara, whose governor had been the famous Peter Stolypin, undoubtedly the most outstanding statesman at the time of Nicholas II). From the embassy, it was not far to walk to the Volga shore. There we used to hire a boat and it was my assignment to row Ksawery across to the beach. It required some exertion. The boat was quite heavy, built to withstand stormy weather; the width of the river there was about two kilometers; furthermore, one had to row against the current. The Volga is a slow flowing river, and one could not possibly compare it with the swift current of my native Wilia (presently Neris), back home in Wilno. On stormy days when the waves were high, rowing across the Volga reminded me of our excursions to Lake Narocz (a lake in the Wilno district). Ksawery, who came from the Ukraine, was very much impressed by my skill in rowing which I had acquired on the rivers and lakes

IN THE SHADOW OF KATYN

of the Wilno district and in Latvia.

During this excursion, it seemed to me that we represented the differences in temperament and lifestyle of the North and the Southeast of the old Polish-Lithuanian Commonwealth. Both of us were recuperating: Ksawery, after being ill from typhus; and I, after being ill from exhaustion and starvation during the terrible winter in the Soviet camps of the far North during 1941-'42. I had been getting slightly better than starvation meals during the last two months in the camp hospital, before my release. Ksawery, from time to time, still had fever. I was smaller built and probably had a weaker constitution than Ksawery, but the water was my environment. The beach at this time of the year was rather empty, even on Sundays. There, Ksawery sometimes used to meet his acquaintances; for example, the family of the secretary of the Chinese embassy. The secretary, who was married to a Polish woman, had seven children who were all brought up in the Catholic spirit and even had some knowledge of the Polish language. He also met Czechs, with whom Ksawery had a particularly close contact. I even suspect that he was romantically involved in that environment. Generally, there were few Russians.

Three names often came up in our discussions: Sikorski, Kot, and Stanisław Mackiewicz. The lattermost was our common friend even though I was very far from Mackiewicz' conservatism, and politically I was connected with the group of Wilno Democrats, who were editing *Kurier Wileński*. Mackiewicz was fighting the Sikorski Government with the same fervor as he had been fighting the Polish Government circles after the death of Marshal Piłsudski. In Poland, his fight against Śmigły-Rydz (Commander in Chief of the Polish Army) and Składkowski (Prime Minister) had led him to Bereza (Polish political prison); his fight against Sikorski and Kot on emigration caused his expulsion from the National Council, which was a sort of Polish Émigré Parliament. He received a monthly stipend, which sounded rather peculiar because it was called "pension of retired member of the National Council."

Ksawery was generally well disposed toward Sikorski and Kot, but he attached more importance to Stanisław Mackiewicz' opinion than anyone else's. Mackiewicz valued the individuality of Kot more than that of Sikorski, but none of them, according to him, had acquired the political intelligence on a grand scale. Mackiewicz thought the only intelligent person among the Polish leaders was General Kazimierz Sosnkowski; unfortunately, he did not possess the will to act. Ksawery expressed doubt about this characterization. He was convinced that Sikorski had a chance of playing a great historical role, perhaps even greater than that of Marshal Piłsudski, whom Ksawery always had admired as a great individual.

In 1942, on the beaches of the Volga, I learned from Ksawery his philosophy of history. At that time he considered that Sikorski was the right man to be Prime Minister of the émigré government in London, conducting war against the Germans; however, he was not certain if he might be considered a great statesman. Ksawery said that a great statesman is one who individually shapes history, who by his policies can delineate the paths in which the nation is going to venture, even after his death. Bismarck was this kind of statesman in the 19th century, as was doubtlessly Piłsudski, who imposed on reborn Poland the Jagiellonian course; so was Ataturk, who broke with the Imperial tradition and transferred Turkey into a new national state. Ksawery considered that the war created conditions for a basic change in the direction from the one in which the

KUYBYSHEV

Polish national and state expansion had been moving.

The union with Lithuania drew Poland into historical competition between Moscow and Lithuanian Boyars. For four centuries, until the partition of Poland [1795], most of the wars Poland waged were against Moscow or Turkey. Our national insurrections – from Kościuszko to the Piłsudski legions – were directed against Russia. On the western border, considerably less blood was spilled than on our eastern border, but at the same time, systematically throughout the centuries, we were culturally retreating from the West. People in the 19th century who tried to liquidate the Polish-Eastern front – as, for example, Wielopolski[10] – had to lose their popularity. Piłsudski, who was permeated with the tradition of the Lithuanian State, and was a strong individual as well, directed Polish politics onto an historically anti-Moscow track.

The present war had to create a new situation. Poland should come out of it mainly as a Mid-European power to take over the role in Europe which the Germans were fulfilling, possibly also inheriting German ambitions in the Middle East. To develop its active role in the West, Poland must have stabilized and have friendly relations on her eastern border. The historical task of Sikorski would be to create the framework for a future Poland and to give the impetus for Polish activity in this new historical direction. If all that could be achieved, Sikorski would go into history as a great statesman. Instinctively, I compared Kot's theories with those of Ksawery while we were on the beaches of the Volga River. For Kot, the Sikorski-Maisky agreement was mainly the means to save the hundreds of thousands of tormented Polish people in Soviet camps and forced settlements, and without doubt, Kot's logic was more convincing to me. For Ksawery, it was the opening of a new historical epoch. It was a writer's vision in which – in my understanding – not everything held together. Possibly in that different interpretation of the Sikorski-Maisky agreement, there was a reflection of two different mentalities: peasant mentality in Kot and that of a nobleman in Ksawery.

I agreed that after a victorious war the Polish position in Mid-Europe would be considerably strengthened. I also agreed that a future Poland must stabilize its eastern borders. I did not believe that this stabilization could be achieved by some territorial concessions toward Russia; however, the Riga border[11] could be negotiable. I considered that between the Polish and Russian nations there was no ethnographic border and that there should not be any direct border at all. I believed that Byelorussians and Ukrainians must be able to create their own countries in those territories where they were in the majority. I surmised that those countries would be willing in one form or other to tie themselves to some broader Mid-European community, and this would also be the policy of the reconstructed Baltic countries. It was self-understood that if the system were to be stabilized, Poland would have to transfer the ethnographic Ukrainian and Byelorussian territories, whose affiliation to the Polish State was accepted on the basis of the Riga Treaty of 1921. I also could not imagine that some new Mid-European combination could be without participation of a renewed Germany. I imagined that if the war were really victorious, then the political

---

[10] Wielopolski, Alexander (1803-1877), Tsar's Polish Minister during the 1863-64 uprising.

[11] The author refers here to the Treaty of Riga (March 18, 1921) after the victorious Polish War against the Soviets, which divided the borders between Poland and the Soviet Republics, and as a result, Poland acquired a considerable part of Belarus and the Ukraine.

organization of Germany would have to return to the pre-Bismarck tradition, meaning a division of loosely joined countries must occur which earlier had determined the First Reich. I also maintained that Russia and Germany were the facts in our geographical position in which not much could be changed, even if the war became victorious. In my judgment, even in spite of all the Hitlerites' atrocities, the farsighted Polish policy should be the creation of conditions that would open the way for cooperation for generations in Poland and Germany. We mentioned also Władysław Studnicki, for whom we had great respect and with whom Ksawery had been in contact in Kraków just before Ksawery's escape from German occupation. From what I understood, Studnicki was living temporarily in Kraków and stayed, on the basis of old friendship, in the abandoned apartment of Kot. I was convinced that my trend of thought was the same as that of Adolf Bocheński, who was fighting near Tobruk, at that time when we were relaxing on the beach.

Strictly speaking, it was not a discussion but rather loud ruminations under the conditions of relaxation in the midst of the raging storm. We were counter-proposing two different visions of the future, but at the same time we demonstrated quite an understanding of one another's position. I told Ksawery that the opinion that Poland committed a mistake by forming a union with Lithuania and moving on Jagiellonian pathways was not new to me. Some time ago, in the beginning of the twenties, the venerable rector of the University of Wilno, Alfons Parczewski, when asked to take part in some discussions among small groups of students, developed the same theme as a debatable question, for which he, as an historian, could not find an answer. Before the First World War, Parczewski played a key role in the Serbian-Lusatian movement, and it seemed to him that the spontaneous Germanization of Western Slavs was somehow connected with Poland's involvement in the East, as a result of the union with Lithuania.

As far as my personal stand was concerned, I told him that I could understand their arguments, but it could not change my conviction about the basic problems of Eastern Europe. Emotionally, my stand was determined by the specific problems of the geographic region where I was born. I am a child of historical Lithuania, even if my ancestors apparently came from Scotland, and in spite of the fact that my forefathers considered themselves to be 100% Poles. Lithuania and Byelorussia were for me autonomous nations, and I cannot look at them as the objects of some kind of policy of either Poland or Russia. I considered that total independence should be given to these countries and that this guarantee of independence should bring them closer to Poland. I could never agree that Russian Imperialism, irrespective of being Red or White, should ever devour those countries.

In this atmosphere of relaxation Ksawery was also inclined to be very tolerant of those who thought differently. We also debated how the world would have looked today if Poland had accepted Hitlerite propositions of cooperation in his Eastern policy, as some of our mutual friends were inclined to do. The acceptance of those proposals could have posed great dangers for Poland, but they could also have brought very real advantages. Stanisław Mackiewicz fought the then Polish Foreign Minister Beck, not because he apparently conducted pro-German policies, but mainly because he did not try to exploit all the advantages that this policy could have given Poland; therefore, Beck's policy was inconsistent. Ksawery considered that it was essential that the

KUYBYSHEV

Western World understood that Poland had a choice; either join with Germany or risk the September debacle of 1939. Our cooperation might have ensured complete victory for Germany in the East, and we could have taken advantage of this victory; but in our stand of 1939, different values had prevailed. What was essential in Ksawery's thinking was that Poland had not only been the victim of German aggression, but as a proud nation had taken a decisive stand in the crucial moment of history. Ksawery maintained that our propaganda should have been so construed that the Western world would have known what we had sacrificed by rejecting the German proposals and entering on the path of war, which in the first stages had to bring us defeat. One could almost say that we had sacrificed ourselves to save Russia, which certainly was not in the plans of Beck, Marshal Śmigły-Rydz, or Mościcki, all of whom had been responsible for the decision. It was an historical paradox. Both of us were in agreement that if Germany would finally lose in Russia, which at that time was not yet clear, it would be mainly due to our firm stand against the temptations which were suggested to us by Hitlerite leaders.

Ksawery had an artistic mentality: he thought in categories of colorful pictures determining certain entireties, but he had not been inclined to analyze them. He was attracted to great ideas and great myths, which acted on the imagination. He was not inclined to think about Poland as a small country, which on the chessboard of political maneuvering by powerful nations had not played a great role, one way or the other. He was not emotionally anti-German, as in our generation a number of Polish political parties were. But it became clearer that his tendency was to take a pro-Russian stand, and even pro-Soviet, though the Marxist philosophy and phraseology were strange to him, as was the Russian culture, which to a great extent had shaped the atmosphere of my youth.

I pondered over the sources of this emotional attitude. Did Republican Spain charm him? Or was it a reflection of the mood of wartime London, from where he came and about which he told me? Or was it perhaps, to a certain extent, the tradition of Polish conservative landed autocracy, which in the 18th century was already inclined to be more favorable to accommodation with Russia? This last supposition was suggested by his references to Wielopolski. Today, from the perspective of time, it seems to me that Ksawery wanted to follow the footsteps of Beneš, who immediately after the explosion of the Soviet-German war in 1941 started a delicate game of positioning his nation to become a satellite of the Soviet Union. The Soviet-Czechoslovak agreement was to a certain extent a model of the Sikorski-Maisky agreement. In the circles close to Sikorski, discussions were ongoing of the possibility of moving the government or perhaps the high command to Russia, from where it would be closer to Poland and the large base of Polish populations that had been deported to Russia. The declaration of General Sikorski at the National Council that he was indifferent to the fate of the Baltic countries was probably a reflection of these various concepts. Pragier writes about this in his memoirs. I am not saying that to simulate the scheme of Beneš did not have, in the context of the situation during the fall of 1941, any sense; but to accept Beneš' stand was impossible and completely strange to me emotionally as long as the case of the missing officers was not solved. That explains Ksawery's reluctance to accept his own proposal when he was presenting his position.

IN THE SHADOW OF KATYN

We represented two different ideals of a future Poland and the whole of Eastern Europe. Neither of us could deny that Russia represented enormous economical and cultural potential. Ksawery believed that this potential would give support to a future postwar Poland. I, of course, wanted friendship with Russia, but only after the nations suppressed by her would receive freedom and the possibility of forming their own countries. I thought in the framework of ideals that were already in existence in the final stages of the First World War.

The dissimilarity in our upbringing and our psychological outlook caused this paradox. Ksawery was an alumnus of Jesuit schools, and I was of a pre-Revolutionary Russian school and Polish underground conspiratorial circles in that school. Ksawery was not inclined to think in categories of social problems; the disputes of the various interpretations of Marx were strange to him. I came to economy through Marx. The first book on economy that I read, still in high school just before the Russian Revolution, was the Russian translation of Marxian theory by Karl Kautski. I never accepted the Marxist philosophy, but I agreed with Stanisław Brzozowski that Marxist theories had great pragmatic values as a kind of method of interpreting social phenomena, political as well as cultural. In the thirties, I had lots of problems connected with the accusations that I had a bad influence on youth by giving too much space in my lectures on the controversy connected with Marxist theory and problems arising from the Soviet economic policy. Ksawery was then a co-worker of *Słowo*, a conservative Wilno newspaper.

Ksawery did not know Russia, and as far I noticed his Russian was very poor. However, his mastery of the French language was excellent. So, he was more a man of Western culture though his cheekbones protruded, reminiscent of the steppes of the Eastern expanses of the old Polish-Lithuanian Commonwealth. I, in my youth, absorbed a large amount of Russian culture. I was an admirer of Russian poetry and Russian Theater. During the days of the October Revolution – when Lenin was fighting for power in what was known as Petrograd – I was a student at the University of Moscow. I always felt very much at ease in the milieu of Russian intelligentsia, their typical controversies and paradoxes.

In that lazy atmosphere of relaxation, in the hot rays of the sun falling on the beach, memories of my boyhood had returned. But toward Russia, either white or red, I was much more uncompromising than this product of Jesuit schooling, who till the last days of pre-war Poland was considered to be a very talented and dynamic representative of the conservative youth. I was afraid that in Ksawery's attitude there was some subconscious or perhaps half-conscious agreement that in case of a Soviet victory, Poland would play the role of vanguard of Russian expansion into the West, with which I strongly and emotionally disagreed.

We submitted various declarations that we wished to achieve in the future, but the future was still covered in a haze. During those ruminations on the Volga beach, it was difficult to foresee how the war would end. It was the summer of 1942, and it seemed that we were quite far away from its solution. That Germany would be defeated, we considered as a certainty; but how the war was going to end for Russia was not easy to envision.

Not long before the war, I published in *Kurier Wileński*, a Wilno newspaper, several articles comparing the potential of the British Empire and the German Reich. I maintained that if a German-English war were to happen, England would need considerable time to develop its potential, but Germany would finally lose. I was influenced by what Hitler himself wrote in *Mein Kampf*, which I read in 1937, when I stayed in Kiel and wrote my book on the economic policy of Hitlerite Germany. I did not mention how our fate would be affected by such a war. I did not consider that such a war would be in our interest. I considered that obtaining British guarantees for Poland (April 1939) was a great diplomatic achievement for Polish Foreign Minister Beck, and which, at the time, presented a strong trump card in eventual negotiations with Germany in the solution of contestable issues, which were suspended by the Treaty of Non-Aggression in 1934. It seemed to me that this treaty had been signed by Marshal Piłsudski so that we should have time to work out some solutions which would calm the hotheads on both sides of our Western border, not that we should go to war against Germany after the date of expiry (1944) ... for which no one had seriously prepared himself in Poland. In 1939, nobody desired an English-German war, except the Soviet Union – and therefore, somehow, I naïvely believed that war would not happen. When that war actually did break out, it was quite clear to me that the (German) pact with the Soviet Union was tremendously increasing the military potential of Germany. When in 1941, I was already in the GULAG in the Far North and learned that Hitler had attacked Russia, it seemed to me sheer madness. Later, at the end of the same year, news arrived that the United States was also engaged in the war. Then, I did not have the slightest doubt that the military fate of Germany was sealed.

In 1942, it was difficult to foresee how the war was going to end for the Soviet Union, and if the Soviet system would last till the final breakdown of Germany. It is true that Moscow was saved, and that Leningrad was still fighting in spite of the German pressure from the South and the Finns from the North; but at that time we did not know that the participation of the Finns was limited to the territories in which they were immediately interested, and that they refused to participate in an attack on Leningrad. On the other hand, the Germans already occupied many of the most important industrial centers. It seemed to me that the Soviet industrial potential was reduced by at least 50%, and perhaps even more.

At that time, we knew that the Germans were moving in the direction of the Caucasus; that meant toward the main centers of the Russian oil industry. It was quite probable that if the Germans were to conquer the Caucasus, then the main center of the war would be Turkey, Syria, and Persia. England was preparing for that. So for this purpose, Churchill obtained Stalin's approval to move the Polish Army, which was being formed in Russian Central Asia, to the British operational territories in the so-called Middle East. On one of the Sundays before we went to the beach, during the morning mass, celebrated at the embassy by Father Kucharski – where Ksawery normally was the acolyte before he became ill – I saw General Anders and his Chief of Staff, General Szyszko-Bohusz, who both had flown in from somewhere in the Middle East. There was already a visible appearance of the influence of the European Colonial Army on their uniform. At that time, I was very excited because it revived in my memory all the discussions on the subject of the assignment of General Weygand in Syria, which we conducted during our time in Kozelsk, in the year 1940. Then, the hope that we could find ourselves over there seemed to me completely unreal. Now new perspectives were opening to actually achieve that which in 1940 seemed to be

IN THE SHADOW OF KATYN

only dreams. The silhouettes of my Kozelsk comrades in misery revived in my memory and the agonizing thoughts about the mystery of their fate started occupying my mind again.

In 1940, while I was still in Kozelsk, we discussed the concept of Churchill's book about the First World War, which Kombrig Zarubin had lent to Prof. Komarnicki, that the fate of the war would be finally decided in the Middle East and the Balkans. It was said then that it was a favorite strategic idea of Churchill. When at the beginning of 1941, I was being investigated in the Butyrki NKVD center in a small room where the wall was covered with the ordnance map of Yugoslavia, speckled with multi-colored small flags, it came to my mind that the Soviet-German agreement could break down because of matters concerning the Balkans. From the period of my studies in 1937 in Kiel, Hamburg, and Berlin, I knew what a great economic role politicians of the Third Reich attached to the expansion into the Near East. As a pupil of the Russian school, I knew of course about the drive of the Russian Empire toward the "warm seas"; that is, toward the Persian Gulf.

So, I decided that if I were going to be at the disposition of the Polish Government in London – as Ambassador Kot told me – I was going to try to stay in the Near East as long as possible. I wanted to be close to the key territories of the war. This I managed to realize shortly thereafter. At the end of 1942, three ministries of our Government in London: Foreign Affairs, Information, and Congressional Work, decided to create a special Bureau of Studies in the Middle East, and I was appointed Chief of this Bureau with its seat in Jerusalem. I supposed that if Germany conquered the Caucasus, then some Russian troops would have to retreat to this strategic region which the English called the Middle East. I pondered what would be the political consequences of that, and how the NKVD would look as émigrés.

In 1942, the internal situation of the Soviet Union was very difficult. A considerable portion of the population was starving. Hundreds of thousands of people worked in concentration camps as veritable slaves. Almost every Russian family had some representatives there. Weapons were not issued to the military units over the minimum, which was required for training purposes. A few years before the war, Stalin conducted a terrible purge among the officers of higher and middle ranks, and as a result the cream of the Red Army commanders had been murdered. It had to have a negative influence in the workings of the military staff. The NKVD controlled everything with an iron hand. In 1941, after the mass surrender of the units stationed in the Ukraine and Byelorussia, the situation seemed to be again under control, but only in the ethnographic Russian territories. But in case of a major defeat, a breakdown would occur again.

There were two basic unknowns, which made it difficult to evaluate the Soviet perspective. First of all, it was not clear what the political aims of Hitler were; secondly, it was difficult to estimate at the time what the material help toward the Soviet Union from the Anglo-Saxons would be. We did not have enough data to estimate the military strategy of Hitler, but his political strategy looked peculiar. Hitler had two great trumps in the Russian campaign, moral and political. On the one hand he could produce the slogan of liberating the nations oppressed by Russia. He would gain great sympathies in the Ukraine, and it would have generated pro-Hitlerite enthusiasm among the nations of the Crimea, Caucasus, and Russian Central Asia, and also a

KUYBYSHEV

preponderant part of the Moslem world. On the other hand, he could play on Russian patriotism. When in the Soviet camps, I learned from the Soviet press about the loss of Smolensk, I was almost sure that the Germans would set up a Russian Anti-Communist Government there, which would take an active part on the further organization of war. Hitler did not take advantage of these trumps. Did he really come to the conclusion that all Eastern Europeans and Asians were "subhuman", destined to perform slave work for German "supermen"? Overlooking the moral aspect of this case, to take this view as a basis for real politics would be madness, which had to lead to defeat. This paranoiac Hitlerite policy tremendously increased the Soviet chances for survival.

It was difficult to reconnoiter the intentions of the Anglo-Saxons. At the beginning of the war in 1941, Stalin gave some kind of press release which was published in the Soviet papers, and which I read about while staying in the prison camp. He said that the final outcome of the Soviet-German war would depend on the ability of both countries to mobilize their industry. It was a very intelligent presentation of the case. Stalin did not have any doubt that with the NKVD, that infernal engine, he would be able to control the human material; that "starving people" taken in the grip of iron discipline would obediently fight, work, and die. But there was the issue whether this war production would be equal to the tremendous German industrial apparatus, which encompassed almost the entire European continent. The conclusion was that the material help of the Western Allies could decide this issue. There was the question: Would Anglo-Saxons be in a position to give material help to such an extent and were they going to be willing to do so? The Russian intellectuals with whom I spoke while still in the prison camps were skeptical. They considered that it would not be in the English interests that the Soviets should have complete victory, but only that the Russian resistance should exhaust the German forces. They believed, however, in the sincerity of the American attitude.

The Soviet Russians, according to my observations, are more inclined to rational, or even perhaps Machiavellian, calculations in the matters of foreign policy than people in the West – whose attitude is more emotional – and more than the ruling circles in Tsarist Russia who had given in to such motives as honor, keeping one's word, et cetera, which in the Soviet Union were looked upon as feudal antiquities. Therefore, the Soviet moves in foreign policy are easier to predict than grasping the directions of wavering Western diplomacy. Western foreign policy is dependent on public opinion, which in the case of America has the character of periodic hysterical explosions of the most opposite tendencies. The mistake of Soviet Russians is that often they ascribe their cynical way of thinking to Western leaders. Therefore, during the last war, there was this common assumption that the help of the Anglo-Saxons was probably calculated to prolong the war and not to allow a complete Soviet victory, which could bring an end to the capitalist system and that of the British Empire, and also the end of liberal democracy.

In the summer of 1942, there was a considerable amount of talk about the possibility of forming a second front in the West. When in the embassy I read in their records about the Sikorski-Stalin talks, I found Sikorski's declaration that he had submitted a memorandum to Churchill about the necessity of forming a second front in the European continent, to which Stalin had replied, "That's fine." I doubt though whether he believed in the sincerity of Sikorski's attitude. I thought myself that

IN THE SHADOW OF KATYN

General Sikorski must have been sincere there because, according to his concept, the Polish Army was going to fight on the Eastern front under the strategic Soviet command. The concept of moving General Anders' Army under the strategic British command in the Middle East came later and had been generated without General Sikorski's knowledge, even though it required his approbation.

To sum up all those elements, I came to the conclusion that the chances for survival of the Soviet system through all those trials were very slim. I imagined that our intelligence services, as well as that of the English, had the same way of reasoning. In the final analysis, it seemed to me that all this was going to depend on the result of the German operation in the direction of the Caucasus. If the Germans were to conquer Persia, the most important route for American supplies would be cut off, even if the Americans were ready to make a maximum effort to help the Soviet Union. They spoke also about a German push toward Stalingrad – about 500 kilometers southwest of Kuybyshev. Ksawery and I were soon to see the push toward Stalingrad with our own eyes, when we were traveling south on the Volga River through those areas. The German push toward this important industrial and strategic point I understood to be an auxiliary operation in order to secure the Caucasus operation, which was of primary importance. General Anders' Army, which now started moving from Russian Central Asia toward Persia and Iraq, could expect very heavy fighting if Germany, after conquering the Caucasus, were to attack in a southerly direction, that is, through Persia and Turkey.

Ksawery did not share my doubts and was quite a bit more optimistic about the Soviet chances of survival. Maybe because he was more a Western man than I, and therefore he thought more emotionally and maybe to a certain degree was under the influence of Western public opinion, even if generally he had little interest in the Anglo-Saxon world.

The following events confirmed his intuition more than my analysis. A few months later, the outline of German defeat in Stalingrad became apparent, and exactly a year later came the battle near Kursk (July 1943), not less important than the battle of Stalingrad. Many times later on, my thoughts returned to our pondering on the beach, and I tried to find the mistakes that I had made in my suppositions there. It has to be assumed that one of the serious deficiencies of my accounting was that I had not known about the scope of evacuation of the basic military plants to the East. After the war, the book by Voznesensky, one of the architects of this evacuation, was a complete revelation for me. He was later shot by Stalin.

If someone in 1942, in Kuybyshev, had told me that this evacuation was being conducted with great success, I would not have been inclined to believe it. I was too much under the influence of my own article about the Soviet industrial problems – published by the Institute of Eastern Europe in Wilno, in 1934. This article was based mainly on the studies of the First Five-Year Plan (1928-1932); while already the period of the Second Five-Year Plan (1933-1937) brought considerable improvement of the Soviet industrial administration.

I did not take into account that considering the tremendous chaos and disorder – which everybody living in Russia had a chance to observe – there was a sphere of industry where during the rule of Stalin the standard of efficiency was brought to the highest level of precision. This was in the area of armaments production. The Soviets had tremendous reserves of artillery equipment and had many educated tank constructors of whom I had met two when I stayed in Lubyanka Prison. American help, which was on a colossal scale, became fully operational only in 1943, that means, after Stalingrad. This help came mainly through the ports in the Persian Gulf. Americans built special highways for this purpose through Persia. If the Germans had conquered the Caucasus and moved into Persia, this help would have been stopped. So, probably during the beach ruminations, I was correct that the key to the situation was the operation in the Caucasus Mountains. It was characteristic that the American help, with which I oriented myself during my three times' stay in Persia in the years 1942-1944, was on a huge scale, but did not encompass, as I was then told, either tanks, or artillery. It consisted mainly of the means of transporting installations for the oil refineries, food, et cetera; the Soviets had enough tanks, weaponry, and ammunition from their own production and from the huge reserves accumulated during Stalin's three Five-Year Plans. This was known, neither to Ksawery nor to me during our discussions on the beach, but Ksawery was inclined to believe that the Soviets would overcome everything, though I was skeptical.

Together with that difference of appraisal between Ksawery and me, there was also a difference on an emotional level toward Russia. For Ksawery it would have been a new deal, in which the Polish Nation should give up all its ambitions in Eastern Europe and concentrate instead exclusively on the problems of the Western borders. Practically, it meant giving to the Soviets the Eastern territories of reborn Poland and a complete withdrawal of the Polish population from those territories, even though Ksawery was not as plain spoken about it. There was something not clearly said in formulating this political line which – according to him – General Sikorski should have imposed on the Polish Nation. It was rather a strange attitude, if one takes into account that several years before the war Ksawery had a case, which I think led to a duel with the greatly respected leader of the Wilno National Democratic Party, Zwierzyński, when some members of the Nationalist Party expressed doubt of Ksawery's readiness to defend the Polishness of the city of Lwów [Lviv].

I countered to him my old ideal, which I professed during my whole conscious political life: to transfer all of Eastern Europe into a kind of Switzerland, consisting of a series of independent countries loosely connected militarily and economically, with full language and cultural tolerance. It would be, according to me, the only honest solution to the ethnically mixed territories, so numerous in the eastern parts of the Polish Commonwealth. For this reason, during the time of so-called Central Lithuania[12] in 1920-1922, I opposed the incorporation of the Wilno district into the Polish State.

---

[12] Wilno (presently Vilnius) during the upheaval of the First World War and Russian Revolution changed hands many times between Germans, Lithuanians, Poles and Soviets. The Red Army handed over Wilno to the Lithuanians on the 14th of July 1920. After the Polish victory over the Red Army in 1920, Piłsudski organized a fictional mutiny in his Polish Army and ordered a march on Wilno to recover the city and established in Wilno and vicinity a central Lithuanian State. After two years of nominal independence the resultant state of Central Lithuania held elections to determine its future. Its request to be incorporated into the Polish Republic was granted by the Sejm (parliament) in Warsaw in March 1922, and was eventually recognized by the Supreme Allied Council, but the Lithuanian Government in Kaunas never accepted it. The takeover by the Polish Army at Wilno in 1920 created tremendous hostility between Poles and Lithuanians and the idea of splendid cooperation, as during the Jagiellonian period, was dead.

IN THE SHADOW OF KATYN

Russian Imperialism, equally white or red, could not agree to the existence of a number of independent countries in Eastern Europe. But the changing course of war might create conditions to realize that which had seemed to me impossible before. I was very much interested in knowing whether there was anybody in London, either among Englishmen or Poles, who would represent this line of thought, but Ksawery could not tell me very much on this subject.

My ideal was, of course, to return to what we called the Jagiellonian tradition. I considered, however, that in our century the rebirth of this tradition must come on a basis of completely different class structure from what it was in the times of pre-partition of the Polish-Lithuanian Commonwealth. The Union of Krewo[13] and the Union of Lublin[14] were the expression of cooperation between magnates and the nobility of Poland, Lithuania, and Ruthenia. In the twenties, when there were so many discussions on the Federalist plans of Piłsudski, it seemed to me that Eastern Europe should have been organized as a Federation of independent peasant republics for which Lithuania could become a model in many respects, even if Poland and the Ukraine had already developed industrial districts.

To rebuild a traditional Polish-Lithuanian Commonwealth, preserving the traditional social structure seemed to me Utopian. In this sense Stanisław Mackiewicz was Utopian, even if he had great intuition in matters of foreign policy. The republic of magnates and nobility had vanished without return, but the geographic reality of the situation of nations in the pass between the Baltic Sea and the Carpathian Mountains had not changed. These nations were exposed to the rapacious waves of invaders, which struck from the great eastern plains. The Union of Poland, Lithuania, and Ruthenia was an attempt to organize a common defense against those predatory waves. The Cossack wars were a distortion of this union of defense, because they were class wars. In the period after the First World War, I believed that the repetition of the situation of the 17th century could be possible only after all these peasant republics conducted a policy of more or less radical land reform as Lithuania and Latvia did. The environment where I developed those ideas was in the *Wilno Klub Włóczęgów* (a political club), to which meetings Ksawery sometimes came as a guest.

At the beginning of the thirties, I started changing my vision of the defense of Eastern Europe. It was the period of the Great Depression in the capitalist world; agricultural countries were suffering in particular because of the artificial price fixing by agreeing cartels. Then I started thinking of the problems of industrialization of this part of Eastern Europe, which was free of Kremlin rule. There was no question of attracting larger foreign capital because those transactions were made by the intervention of either German or Austrian banks. The tariff war with Germany was a

---

[13] On August 14, 1385, at Krewo in White Ruthenia, an agreement was signed between Polish barons and Jogaila (Jagiełło), Grand Duke of Lithuania. Jogaila agreed to convert to the Roman Catholic faith together with the whole of Lithuania in return for the hand of Jadwiga, the Hungarian princess and heiress to the Polish Crown. Thus, the Kingdom of Poland and the Grand Duchy of Lithuania joined in a personal union.

[14] The last king of the Jagiellonian Dynasty, Sigismund August, realized that he would leave no heir and thus there would be no king to unify the two countries of Poland and Lithuania. He called an assembly of Polish nobles and Lithuanian princes at Lublin in 1569, to draft a constitution that would further strengthen the union of these two countries. They decided to call this new creation the Republic of Poland-Lithuania, which would be jointly governed by an elected king.

factor that limited the possibilities of foreign investment in Poland. When that tariff war ended, the Great World Depression took shape. It was clear to me that the industrialization should come as a result of public investments, which eventually would have to be supported by the German investment industry. For that reason, I started studying the economic policy of the Third Reich.

At that time, in the Soviet Union there was starvation and a morally repulsive atmosphere of forced collectivization, but simultaneously they were building a basis for industrial development. I started studying Soviet industrial policy even before studying German economic policy. In my understanding, the Soviet experiment was of tremendous importance to every economist, and it must have led to a revision of a number of generally accepted dogmas of the classical school. But the experimental application of certain suitably reformed Soviet models did not mean, in my understanding, acceptance of Soviet political leadership, not to mention Soviet philosophy.

In the middle of the thirties, I had a common interest in Soviet economic models with the youth group led by Henryk Dembiński and Stefan Jędrychowski. I dissociated myself from this group when they changed toward accepting Soviet political leadership. Dembiński, however, personally never accepted Soviet philosophy. Ksawery was then quite clearly on the other side of the barricade. Now, Ksawery showed a disposition to accept Soviet political leadership without taking any interest in the great historical input of the Russian Revolution, and its blueprints for the quick industrial development of the economically underdeveloped countries. Nor did he show any interest in Marxist philosophy.

The discussions on the Volga beach were for me some sort of ideological and political retreat when I was at the threshold of a new stage of life as a free man. When the war ended two years later, we both remained faithful to our declarations on the Volga beach. Ksawery joined the diplomatic corps of the Polish People's Republic and he became ambassador in the Netherlands. Apparently, his dream was to become ambassador to the Vatican, after the then expected signing of the Concordat with the Vatican. After the war, I became an intellectual rover taking various posts for more than twenty years at the universities of London, Manchester, for UNESCO in Indonesia, and at a university in Canada and in the United States.

The history of Ksawery is an interesting psychological problem. I never suspected that opportunism played any important role for him. He moved under some sort of impulse, whose character was not quite clear to me. The analysis of this psychological process would require a longer article similar to a well-known book by Miłosz about the ways through which a young Polish intellectual in the forties arrived at accepting communism. Miłosz' heroes eventually reached the point of accepting Marxist philosophy. I doubt that Ksawery had come to this. His way was different. It was the path of a youth who started writing for a conservative camp and was attached to its traditional concepts, but gradually, he began to recognize Russian leadership as some sort of historical necessity. He was already on this path when we discussed the historical directions of Poland on the Volga beach.

I do not believe that Ksawery ever accepted Marxist philosophy. I suspect that if he had understood the character of this philosophy, then he would probably not have given his talents to the service of this communist country. Marxism is a very valuable

IN THE SHADOW OF KATYN

method when it comes to the analysis of social relations typical to a certain historical era. But it is of no use when one has to explain political and cultural tendencies, which last through the centuries. It is not easy to explain similarities in the categories of class war existing between the policies of Ivan III, Peter I, and Catherine II, and the Tsarist ministers of the 19th century on the one hand and Stalin on the other. Marxist analysis is particularly of no use when one is trying to encompass the whole history of human civilization as was done by Arnold Toynbee, whom in my later wanderings I happened to meet several times. After finishing his eleven volumes, Toynbee came to the conclusion that the history of humanity is mainly the history of great religions.

Marxist thinking is nonhistoric, as there was nonhistoric thinking among the 19th century classical economists from whom Marx borrowed so much. Ksawery was thinking in images which represented great historical truths; as in the charming short story about the trumpet player in the market square in Samarkand in which he expressed the belief that the freedom of the Moslem nations of Central Asia and the freedom of Poland are closely connected.

Two months after our discussions on the Volga beach, I parted with Ksawery in Tehrān when he flew to London, and I – in agreement with the plan already conceived in Kuybyshev – stayed for the moment in the Near East. Just before D-day Ksawery went back to the army as a press officer. At the very beginning of the fight of the armored division, when he met the column of tanks, he managed to convince some corporal to give up his place in the tank. The tank struck a mine, and Ksawery spent the rest of the war in some continental hospital. I did not meet him before he left for Poland. We managed to contact each other shortly before the car accident in which he lost his life. Some time after, via his brother, I received his letter, written just before his accident, in which Ksawery wrote that on his visit to Poland, he would try to solve the problem that caused me great anxiety.

As to the mystery of the Polish officers in Kozelsk and Starobelsk, Ksawery obviously knew about my description of where, geographically speaking, the Kozelsk officers had been deported, in 1940. But this description did not contain any indication of what finally happened to those officers. It became more meaningful when the revelations of the German radio pointed exactly to the same place. The German revelation came exactly nine months after our discussions on the beach. Ksawery was then in England and I in Jerusalem. During the period June-August 1942, when we saw each other several times daily, I was under the impression from his sayings and reactions that intuitively he was more pessimistic about the fate of our officers than I was.

Once more his hunch proved to be more accurate than my analysis. It is interesting to note that it did not diminish his attitude toward a pro-Soviet orientation.

Chapter VI

JOURNEY TO TEHRĀN

In July of 1942, it became known that Kot, after functioning less than a year as ambassador, was going to leave his position and that the Polish Government was going to appoint a new ambassador. I did not know the exact circumstances for this decision, but after a few weeks of observing the work of the embassy, it became clear to me that Kot was not happy in his position and the Soviet Government considered him unsuitable. Kot, as I said earlier, went to Russia in the early fall of 1941 with two basic objectives. First, to save tens of thousands of people who were suffering and dying in prisons, camps, and Soviet forced settlements, among them many representatives of the Polish intellectual elite. Second, to create conditions of common trust and cooperation between Poland and the Soviet Union.

The Sikorski-Maisky[1] agreement had opened many possibilities. In the districts of the Soviet Union where there were large accumulations of deported Polish citizens, the embassy representatives established outposts, which were supplied with food and clothes, mainly from American donations. At the main railway junctions where the released Polish citizens arrived from the GULAG, recruiting officers were posted who directed people to the locations of the Polish Army. The outposts tried to organize medical, cultural, and religious care, and they also issued Polish passports.

The greatest achievement of the embassy was that it organized a central file of Polish people spread out throughout the Soviet Union. They tried to extract information of the whereabouts of other Polish citizens from the people who came to those outposts and the Army. Through these efforts, in a period of half a year during 1941-1942, they established a whole filing system consisting of many thousands of names including the news of many people who, in spite of the Sikorski-Maisky agreement, were still kept in prisons and camps. In this way, Polish martyrdom was documented during the Second World War. I was told that later on in 1943, when the Soviet Union broke diplomatic relations with the Polish Government, Ambassador Romer managed to take this file with him to the Middle East and deposited it with the Red Cross.

In the buildings of the embassy outposts, priests often said mass. Crowds of people used to gather around these outposts listening to the choral singing inside, astounded by this most unusual display of freedom, in a Stalinist country, allowed to the recently released prisoners and "enemies of the people." News about the priests spread throughout the districts, and there were many cases where Greek-Orthodox peasants traveled tens of kilometers to have their children baptized. During the period when the battle of Moscow was being fought in 1941, Poles behind the frontline organized themselves into a close-knit community, independently of Soviet administration.

According to *Listy z Rosji* (Letters from Russia), published by Ambassador Kot, the Polish Embassy succeeded in establishing 807 institutions with 2,639 employees,

---

[1] On July 30, 1941 an agreement was signed in London between the premier of the Polish Government in exile, Gen. Władysław Sikorski, and Soviet ambassador to London, Ivan Maisky. Diplomatic relations were established between the Polish Government in exile and the USSR. The USSR stated its readiness to form a Polish Army in Russia, to grant amnesty to all Polish internees and to annul the provisions of the Nazi-Soviet Pact regarding Poland.

IN THE SHADOW OF KATYN

giving support to close to 300,000 Polish citizens by February of 1943. It was something unheard of in the Stalinist system, and it obviously irritated the local administration and caused various misunderstandings. One should assume that the provincial authorities complained and gave alarming reports to the Central Government. The case became even more complicated when it was discovered that some of the workers of the embassy were collecting information for British Intelligence. This irritation reflected itself in the attitude toward the Polish Ambassador, who, from the Soviet point of view, was accountable for what was happening in the centers where Polish ex-prisoners and deportees were being gathered.

Ambassador Kot was psychologically unsuited for negotiating with the dignitaries of Stalinist Russia. He did not understand the specific mentality of the Soviet leaders, or of Russians in general, and he did not speak the Russian language. He emphasized his peasant origin all the time, which did not go well with Stalinists leaders. In the eyes of the Soviet Communists, a peasant who had managed to obtain university professorship in Poland must have come from a *Kulak* (a well to do peasant) family, and they had the worst reputation in the Soviet Union. The Polish Peasant Party (to which Kot belonged) in the understanding of communist ideologues was a party of *Kulaks*. During the First Five-Year Plan, Stalin waged war against the rich peasants, which found expression in the policy of forced collectivization. The resistance of peasants to this policy had been broken by methods of extreme cruelty comparable only to the cruelty of Nazis toward the Jewish population. About ten million people lost their lives in one way or another in this greatest social revolution in the history of the world, which took place in the years 1929-1932.

It is interesting that some of the Polish peasant leaders in exile believed that the Polish Peasant Party would become a pro-Russian party in the future Poland. It was a mental conundrum, which later on found its expression in a thesis that, after all, it would be easier for Stalin to exert his influence on Poland through the Polish Peasant Party with millions of peasant supporters, than through the very unpopular Polish Communist Party in which the peasant masses had no confidence. In my understanding, it was one of these ideas that guided Stanisław Mikołajczyk, ex-Prime Minister of the Polish Émigré Government, in his journeys to Moscow in 1944 and 1945.

Kot, whom I met several times in London during that period, apparently supported the policy of Mikołajczyk. He could not put forward any reasonable arguments to defend this policy, except meaningless assurances that everything would be all right. Later on, he became ambassador of the Polish People's Republic in Rome. Did that mean that after staying almost one year in the Soviet Union, he did not grasp the basic directions of Soviet policy? It seems to me that he did this because of loyalty and party discipline. Kot was extremely attached to the Polish Peasant Party. He held various high positions, but it is my impression that he had limited influence on the policies of the party. Afterwards, when he chose freedom and once more became an émigré and spent lots of time in the British Museum, I met with him several times, but we never mentioned those things that divided us immediately after the war.

Another topic of these conversational encounters with which Kot tried to impress his listeners was to emphasize his dedication to democracy. He stated that the times of Piłsudski's dictatorship and his followers had ended, and now the Polish

JOURNEY TO TEHRĀN

Government consisted of true democrats. The Soviet system was a dictatorship of a small, but well-disciplined, group of people who held in their hands a huge apparatus of terror and coercion. The Soviets feel tremendous contempt for all Western liberals and democrats, not excluding those who declare themselves as special friends of the Soviet Union. When Sir Stafford Cripps warned the Soviet Union of the impending German attack, no one took him seriously. However, shortly before, in a closed circle of Hitler's associates, Ribbentrop had gone into ecstasy stating how easy it had been for him to come to an understanding with the Soviet Communists[2] [*"Als ob ich mich unter alten Parteigenossen befunden hätte, mein Führer!"* ("As if I found myself among old party members, my Fuhrer!")]. The best demonstration of the Soviet attitude toward the ideals of Western democracies in Stalin's time was the case of Ehrlich and Alter, described before. Under those conditions, it was difficult to imagine that the Polish ambassador could touch anyone's heart in the Soviet Union by his adherence to democracy and freedom.

Ambassador Kot maintained that he was not a professional diplomat. One could infer from this that General Sikorski had sent his close friend Kot to Russia as an ambassador to indicate a special relationship of friendship between the Polish and Soviet Governments. His actions explained why Kot sometimes abandoned protocol, particularly in the cases of seeking lost Polish citizens and extracting them from labor camps. This attitude irritated the Soviet authorities. The Soviet representatives held receptions for foreign diplomats. In Kuybyshev, there was a diplomatic restaurant where entrance was restricted to only the staff of foreign embassies, and a certain number of selected Soviet dignitaries. One could eat well there and economically. Vodka and caviar were dished out without any limits. I went there several times on various occasions. But at the same time, the Soviet authorities looked rather unfavorably on the mixing of their Foreign Service with the staff of the foreign embassies. Therefore, grounds for the display of friendship with the Soviets were rather limited

I assume that General Sikorski and Kot had decided beforehand that they were going to try to manifest a special warmhearted and friendly attitude toward the Soviet Union. When I was in the Middle East several months later, I was told that when General Sikorski passed through those Middle Eastern countries in 1941, he released several consular employees suspected of being connected with the Promethean movement; that is, the movement of the Caucasus and Middle Asia nations who were being kept enslaved by Russia. In London, at the Polish National Council, he pronounced that the fate of the Baltic countries was of no interest to him. Those were obviously ingratiating moves toward Russian Imperialism. I think, however, that it induced suspicion rather than respect in Russian circles. Later on, when the case of collecting intelligence information by some of the workers of the Polish institutions became known – for which Ambassador Kot could not be responsible – the Soviets concluded that they were justified in their suspicions.

On the other hand, the tendency of Sikorski and Kot to try to develop a friendly attitude with the Soviet leaders was quite understandable. Irrespective of how the war was going to end, the reality of the present situation was that the Soviets were holding

---

[2] Speer, Albert – *Erinnerungen,* Propyläen Verlag, Berlin, 1970, p.183.

close to one million Polish citizens as hostages. Sikorski intended to build the Polish Army outside the borders of the occupied country in order to play a more important role in the final conclusions of the war. The Soviets had in their camps, prisons, and forced settlements enough Polish human resources to realize this plan. Besides, the shortest route for this proposed army to cross the Polish border had to lead through Soviet territory. Politically, it would have been more desirable for this proposed army to attack through the Balkans and Romania, but in 1941 this idea could not be officially promoted if only for tactical reasons. So, if Polish soldiers would have to fight against Germans side by side with the Soviet Army, one would need to create an atmosphere of détente. Whoever would lead the Polish Government would have to look for cooperation with the Soviet Union. Therefore, people like Ksawery Pruszyński, who seemed to sincerely believe in the future of a new epoch of Polish-Russian relations, were very useful for Polish diplomacy during that period. Ksawery's straightforward manners gave confidence, and what he said in journalist circles was undoubtedly reported on the various levels of *Narkomindiel* (Soviet Ministry of Foreign Affairs). So, I think that the choice of Ksawery Pruszyński as a Polish press attaché in Kuybyshev was a proper move from the point of view of the task which Sikorski and Kot were trying to accomplish.

The case of the missing officers, however, made it impossible for further Polish-Soviet rapprochement. Even if Kot had been psychologically more adept at communication with Soviet dignitaries and in creating an atmosphere of common trust, it was impossible as long as the fate of the officers from Kozelsk, Starobelsk, and Ostashkov remained a mystery. Ambassador Kot's duty was to remind the Soviets that he was waiting for their release according to the Sikorski-Maisky agreement. The people he approached about this, even if they had the best intentions, were not in a position to fulfill his desires because these officers were already dead. So, they gave all kinds of evasive answers, thereby creating an atmosphere of common suspicion. The Polish Army's General Staff in the Soviet Union had sent its people to various corners of Russia to look for traces of the missing officers. Our recruiting officers on the railway junctions had also been given definite tasks. All kinds of rumors as to the possible fate of the lost officers started circulating. I am convinced that some of them were even suggested by NKVD agents intent on misinformation. None of them was in agreement with what I had reported to General Wolikowski. The case of Rola-Janicki and other alleged cases of collecting intelligence information for the British were very convenient for the Soviets because they gave the Soviets the opportunity for counter accusations.

Ambassador Kot experienced great difficulties in his position regarding the task he was trying to accomplish. He had high blood pressure and often suffered from severe attacks of migraine. In order to maintain channels of communication with the Soviet Union and to save the institutions of social care which were left there after the departure of General Anders' Army, it was obvious that the only solution for the Polish Government in London was to send an experienced, professional diplomat as ambassador who would adhere to strict protocol, and who would not twist anyone's arm about his personal, political and social ideology. Any fraternization with the Soviets was very difficult as long as the mystery of Kozelsk, Ostashkov, and Starobelsk had not been solved. The Sikorski Government tried to remedy this situation by appointing

JOURNEY TO TEHRĀN

Tadeusz Romer, our ex-ambassador to Tokyo. According to what I later heard from the embassy functionaries, Romer performed his duties with tact, and managed to get the respect and even some kind of sympathy from the Soviets.

Several days before his departure, Kot went to see Vyshinsky. This farewell visit was apparently very courteous. As usual, Kot took an interpreter who recorded minutes. I think that this time legal advisor Mniszek, a professional civil servant of the Polish Ministry of Foreign Affairs, went with him. I never read the minutes, but I was told several times that during this conversation my name was mentioned. Apparently, there is a custom that when the departing ambassador makes a request, as a rule, it is not refused. Kot requested that he be allowed to take Ehrlich and Alter with him. Vyshinsky answered that unfortunately that was impossible. He was probably right as most likely at that time Ehrlich and Alter were no longer alive. Then Kot asked the Soviet authorities if they would allow me to accompany him to Persia. Vyshinsky answered that this might be possible, but he could not guarantee it, and advised that I should make an application for the required exit visa to the proper authorities in Kuybyshev.

From the point of view of Soviet law, my formal situation after my release from the GULAG was as follows: I was a Polish citizen residing in the Soviet Union and employed by the Polish Embassy; I had a Polish passport, which gave me certain diplomatic rights, but I was not protected by diplomatic immunity. In order to leave the territory of the Soviet Union, I had to receive an exit visa from the proper Soviet authorities, which they could grant or refuse. So, immediately I made an application to the militia. I was told to come back a few days later. When I reported back, they told me to come the next day. When I came the next day, they told me again to come the next day and so it went on and on. Finally, the day of departure arrived. In the morning I reported myself to the militia; they told me that the exit visa was not ready yet and advised me to come in the afternoon. I told them that my ship was sailing in the afternoon. Finally, they set a time for me to come about three-quarters of an hour before the departure of the ship. It occurred to me that they were trying to hold me in order to make me miss the ship. I went back to the embassy. The ambassador and those accompanying him were already leaving for the river port. I made an agreement with the chauffeur of the embassy that after delivering the ambassador, he should return immediately without waiting for the *chargé d'affaires* and take me to the militia headquarters, and from there to the river port so that I would be in time for the ship's departure.

After the departure of the ambassador, something happened which I cannot psychologically explain, particularly if one takes into account that by nature I am a nervous man and rather prone to insomnia. I stretched out on a couch and immediately fell asleep like a baby. I awoke after half an hour feeling full of vigor and quite refreshed. It was about three o'clock in the afternoon. They told me a car was waiting for me. They held me at the militia for another half-hour, manipulating something with my passport. Finally, they gave me my visa a quarter of an hour before the ship's departure. I told the chauffeur to speed to the river port with top speed without paying any attention to speed limits or any other signals. I was trembling, afraid that some kind of militia might stop us, even if the car did have a diplomatic flag. We reached the river port, and someone told me that the ship was actually moving away. I showed the

IN THE SHADOW OF KATYN

officer of the NKVD my visa, and he saluted me politely, and I ran with full force through some kind of a garden which was attached to the river port and was surrounded by a pavilion for honored guests. There were plenty of people around, some Soviet dignitaries, plenty of NKVD men in their splendid uniforms and shining leather boots, members of the diplomatic corps, and foreign military *attachés* in the uniforms of their armies. The NKVD functionaries alongside of whom I was running were standing to attention and saluted. It all looked like an *opéra bouffe* in those crucial moments of my war history. The ship, with its engines already in motion, was slowly moving away from the quay and the stevedores were in the process of pulling the gangplank... I ran onto it. There was a space between the gangplank and the deck of the ship of about three-quarters of a meter. I jumped with my suitcase straight onto Ksawery who was standing by the edge of the deck entrance, and he grabbed my left side, afraid I might lose my balance, and a sailor steadied me from the right.

After a while I recovered my composure, and we went for a walk on the upper deck where Ambassador Kot was standing, waving his hat to the Soviet dignitaries and other members of the diplomatic corps who had escorted him. I joined the ambassador's circle, took off my hat, which I had received from the stores of Otto Pehr in Kirov, and started waving. To my mind came the words of a poem written by my favorite poet, Lermontov, which he wrote when Nicholas I ordered him sent to the army operating in the Caucasus (as punishment for another rhyme he wrote on the death of Pushkin):

> Farewell unwashed Russia!
> Country of slaves, country of masters.
> And you, blue uniforms,
> And you, folk obedient to them.

We were sailing south toward the shores of the Caucasus. The NKVD men, who a while ago had been so smartly saluting me, had blue emblems on their uniforms and blue rims on their caps as the Tsarist Gendarmerie used to have, which I remembered from my boyhood years in pre-Revolutionary Russia. In Moscow during the month of March of 1917, a few days after the abdication of the emperor, my high school girlfriend (whose father was a colonel of the gendarmerie attached to the emperor's headquarters in Mogilev) said to me, "I am rejoicing that in our family there will be no more blue color." She was extremely attached to her father.

For the second time in my life, I had the feeling I was leaving behind my stay in this world of gloomy paradox into which Russia had transformed itself. That first time was in Orsha in September of 1918, when I was crossing the border between Lenin's country and the zone of German occupation. Now it is true that we were still in the Soviet Union, but I had the exit visa in my pocket, and it seemed to me quite improbable that they could drag me away from the ambassador's circle, to whom they had waved farewell with pomp a few minutes earlier. The fate of Ehrlich and Alter haunted our minds. As far as I know, neither of the two had an exit visa, even though one of them had been nominated as a member of the National Council in London. So I felt safe, if one could call oneself safe while still in Stalin's country. A great consolation for me was the thought that my family then remained outside the reach of

JOURNEY TO TEHRĀN

the NKVD.

Ksawery stood in the same group on the upper deck, looking very elegant with a red rose on his lapel. I was sure that this red color did not express his attachment to the revolutionary ideas, but was designated rather privately by someone who had said a fond farewell to him. It was his emotional and romantic style. The expression on his face was extremely serious. When the ship had moved to the middle of the river and the contours of the river port started to disappear, Ksawery said with a quiet, assertive voice, "Let's go down."

When we went down near the passengers' cabins, Ksawery stopped and hugged me, while tears started falling down his cheeks. He told me, "I went through several hours of dreadful anxiety, for I was sure that they would never let you out of Russia." Indeed, when the ambassador with his escorts was standing on the upper deck making courteous bows to the people sending him off, Ksawery was standing together with the sailors who were going to lift the gangplank and was waiting, hoping that at the last moment I would appear. It seemed to me that he then stopped the sailors from moving the gangplank when he saw me running through the garden attached to the river port. I was overwhelmed with gratitude for his concern and friendship. At the same time, I realized that on one of the most dramatic days of my life, I had stayed exceptionally composed.

The ship was sailing full speed ahead. The emotions connected with the haste of jumping onto the ship were so stimulating and the satisfaction of achievement so great that during the first hour, I did not take any interest in where I should stay and take my small suitcase. I asked Ksawery about it. He told me that a cabin was ready for me opposite his cabin, and he sent me to the first class deck. The ship was still a pre-Revolutionary one, as most of the passenger ships were, which at that time plied the Volga River. In spite of this fact, there was ideal cleanliness; everything was shining. On one of the well-varnished doors of one of the single cabins, my name was printed on a card in Russian with my professor's title. I understood the NKVD game: because they had promised Ambassador Kot, they had accepted me as a person close to the ambassador's circle on his journey to Persia, and they prepared an elegant cabin for me, yet at the same time they did everything possible to keep me from sailing.

The circle in whose company Ambassador Kot left the Soviet Union was rather varied. Besides Ksawery, who had diplomatic status, the persons accompanying Kot were Bernard Singer, Roman Fajans, and Dr. Julian Maliniak. Maliniak was a very tactful and intelligent functionary, who had been an activist in the Polish Socialist Party in Western Poland, and who had been an ambassadorial delegate in Novosibirsk for some time. He was an older gentleman (in age, closer to Kot than to Ksawery and myself). There was also Mrs. Teresa Lipkowska, whom I mentioned before. She was going to be a secretary and cryptographer to the ambassador. All of them had received their exit visas in the proper time; that is, a few days before the departure of the ship. It underscored even more the game the NKVD conducted in my case. This circle of people signified the concern Ambassador Kot must have had about extracting from the Soviet Union Polish intelligentsia with literary capabilities.

There were two other workers belonging to the embassy that I thought originally came from London. One was the ambassador's personal valet, and the other was the caretaker of the embassy, who had come to the embassy together with the diplomatic

IN THE SHADOW OF KATYN

team. It seemed to me that both of them were conducting money speculations, but they were not the only ones. Both those gentlemen, whose names I do not remember, fulfilled a very important function because they were guarding several bags of diplomatic mail, which had to be watched carefully day and night. They also managed our food supplies, which had been brought with us from the warehouse of the embassy for this rather large team. We were in a situation where the length of the journey was difficult to estimate because of the raging war, more so since we were going to pass the zone on the Volga where the front was close. One had to remember that there was a famine in Russia, and one could not rely on food in the ship's restaurant.

When I got up the next day and went on deck, I was overwhelmed by the charms of nature on the banks of the Volga River at this time of the year. The ship was traveling at full speed in the middle of this huge river. It was a warm but not a sweltering morning. On the nearby meadows, they were cutting and collecting hay. The light wind was bringing the intoxicating scent of herbs that had been cut together with the grass. I understood the bliss of traveling on the Volga, of which I had heard in my school years in pre-Revolutionary Russia.

The source of the Volga comes from the lakes in the Valday uplands, in the western part of Russia near Ostashkov. Between 1939-1940, near one of those lakes, they had held about 6,000 police officers and NCOs from the border corps. It is one of the vanished camps of the prisoners of war, about whose fate various unchecked rumors were circulating. More or less one hundred kilometers to the southwest, there is a place called Velikiye Luki, the site where one of the victorious battles of Stefan Batory[3] was waged against Ivan the Terrible at the end of the 16th century. The Volga, in the upper regions, has a mostly easterly direction with a few deviations, first north and then southeast. Near Kazan – capital of the old Tartar country conquered by Ivan the Terrible – it definitely starts going south. Below Kazan it accepts large masses of water from its left tributary, the Kama River, and from there the river widens itself immensely. Near Kuybyshev, it makes a large loop to avoid the Zheguli Hills and starts flowing in a southwesterly direction all the way to Stalingrad (old Tsarycyn, and present Volgograd). Stalingrad is the most western point in the lower part of the Volga River, and is therefore of strategic importance for any army that attacks from the West and is trying to cut communications between the Caucasus and Central Russia.

We were sailing now in a southwesterly direction, coming closer to the areas engaged in warfare. We stopped in larger river ports picking up new passengers and there was some loading and unloading of goods, even if basically it was not a cargo ship. We watched the stevedores, who when loading heavy objects requiring team effort – for example, engines – accompanied it with a characteristic chant. Those were the famous Volga songs and, in pre-Revolutionary Russia, a whole literature existed on those tunes. Nowhere did I see loading cranes; everything happened by the strength of muscles and the melody in some way helped to produce a coordinated effort. Several times we encountered barges pulled by groups of men walking on the shore, so-called *burlaks* (barge haulers), who also chanted in their characteristic way. This was the traditional Russian way of transporting goods on the Volga, which still existed in the epoch of the steam engine and the diesel. Whether, in the condition of the Stalinist regime, they were so-called "free" people or prisoners from the GULAG, nobody could

---

[3] Batory, Stefan – the prince of Transylvania, Polish King from 1576 to 1586.

JOURNEY TO TEHRĀN

explain. After all, I was too careful to ask questions like that.

The largest river port on the way to Stalingrad was Saratov. Here the Caucasus oil brought by tankers on the Volga River was loaded into railway containers and from there distributed throughout. If the Germans could cut the navigation below Saratov, the Soviet Union would have serious difficulties obtaining oil supplies, even though at that time the Soviet Union already had different sources of oil, still its exploration was in the initial stages. Among others, some were in the Far North, in the Republic of Komi, where the Soviet Union had a great concentration of forced labor camps, and where I had been imprisoned for thirteen months.

Saratov was built on the site of an old Tartar settlement. In the 18th century, Catherine II imported German colonists who had a considerable influence in developing this region. After the Communist Revolution, the Volga Germans were given certain rights of cultural autonomy. They even created a special university where the member of the Central Committee of the German Communist Party, about whom I've written earlier on and who was my comrade in misery in Butyrki prison, had been a lecturer. Part of Saratov, on the left side of the Volga River, was made into a separate town and this town was named Engels; it was the capital of this republic. After Hitler attacked the Soviet Union, a considerable portion (perhaps the majority) of the population of this republic was sent to forced labor camps and forced settlements. In the camps, in the Republic of Komi, in the winter of 1941-42, I met a number of former inhabitants of that German republic, but most of them were deported to someplace in Siberia. Looking at the shores, I thought about some Germans from those areas who worked with me in the same brigade in the GULAG camp half a year ago.

The passengers whom we collected at various river ports were mostly military personnel going to the front, which was not too far from Stalingrad. On the top decks were mostly officers and on the lower decks mostly privates. Officers had with them food rations, which they gave to the cook in the restaurant, who made dinners and suppers for them. The second day after leaving Kuybyshev, Ksawery, after obtaining permission from the proper authorities, organized a lecture for the Soviet officers about the cruelty of the German occupation policy. The lecture, which was given in the crowded ship's restaurant, was very much appreciated. Ksawery spoke with a strong foreign accent and, besides, made a lot of grammatical mistakes. This did not make it more difficult but rather facilitated his contact with the audience. Every foreigner who could speak Russian well was suspected of being a spy. One, who could be assumed to have learned Russian simply because of his diplomatic post, aroused sympathy and confidence.

At one of the river ports, between Saratov and Stalingrad, a work battalion consisting exclusively of Polish citizens embarked on the lower deck. They were about a hundred strong – pressed together like sardines in a can. I went to the lower deck to try to find out something from them. They were young boys, mostly below the age of twenty, in military tunics; they said they received the same food rations as soldiers in the regular units. Those with whom I talked were of Polish nationality and spoke Polish among themselves. Before I managed to collect more information from them, they received the order to disembark at the next river port. They were a surprise to me, as I had not heard before of Polish work battalions being attached to the Soviet Army and that those battalions were being used on the Stalingrad front. It was still another way,

IN THE SHADOW OF KATYN

besides the deportation to camps and forced settlements, of extracting Polish citizens from the territories that had been occupied by the Soviets in the years of 1939-41. How many of them perished by performing various jobs during the battle of Stalingrad – that probably no one will ever know.

We arrived at Stalingrad on the third day of our journey just before sunset. All military personnel disembarked and there was considerably more room on the ship. We were told that the ship was going to stay here for several hours. We were also told that the town was often bombed by the enemy air force, consequently we were definitely forbidden to turn on any lights after sunset, and we were advised not to go on shore. Singer, however, could not restrain himself. His reporter's instinct prevailed, and he wanted to see what the town looked like just before the expected attack. I tried to talk him out of this escapade, maintaining that under the conditions of siege, which as far as I understood had already been formally declared, he could be arrested and it would be so easy to sink into the NKVD abyss. In spite of that he went. He returned after about two hours when it was already completely dark without any great revealing news. According to him everything seemed normal, and he did not notice any symptoms of panic. Our ship stayed in port for the entire night. The expected air attack did not materialize, but throughout the night we could hear artillery sounding like the thunder from an incoming storm from the West. On the basis of my experience from the First World War when, as a schoolboy, I listened near the Dvina River to the sounds of the approaching frontline, I would estimate the distance was between thirty and forty kilometers; that meant, the artillery fire was approximately near the Don River, which at this latitude comes very close to the Volga River.

We left Stalingrad at sunrise. Here, the Volga makes an almost ninety-degree turn from southwest to southeast. We sailed toward Astrakhan and the Caspian Sea. On the ship there was a more relaxed atmosphere, since the military men had gone. The cooks paid more attention to our needs, obviously using our provisions, and receiving food from our supplies as gratuity. We had left the Stalingrad tension behind us; again there was a waft of new-mown hay with the refreshing winds from the steppes.

During this journey on the Volga River, I spent quite a lot of time with Kot. I came to know him better, this man whose individuality considerably influenced Polish policy during the Second World War. Kot was not in good physical or psychological form. He was suffering from insomnia. In the evening, he used to ask Ksawery, Singer, and me to his cabin, and we used to talk till late into the night.

Before the war, I had already heard a considerable amount about him, mostly from those professors and docents who were connected with the Jagiellonian University. I knew that he was an outstanding researcher on the Reformation in Poland, and organizer of the so-called Brest (a town in Poland) protest. This was a protest by a number of Polish intellectuals against the brutal treatment of several politicians arrested and imprisoned who were accused of inciting the movement to abolish by force the then existing government. Among the arrested were several outstanding personalities; one of them, Wincenty Witos, ex-Prime Minister of the Government of National Unity in 1920, who during the days of the Bolshevik invasion received the highest decoration that the Polish Government could bestow, *Orzel Bialy* (The White Eagle). This protest had wide reverberations in the whole country, and particularly at the universities.

A few years before the war, Adam Heydel, Prof. of Economics at the

JOURNEY TO TEHRĀN

Jagiellonian University, told me in great detail about this protest in which he and Kot took an active part. At the beginning of the thirties, the Polish Government pushed for a change in academic legislation through the Sejm (Polish Parliament), which would permit the Minister of Education to remove from the university budget, the positions of Kot, Heydel, and a few other members of the Brest protest from other academic circles. That again caused unrest at the Polish universities. Many of the university professors who, like myself, were adherents of Marshal Piłsudski, were going through some internal soul searching. Kot impressed me as a great political individual, but he represented a different political picture from the one I more or less automatically belonged to throughout my past.

Therefore, direct contact with Kot awakened in me reflections on the controversy in the period between the two World Wars. He proved to be, however, a different individual from the one I had imagined. He was not much interested in the basic problems of the country's raison d'être, and in its ideological and philosophical justification of political programs. He took great interest in people, and he was a gregarious person. It was not his inclination to deduce the general type of a person in a cultural setting as, for example, in the works of Werner Sombart or Max Weber. But he was interested in real people with their virtues, vices, and passions. Therefore, he liked to collect gossip and spread it. He had a passion for meeting new people. I found this out in Tehrān and Jerusalem where he used to invite various individuals – unknown to him – and had long conversations with them.

During the evening talks in Kot's cabin, which we also continued in Baku, the greatest source of information about people and the relations among them was Singer, who knew more people than any one of us. Singer could even talk about the virtues and vices of some representatives of the Roman Catholic clergy. It appeared to me that Kot contributed as an historian, not by trying to discover general trends, but by shedding light on the character and role of individual people who were forming the history of Polish culture. We both belonged to the academic world; we had many common friends and acquaintances, so naturally we had much to say to each other.

Kot was interested in knowing about the role of freemasons in Wilno in the period after Poland received independence. I told him everything that I thought I knew and was trying to guess, adding that I considered the group of Wilno Freemasons, led by Witold Abramowicz (as it was generally assumed), as the most decent, sensible, and trustworthy team in the land of the former Grand Duchy of Lithuania. I also told him that personally, I had taken part in some actions conducted by that group, even if I considered myself to be a practicing Catholic. Then I added also that it seemed to me that the composition of Polish Freemasonry Lodges had been thoroughly decoded by the NKVD. Col. Wacław Koc, with whom I shared the same cell in Butyrki Prison in Moscow after I received my verdict, told me that during the investigation after he had admitted various anti-Communist aspects of his activities, they countered that he was hiding his membership in Freemasonry. Upon which Col. Koc answered that he was only asked about membership in organizations of political character, while masonry was mainly a cultural organization. The tribunal judged Koc, and he received the death sentence, which was commuted to ten years of forced labor.

The second surprise for me was that Kot did not have much interest in foreign policy, even if the so-called Front Morges, with which he had been connected before the

IN THE SHADOW OF KATYN

war, based a considerable amount of its opposition to the rule of Marshal Piłsudski and his followers on foreign policy. Front Morges (S. Stroński, W. Sikorski, and I. Paderewski) tried to maintain the post-Versailles power structure, in which Poland would be a kind of French satellite. Marshal Piłsudski tended to a certain amount of flexibility in foreign policy; he tried to talk directly to the Germans, maintaining at the same time our military alliance with France. Could he have succeeded if he had lived? No one is able to ascertain this. Stanisław Mackiewicz wrote about the possibility of the Paris-Berlin-Warsaw axis. After the death of the Marshal, Beck conducted a rather inflexible policy, based on the assumption that Poland was a major power capable of defending its own interests. In reality it was a policy of bluff. As an economist who was studying the economies of Russia and Germany, I had full realization of how incredibly weak we were in comparison with our big neighbors. Now, in the present circumstances, as an Émigré Government, we became an English satellite. I was interested in knowing whether we would have any influence on postwar plans, particularly as it was suggested that I had to go to London to the Ministry of Congressional Work. That was the Ministry preparing work for the Peace Conference. In my opinion we were interested in England maintaining its traditional policy of balance of power on the European Continent. My curiosity wanted to know how the elements directing the Émigré Government perceived this situation.

Kot, however, was not inclined to pay attention to this topic. He was mainly interested in Polish internal affairs and those groups that were fighting for influence, equally in the Polish Home Army as in the émigré circles. I learned considerably about the intensive political life, which sprouted in the country in spite of the occupiers. These were the things that I had not heard any news about during those years when I was in the prison and labor camps of the Soviet Union. The thing that was interesting psychologically was that we did not touch on the military situation and possible results of the battle, the echoes of which we heard in the port of Stalingrad. We did not have enough information to produce any complete judgment about what was going on in the relatively close by theater of war. We were not conscious of the fact that we were approaching the momentous days of history on which the fate of Russia, Europe, and Poland depended. On this ship, which was sailing on the middle of the Volga, we were reminiscing about minor events and people of the not so distant past.

In this rather escapist mood, we sailed into the delta of the Volga River. One could assume that the delta of the Volga River starts in Stalingrad, because there it begins running into parallel riverbeds. About thirty kilometers before Astrakhan, mostly from its eastern side, it fans out into a number of streams for about a hundred kilometers and runs into the Caspian Sea. From the ship, it looked like a vast amount of water whose banks could not be detected with the naked eye, but there were numerous islands.

The refreshing gusts of the warm July wind, after leaving Stalingrad, had caressed our lungs; now in the delta, we were overwhelmed with a terrible nauseous stench which penetrated through everything. I suddenly remembered a joke, told in the GULAG, that the Soviet Union is like a ship on the high seas, "it nauseates you and there is nowhere to run." This stench was coming from the world famous factories producing caviar. The Volga delta is the main center of this production. During the process, the entrails of the fish are thrown out and they rot in the scorching sun of the

JOURNEY TO TEHRĀN

south, poisoning everything around with its odor. Among those stinking vapors, we entered the port of Astrakhan.

Once upon a time, Astrakhan was the capital of a separate Tartar country whose ruler was Khan of Astrakhan. Ivan the Terrible, after liquidating "The Empire of Kazan," conquered this country. The conquest of Astrakhan finalized the process of conquest of the Volga by Moscow. This process had two main stages. In the first stage Ivan III conquered the Upper Volga down to the mouth of the Oka River, which was conquered in the fifteenth century in his war against the merchant Republic of Novgorod. Novgorod was a member of the Hanseatic League and its merchant empire stretched over the whole part of European Russia. This process would probably have been stopped if the Jagiellons (Polish-Lithuanian kings) had given Novgorod the necessary military help. The second stage was in the sixteenth century when Ivan the Terrible conquered Kazan and Astrakhan, and in this way subjugated the middle and lower part of the Volga River. Ivan the Terrible was losing in the fight with the Polish-Lithuanian-Ruthenian Commonwealth led at that time by the Hungarian genius, Stefan Batory; however, Ivan had great military successes in liquidating the remainder of the Tartar Empire.

Many times in my childhood and during the First World War, I heard very popular songs of charming melodies which express, it seems to me, all the contradictions of the Russian soul, and at the same time were a reflection of the artistic genius of that nation. One starts with the words:

> "Volga, Volga mother, who gave us birth
> Volga, oh, you Russian river."

The Russian character of this river is rather relative. Even now, non-Russian and non-Slavonic nations and tribes inhabit her banks. In the Upper and Middle Volga since time immemorial all kinds of Ugro-Finnish nations inhabited the area, including Mordvinians, Cheremisians, and Chuvashians. Below Gorki, where I started my journey on the Volga, in the middle and lower part of the river, among the natives there were still many Tartars, Kalmuks, and Bashkirc. After the Second World War, Stalin resettled the Kalmuks and partly liquidated them. The rebellion of Stenka Razin, who in the second half of the 17th century subjugated the whole Volga River from Astrakhan to Samara (Kuybyshev), and of Emelian Pugachov, in whose old cell I was kept in the Butyrki Prison, had the character of an insurrection of colonial people fighting against the exploiting imperial power.

The first great attempt to colonize the banks of the Volga was achieved by Ivan III, who deported almost all the inhabitants of the capital of Great Novgorod to the vicinity of the mouth of the Oka River. In this manner they created a town, Nizhni Novgorod (Lower Novgorod). The name was changed during Stalin's time to Gorki. Therefore, Ivan III started this basic method of building the Russian Empire, which was based on destroying centers of civilization in the West and transferring the conquered population to virgin territories in the East. Great Novgorod had been more civilized and better developed economically than Moscow in the 15th century, and had all the attributes of becoming a Northern Venice. Of all the rulers of Russia who deported people to the Eastern territories, none did this on as massive a scale as Stalin.

IN THE SHADOW OF KATYN

Colonization on a larger scale of the Middle and Lower Volga did not start until Catherine II. After the rebellion of Pugachov, she imported a number of German settlers into the region of Saratov and she transferred to the Volga some people from the Eastern Ukraine. Also a military settlement was started with the settlements of the Astrakhan Cossacks. Cossacks around Astrakhan, as well as near Don and Kuban, were free people (that means, they were free from villein service); they received land and limited self-government in exchange for performing military duty in special Cossack regiments.

In Astrakhan, the governor was usually an Ataman (Cossack chief) of the local Cossack forces. During the revolution of 1905, General Grąbczewski was Ataman there, a Pole in the service of Russia who was a great traveler and cartographer and performed great services in the establishment of Russian rule in Middle Asia. At one time, he went to Emperor Nicholas II with the request that for his great services to the Russian Empire, he wished to buy back the estate that had been confiscated from his family during the Polish national insurrections. His request was refused. Grąbczewski survived the Bolshevik Revolution and spent his old age in Poland. Several years before the war, I read his memoirs with great interest.

In Astrakhan, we were supposed to transfer from a flat bottom river ship to a seagoing vessel. The town itself did not make a pleasant impression on us. The odors, though not as intensive as in the Volga delta, seemed to have penetrated all the walls of this town. We were placed in an unattractive hotel, and we were told that the next day a ship would go to Baku. Taking advantage of the fact that we were on firm ground and that we had access to the post office, we wrote a number of letters and postcards to those remaining at the embassy, and also to our friends, which so many of us had in the Soviet Union.

The next day when we arrived at the port, we found a rather dense crowd standing opposite a shabby looking ship. We were told to join this crowd. Opposite us there was a sort of platform on which an NKVD man appeared after approximately half an hour, and started to read the names of the people that were allowed to go aboard. When somebody's name was mentioned, he was to raise his hand. The crowd we had joined was not much different from the GULAG dwellers being moved from one camp to the next. I watched from the side how the ambassador of the Majestic Polish Republic, at the sound of his name, raised his hand by stretching two fingers, as if for the oath. I wondered whether pushing us into this crowd was the result of instructions from the higher authorities or just an ordinary display of boorishness by the local administration. In light of what I learned in the following few weeks, I am inclined to think that it was a conscious effort to show how little respect the Soviet Union had for the Émigré Polish Government in London.

Astrakhan is not situated immediately by the Caspian Sea, but on the banks of the Volga delta, which is still the lower part of the river. It is difficult to see where the river ends and the open sea begins because the delta is so wide that one hardly descries the shore. There, the Caspian Sea is very shallow and our ship sailed into a narrow canal, set off on both sides by tall poles. Our cabins were uncomfortable and stuffy. Though there was some sort of restaurant, we ate in a special cabin, probably the crew's dining room, where between the narrow table and narrow benches we felt sqeezed in when we sat down to eat our supper, which the cook had prepared for us from our

JOURNEY TO TEHRĀN

supply of canned food.

After about thirty-six hours, we passed Derbent at sunrise. It is one of the two main towns of Dagestan – an eastern province of the Caucasus, existing as an autonomous republic with the capital in Makhach Kala, and belonging to the Russian Federal Republic. Obviously this autonomy is fiction. In my young years as a student, I read a considerable amount of prose and poetry about the beauty of the Dagestan valley. These valleys had formed a trail through which the Russians used to invade the Caucasus since Tsar Peter I. The population of Dagestan consisted of many highland tribes, mostly speaking in all kinds of Turkmen dialects. They are of the Islamic faith, and they hate the Russians with all their hearts, particularly the Bolshevik kind. Their patriotic ideal is union with Turkey. From the time when Russia started penetrating the Caucasus, there were guerrilla fights, which in the middle of the 19th century transferred themselves into regular war, particularly when the Caucasus religious leader Shamyl called upon all the Moslem world to start a holy war against Russia. Immediately after the Revolution, Soviet historiographers represented Shamil as an exceptional leader in the fight for the freedom of the Caucasus. During the Stalin years, he was described as an English and Turkish agent because he emigrated to Syria.

In the fights to conquer the Caucasus, a number of Poles distinguished themselves serving in the Russian Army, among them Zygmunt Sierakowski, who was on the way to an exceptional career in the Russian General Staff, when in 1863, he took charge of the insurrection in Lithuania. After the insurrection had failed, he was publicly hanged in Łukiski Square in Wilno. Such is the paradox of Polish fate.

Stalinist Russia was slowly liquidating those Caucasus tribes, filling the GULAG with them – as I mentioned before. They were not necessarily pleasant comrades in misery; they were eager to pick a fight, especially Chechens. Once, in the GULAG, I had a rather difficult confrontation with them, when I stood by a Russian with whom I shared a bunk and whom they wanted to harm. Poles and Ukrainians thrown into the jungles of the GULAG, or forced settlements in Asian Russia, often had to cosy up to Russians, and therefore became an assimilation factor. It is another example of the paradox of Polish fate.

The first impression of Baku was unexpectedly pleasing. I thought it would be like the Polish oil town of Borysław (presently in the Ukraine) which I happened to visit on one of the scorching June days in 1929. In Baku, at least in the part of the town where we were placed, in contrast to Borysław, one could not smell the oil. In spite of the hot July day, pleasant gusts of wind brought not only the scent of the sea, but also the scent of the desert on the other side of the Caspian Sea. The streets were wide and planted with shady trees. Everywhere one could feel the influence of Persia. On the street, we saw many eastern, sharp, and delicately shaped faces, so different from the crude Slavic-Mongolian features, which were prevalent in Russia. It created an appealing atmosphere. We were on the outskirts of this part of the East, which I had always wanted to see.

We stayed in a rather magnificent, newly built hotel of Intourist (Soviet Travel Agency). There were some problems with the bathrooms: in some of them the water would not come from the taps, and in the others where the water would come out, it went straight to the floor, soaking our feet. This was the usual result of Soviet buildings in those days, about which there was plenty of information in the back pages of the

IN THE SHADOW OF KATYN

Soviet papers after mentioning all the great achievements on the front page. They told us that no ships were expected to go to Pahlavi in Persia in the next few days, which was our final destination port in the Caspian Sea. They also told us that during our stay in this hotel, we could order caviar and vodka without limits, and that our hotel would supply us with tickets to the theater and concerts.

I do not remember exactly how long we stayed in this hotel. It seems to me about one week. Ambassador Kot tried to communicate with the embassy in Kuybyshev or Tehrān, but the long distance telephone connections strangely did not work, and he received no replies to his telegrams. Only at the end of our stay in Baku did the idea come to us that they were keeping us "interned" under luxurious conditions. We could not understand what was behind this strange behavior of our Soviet host. Again we resumed our long evening discussions to which Ksawery, Singer, and I were invited.

In the meantime, we took advantage of the conveniences and privileges that were given to us. I went with Ksawery for swims in the Caspian Sea. Because the sea was quite shallow, we had to walk on a long and rather wide wooden pier. After a quarter of a kilometer, we would manage to reach a place where we could buy a ticket and receive a key for a locker. By descending wide steps we reached the water, which came to our waist. A number of people would come to spend the scorching July days near the water while sitting on the benches on both sides of the pier.

Once, my attention was drawn to a young woman of typical eastern beauty with a small child of about two years on her knees. The child with big black eyes had exceptionally noble features. I slowed my pace, looking at the object of my admiration. I said to Ksawery, "What a magnificent model for a painter or amateur photographer." The woman, when she noticed my gazing at the child quickly threw her scarf over the child and screamed in Russian at me, "I beg you, don't look, don't look!" She tried to cover her face as well. I understood. She obviously thought we were Russians. The eye of Russians on them, occupiers who conquered this country, was a bad omen, which brings ill fortune. They believed an eye like that could cast a spell over a child. So, in the belief of their folklore there is a reflection of Russian colonialism whether red or white.

In Baku, I experienced one of the strongest musical sensations in my life. Baku has a "Palace of Music," which consists of terraces descending to the Caspian Sea. On those terraces there are wide platforms for concerts under the open sky. We were informed that the Russian pianist, who before the war received the first prize in the Chopin International Competition in Warsaw, was going to perform on one of the terraces in the Palace of Music. Ksawery and I applied for the tickets. It was an unforgettable experience. In the town, a blackout was ordered. Three hundred kilometers north, near Groznyj, on the northern outskirts of the Caucasus Mountains they were fighting. It was a warm, calm night. The moon was rising. On the grand piano only two candles shed light on the music. I do not belong to the group of people who were educated in music. I do not have innate artistic abilities for music, nor for painting. I am rather tone deaf. The piano and violin lessons I had started in my childhood were interrupted by the outbreak of the First World War. In spite of all that, music overwhelms me; it transfers me into a different world, and it stimulates my imagination and mental faculties. On this particular night, I felt all the charms of the

JOURNEY TO TEHRĀN

old romantic era, so far removed from everything that is the brutal Soviet reality.

The terrace on which this concert was given was not a large one. It could accommodate only a few hundred people. It is characteristic that among the public I saw hardly any Armenian or Tartar faces, even though the Azerbaijani Tartars and Armenians are the mainstay of the population in this part of the Caucasus. I saw only Russians around me. There were many officers, mostly of higher ranks and mostly in the company of cultured women. They all seemed to be under the spell of this concert. When I looked at the faces of these people in the moonlight, I automatically remembered the cultural circles of pre-Revolutionary Russia among whom the best part of my childhood was spent.

At the moment when I am writing these words, I remember another Chopin concert, also in a colonial setting. It took place in Singapore when it was still a British colony. The intellectual cream of the British administration was also present there, but the percentage of Malayans, Chinese, and Indians was much higher than the percentage of natives at the concert in Baku. In spite of the separation from the natives in the colonies, British Imperialism attracted conquered nations to the spiritual and artistic values of western civilization more than Russian Imperialism, which destroyed local spiritual values and at the same time barred its colonies from western culture.

The day after the concert, we went with Ksawery and Singer to visit the local museum where there were many exhibits illustrating the history and ethnography of Azerbaijan, as also the development of Baku as a great industrial center. A young, intelligent museum guide, who had finished historical studies, conducted us through the museum. Full of life and with a good sense of humor she answered our questions. She was very good-looking. I contemplated on her ethnic background. She did not look Russian and she definitely was not a Tartar or Georgian, nor was she the descendent of some Caucasus mountaineer tribe. She was of middle height, a brunette, her light complexion not blemished by the rays of the southern sun, her figure attractive, and her dark eyes sparkled with intelligence and humor. In Europe, she could pass as being from the south of France; in Kraków or in Lwów, she would be considered Hungarian. So, I decided that she most likely was Armenian. The Armenian Republic, with the capital, Yerevan, borders on the western part of the Azerbaijani Republic. Armenians have a higher percentage of intelligentsia than any other nationality in the Soviet Union except for the Jewish population. In the middle ranks of Soviet economic administration one can find many Armenian engineers, managers, organizers of technical research, and so on. We came to the conclusion that the best exhibit of the museum was our cicerone. We posed various questions so we could prolong our conversation. Shaking her hands when we said goodbye, I asked, "Are you Armenian?" I wanted to add that we, in Poland, also have an autonomous organized Armenian Society.

She replied, "My roots are the same as yours." Apparently, she was the granddaughter (or perhaps the great-granddaughter) of some participant of the Polish Insurrection, who after doing his time was sent to settle somewhere in the Russian Empire.

One evening, they announced that the next day a ship would be sailing to Pahlavi, a Persian port on the south side of the Caspian Sea. The journey would take twenty-four hours. The ship was very small and similar to the one in which we sailed

IN THE SHADOW OF KATYN

from Astrakhan. In the cabins it was extremely sultry. I happened to sleep on the upper bunk, but do not remember anymore who slept on the bottom. I thought that in this stifling atmosphere I would not be able to fall asleep, so I went on deck. It was a bright night, full of stars, and the sea was calm; the ship was going full speed ahead plowing the waves with ease. I settled rather comfortably on the coiled ropes. Not far away on another coil of ropes two people were sitting, and they spoke in a language not known to me; it could have been Azerbaijani, Persian, Armenian, or perhaps even Georgian – the mother language of Stalin. I listened to the sounds of the words that were strange to me, and to the sound of the waves hitting the side of the ship. I fell asleep on those ropes in a sitting position. When I awoke it was already dawn, and on the horizon I could see the banks of Persia. In the light of the daybreak, the contours of the port of Pahlavi appeared. Rising from the East, the orange sphere of the sun was throwing its rays on the town as we approached the port. The ship dropped anchor and rested two hundred meters from the landing stage. They lowered a boat, and another boat approached the ship. Some were quarreling and haggling with others. We could see with the naked eye what was happening in the harbor. Among the assembled people over there, we could see two military men in tropical outfit, and someone suggested that it could be Polish officers who had come from Tehrān to meet the ambassador.

After about two hours, we moored alongside the quay. Persian longshoremen started unloading the ship. Those from our team who did not have diplomatic passports were directed to Customs. Everywhere there was order and cleanliness; everywhere the portraits of the young Shah were displayed. Since 1941, Persia was under common English-Soviet occupation. The occupiers compelled Shah Reza of Pahlavi to abdicate in favor of his handsome young son, who had a European education. Shah Reza was one of the most distinguished rulers in our times. He started his career as a noncommissioned officer in the regiment of Persian Cossacks led by Russian instructors. In 1917, he became the leader of the movement to fight for removal of Russian influence in Northern Persia. He soon achieved high rank in the military, and then he became Minister of Defense and Prime Minister. In 1921, after the abdication of Shah Zia ad-Din, the last member of the dynasty which ruled Persia since the 17th century, Reza was pronounced Shah by parliament, and he started the new dynasty under the name of Pahlavi. Between the two wars, he ruled the country with an iron fist bringing order to the administration and holding the rebellious mountaineer tribes in line. He was trying to develop his country based on German investment and therefore he was considered to be pro-German. The occupation of Persia was a military necessity to secure American supplies for the Soviet Union, which were going through the Gulf of Persia to the Soviet border. The Russians were occupying Northern Persia and mainly Persian Azerbaijan, which bordered Russian Azerbaijan. The British were occupying the South. Tehrān was jointly occupied by the Soviet and English forces.

In Pahlavi, they were disembarking military transports of General Anders' Army, which were moving from the Soviet zone in Central Asia to come under the British command in the Middle East. Those transports were going mainly by sea from Krasnovodsk, a port in Turkmenistan on the eastern shores of the Caspian Sea. Together with this army, about 25,000 military families were evacuated from Russia. Obviously, the notion of military family was understood widely, because the Polish authorities were trying to extract from the Soviet Union all Poles who managed to get to

JOURNEY TO TEHRĀN

the area where the Polish Army was concentrating. In Pahlavi there was even a temporary transit camp from which non-military – those who had been attached to the Polish Army and were not able to perform military service – were transferred to large camps near Tehrān. From there they were trying to transfer them to the British colonies in India and Eastern Africa. Mainly, they were women with children and older people. In 1940-41, the Soviet Union deported tens of thousands of whole families from Eastern Poland, not excluding eighty-year-old family members. As a matter of rule the head of the family was sent to a concentration camp, mostly in the Far North; but women, children, and old people were thrown on the so-called forced settlements in Kazakhstan, where many of them (probably the majority) were dying from typhoid and starvation. They had deported particularly the wives and children of Polish officers and noncommissioned officers, whose husbands and fathers were in German prison camps and in the Polish Army under Allied Command. The deportees, who had managed to survive in Kazakhstan till the end of 1941, were trying to move south to the areas where the Polish Army was concentrated. Kazakhstan was closer to the Polish Army location than other areas in the Soviet Union. For example, an old woman, maybe from Nowogródek or Łuck, who during her life had never moved outside her village was unexpectedly grabbed by the NKVD as a member of a military family, because her son happened to be an NCO in the Polish Army and had become a prisoner of war in Germany. Therefore, she was thrown into a forced settlement in Kazakhstan. If she was lucky, she then managed to get to the Polish Army in Uzbekistan, from where she was transported to Persia, and then she had to journey to Kenya or Tanzania, names she had never heard of in her life. The Near and Middle East suddenly became the area where the Polish language was resounding.

When we as so-called "previous Soviet prisoners" – who were accompanying the ambassador on his journey – were settling our formalities with the Persian authorities in Pahlavi, Kot and Ksawery went to visit the temporary transit camp. After finishing the formalities and a very superficial search of our belongings, we were directed to a one-storied building, not far from the port, which during the period of occupation was the English officers' mess, and where we had dinner after the return of the ambassador. When we arrived in the officers' mess, only one member of the British military was present. He had the rank of major; he was a military doctor with a beard, and he wore a turban. I observed him with great interest. It was my first meeting with a representative of the British imperial power and on the territory which for many years was an area of potential conflict between the Russian and British Empires. Whatever happened to be the attitude of nations that were part of the British Empire toward the English, the intellectuals from the Caucausus and Middle Asia with whom I made contact were awaiting the liberation of their nations should a Russian-English conflict occur. They viewed British Imperialism as a liberating force from Soviet oppression.

After dinner, we found out that we were going to Tehrān on the newly built and little used highway through the mountains; it was called, "The Road of the Shah", because he was a keen hunter and used to travel this way to his palaces. This road was quite far to the east of the pass through which transports of General Anders' Army and of military families were going in the direction of Tehrān. The military transports were going from Pahlavi to Qazvin, a large Persian town, and northwest of Tehrān. The Polish units, which were going to protect the oilfields in Northern Iraq, did not

IN THE SHADOW OF KATYN

necessarily have to go to Tehrān. But the transports of military families were turning in Qazvin southeast to a large distributive camp near Tehrān. The road of the Shah wound over the precipices and valleys surrounding Damavan, the highest mountain in Persia (18,549 feet), whose snowy cap, ruling over the whole mountain chain of snowy peaks, was visible from Tehrān. In one of the palaces near this road, preparations had been made for us to spend the night.

We were traveling in two cars. A passenger car that ambassador Kot, Mrs. Lipkowska, and someone else from Tehrān took. The other, a truck in which the rest of the company traveled, including an officer who had come from Tehrān and was armed with all the necessary documents. This was extremely important because this part of the country was still under Soviet occupation. On the truck we sat comfortably on benches and took advantage of the refreshing gusts coming on one side from the sea, and on the other side from the Elburz Mountains that separated us from the Persian plateau.

The first larger town through which we passed was Rasht – some forty kilometers south of Pahlavi. The town made a positive impression on us. People were reasonably well dressed and appeared to be reasonably well-fed, and abject poverty did not strike our eyes which, in later years, I saw in many towns in India. The major difference in comparison with Russia was the relaxed atmosphere. Despite the fact that the country was under foreign occupation, people were not so frightened as everyone else, including Party members, was in the Soviet Union. The Persian administration seemed to be functioning normally. I did not hear of any massive deportations here as had happened in Eastern Poland and the Baltic countries. It seemed to me that the behavior of the Soviet occupational forces was regulated by some sort of agreement with England. Besides, there was not that constant rush which was a characteristic of all activities in Stalinist Russia.

From Rasht, we went in an easterly direction. All around us were green gardens and vineyards. For the first time in my life, I saw rice fields. After traveling for a considerable length of time, the road started winding and the area became hilly; I had the impression that we entered the mountains. In the darkness of the August night, it was difficult to see the contours of the palace where we were to spend the night. When after supper the uniformed servant took me to my room, the luxurious furnishings stunned me. I was most impressed with the bathroom, which was completely done in pink marble, but I can not swear that it was made from real marble. The delight of bathing in this bathroom after the dust of the scorching highway was extreme. When I woke up before sunrise, I repeated this pleasure and then for a third time when it was time to get dressed. It was an exceptional occasion for a man, who, not quite half a year ago, was at the depths of human degradation as a prisoner in the Soviet slave labor camp. Looking out the window, I was very surprised. When we arrived here during the night, I was sure we were deep in the Elburz Mountains. However, at the bottom of the hill on which the palace was built, a bluish-green slab of Caspian Sea was shining in the morning sun. I walked out to the well-maintained park wherein steeply sloping terraces descended toward the sea. Shortly, we were called for breakfast.

An abundant breakfast in the English style was given to us on a large round table in one of the smaller halls of the palace. We were in excellent spirits and exchanging political jokes. Singer, who knew the history of the Soviet Revolution quite

JOURNEY TO TEHRĀN

well, began to tell something about Lenin's life, calling him at the same time, "grandfather of nations." In our time in the Soviet Union, it was popular to call Stalin, "father of nations." From this Singer deduced that Lenin, posthumously, should be given the title of "grandfather of nations." Listening to this talk and turning toward me, Kot jokingly said, "You, in Wilno also had your grandfathers." He was referring obviously to Józef Piłsudski, who was called "grandfather" during the First World War by legionnaires of the First Brigade.

I retorted sharply, "Our grandfather is indispensable in recent Polish history, and, unfortunately, he did not leave anyone behind whom we could call father." Ksawery enthusiastically supported my answer and continued to develop it further while Singer also agreed; and Teresa Lipkowska, without any hesitation, also expressed her admiration for Józef Piłsudski. We found out that Kot, who had the reputation of being a tenacious enemy of those groups of people whom Piłsudski brought to power after the 1926 coup, had collected for this journey as his closest companions all the admirers of Piłsudski. At that moment, a servant came in to announce that a messenger had arrived from Tehrān with urgent mail for the ambassador. Kot interrupted his breakfast and went to see the messenger. The so carefree atmosphere now became charged with apprehension, and we finished our breakfast in silence.

After breakfast, I went to the park. Because our departure was announced to be about noon, I wanted to go down to the beach to take a farewell swim in the Caspian Sea. Shortly, I realized that the closeness of the sea was a delusion. To get to the shore, one had to walk about three kilometers and to walk back under the scorching rays of the southern sun would be very tiring. I returned. Approaching the palace, I met Teresa, who told me that the mail had brought tragic news. They communicated from Kuybyshev through Tehrān that the Soviet authorities, immediately after the departure of the ambassador, had begun to liquidate the embassy delegations in various districts of the Soviet Union. They had taken the canned food storage, medical supplies, and clothes that had been sent from America to give to the Polish deportees. Many workers at the outposts had already been arrested. The workers in those outposts, as a rule, were not protected by diplomatic privileges, except for a few people who had arrived from London in 1941, though in 1942 most of them had already been replaced with ex-prisoners of Soviet camps. Kot – as I mentioned before – had been attracting outstanding people to the embassy from among the released prisoners, and those people who had some administrative experience had been redirected to the outposts. Now again, these people were imprisoned. The shadow of Ehrlich and Alter was again hanging over the embassy co-workers. Kot, as Teresa told me, was completely heartbroken by the news. He had considered as his main task the formation of a network of social care for the hundreds of thousands of Polish deportees in Russia. Now, this network was in total ruin.

At this time, the reason for keeping us in Baku became obvious to me. It was more than likely that for some time the Soviet authorities had a liquidation plan for the Polish network of social care, and for taking the supply of food from the embassy outposts. The case of Rola-Janicki gave them a comfortable excuse. They chose to perform this blow at the moment when the representation of Polish interest in the Soviet Union was weakened by the absence of its ambassador. It was much easier to go over the protest of the *chargé d'affaires* than that of the ambassador. Until the arrival of the

IN THE SHADOW OF KATYN

new ambassador, our *chargé d'affaires* was Henryk Sokolnicki, a civil servant in the foreign service, our ex-envoy from Finland; but according to the common opinion not a very active man. As far as I know, he made a formal protest against the breaking of the Polish-Soviet agreement of 1941. Could he have done something more and failed to do so? I am not in a position to judge.

One could have tried to manipulate foreign opinion. It was still a period before Stalingrad and before American aid had acquired full strength, and when the Soviets had to pay attention to foreign opinion, particularly American opinion. In this situation the press attaché who would have had contact with American and English journalists could have been a very important factor in stimulating protests. In the meantime, our attaché, who had experience with the Soviets and could have informed his Western colleagues about the whole affair, was together with the ambassador on the road between Kuybyshev and Tehrān. People who were especially distraught by this case were looking for contact with the ambassador, thinking him to be the person who would have been the best informed. Various diplomatic and press moves were delayed because they were waiting for explanations from Ambassador Kot, who during the first year of the Soviet-German war was the main contact between the Government of General Sikorski in London and the Soviet Union. Meanwhile, the Soviet authorities paralyzed him in Baku, cutting him off from any contact with the outside world. Formally, in Baku we were specially privileged travelers, but in reality we had been interned. Now, in 1974, while I am writing this in Halifax, Canada, I am not in possession of the list of the workers from the outposts who were executed after their arrest. Their names, which Ambassador Romer managed to remove from the Soviet Union, must be in the embassy archives. I know some of the arrested were released. Others were lost, probably also executed. We are faced with a case like Katyn, which is waiting for its historian. Katyn is the name of a geographical place. But Katyn also became a symbolic word, meaning all the group executions of the citizens of the conquered nations by the Soviet authorities. On the basis of these data and from an historical perspective, we can say that there were big Katyns and small Katyns. Then, however, in August of 1942, we did not yet know the name of Katyn, even though I could point to the place where the prisoners of Kozelsk had been deported in April of 1940. At that time, we were still in the irritating clouds of mystery.

One other urgent case that preoccupied Ambassador Kot, and that people in his closest circles whispered about among themselves, was the appointment of a commander-in-chief in the East. The Polish Army was exiting Russia in order that it could join other elements of Polish forces, which were already in the Middle East and in North Africa. The need for a commander was important, not only from a military, but also from a political point of view. Communication with London was difficult; therefore, it was necessary for an army commander to make political decisions independently of consultation with the Polish Government in London. For example, General Anders, deciding to exploit the presence of Churchill [in Russia] moved the Polish Army out of Russia. Apparently, Sikorski supported the candidacy of General Zajac, while Kot defended the candidacy of General Anders.

Around noon, they gave us a light lunch, which we ate in silence. Immediately after, we resumed our journey, and this time we really went into the mountains. The winding road with its wide bends led south. At one point we were stopped by a Soviet

JOURNEY TO TEHRĀN

patrol. The accompanying lieutenant who had come from Tehrān showed them the necessary permits. Several Red soldiers climbed on the truck and looked under the benches, after which they allowed us to proceed. Suddenly, we realized that, to a certain extent, we were still in the claws of the Soviet Union. Then, we spent another night in a building in the mountains where we arrived well after sunset.

The next day, early in the morning, we journeyed again and the road ascended even more steeply than before. From a tourist's angle, the views were magnificent. I can compare it only with what I saw several years later, when I was traveling with my wife by bus through the Himalayas to Srinagar, the capital of Kashmir. It was getting colder all the time. When we reached the mountain pass, on both sides there was hard packed snow. The pass was above 3,000 meters. Looking down from there at the road behind us and the road ahead of us, we pondered over the contrast between the northern and southern slopes of the Elburz Mountains. The northern part was rich in greenery and the southern part, into which we were about to descend, was bare and sharp. The views on both sides were magnificent but different in character.

At dusk when we were already on the plateau, which was something in between steppes and desert, I drew the attention of my fellow travelers to the wolves that were running 150 meters from the road. They enlightened me that those were not wolves but hyenas, which meant that we were approaching populated areas. Soon after we saw the lights of Tehrān. There was no blackout there. We were struck by the flashy advertisements, which I had not seen for about three years, and it gave us the feeling of entering a large modern city. We stopped in front of a garden surrounding the building of the Polish legation. The secretary of the legation, Michal Tyszkiewicz, whom I knew before the war, and who also went through the Soviet GULAG, met us. When I told him about the positive impression that Tehrān made on me, he answered, "I am also contemplating whether Tehrān reminds me more of Wilno or Paris." He compared in this way the capital of Persia to two towns to which he had a particular sentimental attachment. My journey from the ominous forests near Katyn to the world of free people had reached its destination.

Chapter VII

THE REPORT ON THE MISSING OFFICERS

In Tehrān, Ambassador Kot established himself in the legation. It was a villa with a large veranda and a big garden in which, besides the main house, there were two annexes where the offices were. The remaining members of the team were placed in hotels. Ksawery, Singer, and I stayed in a hotel, which not considered first class, nevertheless was quite comfortable. The hotel was built in a quadrangle and had an inner courtyard with a restaurant. Rooms with windows facing the garden had large verandas. The food was excellent.

About one week later, owing to the help of one of my ex-students from the University of Wilno, I found a very comfortable room in a traditional Armenian household. The bungalow had an interior, very well kept garden with a fountain. My windows were facing the fountain and were so constructed that the sun's rays almost never entered my room at noon. During the scorching days one could rest there very comfortably. It was only a ten-minute walk to visit a Catholic Church in which the priest said mass in French. Still closer by, there was a learning institution for girls who were the daughters of Persian aristocrats; that is, Moslem girls. French nuns ran this establishment with French as the language of instruction. In this school mass was said in the chapel at 6:15 every morning. On leaving this chapel and entering the hallways of this place, the aroma of coffee the nuns had prepared for the priest tickled one's nostrils. When I returned home, a young Armenian servant brought me a kettle of boiling water, cheese and butter. Only one who went through Russia and saw what I had seen can appreciate the luxury of the freedom to pray.

In Tehrān, there was also an office registering all Polish citizens who were of military age, but for some reason were not in the army as yet. Since I came to Tehrān as a civilian, I went there to register. The atmosphere of a typical Polish pre-war recruiting center struck me, and I felt as if I were somewhere in Lida or Nowogródek. The place was rather badly furnished; several sergeants were sitting by small tables, and one sat behind a typewriter. There was a small group of clients: some Poles who had managed to leave Russia without formally being in the army, and several Polish Jews who had already lived in Persia for years. I was being questioned by a major, a typical military bureaucrat; he put down all my personal data, my military service, dates of promotion, decorations, et cetera. Toward the end, he became interested in my intellectual qualifications. He asked me, "Do you have matriculation?" I answered that I was a university professor. The major sharply interrupted, "I am not asking you who you were, but I am asking if you have matriculation." I hesitated for a while; then, in order not to complicate the issue with unnecessary details, I answered in the affirmative. It was not strictly correct, because, actually, I did not have what is called Polish matriculation. I never attended a Polish school. I was accepted at the University of Wilno in 1919 on the basis of my matriculation from the University of Moscow and my studies there in 1917-18. In those days the Polish universities accepted people with those qualifications under the condition that within a year they would pass matriculation exams of history and Polish literature. I was not asked to do so; therefore I could not with absolute certainty claim that I had Polish matriculation.

REPORT ON THE MISSING OFFICERS

When I returned to the legation, I entertained Kot and Ksawery about the story whether I possessed the necessary intellectual qualifications to hold the rank of officer in the Polish Army. Later, I sat down on the veranda, and my thoughts wandered to the days almost exactly twenty-three years ago when I applied to be accepted as a student of Wilno University. It was also connected with the war experiences. In the fall of 1919, when Wilno was getting ready to revive after closure of the Wilno University by the occupiers, I served as a volunteer in the light artillery battery, which took an active part in our September offensive near the Dvina River. From frequent firing, the barrel of one of our guns expanded, and the commander of the battery sent me to Wilno to bring this gun to the artillery workshop. After fulfilling my assignment, I walked out on the street. Wilno in those days – after the emotional happenings of the well remembered Easter experiences when the Polish cavalry soldiers, under the command of Belina, threw the Bolsheviks out of Wilno, liberating the town – was a joyful place far away from the frontline of the Dvina and Berezyna rivers. From the newspapers, I found out that they were enrolling students at the university. I decided to submit my documents. I was told that I should see the Dean of the Faculty of Law. The dean's office was in one of the side wings of the university where later on seminars would be conducted. In front of the dean's office there was a rather long line-up: many girls, a number of men of a more than mature age, and some young men of Semitic background. There were no young men of Slavonic origin because they were all in the army. The Wilno Jews did not participate in the fights being waged on the territories of the previous Grand Duchy of Lithuania; they were staying neutral, and therefore had time to study. At that time, there was a custom in Wilno that military men did not have to wait in line-ups. I passed by all these applicants and barged into the dean's office, as I was, extremely dusty with an Austrian cavalry rifle on my back. In the middle of the small room behind a table sat a round-faced, dark-haired man, perhaps over thirty years of age. He was not tall and gave the appearance of being French or Italian rather than that of a typical Wilno inhabitant. I told him that I had just arrived from the front and that I would be in Wilno for only a few hours; therefore, I was taking the opportunity to apply for studies in the department of law and social studies. This same man asked me for the documents. I put my rifle in the corner, unbuttoned my uniform, and took from my neck the pouch that my mother had sewn for me in Dyneburg (Daugavpils), producing the required papers. I showed him the diploma of the Mathematical Gymnasium (high school) in Orel; proof of exams in Latin, as required by the school authorities of the Moscow district; and proof of my studies at the University of Moscow in the academic year 1917-'18, the year of the October Revolution. The dark-haired man said that everything was in order, and that I was accepted as a student. He got up and shook my hand. We looked into each other's eyes, and it seemed to me that a certain bond had formed between us.

It was undoubtedly a crucial day in my life. Today, from the perspective of half a century, I know that this bond to a certain extent intertwined our fate. I found out only after departing from the dean's office that this same individual was Professor Władysław Zawadzki, then one of the pioneers of mathematical economy. In the winter of the academic year 1919-20, when the frontline was relatively quiet, I came to Wilno and began to attend the university. I became one of the more earnest listeners of Prof. Zawadzki until fate threw me again on the front in 1920, this time in the infantry. Upon

IN THE SHADOW OF KATYN

receiving my master's degree in 1924, I immediately became senior assistant to Prof. Zawadzki. Afterwards, in the early thirties when he became a Cabinet Minister of Economics and Finance, I took over all his lectures as a docent at the university. At the beginning of 1939, in one of the courtyards of the Wilno University, I delivered the eulogy over his coffin as the representative of the university to which he had accepted me, disregarding some of its regulations.

Why did Prof. Zawadzki, on that September day, not require additional Polish exams in addition to my Russian matriculation as a condition of admission? Perhaps he forgot or perhaps he had some kind of intuitive empathy as I felt at the time. Most likely, he did it consciously and purposely. The conditions of additional Polish exams were required selectively. When a young man arrived from a unit actively operating on the eastern front, and would produce matriculation given to him by the occupiers, this matriculation was generally considered equal to Polish matriculation. Here in the chaos of the present war, my thoughts had gone back to the recollection of student volunteers in the 1918-1920 war. The experiences from that period had some meaning for the present because the Polish Armed Forces that were fighting after the September defeat in 1939, on all fronts of the Second World War, were based almost exclusively on the volunteer element.

During 1918-1920, at the student rallies in the various institutions of Polish higher education, they passed the resolution that it was the duty of all students of Polish nationality, capable of bearing arms, to volunteer in the armed forces. Those who did not fulfill this duty were likely to be shunned from academic society. Not all of them could adjust themselves to the conditions of military service. There were many jokes on the subject of intellectuals in the army, but most of them quickly managed to advance themselves to NCOs. It was probably one of the most peculiar armies because well-trained Polish officers had come mostly from Imperial Austrian and Tsarist Russian Armies that had occupied Poland for more than 100 years. They were not always of high intellectual ability, while among the NCOs there was a high percentage of academics, who represented various ideological movements, but all were imbued with the drive to build and defend an independent Polish State. The NCO Corps determines to a high degree the morale of an army. In 1918-19, when the whole of Middle and Eastern Europe was in chaos, Poland was the only center of law, order, and discipline because of its improvised army. This army, during a severe battle in 1920, stopped swarms of Bolsheviks deployed by Lenin to conquer Europe. Today it is difficult to determine how much this very specific NCO Corps helped to counter the balance in our favor. However, without a doubt, the role that the "academic" corporal played during the memorable days of August and September of 1920 was of great significance.

Several years after the war, the volunteers with qualifications from the period 1918-1920, who had a certain minimum frontline experience, were being promoted to second lieutenants of the reserve force. During mobilization in 1939, many, if not the majority of those aged volunteers from the war of 1920, were called to active service: some to the frontline, and some to do administrative work. Many of them ended up in Kozelsk. The NKVD tried to get very detailed records of each of the prisoners. Undoubtedly, they discovered that among the prisoners were the many volunteers of the year 1920. This was a standard question during the interrogation which every prisoner

REPORT ON THE MISSING OFFICERS

of Kozelsk underwent. This was most likely on instructions from Moscow. Some of the prisoners denied that they had performed voluntary service during the Polish-Bolshevik war of 1918-1920. I think it unlikely that the NKVD believed them. The Soviet *sledovatyels* were very well informed about the fact that all the older first and second lieutenants of the reserve, who came to Kozelsk and Starobelsk, were the previous volunteers of 1920. I pondered over the fact that the high percentage of these volunteers might have had some influence on the fate of the Kozelsk camp.

During my ruminations in Tehrān, the truth about Katyn was not yet known. Today, I have no doubt that the Katyn massacre was to a certain degree a settling of scores for 1920. In the summer of 1920, Bolshevik Russia was marching to conquer Europe. Lenin believed that after conquering Poland, the torch of the Revolution would be lit in Germany, France, and among Czechs. Our victory close to Warsaw, and then near the Niemen River, stopped this march for more than twenty years.

They were the victories of an isolated army. Today we all know that the entrance of the Soviet Union into Central Europe in 1945 was done with the active connivance of the West. Roosevelt and Eisenhower bear a tremendous historical responsibility for this. Also in 1920 the West had been quite ready to self-destruct. Not only Lloyd George, but also Ernest Bevin – leader of the trade unions – was against us. The English workers refused to load the ships with armaments for Poland. The Czechs refused to let transports with weapons pass through their territory. The Polish General Staff, who was conducting mobile warfare, had several French generals experienced in trench warfare hobbling around, but these generals did not represent any real help. But we won that war owing in a great degree to the psychological attitude that this "corporal-academic" represented. In the forest of Katyn and in some other unknown place of torment – probably not far from Kharkov – there was the settling of scores by the Soviet Union with this "corporal-academic."

After several days in Tehrān, Ambassador Kot invited me to the legation for a long conversation, during which he suggested that I should prepare a paper about the missing officers. Kot was not only worried about the ongoing investigation of the case, but also about the role the embassy had played in trying to find the missing officers. In our army, which at this moment was moving out of Russia, there was considerable bitterness because of the alleged sluggishness of the embassy in pressing the Soviet authorities to release the officers or to give reliable information about them. Among the Polish civilian population in England and the Middle East, this was pointed out as proof of Sikorski's failure in his Russian policy. It was known that Gen. K. Sosnkowski – the most influential among the still living cooperators of Marshal Piłsudski – and the Minister of Foreign Affairs, August Zaleski, were sharply critical of Sikorski's policy and had left the government. Kot told me that when leaving Russia, he had taken with him a number of documents pertaining to the activities of the embassy, and that he was going to make them available to me. The intention of Kot was to send this proposed paper to the Polish Government in London, and also to Washington to Ambassador Ciechanowski, so it could be used for the enlightenment of the United States.

From then on, I sat in the Polish Legation, in a corner of the veranda, where I organized for myself a work place to study the contents of the files. They pertained to the correspondence of the missing officers, and generally were in regard to the case of enforcing the Sikorski-Maisky agreement of July of 1941. About noon, I would hire a

IN THE SHADOW OF KATYN

horse-drawn droshky to take me to the swimming pool where there was also a restaurant. When I would come back to work, I used to hang my bathing trunks and towel on the railing of the veranda to dry. One day when I was engrossed in my work, a car arrived and the Polish envoy to the Government of Iran alighted from the vehicle. It was Karl Bader, who probably had been on some official visit and looked, as always, very distinguished and authoritative. Several years before the war, I had met him in passing. With disdain he looked at my bathing trunks, and there was such an expression of disgust in his face that I realized immediately that my trunks were not the proper decorum for the main entrance of the legation of the Polish Government. From then on, I hung them in a less conspicuous place.

The contents of the files that I was studying consisted of correspondence with the Soviet Ministry of Foreign Affairs (*Narkomindiel*). There were also records of the conversations of Sikorski with Stalin and of Kot with Stalin, Molotov, and Vyshinsky; there were records of correspondence that our Ministry of Foreign Affairs in London had sent to the Soviet Ambassador Bogomolov. Then there was a report made by cavalry Captain J. Czapski, who had been delegated by General Anders to visit several top dignitaries of the NKVD, in the hope that he would get some indication on the whereabouts of the officers who were expected to arrive, but never did. I also found a note to the Soviet Ambassador Bogomolov about my case, signed by then head of Ministry of Foreign Affairs, Kajetan Morawski.

I do not intend to dwell on them here, because immediately after the war, most of them were published by the Polish émigré authorities and by Kot himself; the main points were known to anyone who was interested in the case of Katyn. But at that time (the end of the summer of 1942), the study of those documents made it easier for me to realize the complexities and complications connected with the efforts to penetrate the mystery of our officers – and to realize the uniqueness of my own fate in the context of this drama. The man who is being carried away by a flooded river cannot estimate the size of the deluge. In order to do so he has to stand on the shore. Kot, by entrusting me to work on the case of the lost officers, to a certain extent, put me in the position of the outside observer of this drama in which I was unknowingly an actor.

The standard answer of Soviet dignitaries when they were questioned was this: "All Polish military, as well as civilian prisoners, have been released; however, if not all of them reported to the newly created Polish Army, then the Soviet authorities can not bear responsibility for that." This answer made a reasonable amount of sense when you take into account that a certain number of soldiers and officers, who for a specific time had been interned in Kozelsk, Starobelsk, and Ostashkov, actually reported to the Polish Army. The Soviet authorities were playing a time game based on the fact that in the same places in the period 1939-41, there were various kinds of camps. As far as Kozelsk was concerned, there were actually three internments:

1) In October of 1939, there was a camp of privates. These privates had been sent there to work, and some of them were possibly released.
2) At the beginning of November 1939, the Soviet authorities brought 4,200 Polish officers and approximately 300 NCOs and civilians, who remained there till April-May of 1940.
3) After the liquidation of the second camp in April, in the summer of 1940 they brought to Kozelsk more than a thousand officers who had previously been

REPORT ON THE MISSING OFFICERS

interned in Lithuania. These ex-internees from Lithuania were then taken from Kozelsk to a camp in Grazovetz, near Vologda, where 3% of the previous prisoners of Kozelsk, Starobelsk and Ostashkov were already staying since June of 1940.

Also one has to remember that a certain number of officers (probably not more than a dozen or two), who had been in Kozelsk camp No. 2, but not in Grazovetz, had joined Gen. Anders' Army. They were those who were taken individually from the Kozelsk camp and had been tried according to the Soviet penal procedure, and they were released on the basis of the amnesty of 1941. But, except for myself, there was no one from those who were taken by regular transports (more or less about 300 people every few days) in the period of April-May 1940. The situation of Starobelsk was similar. Not so clear was the method and time of transport from Ostashkov, the most populous camp (about 6,500), where they had concentrated mostly police, military police, and officers and NCOs who had belonged to the border corps. The fate of the prisoners taken from the camps by normal transports (95% of the content of the camps) caught the extreme attention of the embassy and also of General Anders' staff. Even the direction of those transports was difficult to establish, but it was generally assumed that they had gone in an easterly direction. It was estimated that those regular transports from Kozelsk, and Starobelsk (not counting Ostashkov) were comprised of about 8,000 officers. What distressed us most was not that they were not coming, but that the Soviet authorities, during the winter of 1941-42, refused to give any information of their whereabouts. In Russia, there were forced labor camps from which transport is only possible during the time of navigation on the great Siberian rivers: Irtysh, Ob, Yenisey, Lena, and Kolyma. There are forced labor camps in Siberia situated 2,000 kilometers north of the Trans Siberian Railway, for example Norylsk, Dudinka, and Igarka on the Yenisey River. Transportation from Kolyma is possible only during the period of navigation on the East Siberian Sea. Sikorski in conversation with Stalin, and Kot in conversation with Vyshinsky, put forward the question whether our officers could be stuck in Northern Siberia. The answer was that the officers were definitely not in the Far North. So where could they be?

We knew definitely that the Soviet authorities had complete lists because the transports, moved from Kozelsk, were centrally regulated from Moscow. The Kozelsk command, as previously described, received the lists of names of those who were to be moved that day only several hours before each transport left. The NKVD, in its archives, must have had precise information on the dates, direction, and names of those transports. Why then did the Soviet authorities refuse all information about the names of the prisoners, and the direction of those transports? There definitely lay a baffling mystery.

Only after studying the documents from the files I received from Kot did my part in this case become clear to me, and the meaning of the special precautions which Otto Pehr had undertaken in organizing my transport from Kirov to Kuybyshev. I was the first and only person from those transports about whom the embassy had received precise information concerning my whereabouts. As to the particular 8,000 missing army officers, of whom I was one, the Soviet authorities refused to give any information. It was also proof that Stalin's assertion that all Polish military prisoners were released had been false. They were expecting that I might be in possession of

IN THE SHADOW OF KATYN

information on the fate of some other officers, or perhaps that I might have the key to the solution of the whole mystery. The Polish authorities then mobilized all possible manner of pressure in order to obtain my release. Ambassador Kot informed our Polish Ministry of Foreign Affairs in London, whereupon a note signed by Kajetan Morawski for Edward Raczyński, who was at that time in Washington, was presented to Ambassador Bogomolov. From the time of the resignation of August Zaleski, the Polish Government in London did not have a foreign affairs minister, but only a temporary caretaker, Edward Raczyński, who was ambassador to the Court of St. James. It appears that it was the only case where the Ministry of Foreign Affairs had been able to present a note about one particular prisoner of the campaign of 1939 to the Soviet Government. The Soviets had no alternative but to release me.

I brought the information that the transports from Kozelsk (or at least part of the transports in April 1940) did not go in an easterly or northerly direction as was assumed, but in a westerly direction to Smolensk, but that the prisoners had disembarked several kilometers from Smolensk. And here all traces of the transports disappeared. As a consequence of this information, instructions should have been given to the Polish Home Army intelligence service to collect information from the local population near Smolensk and from the railway men about what had happened to those transports. Among the documents that I received from Kot there was no indication that my report had been used this way, but the Poles under German occupation played, as far as I know, a considerable role in discovering the Katyn graves. Polish workers mobilized into the organization Todt[1] were the first to find out from the local population about these graves. According to the local population, they also placed a cross at the site of those graves. This case interested the Germans whose intelligence obviously had been informed of the fact that the Polish high command in Russia could not account for about 15,000 officers and policemen who had been taken prisoner by the Russians.

Kot wanted me to put special emphasis on the list of lost officers in my paper. Kot maintained that all the interventions of the embassy would have been easier if the army would have given him a more detailed list with the first name, last name, and rank of the lost prisoners. Kot had approached the army several times, mainly Col. Okulicki, who for a period of time was the Chief of Staff for the Polish Army in the USSR. To prepare such a list was not easy. The Polish Army in the USSR was not in possession of the lists of personnel of the Polish frontal units who had been taking part in 1939, nor were they in possession of the lists of personnel of military hospitals that had been evacuated to the east. The only sources of information were from those who had been in Kozelsk No. 2, Starobelsk, or Ostashkov, and who were transferred to Grazovetz, reporting upon their release to the Polish Army in Russia, and were able to give some of the names of their missing colleagues. It was relatively easy to determine the names of high-ranking officers who were generally well known. It was much more difficult when it came to junior officers, mostly in the reserves. People remembered those with whom they shared the same bunks, and also those with whom they had a closer contact. In relation to those whom they knew less well they remembered generally their last names

---

[1] The Organization Todt: Leaders - Fritz Todt (1938-1942) and Albert Speer (1942-1945). A German organization, operating in the Third Reich and countries occupied by Germany, created as an organization of technical support for the Army. Todt had its own work camps and also used prisoners.

REPORT ON THE MISSING OFFICERS

and ranks, but had forgotten their first names. In spite of that, in the autumn of 1941, the army managed to compose a list of 4,000 names, which General Sikorski handed over to Stalin during his conversation with him in December of 1941. The total list with all the names of those officers who were lost in Russia has never been fully completed. Major Adam Moszyński, who in 1948 edited *Lista Katyńska* (Katyn List), which consisted of about 10,000 names[2], made the greatest individual effort in this field. I published a review about this list in *Kultura* under the pseudonym of Jerzy Lebiedziewski.[3] However, as far as I knew, nobody tried to compose a list of the policemen who were concentrated in Ostashkov and numbered at least 5,000. At that time (August 1942), Kot's main concern was to satisfy the opposition and to prove to future historians that the embassy in Kuybyshev did everything that was humanly possible to obtain from the Soviet authorities the release of the lost members of the Polish Armed Forces. The documents supplied by Kot confirmed this.

I was particularly intrigued during my work on this project that among the officers, who were found and had joined Anders' Army, a number of them were exceptionally antagonistic toward the Soviet Union. This was so, mainly because they had been connected with intelligence, with some political action that was hostile toward communism, or they had participated in the underground conspiracy during the occupation of 1939-1941. On the other hand, it seemed to me that quite a smaller percentage of this type of officer was among those who had perished.

From the time that I was released from the camps, that is, in May of 1942, I continuously learned about people whom I had known before, who had been hostile toward communism that were now in the army of General Anders. For example: Major Władysław Kamiński had become a Lieutenant Colonel, an old legion officer, who after the First World War left the army. He completed his studies in law at the university in Wilno and was elected president of the Union of Military Settlers; then he was elected to the Senate of the Wilno district, and during the Soviet occupation he was second in command of the Wilno district Home Army. He ended up commanding a battalion in the Polish Army in Russia and was highly respected as one of the best organizers in this army. And then there was Lt. Col. Wincenty Bąkiewicz, who worked for the General Staff and was Chief of Intelligence on Russia, and became Chief of Intelligence in the staff of General Anders. Another person I knew was Lt. Adam Telmany, with whom I was a friend in the GULAG and who was the adjutant to the commander of the Home Army in Lwów [Lviv], who now came to Central Asia as an intelligence officer of the Polish Army in Russia. Col. S. Lubodziecki was a military prosecuting magistrate in pre-war Poland, who was taken from Kozelsk as a typically burdensome person against the Soviet Union, and he served again in the judiciary in the Polish Army in Russia.

Not one of those I remember from the perished prisoners of Kozelsk and Starobelsk had engaged in anti-Soviet work. I did not know whether any of my colleagues from Silesia, who in the last days of September 1939 irritated me so much with their sympathies toward the Soviets, were enlisted in Anders' Army. None of the

---

[2] Moszyński, A. – *Lista Katyńska*. Jency oborów Kozelsk – Ostashkov – Starobelsk zaginiem w Rosji Sowieckiej. (Katyn List. Prisoners of camps Kozelsk – Ostashkov – Starobelsk perished in Soviet Russia) London, 1949.

[3] *Kultura* 1949, no. 2/28 – 3/28.

officers with whom I worked closely in September of 1939, and who then fell into Soviet hands – Lt. Col. Nowosielski, Captain Pawłowski, Captain Kowszyk, Lt. Sielicki – were sympathizers of Soviet communism, but not one of them had in their account any special anti-Soviet activities. None of them had managed to join Gen. Anders' Army and they all were among those who perished.

The case appeared to be as follows: The Soviet authorities during their very detailed investigation of the prisoners, about which I wrote before, divided them roughly into two groups:

1) Those who could be charged because of some connection with intelligence or political activities.

2) Those who had some kind of professional, military, or civilian qualifications, but in no way were connected with anti-Soviet activities.

The greater part of the prisoners belonging to the first category were taken from POW camps and placed before the Soviet judiciary. When in July of 1941, the Sikorski-Maisky agreement was signed bringing about the so-called amnesty, those from the first category – incarcerated together with the Soviet political prisoners – were close at hand in prisons and camps; therefore, they were released immediately.

The officers' corps in Gen. Anders' Army consisted mainly of two groups. First, there were officers and officer cadets from the camp in Grazovetz. Secondly, there were various people freshly released from prisons, camps, and forced settlements who possessed officer rank in the Polish Army, but had mostly been deported as civilians during all kinds of "purges" conducted by the NKVD on their newly acquired territories in Poland. Some of them were not capable of active military duty, but they could not be rejected because of humanitarian considerations, as it was the only way for them to survive this terrible exile in the Soviet Union. Anders was facing a tremendous task of creating from this variety of elements a coherent army capable of warfare. However, in Kozelsk and Starobelsk, there had been trained cadres of all kinds of frontline and supply units. In our team of the 19th Infantry Division everybody knew his place if we had to organize new battalions and supply units. The same thing could be said about many other units. The cavalrymen with whom I was in Kozelsk in the same hall represented an extremely coherent and harmonized group that was ready for action.

In 1939, the Soviet occupation had engulfed many hospitals whose staffs were taken as prisoners. In Kozelsk alone there were about 300 medical doctors. Those cadres could have been made useful if given the necessary equipment, which we could have received from the West through the Persian Gulf, White Sea, or the Far East. Hospitals could have been useful, not only for Polish units, but also for the Russians. In English formations in the Middle East there was a shortage of medical doctors, and we had indications that the British high command was interested in the Polish doctors who were being kept in Russian prisons.

Then, what had happened to all these officers and all kinds of experts necessary for the present day military machinery? In the summer of 1942, when I was in Kuybyshev, I often heard the opinion that most likely they were no longer alive. The high command of the army of Gen. Anders and the Polish Embassy still had the hope that the lost officers were somewhere in the far north of Asian Russia in spite of the contrary statements of the Soviet authorities. The probability that they might have been

REPORT ON THE MISSING OFFICERS

murdered after eight months of relatively decent treatment in Kozelsk and Starobelsk was difficult to comprehend for either the people I talked to, or for myself. Besides that, there was also the experience of Grazovetz, where the treatment was even better than in Kozelsk or Starobelsk. I also had behind me my experiences of two years of internment in prisons and Soviet camps after I had been taken away from Katyn. This experience, so very gloomy, had proven to be less terrifying than what I was imagining about the Stalinist system before the war. I came out of the GULAG in April of 1942 with the conviction that, in spite of all Dante's hellish scenes, which I witnessed, there was in the NKVD some margin of respect for human life.

There was still in my mind the fact that in March of 1940, before the liquidation of the Kozelsk camp, they conducted an immunization against typhoid and cholera. It was done in a proper way because after the first inoculation, we still had a second shot which would give us full protection. How could it make sense to organize an action of immunization for people who were going to be executed? I excluded the possibility that execution could have happened in April or May of 1940, in less than a month after receiving these injections. On the other hand, I had been quite perplexed about the severely increased security that I observed through the window in the prison carriage when they took the officers from the train into the bus.

The rumors that more than 90% of the prisoners were lost at sea in the process of transporting them to some far away islands in the North could be plausible. We even found some witnesses to this catastrophe, probably planted by the NKVD. They had apparently seen the departure of the transports, and then they heard about the drowning. In the files that Kot had given me, there were even depositions of those witnesses. My statement that the transport from Kozelsk was going west, and that the prisoners were exiting shortly after passing Smolensk was to a certain degree a contradiction of the rumor about the drowning, in any case as far as the Kozelsk camp was concerned. It seemed rather strange that, in spite of the strong pressure from General Sikorski, the embassy, and the high command of the Polish Army in Russia, none of the Soviet dignitaries said anything about those transports which had traveled to the vicinity of Smolensk in the early spring of 1940. I was rather surprised to find out that my statement about the unloading near Smolensk must be buried somewhere in the embassy papers, because it was not among the documents which Kot gave me as a basis for my project.

I do not have a copy of my report; I think it must be in some of the archives left behind by the Polish Government in London, or with the archives left behind by Ambassador Ciechanowski in Washington. After so many years, I do not remember the details of the report that I wrote then, but I remember well the general direction with which I approached this task. Of course, I presented the essential parts of the whole case and the history of the embassy's intervention with the Soviet authorities. But I was very careful about drawing any conclusions. I expressed the hypothesis that a large part of our officers in captivity was simply murdered. But I had some reservations. I emphasized that my experience of Soviet camps and prisons pointed against such a supposition, and I pointed out a number of controversies in the existing materials. How could one agree with such a supposition along with the fact that in the camp in Grazovetz prisoners were treated decently? Why should they have murdered the prisoners with less of a political disposition, when they kept alive the people with

IN THE SHADOW OF KATYN

obvious anti-Soviet attitudes?

Somehow during that period, encompassing more than a year from August 1941 through September 1942, it was difficult to imagine that, if our officers were still alive in some far regions of this huge country, not even one of them could find a way of communicating with the embassy or the headquarters of the army of General Anders. It was also difficult to reconcile the detailed telephone messages in April of 1940, on the departure of each prisoner controlled from Moscow (to which I was a witness myself) with the refusal of the Soviet authorities in 1941 to communicate to Gen. Sikorski, or Ambassador Kot as to where these prisoners were taken. We were facing a mystery here for which it was difficult to find a definitive answer.

But even if we were to assume that our lost comrades in arms were not alive, that did not mean that they had been murdered with premeditation. However, if there had been some natural calamity that had engulfed them, then what would be the purpose of covering it up? Could this be another mystery? My report, even while strongly confirming the efforts of the embassy to obtain any information on the fate of the lost officers, did not put forward suggestions as to what could really have happened. I did not have any doubts that the NKVD had the key to this mystery, but for some reason did not want to unlock it. This mystery was revealed eight months later, in April of 1943, when Berlin radio announced the discovery of the graves of Polish officers in a place called Kosogory, sixteen kilometers west of Smolensk. I was then in Jerusalem as the head of the Bureau of Studies attached to the Polish Center of Information in the Near East. One day, a Lieutenant Colonel Krajewski, who was monitoring the German radio, came to our bureau and informed the members of the bureau of the news he had just received. The German communiqué agreed exactly with the description of the geographical position of the location to where the Kozelsk officers had been deported which was in my report of June 1942 to General Wolikowski, who was then the chief of the military mission in the USSR.

Various circumstances of the liquidation of the Kozelsk camp which I could not understand then – extreme precautions in formulating the transports, the brutal behavior of the guards, the precise orders from the central authorities in Moscow on who was going to be in each transport, and then, in 1941, the refusal to give Gen. Sikorski any data as to the direction of those transports – became all too clear now.

Something else also became quite clear. I understood that in spite of everything that I went through in the Soviet Union, and in spite of "Dante's infernal scenes" which I witnessed in the GULAG, and in spite of everything I read about the trials from the thirties, I still had held a rather optimistic judgment about the moral essence of the Soviet State; and I had still believed that somewhere in the upper regions of the Soviet authorities there existed some remnants of respect for human life and human dignity as well as for the moral principles, generally accepted in the civilized world. I had remained under the influence of stories told to me by my fellow prisoners in Lubyanka who maintained that – after the removal of Yezhov and the ascendance of Beria – there was, to a certain degree, a humanization of the Soviet Security Services. Therefore, when I wrote my report in September of 1942, in Tehrān, I had shuddered to put forward an assumption that my colleagues could have been executed. Immediately, I sent a coded message to Kot, who was then the Head of the Ministry of Information in the Polish Government in London, informing him that the German revelations were in

REPORT ON THE MISSING OFFICERS

complete agreement with the report which I, in June of 1942, submitted to the Polish Embassy in Kuybyshev on the direction of the transport of Kozelsk officers in April of 1940, and their unloading west of Smolensk. I assume that Kot showed this wire to General Sikorski, and to General Kukiel, who was then Minister of National Defense in that government. I do not know if it had some influence in the decision of the Polish Government to turn to the International Red Cross with the request to investigate the Katyn graves. This decision, taken April 18, 1943, became the reason why the Soviets broke diplomatic relations between the Soviet Union and the Government of General Sikorski in London.

Chapter VIII

KATYN FROM THE PERSPECTIVE OF THIRTY YEARS

Unraveled Aspects of Katyn

The previous chapters gave a factual account. They were mainly concerned with what I had seen and gone through, and the chain of events which brought me close to Katyn and from there through Lubyanka, Butyrki, and the camps to the Polish embassies in Kuybyshev and Tehrān. I tried also to give characteristics of the various people whom I met on this journey. Now, looking back with the perspective of time, I would like to attempt an analysis of the whole case of Katyn – to the place where I happened to come so close. I would like to take into account, not only my experiences, but also various things about which I did not know when I was being swept up by the current of events, and from which I was separated by prison walls or camp wires.

From my entire experiences and from the printed records that I read afterwards, there are certain aspects of the Katyn case that seem to be completely clear. There are also others which are still surrounded by mystery, and they are going to stay that way until Russia makes the archives pertaining to the period of Stalin's rule available to historians.[1] It seems certain that the NKVD committed the crime, which means the decision and its execution were made centrally by the Soviet Security Police. However, it does not seem appropriate that the Red Army, which took these officers captive, but then had to transfer them into the hands of the NKVD, should be burdened with this crime. The earlier described Putyvl camp was a transfer camp from where the army transferred us into the hands of the NKVD. What is not clear is the question of how the Katyn execution was connected with the logic of internal and external policy of the Soviet Union at that time. I would like to spend more time, equally, on the aspects that are clear, and on those that allow quite a different interpretation.

The answer to the question of who committed the crime of Katyn is based not only on the conviction of former inmates of Soviet prisons and camps who happened to be connected with various circumstances accompanying the disappearance in the Soviet Union of 15,000 of their comrades in misery, but also on the reports of three commissions (a German Commission, the Polish Red Cross, and an International Medical Commission) which investigated the Katyn graves. We also have the result of objective studies conducted in the last years by a number of people who were not directly connected with the case: Poles, Americans, Englishmen, and Frenchmen.

First, one has to mention five volumes of the materials published by the Select Committee to Investigate the Katyn Forest Massacre, appointed by the Congress of the United States in September of 1951. After studying all these materials, all members of the commission (four Democrats and three Republicans) came unanimously to the decision that the Russians did commit the crime. The verdict was announced in December 1952.[2] From the collection of materials published in 1948 under the

---

[1] After President Boris Yeltsin came to power, many documents from the Russian Archives have been released and some have now been included in this book.

[2] U.S.A. House of Representatives. Select Committee on the Katyn Forest Massacre. *The Katyn Forest Massacre.* A hearing before this Committee to conduct an Investigation of the Facts, Evidence

KATYN FROM THE PERSPECTIVE OF THIRTY YEARS

editorship of Zdzislaw Stahl, *Zbrodnia Katyńska w Świetle Dokumentów*, this publication had come to the same conclusion. General Władysław Anders in the introduction to this book particularly stressed the fact that the International Tribunal at Nuremberg, which in 1946 investigated German crimes, did not accept the Soviet prosecutors' application to include the Katyn massacre (as a German crime) among those crimes. So, if the Germans did not commit this crime, then who could be responsible for it? Only those who politically and administratively had been ruling over those territories could have conducted the execution on such a scale. And except for the Germans, only the Russians were in control of those areas during this war.

The first larger individual work on this case is the book by Jozeph Mackiewicz, edited in London in 1951, with the introduction by Arthur Bliss Lane, ex-ambassador of the United States to the Polish People's Republic.[3] Bliss Lane was well acquainted with matters concerning Eastern Europe and was quite blunt in telling whom he considered were the perpetrators of this crime; that is, the Soviet Union. Mackiewicz' book, besides its great literary values, has the additional merit that it was written by a man who was at the Katyn Forest during the exhumation of the Kozelsk prisoners of war. He had the opportunity of point-blank and unrestricted conversations with witnesses from the local population, of whom two Russian peasants who were living near the scene of crime should be mentioned: Parfeon Kisselev, and Ivan Krivozertsov.

Even before the Germans found out about the graves, Kisselev had already mentioned the executions to the Polish workers, mobilized with the organization Todt, who then placed a cross [near the burial ground]. Mackiewicz included a photograph of Kisselev in his book, taken at the moment when he speaks to a member of the International Commission, Professor Orsos, who could speak the Russian language. Professor Orsos was at that time a Professor of Forensic Medicine at the University of Budapest. It was at the end of April 1943, when Hungary was not yet under German occupation.

Krivozertsov was the one who at the beginning of 1943 was the first to inform the German authorities about the graves of the Polish officers. He was younger and sharper than Kisselev and other local members of the collective farm, whom the German authorities were questioning about the Katyn crime. He knew exactly what would await him if he should fall again into Soviet hands; so, in 1943, when the Soviet Army was approaching Smolensk, Krivozertsov took his mother and niece with whom he was living and went west. In the Polish territory, during the chaos of German evacuation and the Russian offensive, his mother and niece went missing, and he never found them again. Krivozertsov himself managed to walk through Germany and reported himself to the authorities in the American zone, thinking that information in his possession could stir some interest with the Americans. The American officers with whom he spoke through interpreters could not understand what he was trying to convey; consequently, they decided to deport him to the Soviet allies where the suitable authorities would be able to evaluate properly his revelations. Krivozertsov, however, managed to escape from the protective wings of the Americans and found the Polish

---

and Circumstances of the Katyn Forest Massacre. 82nd Congress, 1st-2nd Session 1951-'52. Washington, US Government printing Office, 1952 --- 2362 pp

[3] Mackiewicz, J., *The Katyn Wood Murders*, London 1951.

units, where his testimony about his Katyn observations was properly recorded. His testimony has been included in the previously mentioned collection of documents under the editorship of Prof. Stahl. From Germany, he was sent to the Polish Army in Italy from where, together with Polish units, he managed to get into one of the refugee camps in Great Britain. He was registered there under the name Michal Loboda.[4] Mackiewicz managed to find him somewhere in the west and had a long conversation with him, and he described the whole biography of this Russian peasant whose family suffered immensely because of collectivization.

This most important witness of the Katyn massacre supposedly ended his life in very mysterious circumstances. He was in England in a refugee camp and was making a living when some Russians approached him. They had been ex-Russian prisoners in Germany, who had managed to escape re-evacuation to the Soviet Union. One day, in October of 1947, he was found hanging in one of the barns. The British police concluded that it was suicide. Mackiewicz wrote a couple of articles on the subject of his death.[5]

Mackiewicz' book has the character of an excellent report made by a professional journalist. It superbly introduces the reader to the essence of the matter, and includes many personal impressions from a direct witness of the unearthing of the Katyn graves. It also points out the inconsistencies of the Soviet version of the Katyn massacre. It was translated into several languages, and it fulfills its task in a sense that it enlightens a number of people as to the essence of the Katyn massacre. However, as with so many books that have a journalistic character, it had a relatively short life. The book has no index, and does not give a review of sources and literature on the subject, which is a standard requirement of scientific and documentary books.

The book by J.K. Zawodny, on the other hand, has a strictly scholarly character. At the time of editing this book, Zawodny was a professor of Political Science at the University of Pennsylvania.[6] This work was based on the study of all the accessible documents and the entire literature existing on the subject at that time – not excluding, of course, that which was published by the Russians – and also was based on a number of conversations with people who were in some way connected with the Polish POWs in the Soviet Union. The first five chapters give all the facts. Chapter VI gives the analysis of the evidence. As a result of this analysis, Prof. Zawodny rejects the possibility of accusing the Germans and comes to the conclusion that the Soviet Security Police (NKVD), functioning according to the instructions of the Central Government, committed the Katyn crime. In his chapters VII and VIII, Prof. Zawodny tries to reconstruct the method of executions, and at the end he gives a list of the people about whom evidence exists that one way or another they were connected with the Katyn massacre.

At the beginning of the seventies, the book by Louis FitzGibbon, *Katyn: a crime without parallel*, received considerable acclaim. The book gives a clear presentation of the Katyn case, and it includes the appeal to the International Tribunal to pronounce

---

[4] *The Crime of Katyn, Facts and Documents*, London 1965, p. 239-240.
[5] Polish émigré weekly *Wiadomości* (News), 20 April 1958; *Dodatek Tygodniowy Ostatnich Wiadomości* (Weekly Supplement to the News), 12 October 1958.
[6] Zawodny, J. K. *Death in the Forest. The story of the Katyn Forest Massacre*, University of Notre Dame Press,1962, English Edition by Mac Millan, 1971.

KATYN FROM THE PERSPECTIVE OF THIRTY YEARS

some judgment of this particular war crime, omitted in the verdicts of the Nuremberg Tribunal. FitzGibbon's criticism of the pronouncements from the Soviet Commission, called up in the fall of 1943 to investigate the Katyn case, is shattering.

Zawodny and FitzGibbon supplied us with very interesting information about the Minsk NKVD records pertinent to the liquidation of three camps of Polish officers, published in West German papers. This report, taken from the Minsk archives during German occupation, stated the dates of the fulfillment of the plan and also the names of the formations that provided the security during the liquidation operation. The date of this report was June 7, 1940. The photocopy was reproduced in the weekly, *7 Tage*, edited in Karlsruhe in Baden-Wurttemberg on July 20, 1957. It also mentions the districts where the two other camps (besides Kozelsk) were liquidated: Starobelsk in the region of Kharkov, and Ostashkov in the region of Velikiye Luki.

FitzGibbon's book reverberated in the English press and parliament, strengthened by the fact that its edition coincided with the documentary film on Katyn by BBC 2, and with the English edition of Zawodny's book. On April 21, 1971, a member of the British House of Commons, Airey Neave, tabled a petition that Her Majesty's Government should submit a proposal to the General Assembly of the United Nations that they appoint a commission to investigate the Katyn massacre. Two hundred twenty four (224) members of Parliament, Conservatives as well as Labour, and three members for Ulster signed this petition.

On June 17, 1971, in the House of Lords, at the request of Lord Barnby, there was a debate on this subject, which lasted two hours and had several speakers. None of the speakers had any doubt about Russia's guilt; however, doubts were expressed about the purpose of bringing forward this case. In July of the same year, Congressman Roman Pucinski put forth the case of Katyn, calling on the Government of the United States to proceed with the recommendations of the Katyn Commission of 1952, and bring this case to the United Nations. Shorthand notes of the debate of the British House of Lords were included in the publication of the Congress of the United States. In September of that same year, Senator Kane started a similar action in the Australian Senate.

At the same time, a number of letters in the British press appeared, mostly in solidarity with the position taken by FitzGibbon, but having various reservations. Some of them questioned the advisability of handing over this case to the United Nations. The discussion in the press had begun. Mr. Felix Alexeyev, correspondent of the Soviet Press Agency, "Novosti", in a letter to the *Times* stated, that the case of Katyn was already clarified by the verdict of the Nuremberg Tribunal. This was definitely not true, because the Nuremberg Tribunal, as it was stated before, contributed considerably to enhance the Katyn mystery because it did not accept the Russian Prosecutor's proposal to include the Katyn massacre to be registered as a German atrocity.

The discussions in the press, caused by FitzGibbon's book, created the possibility of explaining the confused notions of the Nuremberg Tribunal, which could not find any basis on which to accuse Germans of this crime. Since the time of this Tribunal, no new elements have come to light that would allow Germany to be incriminated. However, a number of new traces began to point to the Russian guilt.

The increased interest in the Katyn case, thirty years after the massacre, was probably the reason that the Foreign Office decided to release the documents pertaining to this case from its archives. There were two reports from Sir Owen O'Malley, the British Ambassador to the Polish Government during the war. One was dated May 25, 1943, and contained 24 points;[7] the second of 1944 contained 12 points, also addressed to Anthony Eden, who was then the British Minister of Foreign Affairs. In both reports O'Malley comes to the conclusion that the information collected by him showed the Soviet culpability.

These publications awakened a personal memory in me, because in 1944, I had a long conversation with Ambassador O'Malley on the subject of Katyn. This meeting took place at the home of British journalist Irma Dargenfield. Besides the hostess and the two of us, Rowmund Piłsudski was also present. At that time, among the Poles close to the Polish London Government in exile, rumors were circulating that Ambassador O'Malley was preparing some kind of statement by special request of King George VI, who apparently was much disturbed by the case of Katyn. During this conversation, I was overwhelmed with the excellent mental grasp of Ambassador O'Malley. I had nothing new to add, as there was nothing he did not already know. I had the impression that by asking me various questions, he wanted simply to verify his conclusions.

To the first of these reports from May of 1943, added commentaries were written by high officials of the Foreign Office as this was transferred up the ladder of the British Foreign Service to Sir Alexander Cadogan, who as Undersecretary of State was the highest official in the Foreign Office. In all of those commentaries, formulated for internal consumption, was the striking perplexity between the moral notion of a gentleman, and the necessity to cover up the Soviet atrocities and crimes because of the political and military situation at that time. Sir Owen O'Malley, in the final points of his report, writes of the future "darkened vision" in the wake of the Katyn case. This moral tone emanates through all the commentaries. It is as if the end of a veil is lifted to uncover the confidential discussions of the Foreign Office. This regard for arguments of a moral nature, is to a certain amount, in contrast to what I heard so many times in my life about the cool, uncompromising British State's *raison d'être*. It stands out positively as opposed to what we know about the cynicism of Roosevelt, or the vulgarity of Nixon in confidential talks with his closest co-workers, exposed recently during the Watergate investigations.

On the other hand, those documents revealed that the British Government knew the truth of Katyn at the beginning of 1943. Zawodny's book demonstrates that American Intelligence, and that means also Roosevelt, had enough information to be quite clear about who the perpetrators of the Katyn massacre were. **It means that during the Tehrān conference and later at the Yalta conference two great Anglo-Saxon powers knew very well to whom they were giving half of Europe.** Such were those "darkened visions" about which, in the spring of 1943, Sir Owen O'Malley had forewarned in his report. It is quite possible that the exposition of truth about Katyn, at that time, would have caused a crisis in relationship among the allies. But it would not have stopped the final defeat of Hitler. However, it could have accelerated the consolidation of anti-totalitarian forces on both sides of the frontline. In 1972, Louis

---

[7] Mr. O'Malley to Mr. Eden. (Received May 31) British Embassy to Poland, 45 Lowndes Square, S.W.I., May 24, 1943. Warren Kimball: *Churchill and Roosevelt, The Complete Correspondence*, 1984, Vol. 2 p. 389.

KATYN FROM THE PERSPECTIVE OF THIRTY YEARS

FitzGibbon published his second book on Katyn,[8] in which he addressed the reactions of his first book, and he mentioned new facts pertaining to the Katyn tragedy, which had been revealed in the meantime.

Among others, he writes about the revelations of Abraham Vidra, a Polish Jew, living in Haifa, who went through the Soviet camps, and who had managed to extricate himself to Israel. There in the Hebrew press he published revelations concerning his conversations with Soviet officers who had taken part in the massive execution of Polish officers, and who had become his comrades in misery in the GULAG. According to his revelations there were cases of nervous breakdowns and even suicides among the soldiers after having been assigned by the Soviet authorities to perform the execution.[9] I am prepared to believe this when I reminisce about that deep emotion with which my guards, who were escorting me from Smolensk to Moscow, whispered something about the fate of the Polish officers. I described this incident earlier. Not all the people who are ordered to be executioners are brutal by nature. In some people, there is an instinctive disposition toward cruelty, but in the majority there is an innate consciousness of respect for human life. Systematic disturbance of this feeling, particularly while engaging in the executions conducted on the scale of Katyn, could lead to psychological breakdown. It probably explains the breaks of several days in the transports from Kozelsk to Katyn. Possibly the authorities of the NKVD considered it necessary to give some kind of psychological rest from time to time to the teams of executioners. In the summer of 1972, I watched the appearance of Vidra on German television. I could not understand what he said in Hebrew, but it was translated into German. The full text is probably available in the archives of German television in Wiesbaden.

The revelations of Vidra caused rather unexpected reverberations. According to the *Deutsche Nationale Zeitung* of July 31, 1971, Dr. Mosze Sneh, leader of the Communist Party in Israel declared that at the beginning of the war, as a Polish reserve officer, he was taken to Russia as a prisoner of war. He escaped the massacre because in 1939 he had managed to flee from the transport of prisoners.[10] This revelation again awakened in me many personal memories. I had met Mosze Sneh in 1943 in what was then Palestine under British mandate, and I had several lengthy conversations with him. In Poland his original name was Kleinbaum, by profession a medical doctor, and he played a great role in the Zionist movement. When I met him, he was the youngest member of the Zionist executive. I also knew that he was one of the leaders of the partly conspiratorial Jewish military movement, Haganah. During our conversations, he told me that he had been taken to Starobelsk. He never had any doubts that the Katyn massacre had been executed by Russians, but at the same time he emphasized, on numerous occasions, that in his understanding the main source of Jewish immigrants to a future Israel (which did not exist at that time) was still in Russia. So immediately after the war, when I found out that Kleinbaum went over to communism, the logic of his political about-face became quite clear to me. Probably, he hoped that in this way he might be able to remove the obstacles of emigration from Russia to Palestine. The help which, immediately after the war, the Jewish anti-English underground received

---

[8] FitzGibbon, L., *The Katyn Cover-Up*, London, Tom Stacey, London, 1972.
[9] Ibid. pp. 42-44, 46, 134.
[10] Ibid., p. 46.

IN THE SHADOW OF KATYN

from Russia via Czechoslovakia seemed to give full justification to his hope. I do not have the text of Sneh's pronouncement published in the German press, but knowing the man, I can easily imagine his reactions to the revelations of Vidra, particularly when it was not long before his death, which Doctor Sneh must have known was imminent. He died in 1973. Our common friends told me about his funeral.

Tadeusz Wittlin made a valuable contribution by writing a number of literary sketches on the subject of various events connected with the Katyn tragedy.[11] Wittlin himself went through Russia and was in the army that General Anders formed in Russian Central Asia in 1941-42. Therefore, he had a feeling for the atmosphere in which the Katyn drama was played out, and he went through the same anxiety the whole army experienced when 15,000 officers and NCOs were found to be missing about whom Soviet authorities refused to divulge any information. At first, the title sounds strange: *Time stopped at 6:30.*

This title was taken from one of the most moving Katyn mementos: the diary of Major Solski [found on his body]. That is the time when Major Solski on April 9, 1940, made the last note in his diary. It was written after entering the area of the Katyn Forest, where the guards searched the about to be shot officers once more, taking away their watches, wedding rings, and other valuables, but not touching their papers and diaries. Before they took the watch from him, Major Solski had managed to write in his diary the time: *6:30 p.m.* Tying their hands with wire happened most likely several minutes later, preceding the execution itself. For Major Solski time stopped. The excerpts from his diary were placed in the files of the United States Congressional Commission. I remember Major Solski always with great affection. I met him a few times in Putyvl and Kozelsk. As far as I could deduce from talking with him, he belonged to the staff of General Dąb-Biernacki during the September campaign.

I was in prison near Putyvl with Major Solski in the small house of that collective farm where they grew beetroots. He made an impression on me as a man of high ideals, pale faced with rather sharp features and a flame in his eyes. I do not remember how tall he was, because he was lying on the upper bunk without boots, which he had by his head, but had his feet in warm woolen socks. I asked him what he was writing all the time; he answered ... a diary. I expressed a certain skepticism if this effort had any purpose because it was difficult to imagine how one would be able to take such a manuscript outside the borders of the Soviet Union. How could one even think at that time that the excerpts from the diary of Major Solski were one day going to be published in the official publications of the Congress of the United States? Today, with shame, I consider that my remarks about the writing aspirations of Major Solski were a reflection of a certain attitude of resignation in the face of the enormity of the catastrophe that had befallen us. Major Solski, however, did not give up fighting. Not able to participate in military action, he remained combative by writing his diary, and thanks to unfathomable decrees of Providence his diary became an historical document.

Major Solski was not the only officer who wrote a diary in captivity. He was, however, one who managed to bring his notes up to the point of disembarkation in the Katyn Forest, and to the last search where they took away all the valuables. It is possible that the guards confiscated the valuables immediately before the execution, supposedly taking place at the lip of the dug grave, and after the murder, the body

---

[11] Wittlin, Tadeusz, *Time Stopped at 6:30*, The Bodds Merrill Co., New York, 1965, 317 pp.

KATYN FROM THE PERSPECTIVE OF THIRTY YEARS

automatically plunged into the ditch. A diary was also found on the body of Lt. Wacław Kruk. Wittlin states that Second Lt. Henryk Bruno Kuminek, a journalist from Bydgoszcz, and Captain Alfred Wilecki, also a journalist who had been Editor-in-Chief of the Polish Press Agency, were both writing diaries. Reserve Lt. Kruk, teacher by profession, wrote in his diary to the point of disembarkation near the station of Gniezdovo; the excerpts from his diary also found their way to the annals of the Congressional Commission of the United States.

Wittlin, as a member of the press, was present in Washington at the sitting of the Congressional Commission of the United States while it was investigating the Katyn massacre. The depositions of Col. Van Vliet, a professional American officer, made a special impression on him. Wittlin wrote two sketches out of these depositions. Col. Van Vliet fell into German hands during the American invasion of North Africa. In 1943, the Germans, without asking his permission, took him to Smolensk to look at the Katyn graves. Having antipathy toward the Germans, he was not inclined to believe them. The Germans maintained that the Russians committed the murder during the early spring of 1940. The Russian thesis proclaimed that Germans had committed the murders immediately after taking over these territories in the summer of 1941; and, in the meantime, from April 1940 till August 1941, the Polish officers had worked in the Smolensk district building roads. Col. Van Vliet, an experienced infantry officer had looked at the state of the boots of the exhumed bodies even though at the time he did not know the Russian thesis. The boots of the officers were in good condition. If after April 1940, the imprisoned officers were to have worked for fifteen months, in the autumn mud and spring thaw, while building roads, their footwear should have been in a deplorable state. That means that the Russian thesis was a lie.

While Col. Van Vliet was in captivity, he did not talk about his conclusions in order to avoid being in solidarity with the Germans. As soon as he managed to reach the territories occupied by the Americans, he immediately reported to the proper American Intelligence Authorities in order to tell them about his experiences in the Katyn case. As a result, he was directed to the vice-Chief of Staff, General Bissel, who told him to write a strictly secret report of his conclusions from the observation of the bodies of the murdered Polish officers, and he gave him strict orders that during his hours of duty or while on leave not to talk about this. Col. Van Vliet, having special information on the Katyn case, was now muzzled by the higher authorities. He was, however, not the only American officer to whom this happened; for it occurred in similar circumstances to George H. Earl, President Roosevelt's special emissary to the Balkans, who during his mission managed to get various information on the Katyn massacre. Roosevelt forbade him to share this information with anyone, and when he, in the grip of a moral dilemma, decided that he could not keep quiet any longer, Earl was ordered to the island of Samoa in the South Pacific as a naval officer from where he could come back only after the death of Roosevelt. Col. Henry J. Szymanski, an American officer of Polish descent, who had been attached to the Polish Army in the Middle East as a liaison officer, and who reported various materials in the Katyn case to his superiors, was severely ostracized[12] for his report. Those cases became known during the investigation of the Congressional Commission and are published in the

---

[12] Zawodny, J.K., "*Death in the Forest*, The Story of the Katyn Forest Massacre", University of Notre Dame Press 1962. pp. 178-182.

chronicles of the Commission.

Wittlin's sketches did not bring any new facts to the present day investigators of the Katyn case, but by creating literary exposés of the events concerning Katyn, he has brought into prominence many aspects of this case. Wittlin in his sketches based on a thorough study of the materials, of which a bibliography is given at the end of his book, tried to reach deeper and managed to penetrate the psychology of the actors of the Katyn drama. In my view, Wittlin's book would be an excellent basis for the production of a screenplay.

All the above mentioned papers also give the essence and analysis of Soviet Commission pronouncements pertaining to the explanations of the circumstances of the Katyn massacre. This Soviet Commission was called immediately after the territories were taken away from the Germans in 1943. They accepted the premise that Germans had committed the murder. The terms of reference for the commission was to establish only the details. The Chairman of the Commission was a member of the Academy of Science, Dr. Burdenko, the personal physician of Stalin. Besides him, there were Metropolitan Nikolai, and Aleksei Tolstoy; the latter a known writer of aristocratic origin, who was well favored by Stalin, and a few other high Soviet functionaries. Not a single one of the Polish communists was invited to be a member of this commission, even though, at that time, there was a Polish Communist Committee in Russia operating with Wanda Wasilewska as Chairperson, and they were forming military units under the command of General Berling.

In all probability, the function of the Commission was only to sign a communiqué already prepared by the NKVD. The complete text is published in *The Crime of Katyn*.[13] It is a document full of contradictions, and a thorough analysis of this would take too much time here. I am limiting myself to commenting on only several of the most important points.

First, the Russian thesis declared that in 1940-1941, the Polish officers were in camps near Smolensk and that they were overtaken during the offensive in July 1941, by German troops who then must have proceeded with the mass execution. The question arises as to why, in 1941-42, the Soviet authorities did not convey this to General Sikorski, General Anders, Ambassador Kot, and Captain Czapski, when they were asking insistently about the fate of the Polish officers imprisoned in Kozelsk, Starobelsk, and Ostashkov.

Second, the Soviet communiqué declared that in 1942-1943, the Germans decided to exploit the Katyn grave as anti-Soviet propaganda. They exhumed 11,000 corpses, took from their pockets all the documents dated after May 1940, buried them again and then they announced the news of finding the graves of Polish officers, murdered in the early spring of 1940. It appears that for this exhumation and second burial, they used about 500 Soviet prisoners whom they later executed. If the Germans had really decided on such a complicated and troublesome operation of exhuming 11,000 corpses and searching their pockets, it would be quite incomprehensible that the Intelligence of the Polish Home Army would not have known about it through the Polish workers near Smolensk, conscripted into the organization Todt, who actually, through contact with the local population had found those graves.

Third, if they had used Soviet prisoners for this operation and then executed

---

[13] *The Crime of Katyn, Facts and Documents*, Polish Cultural Foundation, London, 1965, pp. 139-171.

KATYN FROM THE PERSPECTIVE OF THIRTY YEARS

them, the graves must be somewhere in the vicinity, and such graves were never found.

Fourth, the Commission of the Polish Red Cross found out that there were at most 4,500 not 11,000 corpses, and these were exclusively Polish prisoners who had gone through the Kozelsk camp. The Germans announced the number as 11,000 in their first communiqué, before they started a more detailed investigation. Why does the report of the Soviet Commission adhere to the original German mistake? The answer seems to be clear. This number includes, to a certain degree, the answer to the question: What happened to the prisoners of Starobelsk and Ostashkov? The names announced on the list explain only the fate of the Kozelsk camp. The report of the commission is so construed as to evade all further attempts to explain the mystery of Starobelsk and Ostashkov.

Fifth, the Soviet investigating commission does not explain why the shoes and footwear were in such good condition despite the supposed lengthy period of highway construction work. The commission does not explain why they directed invalids to this supposed road construction work as, for example, the retired Generals Minkiewicz and Bohatyrewicz, who after the occupation of Eastern Poland were taken from their homes by the Soviet authorities. In Kozelsk and then in Grazovetz, the officers were treated generally in accordance with the Geneva Convention, and they were not required to work. It is characteristic that the communiqué of the Soviet Commission talks about the camps N1-ON, N2-ON, and N3-ON, avoiding mentioning the more exact geographical location of those camps. There is doubt that these camps existed at all.

Sixth, the report of the Soviet Commission, which describes the period of Katyn executions as July-August 1941, does not explain why the post-mortem examination points out that the murders must have happened in the season where cold weather prevailed. The officers were in coats; many of them were wearing warm underwear. July-August, in the continental climate of Russia, is a period of torrid temperatures. In the meantime, in the Katyn grave, they could not find any insects which are characteristic to this period of the year, while April is rather a cold month. The day, April 30, 1940, when I was brought near Katyn was sunny and rather warm, but in the field there was still snow. It is not surprising that the prisoners, as well as NKVD soldiers, were wearing their coats. The Commission of the Polish Red Cross discovered that there was one rather small grave where murdered officers were lying without coats and were only in uniforms. They most likely were those who, when I left Kozelsk on the 29th of April, 1940, were still in the camp, and whose execution happened to be several weeks later in May when spring was already in full progress.[14]

Seventh, the Soviet Commission did not produce any convincing evidence of any papers found after May 1940. In Kozelsk, Starobelsk, and Ostashkov, and later on in Grazovetz – correspondence with the families was allowed. Correspondence with persons, who were later on found on the Katyn list, stopped abruptly in the spring of 1940; among their families in Poland it caused considerable anxiety. This fact and also the fact that neither the German Commission, nor the International Commission, nor the Polish Commission of the Red Cross could find any documents of later dates on the corpses, points to the execution being committed before the summer of 1940. The Soviet Commission declared that it possessed nine documents dated after May 1940, among them three letters. Józef Mackiewicz analyzed those letters and concluded that

---

[14] Ibid., pp. 191-228.

IN THE SHADOW OF KATYN

in two cases they were letters that arrived after the execution and could not be given to the addressees. The third letter was from an officer who never was at Katyn. It was a letter from Stanisław Kuczyński to Irena Kuczyńska, dated June 20, 1941. Stanisław Kuczyński was not among the identified corpses of Katyn. Probably it was a letter from cavalry Captain Stanisław Kuczyński, who was in Starobelsk and who had been taken from the camp before the beginning of the liquidation of the camp. It is possible that in June 1941, he was still alive in some prison or other camp. Possibly, he tried to send a letter to his wife, which had been confiscated by the censor. There is no indication that cavalry Captain Kuczyński was attached to the Kozelsk prisoners who were murdered in the Katyn Forest.

In the Katyn grave they found the body of Lt. Stefan Kuczyński, who had on him a letter to his wife Danuta Kuczyńska. It is clear that we are talking about two completely different individuals here. Two of the documents had the appearance of receipts given by the Soviet organization that bought valuable things from prisoners or was an intermediary in selling these things for them. The receipts were from December 1939, but on the back of the receipts were stamps of the organization showing the transaction had been performed in March of 1941. It is easy to imagine that after taking the receipts from the pockets of the victims this organization, which was after all one of the branches of the NKVD, could have easily stamped it with the required date. The members of the Commission might not have known about this. If even one of them had some doubt – as anyone who knew Stalinist Russia understands perfectly well – he could not question the documents presented by the NKVD. After all, it would not be of any use, for the terms of reference of the commission was not to find out who committed the crime, but how the German Fascist invaders performed this crime. Three other cases also contained receipts of small payments. These pieces could have been easily produced in the proper laboratories and added to the exhibits found in the Katyn graves. The ninth document, mentioned in the report of the Soviet Commission, was a picture of Jesus Christ on which there was a handwritten date, April 4, 1941. Obviously this date could have been added after taking the picture from the grave. The whole case of the documents, apparently taken by the Soviet authorities from the Katyn burial ground, cannot be interpreted as anything but a farce.

Eighth, the Soviet communiqué does not advance any explanation of why the pierced wounds on some of the bodies were given by the typical Russian bayonet that has the shape of a spike, and not by the German bayonet, which has a knifelike shape.

Ninth, the Soviet communiqué does not explain why the age of the trees planted on the graves – according to the expertise of the members of the Polish Red Cross Commission – was three years (spring 1940-spring 1943).

Tenth, there is evidence that Dr. Nicolai Burdenko, the Chairman of the Soviet Commission, told his personal friends in 1946, shortly before his death, that he took on the chairmanship of this commission on the personal order of Stalin and signed the communiqué [1944] under duress, adding at the same time that he was convinced that in the territory of Russia there are a number of Katyns. According to his opinion the bodies were in the graves for about four years, which means that the murders were committed in 1940. This conversation with Dr. Burdenko was described by ex-university professor from Voronezh, B. Olshansky, in a letter to the editor of the monthly *Socialistitheskei Viestnik*, published by Russian Mensheviks in New York.

KATYN FROM THE PERSPECTIVE OF THIRTY YEARS

This magazine was started by Abramowicz, an old friend of Lenin, and was printed for several years by Russian exiles, and was scrupulously read by all who were studying Soviet Affairs because it had bountiful information on behind the scenes Soviet politics. The letter appeared in this magazine in June of 1950. Several months after this conversation, which took place in 1946, Dr. Burdenko died. Prof. Olshansky, who was assigned to Eastern Germany, managed to cross to the West. Prof. Olshansky also testified before the Congressional Commission of the United States.[15]

Anyone who takes the trouble to study all the documents and significant works on Katyn gathers such an accumulation of clues that any doubt about the Soviet's guilt must disappear. This is also the opinion of all outstanding Western Sovietologists.

Ronald Hingley, Fellow of St. Anthony's College in Oxford, in his book on the secret police in Russia writes, that the responsibility of the NKVD for performing the Katyn massacre was established without a shadow of a doubt.[16]

Expressing themselves in the same spirit are Adam Bruno Ulam; professor of Harvard University, and author of many works analyzing the most recent history of the Soviet Union;[17] Robert Conquest, well-known Sovietologist;[18] Henri de Montfort, professor of the *Institut des Hautes Etudes Internationale*, in his book, edited in 1966, *Le Massacre de Katyn: crime russe ou crime allemand.*[19] Julius Epstein of the Hoover Institute, on War, Revolution, and Peace, expresses a similar opinion very firmly in a number of articles in the American and Swiss press. Dr. Epstein contributed considerably to the decision of the Congress of the United States to form a Commission to engage in the case of Katyn. In April of 1974, he published an article in *Die Welt*,[20] in which he gave information (which still has to be verified) that the Katyn execution for some unknown reason was filmed by the NKVD, and that the film – in unknown circumstances – was found in the possession of Chinese communists in various periods in Chinese embassies in Paris, London, and Warsaw.

Solzhenitsyn maintains that some of the details of the techniques of mass execution applied in Katyn – as for example, tying the hands with wire – were already established at the time of Dzerzhinsky.[21] Svetlana Alliluyeva, beloved daughter of Stalin, writes that after the Katyn murder, whenever her father listened to the opera, *Ivan Susanin*, he used to get up and leave the theater when it came to the scene of murder in the forest. Alliluyeva seemed to believe that her father had attacks of remorse because of Katyn as, apparently, Ivan the Terrible used to get nervous breakdowns whenever he remembered some victims of the explosion of his murderous passions.

---

[15] Zawodny, J.K., *Death in the Forest, The Story of the Katyn Forest Massacre*, University of Notre Dame Press, 1962, pp. 157-159.
[16] Hingley, R., *The Russian Secret Police*. Hutchinson, London, 1970, p. 186.
[17] Ulam, A.B., *Expansion and Coexistence*, Praeger Publishers, New York 1974, pp. 343-344.
[18] Conquest, R. *The Great Terror, Penguin books,* London, 1971, pp. 643-645.
[19] de Montfort, Henri, *Le Massacre de Katyn: crime Russe ou crime Allemand*, Edition de la Table Ronde, Paris, 1966.
[20] Epstein, J., *Die Welt*, "Zur Wahrheit über Katyn" (The truth about Katyn), April 1, 1974.
[21] *Survey, 1974*, "The Autumn Issue", p. 153.

Chapter IX

THE DIALECTICS OF KATYN

The explanation that the NKVD, on the order of the Soviet Central authorities, committed the Katyn massacre reveals only a part of the Katyn mystery. In order to understand the historical sense of this tragedy, one has to address the question as to *WHY* the decision was made to liquidate the Polish prisoners of officers' rank. This question also torments Prof. Zawodny, who projects several hypotheses.

At first sight, the answer seems to be simple. Constantine FitzGibbon writes in the introduction to her brother's book on Katyn, that the murder was part of an action to eliminate the leadership of the Polish Nation. In Russia, Stalin was destroying everybody who seemed to represent a potential danger to his authority. Therefore, in the years 1937-38, they murdered a number of outstanding communists, old friends and co-workers of Lenin, and the majority of high-ranking officers of the Red Army. The Polish officers taken during the Soviet invasion in September 1939 represented a class that could potentially be an opposition factor against Soviet aims in Middle and Eastern Europe. They were part of the elite of the nation that had defeated Russia in 1920 and, therefore, they had to be destroyed. This answer, however correct, is not sufficient to completely explain the Katyn tragedy.

The Soviet foreign and internal policy is equally permeated with hypocrisy, wrapped in the coat of dialectic casuistry. The dialectics of Hegel and Feuerbach, that is placing everything in categories of thesis, antithesis, and synthesis, determines the basis for Marxist philosophy, which has been elevated to a State Religion in the Soviet Union. The whole Soviet educational system in the area of social and political studies is supported on the basis of these dialectics. In the times of Lenin and Stalin, the internal as well as foreign policy had a dialectic character, surprising its observer by these constant inconsistencies.

These aberrations were particularly striking when one confronted the propagated theory with the stark reality. The doctrine portrayed the gradual demise of the State, while the social system was transferring toward communism. In the meantime, the Soviets created a centralized totalitarianism, interfering in the smallest details of the private life of the citizens. They explained that the dialectics required that the country should be strengthened before it starts its process of the State's demise.

The USSR pronounced anti-military slogans and, at the same time, was creating a powerful army; thus giving impetus to the armaments of the European countries that demobilized themselves mentally after the First World War. The great rearmament program by Hitler did not start until 1934, but many years earlier in the twenties, the diminished German General Imperial Staff was already conspiring with the Soviet leaders on the subject of tactics, organization, and techniques of panzer units.

Immediately after the Revolution, they divided land among the peasants, in this manner increasing a number of small independent peasant plots. At the end of the twenties, however, they compelled the amalgamation of these holdings into collective farms, taking away from individual peasants a large amount of their tools and livestock and creating a system that, in many respects, reminded one of the old feudal system.

THE DIALECTICS OF KATYN

The Communist Doctrine declared the right of each nationality to develop its national culture. The Revolution transferred the Old Russian Empire into a union of nationalistic socialist republics. For the minor nationalities of the less advanced and culturally developed people, they created a number of autonomous national regions. Schools and universities were springing up based on the national culture of the given region. The Stalinist Constitution of 1936 even allowed for the individual republics to secede from the Soviet Union. Yet, several years earlier, at the end of the twenties, thousands of cultural activists of various nationalities went to the GULAG for "nationalistic deviations" – including national leaders of the communist parties. I previously described how, at the beginning of 1941, I was transported to the GULAG in the Far North in the company of the Central Committee of the Kazakh Communist Party, condemned for "nationalistic deviations." In the first half of the twenties, after formal incorporation into the Polish State of so-called "Middle Lithuania" (district of Vilnius), when the Polish authorities were liquidating the Byelorussian schools – a number of Byelorussian cultural activists went to Minsk (Capital of the Socialist Byelorussian Republic), where they received positions at the university or at recently created Byelorussian academies of sciences. After several years, almost all of them found themselves in the GULAG, and some of them were even shot.

The case of Katyn also has dialectic overtones. The prisoners, after being taken into captivity, were rather reasonably treated. The conditions of life in the Kozelsk camp were not pleasant, but one could say bearable. The prisoners were looked upon as individuals. Everyone was addressed politely, sometimes even in a friendly manner, and would be asked about his profession, conditions of work, family and friends. Some of the prisoners coming out of the individual talks were extremely surprised to find out how much the NKVD investigating officers knew about their lives. The individual files in the camp were getting thicker. The prisoners had the right to write letters. Letters to family and friends were answered and received.

When it became known that the investigation of prisoners had been completed and that the camp was going to be liquidated, and that transport was awaiting the prisoners, everybody received injections against typhoid and against cholera — but immediately after which, more than 95% of the prisoners were taken for execution. After the massacre, they organized a camp in Grazovetz for those (about 3%) whom they had spared, and added a subsequent number of 1,000 officers and officer cadets seized during the occupation of Lithuania in the summer of 1940. Their lives were also saved. Again, reasonable treatment was given. Furthermore, several officers, especially selected from Kozelsk and Starobelsk, were placed in the so-called "villa of bliss."[1]

---

[1] After investigating all Polish officers, the authorities of the NKVD selected 395 officers who were spared execution and sent to the camp in Juchnov, from where they were transferred to the camp in Grazovetz. How the selection was done is still a mystery, for the many that were spared from execution were not necessarily sympathetic to the Soviet Union. Among them a small group of officers showed their dedication to the Soviet authorities and they were sent to a villa in Malakhovka, about forty kilometers from Moscow. The conditions in this villa were quite reasonable compared with the other camps. Officers called this place the "Villa of Bliss." Colonel Berling was one of the most prominent officers in this villa. After the Polish Amnesty in 1941, when all Polish officers joined General Anders' Army, he refused to leave the Soviet Union with this Army and stayed behind to form a Polish Communist Army under Soviet Command.

IN THE SHADOW OF KATYN

How does one explain these contradictions? Were they an expression of certain general principles? Or, perhaps, were they the result of uncoordinated decisions? The potential pro-German attitude of Stalin, and the impetuous anti-German attitude of the Party cadres could have caused conflicting concepts regarding a Soviet policy toward Poland. The mystery of Grazovetz is just as puzzling as the mystery surrounding Katyn.

The thesis that Stalin wanted to murder all the intellectual elite of the Polish Nation seems to be logical; on the other hand, the cream of the intellectuals were also among those who were selected to go to Grazovetz and who were spared. In Kozelsk, they selected Prof. Wacław Komarnicki, a specialist in international law, an outstanding member of one of the pre-war political parties, ex-dean of the faculty of law of the University of Wilno, ex-member of Polish parliament, and one who could not be suspected of having any inclination toward radical socialism. From Starobelsk, they selected Józef Czapski, a well-known painter from an aristocratic family. From Ostashkov, they selected Captain Bronisław Mlynarski, son of the famous composer.

The question also remains why they wasted so much immunization material on more than 4,000 prisoners before they executed them. It is possible that the NKVD apparatus, which was administering the evacuation of the camp, had no idea of the purpose of the transport. Possibly some instructions existed that because of fear of an epidemic all prisoners designated for transport had to be inoculated against typhoid fever and cholera. So, automatically they immunized those who were going to be executed after one day of travel.

The symbol of the puzzling dialectic of Katyn was, to a certain degree, the figure of Kombrig Zarubin, whom I also characterized in *The Crime of Katyn*, and about whom I wrote in previous chapters here. The possibility that he was the originator of the dialectic solution of the fate of the Polish officers cannot be excluded; that is, the concept of Katyn, the concept of Grazovetz, and the concept of Malachovka (villa of bliss). Let us hope that some future historian will be able to clarify this mystery.

It is interesting to note that those whom Zarubin called more often, and with whom he liked to talk, mostly avoided the Katyn Forest massacre. This was the case of Prof. Wacław Komarnicki, for whom Kombrig Zarubin had a special regard. Prof. Komarnicki, who was approaching the age of fifty, was inducted as a second lieutenant to the judicial corps, and in this way he became a captive. As I mentioned before, the Kombrig ordered him to be separated from the junior officers, moved him to the colonels' quarters, and granted him all the privileges which were given to staff officers. At the same time, they brought to the Kozelsk camp a number of judges and attorneys; among them was Judge Pohorecki, the second chairman of the highest court of Poland. In the hierarchy of social life and as a moral authority, Judge Pohorecki was of at least equal stature to Prof. Komarnicki. Age-wise Judge Pohorecki was one of the oldest in Kozelsk. However, Zarubin was not interested in him. Pohorecki slept on the bunks together with young officers and officer cadets, and he suffered considerably because of various ailments connected with old age. My impression was that Zarubin's interest in Komarnicki was mainly because he had been an outstanding representative of *Stronnictwo Narodowe*, a political party which historically was pro-Russian, even if, of

THE DIALECTICS OF KATYN

course, it was far removed from Marxist ideology. Zarubin was trying to orient himself to what degree persons of this type could be used in the future political game. I am basing my impression on what Kormanicki told me about his conversations with Zarubin. Those talks produced such a result that Komarnicki began to believe that the period of terror had gone and that the Soviets, in their lifestyle and habits, had started moving closer to the Western Powers.

Another officer who enjoyed a particular respect from camp authorities was Col. Künstler. During the September campaign, he was the commander of artillery in the army of General Dąb-Biernacki. In the last days of the campaign, he commanded his own unit which destroyed the bridge on the Bug River near Dorohusk, in order to make it more difficult for the Germans to retreat from Volhynia to the West. Col. Künstler had the style of a professional officer and in his manner, more than anybody else in Kozelsk, he resembled General Anders. As far as I could draw my conclusions from the various responses of Soviet political officers, they considered him a man of great potential. Kombrig Zarubin had several conversations with him.

I remember that Col. Künstler was connected with Col. Tyszyński, who also belonged to the army of General Dąb-Biernacki, where he was commander of the engineers. He did not appear to have the style of a military man, but gave me the impression that he was a competent engineer. I became closer acquainted with those two officers in the cattle train, which took us from Putyvl to Kozelsk. Col. Künstler was not very talkative and did not say anything about himself. Col. Tyszyński was a descendant of Polish landowners who owned the Plebania estate in the district of Mołodechno. It was some twenty kilometers from the estate of my father-in-law in the same district. On August 15, that means two weeks before the outbreak of the war, I was with my wife and children at the yearly fair in Plebania.

We started a conversation, recollecting our common acquaintances, especially University Rector Marian Zdziechowski, who was also from the Mołodechno district. Then in Kozelsk, I met on occasions with Col. Tyszyński, and we used to exchange a few sentences. One sunny day, in March 1940, Col. Tyszyński and I met in a spot sheltered from the wind while we relaxed in the sunshine. I sat close to him and asked whether he knew anything about the fate of several high-ranking officers about whom some colleagues in my hall were very concerned. Col. Tyszyński answered with slight irritation that nothing bad had happened to any of them, that they were all in Starobelsk and that there was contact with that camp. In his voice I detected a tone of confidence as if he believed in the wisdom and decency of our Soviet hosts. I do not remember exactly what he told me, but I understood that not long ago he had spoken with Zarubin, who filled him with optimism. It was our last meeting before the liquidation of Kozelsk.

I was not too surprised when, after leaving the Soviet Union, I discovered that both colonels Künstler and Tyszyński had been selected to go to "the villa of bliss." When in 1943, I accidentally met Col. Künstler in a café in Cairo, he told me then a little bit about his history after the liquidation of Kozelsk. When he realized what the purpose of the discussions was in the group of officers in Malakhovka (villa of bliss), he tried to withdraw from there forthwith. He made some declaration to the Soviet authorities, after which he was put in prison in Moscow, and then he was taken to Grazovetz.

IN THE SHADOW OF KATYN

Today, from the perspective of years, it seems to me that I begin to understand the dialectics behind the three different aspects: Katyn, Grazovetz, and Malachovka. The investigation of prisoners had shown that the junior officers, in the same way as most of the privates, had a hostile attitude toward the Soviet Union, or in any case toward communism. Therefore, if after the liquidation of the Polish State (which was the thesis of the USSR) the Soviets were to form Polish military units, these units would be inclined to attempt all kinds of conspiracies and coups. The memory of the year 1920 was very much alive among the Kozelsk prisoners; there were many veterans of the campaign of that year. The way in which the day of March 19, 1940, the name day of Piłsudski was celebrated in Kozelsk was an obvious proof of the feelings that were alive among the veterans.

In any case, if the Soviet authorities decided to play a Polish card by forming a Polish military unit under Soviet command, it would not be an enterprise on a large scale and only a small number of prisoners would have found regular positions there. In the last month of the existence of Kozelsk, the interest of the NKVD in this multitude of prisoners had diminished. However, there were still attempts to talk to some of the staff officers who had the potential of forming a well-disciplined unit. Mainly, they were the staff officers of the Polish Army unit called "Prusy", of whom (except the commander himself) almost all found themselves in Soviet captivity. In this way Col. Künstler and Tyszyński were considered to be especially favored prisoners, which – as far as I understand – led to aggravated circumstances when it came to their positions in the army of General Anders. Undoubtedly, they made extensive depositions, which must be somewhere among the documents of the Polish Army in the Middle East. By becoming acquainted with those depositions one might shed some light on how Soviet rulers understood Polish problems in the years of 1940-41.

To understand the dialectic decision of Katyn is important, not only because it illuminates the attitude of Russia toward Poland, and not only because of moral considerations, but also because it is a sociological problem. To comprehend these dialectics might facilitate the ability to mentally grasp the difference between pre-Revolutionary Russia and the Russia of Lenin with his followers. The policy of Tsarist Russia did not have a dialectic character. It was often brutal, which to a certain extent was moderated by the liberalism of the upper strata of society. However, in its attitude, particularly toward Poland, the class solidarity among landowners and aristocracy was often stronger than the feeling of nationalism and historical antagonism. This last – that is, the multiple connections of Polish aristocratic families with the Russian aristocracy and Imperial Court – could not change the basic direction of Russian policy (in spite of efforts by Czartoryski[2], and then Wielopolski[3]), but it contributed to mitigation of this policy in individual cases and its application. Generally, the Tsarist policy was straightforward.

Hitler's Reich also had a straightforward policy, despite that Hegelianism was pressing on the national-socialist movement. The contradictions of German policy

---

[2] Polish Prince Adam Czartoryski (1770-1861) became foreign minister and a confidant of Tsar Alexander I. He promoted Polish education and pressed for an autonomous Poland under the protection of Russia.

[3] Wielopolski, Alexander (1803-1877), a Polish nobleman who attempted, as a Minister of Tsar Alexander II, to gain concessions for Poland by staying a faithful subject of the Tsar.

THE DIALECTICS OF KATYN

during the occupation of Eastern Europe, which is very well portrayed by Alexander Dallin in his studies of this policy, [4] and Józef Mackiewicz in his novel *Nie trzeba głośno mówić* (One should not speak loudly), were the result of inconsistent concepts which individual dignitaries tried to realize on their own, but none of which were acceptable to Hitler. The disorder of German policy with all of its unprecedented cruelties was the result of oscillations in not taking a unified course, while the paradox of Soviet policy was the result of the system. To what degree this system was connected with the philosophy of dialectic materialism is one of the most fundamental questions for those who want to deeply understand the essence of the communist movement. Therefore, the dialectics regarding Katyn is a subject that must be of particular interest to Sovietologists.

---

[4] Dallin, A., *German Rule in Russia 1941-1945*, London 1957

Chapter X

DID KHRUSHCHEV WANT TO PUBLISH THE TRUTH ABOUT KATYN?

The behavior of post-Stalinist Soviet Governments is ambiguous with respect to the Katyn tragedy. The most puzzling aspect of all is that the Soviet Union did not take advantage of the opportunity to unburden itself of the case of Katyn by adding it to the Stalin crimes, which Khrushchev exposed in the confidential sitting of the 20th Congress of the Soviet Communist Party in February, 1956.

The content of this speech is widely known. Its text was sent to the outstanding communist activists in the satellite countries and almost immediately found its way into the hands of the Western press. In this speech Khrushchev exposed the extermination of prominent members of Soviet communism which had been the essence of various Stalinist "purges." In 1934, for example, from among 139 persons who were elected to the Central Committee of the 17th Congress of the Party, 98 of them – in other words 70% – were arrested and executed, mostly in the years of 1937 and 1938. From among 1,966 delegates of that Congress, 1,108 – the obvious majority – were arrested in the next few years under the pretext of various political crimes. Khrushchev did not mention how many were executed. He pointed out, however, the extreme weakening of the fighting ability of the Red Army just before the war. The liquidation of a considerable number of high-ranking commanders, beginning with company commanders and ending with marshals (three from among five)[1] and vice-commissars of war caused this weakening. All were killed on the orders of Stalin.

After Khrushchev's speech, a movement was started among the high Soviet military to exonerate the most outstanding commanders who, at an earlier stage, had been annihilated by the orders or intrigues of Stalin. A commemorative book was issued to honor Marshal Tukhachevsky; there was a project to erect a monument for Marshal Blücher, one of the most distinguished military talents, who showed his military capabilities during the civil war and the first years of the Revolution. They counted the approximate number of victims. Apparently, it came to 35,000 Soviet officers of various ranks, murdered in the years 1937-1941.[2]

If officially they had added 10,000 Polish officers and 5,000 policemen to that total, it would not have changed in any glaring way this gloomy balance sheet, and then to a certain extent the Katyn case would be closed and the Katyn massacre would not still stab at the international conscience. The moment when the Soviet Government accepts the responsibility of its predecessors for these crimes, condemns them, and agrees to pay some compensation, then this hideous case will stop being the subject of international controversy.

Why then did the Soviet leadership not do it, but instead identified with the

---

[1] Stalin executed marshals Tukhachevsky, Blücher and Yegorov. Marshals Voroshilov and Budyonny, whom Stalin trusted, were left alive. Neither of the two knew anything about modern mechanized warfare.

[2] Shapiro, Leonard, *The Communist Party of the Soviet Union*, Vintage Books, London 1960, p. 420; R. Hingley, *The Russian Secret Police*, Hutchinson of London, 1970, p. 170.

DID KHRUSHCHEV WANT TO PUBLISH THE TRUTH

indefensible thesis of the Stalinist Commission that in 1941 the prison camps were taken over by the German Army, and that the Polish officers were murdered by them?

In the sixties, there was a widely spread rumor that Khrushchev had proposed to Gomulka[3] to add the Katyn case to the other crimes committed by Stalin, but Gomulka had dissuaded him. He feared that if the existing prohibition of discussing the Katyn massacre were removed, he might not be able to control Polish opinion in his country. What really happened was only for the people privy to it to know. From the text of Khrushchev's speech at the 20th Congress, there was no condemnation of Katyn. This speech was almost exclusively concerned with the murders performed by the Stalinist police on the members of the Party. Khrushchev, for example, expressed strong disapproval of the physical liquidation of old Trotskyites, who already had denounced their mistakes and come back to the "Leninist position"; but he left open the question of what to do with those who were still clinging to the Trotskyist heresy. From the analysis of this speech, it could be concluded that Khrushchev, in essence, did not exactly condemn a system of mass executions, if the reasons for this would be in the interest of the State. It is obvious that in the context of Khrushchev's speech at the 20th Congress of the Party, there could not be a place for Katyn.

The possibility cannot be excluded that in later years Khrushchev had the intention of disclosing the truth about Katyn. There are several indications that point in this direction. First of all, after the 20th Congress of the Party, there was a change in attitude toward investigating the most recent history in the Soviet Union. During Stalin's time, almost anything that had been written in this sphere was a lie. After the famous speech by Khrushchev, they started working on the problems of the recent history, if not with full objectivity, then at least they tried to preserve a certain semblance of objectivity. Writing and speaking about the final stages of the war, it was not possible to omit the question of Katyn, which was the cause of international friction and had been a subject discussed by the Nuremberg Tribunal. In the meantime, the presentation of Katyn in the report of the Soviet Commission was so unconvincing and so full of contradictions that the Soviet citizen who was experienced in reading between the lines would very quickly guess who the real culprit was. Alexander Werth,[4] one of the most pro-Soviet, Western publicists, who on the fiftieth anniversary of the Revolution traveled extensively through the Soviet Union, writes in his book, which he published after his journey, that for the politically informed Russian the case of Katyn is an open secret. "It is a festering ulcer which we do not like to touch," said one of the leading Soviet writers. A second person with whom he had a conversation, at the mention of Katyn, added additional information about another mass murder committed in 1945, involving many thousands of North Koreans, who previously had apparently been collaborating with the Japanese. He also said, however, that the mass executions were rather an exception in the Stalinist method of extermination of real or imaginary opponents. Naturally, the question must have arisen: Would it not have been better to excise this ulcer by an official admission of the truth?

The most important consideration for admitting the truth about Katyn would have been Khrushchev's self interest if he had wanted to cling to power. Khrushchev,

---

[3] Polish Communist Party leader.
[4] Werth, A., *Russia: Hopes and Fears*, Pelican Original, 1969.

IN THE SHADOW OF KATYN

however, because of his speech at the 20th Party Congress, found himself in a situation in which his own political future and his historical role were dependent on the progress of de-Stalinization. To tell the truth about Katyn could have created a positive atmosphere for the further development of this action which – however popular in the beginning – in later stages found itself against strong resistance from the Soviet apparatus of Party bureaucracy. This apparatus consisted in Russia of the ruling class that enjoyed many privileges in living standards and the possibility of social advancement. More or less fifteen years ago, Milovan Djilas, former Vice President of Communist Yugoslavia, gave an excellent characteristic of this class in his famous book, *The New Class*. Party bureaucracy, together with the political police known in different times under various names (Cheka, OGPU, GPU, NKVD, MVD, and KGB), created a vise which held the nation of the Soviet Union in the grip of Party dictatorship. Western researchers calculated that during Khrushchev's rule there were about a quarter of a million paid Party functionaries.[5] Stalin, who had been General Secretary, that is, chief of the administration of the Party, had created this enormous apparatus. For more than thirty years Stalin physically liquidated old communists, former comrades of Lenin, and people of revolutionary psychology who could think independently, and replaced them with young people of clerical mentality who were conservatives (conservative toward the order of things in which they were brought up) and subserviently obedient. During the 18th Congress of the Party in 1939, Stalin declared that since the previous Congress, approximately 500,000 members of the Party had advanced into various leading positions. Solzhenitsyn describes to a certain degree in his book, *The Cancer Ward*, a cross section of today's (1976) Soviet society, at the same time depicting the psychology of the people belonging to this ruling class.

This class accepted Khrushchev's speech in the 20th Congress almost positively, because it declared a certain amount of personal safety for the members of the Party bureaucracy. During Stalin's time, many of the people who had just been promoted found themselves in the GULAG camps while others took their place. Some limitations of power in the secret police were in the best interest of this class. However, when Khrushchev started to cancel the decorations previously given to the KBG men for their very base deeds (among them his protégé General Serov, called the butcher of Lithuania and Hungary), many people belonging to the Party bureaucracy started feeling that their own social position was in danger. The de-Stalinization had turned into a deeper dimension, and they became afraid that this action might transfer itself into the liquidation of the system of Party dictatorship.

One also has to remember that in the Soviet Union people of this generation were brought up in the cult of Stalin. Many of them considered that the wisdom of this Statesman and leader of the World Revolution, to a certain degree, counterbalanced the human suffering resulting from his cruelty. The moral notions that were inculcated into these people were different from those that prevailed in the West. Soviet Marxism is to a great degree devoid of the elements of humanism, which permeated Western Marxism and also among the old Bolsheviks, Mensheviks, and Social-Revolutionaries, who were annihilated by Stalin. Communist ideology excludes exploitation of human work for the purpose of private gain, but it does not exclude the murder of people when it seems

---

[5] Shapiro, L., *The Communist Party of the Soviet Union*, Vintage Book, London, 1960, pp. 525, 573.

DID KHRUSHCHEV WANT TO PUBLISH THE TRUTH

to its leaders that it suits the purpose of the revolutionary raison d'être of the State of the "proletarian country."

Tsarist Russia also used to be ruthless and cruel. The cruelty in that period was somehow mitigated by the official recognition of the Christian religion. The Greek Orthodox Church – even though it was quite corrupt and since the reign of Peter the Great completely subjugated to the State authorities – played a significant moral role because it established certain concepts about the difference between good and evil. For example, Greek Orthodox belief demanded that prisoners had to be visited especially during the most important religious holidays. As a child I witnessed how rich merchants sent carts full of gifts to the local prison during Easter time. When I was a teenager at the time of the First World War, I saw how ladies from high society in the military hospitals looked after German and Austrian prisoners with the same tenderness as they looked after Russian soldiers.

During the Stalinist collectivization, when a child of a *Kulak* (well to do peasant) was thrown out into the village street and was dying during the cold night from hunger and exhaustion, any peasant who would bring the child a piece of bread and a mug of water risked the accusation of being a *Podkulatschnik* (Kulak lover) and faced possible deportation to the GULAG. The present day generation of Party bureaucracy was brought up in the conviction that the period of Stalinist collectivization, with all its senseless cruelty, was a heroic period in the history of Russian communism. It is a great historical contribution of Polish communists that when Poland, abandoned by its Allies, was delivered as prey for Stalinist experimentation, these same Polish communists managed – till now – to save the Polish villages from those kinds of cruelties.

In order to completely understand this strata of Party bureaucracy which resisted attempts of de-Stalinization, one has to remember that even in the eyes of those representatives of the administrative apparatus who agreed that Stalin was a moral monster, he was at the same time a leader who had added great industrial and military achievements to his name. Stalin, by ordering the great purge in the years of 1937-38, disorganized – according to the common opinion of all pre-war intelligence services – the Red Army, but several years later, this army under his leadership achieved the greatest triumphs. Stalin physically liquidated a number of the closest comrades and collaborators of Lenin, but the Soviet State under his leadership achieved the position of Super Power. Stalin was a criminal without parallel, but he also symbolized the road to power. Evidently, Khrushchev himself had become perplexed and kept contradicting himself when he talked about Stalin. What will come out of the proliferation of crimes we do not know, but we should try to understand the way people think and reason in that sphere of environment, for they are in their way honest people.

Therefore, it is psychologically understandable that the cult of Stalin resurfaced in the Soviet Communist Party. Those tendencies quite naturally impeded tremendously any further attempts of de-Stalinization begun by Khrushchev. Together with the action by members of the Party to restrain de-Stalinization, one could scarcely expect Khrushchev to tell the world the truth of Katyn, even if he had so desired.

Chapter XI

KATYN AND THE SOVIET-GERMAN ALLIANCE

At the time when the Katyn massacre was being committed, the Soviet Union was a faithful ally of Nazi Germany; it was executing scrupulously all the obligations resulting from the agreement of August 1939. The question arises: Did this alliance somehow weigh on the decision of Katyn undertaken by the rulers of Russia?

After his escape to the West, Stanisław Mikołajczyk, who had been Chairman of the Polish Peasant Party for some time, and had been Vice-Premier of the Russian satellite government in Warsaw, told J. K. Zawodny,[1] as he was gathering material for his book, that it was known to him that in the period of 1939-41 an agreement existed between Germany and Russia to exchange Poles and Ukrainians, but the Germans decided not to accept Polish officers in this exchange. This statement by Mikołajczyk agrees with my observations as a prisoner in Kozelsk. In Kozelsk, all the time rumors were circulating that we were going to be handed over to the Germans. This information seemed to contradict basic logical thinking. Why should the Germans burden themselves with the care of thousands of Polish officers whom – according to the Geneva Convention – they could not use for forced labor? These news flashes were so persistent that our generals instructed our younger officers to protest if they were being taken to the Germans. A certain probability was ascribed to the rumor that only officers from Central and Western Poland were going to be given to the Germans – only those who were concentrated in the monastery, but not those in the "Skit" where they had garnered officers who were from the territories incorporated into the Soviet Union. It cannot be excluded that the officers of the NKVD who were suggesting the possibility of sending Poles to Germany had been completely sincere. It would appear that the concept of execution came later when the Germans refused to accept this "gift".

There had been some cases of the transfer of Polish officers in the opposite direction – that is – transferring officers from German into Soviet hands. In Kozelsk there were about seventy officers taken prisoner in the region of Brest who, toward the end of the September campaign, had been transferred to the Red Army according to the Soviet-German agreement when the German Army, after conquering Brest, moved west. I do not remember today (1975) the names of these officers, but I remember vividly what they said about their experiences. The defense of the Brest fortress had been very stubborn; the crew of the fort after being completely surrounded by the Germans still fought for several days and surrendered only when they ran out of ammunition. After the surrender, the Germans treated the Polish officers with great courtesy. The German general who had commanded the troops that took fortress Brest made a speech to the prisoners in which he expressed his admiration for the military valor exhibited by the Poles during this fight. After several days, the German major who commanded the POW camp collected the Polish officers and announced that he wanted to bid them farewell because he was moving away, and that soon different units would arrive who would perform guard duties. Shortly after, the German guards were

---

[1] J.K. Zawodny, *Death in the Forest, The Story of the Katyn Forest Massacre*, University of Notre Dame Press, 1962, p.128

KATYN AND THE SOVIET-GERMAN ALLIANCE

relieved by the Soviets, and those officers then found themselves in Kozelsk.

They also told me about an interesting occurrence. Among the prisoners in Brest, there had been the Polish ex-Prime Minister Świtalski, who had come from Warsaw to Brest in his own car with his brother or perhaps brother-in-law, and from what I know both of them were in military uniforms. So, they were added to the prisoners. The Germans informed Colonel Świtalski that these new guard units were going to be Russians, and as an exception they allowed him and his companion to return to Warsaw. In this manner Col. Świtalski managed to avoid Kozelsk and Katyn.

It is possible that the German-Soviet relations on a different plane also had some bearing on the fate of the Polish officers. In the Soviet Union, immediately before the war, there existed between Stalin and the Party intelligentsia a difference in attitude toward Germans. I saw Russia during both World Wars. In 1940, before the German attack, I had the impression from talking with my fellow prisoners that among the Russian intelligentsia the hostility toward Germans was stronger than during the First World War. I have to emphasize that here I am writing about the intelligentsia and Party cadres, not about the masses; and about the Russian intelligentsia, not Ukrainian nor those from the Caucasus. The latter were inclined to expect that the Germans would bring them national liberation.

At the beginning of 1941, I was taken to the GULAG in the north together with a Russian general, a commander of a division. He had been arrested not too long before; so he had experienced the opportunity of observing scrupulously all the operations in the West during the summer and fall of 1940. He was convinced that as soon as Hitler gave up the idea of invading the British Isles, it could be considered that for Hitler the war was lost in spite of all his apparent impressive successes in France. This commander of a division was emotionally anti-German and in this respect was not much different from my colleagues in Kozelsk. I was under the impression that he would very easily have come to an understanding with our Polish officers.

In the meantime, Stalin's aspiration was to strengthen the ties of the existing agreement with Germany, resulting from the pacts signed in August and September of 1939, which de facto had the character of a military alliance. There are many indicators that the question of the alliance with Hitler had not only political values but also emotional ones for Stalin. A well-known historian and Sovietologist, Ronald Hingley, fellow of St. Anthony's College in Oxford, writes that Hitler was probably the only man in whom Stalin had complete confidence.

The Soviet historian, A. M. Neckreech, coworker at the Institute of Marxism and Leninism, and the Institute of Soviet Academy of Sciences, published in 1965 a book in Moscow in which he tried to establish the blame for the initial defeats of the Red Army in the campaign of 1941. According to him, the main responsibility rests with Stalin, who stubbornly ignored the reports of Soviet Intelligence about the colossal German concentration near the border agreed upon by the Ribbentrop-Molotov Pact in 1939. Those reports irritated Stalin and his anger turned against its authors with a vengeance. When at the end of May in 1941, the German ambassador in Moscow, Schulenburg (later on executed by Hitler), who made desperate attempts to prevent a Soviet-German war, decided to forewarn the Soviet ambassador in Berlin about the true intentions of Hitler, Ambassador Dekanozov refused to inform Stalin of this news. Dekanozov (executed later on in connection with Beria) probably was well acquainted with the fact that he could bring the wrath of Stalin on his neck.

Marshal Tukhachevsky, in his report to the Central Executive Committee of the USSR in 1936, stressed the gravity of the dangers facing the Soviet Union resulting from the Hitlerite rearmament. Consistent with the hypocrisy characterizing Stalinist Russia, he was shot in 1938, supposedly for secret cooperation with the Germans. This exceptionally able officer of the Imperial Guard had joined the Bolshevik Insurgence and was considered by many to be the Napoleon of the Russian Revolution. Obviously, Stalin had to move him out of his way.

It is difficult to know, of course, what kinds of emotions did beset Stalin. It seemed strengthening the close agreement with Hitler must have been the only logical route to take after the great purges. I am not sure if purges should be considered as an indispensable element of every totalitarian system as Zbigniew Brzezinski[2] seems to think. Considering the purges of the years 1936-38, they seemed to have been the result of the gulf that originated between Stalin and the Party cadres in the middle of the thirties. It was a crisis of confidence involving Stalin and the enormous apparatus of Party bureaucracy of his own creation. It expressed itself in various unimportant facts (for example, during the 17th Congress of the Party in 1934, Stalin's title since 1922, "General Secretary", was changed to "First Secretary") and in several critical pronouncements from representatives of the central organs of the Party or of the government as, for instance, the declaration by Postischev, secretary of the Ukrainian Party, about whom Khrushchev spoke in his speech during the 20th Congress. During the 17th Congress in 1934, the most admired by the public was not Stalin, but S.M. Kirov, handsome secretary of the Leningrad Party, favored by the majority to succeed Stalin.

Stalin answered those critics with decisive repression even before a new opposition managed to organize itself. Under the knife went principally old Bolsheviks, people accustomed to a certain amount of independent thinking, party intellectuals, Marxist theoreticians, and many commanders who had distinguished themselves during the civil war. Leonard Schapiro, in his fundamental book, *The Communist Party of the Soviet Union*, describes those events in the 22nd chapter under the title, "Victory of Stalin over the Party."

It was clear that the great purge in the Party created not only internal consequences but also influenced the international policy of the Soviet Union. The logic of the situation inclined the dictatorial system of Stalin to move away from the democratic countries – and that in spite of the victory of the people's front in France in 1936. Instead, it created a favorable climate for approaching countries with a system of totalitarian leadership like Nazi Germany. We do not know exactly when the first contacts were made between Stalin and Hitler. Evidently, it happened some time before the signing of the Ribbentrop-Molotov Pact.

Apparently, the first attempt to establish a closer contact with the ruling circles of Hitlerite Germany was made through David Kandelaki, a member of the personal secretariat of Stalin, who visited Schacht in December of 1936; however, von Neurath, Hitler's Minister of Foreign Affairs, did not express much enthusiasm for the continuation of those contacts. Kandelaki eventually found his way to the GULAG and

---

[2] Brzezinski, Z., *The Permanent Purge*, Harvard University Press.

KATYN AND THE SOVIET-GERMAN ALLIANCE

no more was heard of him.[3] At the same time, the NKVD prepared Marshal Tukhachevsky's case of "treason" and of other Soviet generals who supposedly had made contact with the German General Staff. It all was in accord with the dialectic method of Stalin's policy. When the full agreement between Stalin and Hitler would be realized, their own generals could present a danger to either dictator.

At the beginning of 1939, people close to the Trotskyite centers in Poland observed that Soviet policy was seriously looking at the possibility of an alliance among Stalin, Hitler, and Japan in order to divide the British Empire. The huge industrial machinery, built in the Soviet Union with incredible human sacrifices and costs, was destined to move into the grip of the darkest forces of international relations.

It is interesting that a certain amount of affinity existed between the dictators of Germany and Russia; however, it did not mean that Hitler intended to give up his aims in the East. Speer writes in his memoirs that in August of 1939, Ribbentrop, on his return to Germany after signing the pact with Molotov, was elated by the reception he had received in Moscow. In the presence of Speer, he told Hitler that with Stalin and his closest surroundings he had felt at home, as if he had been with his old party comrades. During the Soviet-German war, after the pact had fallen apart, Hitler confided to Speer that in Russia he only valued Stalin, and that after the final victory, he was prepared to make Stalin administrator of Russia under the jurisdiction of Germany, of course.

The purges of 1936-38 had been intended to remove internal obstacles for the eventual alliance with Hitler's Reich; however, the more conscious preparation for the groundwork probably started in 1938 or 1939. At that time, Stalin started paying special attention to the existence of foreign communists, particularly the communists from countries neighboring Germany and the veterans of the Spanish War. They called to Moscow the leaders of the Polish Communist Party in order to murder them and in that way almost completely eliminated the Central Committee of the Polish Party. In 1940, my fellow Russian prisoners in Lubyanka maintained that almost all of the Hungarian communists, who found themselves in Russia at that time, had been locked up. Evidently, the most prominent leader of the Revolution of 1919, Bela Kun, was still alive and was kept in a prison somewhere in Southern Russia. I met Matias Rakosi in 1941 in the GULAG camp in the Far North. I have the best of memories of him.

At the beginning of 1941, a German communist, a member of the Central Committee of the German Communist Party, was with me in Butyrki Prison. At the end of 1941, in one of the camp hospitals in northern Russia, I met a young Soviet officer who had fought with the international brigades in Spain and he, upon returning to Russia, had been immediately arrested. His father, a Soviet general, had perished in the purges of 1938. This boy was quite openly cursing Stalin for the betrayal of the Spanish Revolution. George F. Kennan, one of the best American specialists on Russia and ex-ambassador of the United States to Moscow, maintains that almost 100% of the top Soviet military had become victims of the purges on the eve of the 1939 war.[4]

Foreign communists and veterans of the Spanish War did not present the most important internal obstacle to the Soviet-German alliance. This obstacle also existed in

---

[3] Conquest, R., *The Great Terror*, Penguin Books, London, 1971, pp. 298-300.
[4] Kennan, G.F., *Russia and the West under Lenin and Stalin*, Boston, 1961, p. 292.

the attitude of the vast majority of the Russian intelligentsia, and in the party bureaucracies, which were opposed to Hitler and generally were anti-German. To complicate matters, Stalin did not possess a clear ideological concept that could explain the direction of his foreign policy toward an alliance with Hitler. The huge Soviet propaganda apparatus was still operating with their well-established slogans of warfare against fascism, loyalty to the Leninist tradition, et cetera; however, reading Lenin's publications had been forbidden when I was in Soviet prisons.

In 1940, I had the exceptional opportunity to compare how the Polish officers interned in Kozelsk and the representatives of the Soviet administration, of whom I met so many in Lubyanka, viewed the world situation. The Polish officers were imbued with the will to fight the Germans and a great majority considered that in this respect Poland and Russia had a common interest. The Polish officers were little interested in the Marxist analysis of social and economic structure, but their attitude toward Hitler's Reich was the same as that of the average Russian party intellectual in 1940.

This similarity must have found its way in the report which Kombrig Zarubin had prepared for the higher authorities. We can also presume that it was taken under consideration when the fate of Polish officers was being considered at the highest level, which means Beria and Stalin. If Polish officers were to stay longer in the Soviet Union, they would have to find some kind of application for their professional qualifications. In Kozelsk there were about three hundred doctors and also a large number of engineers, agronomists, and all kinds of technicians. The same applied to Starobelsk. To direct those specialists into Soviet hospitals, factories, and laboratories, when the highest leadership of the Soviet Union had tried to consolidate the just acquired pact with Hitler, could have created conditions for them to spread the belief that Hitler was equally an enemy of Russia as of Poland. It could have increased the already existing agitation among the Soviet intelligentsia in connection with the pro-Hitler policy of Stalin. Obviously, this was probably not the only argument for the physical liquidation of Polish officers in the framework of Beria's system of rationalized cruelty. Stalin had the tendency to shift toward the Hitlerite position with respect to his attitude toward the individual man, and with respect to his international contests. This was in total disagreement with the ideals of the Russian Revolution. So, it was a counter-revolutionary action. Trotskyites called this policy the policy of "Thermidor," referring to the consequences of the French Revolution. It is somehow an historical paradox that Polish officers, people who were mostly very far removed from the Marxist controversies, had become victims of those currents, which in reality were counter-revolutionary in the history of the Russian Revolution. The motives for their execution could have been partly the same as the motives for the execution of the leaders of the Polish Communist Party.

Summing up, I consider that we have enough elements to recreate the logic of the Katyn decision:

1) The decision to murder the Polish prisoners was probably taken by Stalin himself somewhere near the end of February or in March of 1940. It is difficult to imagine that Beria or Merkulov could have been responsible for such a decision. One must assume that Stalin's obsession with the Soviet-German Alliance played a certain role here. So far, we do not have any indications that the German allies had been informed of this decision.

KATYN AND THE SOVIET-GERMAN ALLIANCE

2) I do not think that Grazovetz or Malakhovka required the personal decisions of Stalin; they were simply the result of a general dialectic treatment of each case. Besides, extreme care had been taken to wipe out any traces of the murder. Those who survived would constitute living contradictions to any possible rumors about the execution. When they liquidated the leaders of the Polish Communist Party, some Polish communists – from those who at that time were in Russia – survived this period. Some future historian might explain what path Bierut [Polish Communist President after 1945] had been walking at that time.

3) Shortly after the Katyn murder in the second half of 1940, a perceptible change toward the Poles in the method of interrogation took place. It was my impression that torture was not as frequently applied as it was to Russians with whom I happened to have been in Lubyanka and Butyrki. I have heard of many instances where there was a reprieve of the death sentence.

Party cadres at the highest level of the ruling apparatus started questioning the rationale behind the decision of the mass execution of Poles. It is possible that Merkulov was being completely frank when he told Berling and his comrades that a "grave mistake" had been made with the officers from Kozelsk and Starobelsk. About a thousand officers and cadet officers who had been interned in Lithuania and had been seized by Russians in the summer of 1940 were not handed over to the execution squads, but were taken to Grazovetz. I suspect that the factor that contributed to the mitigating course against Poles was the occupation of France by Hitler. Hitler was engaged in war in the West and was no danger to the Soviet Union. Should Hitler become master of Europe, then he would be a definite threat. Poles could become useful during some future strife against Hitler; therefore, from the point of view of Beria's system of rational cruelties, genocide of the upper strata of the Polish nation was not recommended. In February of 1941, in a rather relaxed atmosphere and in the process of closing the investigation in my case, the investigating magistrate engaged me in a talk on general subjects. I noticed a lack of faith in his opinion of the German-Soviet Alliance. Looking at the ordnance map of Yugoslavia spread out on the wall and heavily seeded with small flags, which probably meant the network of Soviet agents in that country, I thought that this interference in the path of German expansion must have irritated Hitler.

It happened during the time when Stalin was making desperate moves to maintain the Soviet-German Alliance. I still keep asking myself the question of whether Stalin realized that his intelligence and propaganda services were provoking Hitler. Hitler was not a statesman. He was a man possessed by a wild passion that inflamed and carried the German people. Constantly, he had talked and written about his far-reaching visions, but his decisions were usually emotional. Much more than Stalin, Hitler was a slave to his own phraseology, easily losing his temper

Thus, to avoid a military confrontation with Hitler, one had to be very careful not to trespass on the immediate objectives of German expansion. In spite of the pro-Hitler attitude of Stalin, the German-Soviet relationship had an uncertain character. A full understanding of the dialectics regarding Katyn is possible only then, when one takes into account the fluctuations that existed in the precarious balance of the Soviet-German Alliance.

Chapter XII

RUSSIA vis-à-vis POLAND

An explanation regarding the mystery of Katyn is necessary when taken in the context of the historical problems between Poland and Russia – two nations whose relations with each other throughout the ages were loaded with emotionally explosive material. I do not believe in the existence of "hereditary" or "age old" enemies. But one must agree that certain historical facts may burden the relations between nations throughout the generations, and that those facts, from an historical perspective, may develop into a greater expressiveness and greater meaning. They may also weigh heavily in moments of important decisions. One has to admit that emotional conflicts could give way to explosive reactions. On the other hand, many disagreements can be solved through negotiation and may even induce cooperation and friendship between nations.

There is a certain inaccuracy in public opinion about the historical conflict between Poland and Russia. An historical conflict existed at least since Ivan III between Moscow and the Grand Duchy of Lithuania. When the Great Dukes of Lithuania became Polish Kings and when the Lithuanian-Ruthenian nobility started to become Polonized, this conflict acquired the character of a Polish-Russian conflict. Even after the partitions,[1] a considerable number of the Polonized nobility thought in categories and interests of the Grand Duchy of Lithuania, a country which had ceased to exist and which did not have a clear-cut ethnographic base for rebirth – such as Poland had.

Pushkin, in his famous rhyme about the November Uprising, wrote about the revolt of Lithuania. Józef Piłsudski tried to rebuild the unity of the old Grand Duchy of Lithuania, independently of the Polish Parliament and Government in Warsaw, in the years 1919-20 when the Polish Army was moving east. After the defeat at Kiev, in May of 1920, those attempts had to be abandoned. My arguments with Ksawery Pruszyński on the Volga beach, as I described before, had as its bone of contention that Ksawery was prepared, in the name of friendship with Russia, to forego our historical and traditional ties with the Grand Duchy of Lithuania. However, I considered this tradition as an intrinsic part of my own affection for this part of the world where I was born and which I considered as my more rightful motherland. Today, the Grand Duchy of Lithuania, whose rebirth seemed to be real in 1919, belongs clearly to the past. The drive for complete independence for the Ukraine, Byelorussia and the Baltic countries has become a growing concern. I personally attach a high priority to this problem. How it will weigh on Polish-Russian relations is difficult to foresee. While Poland under Pilsudski had still emotional ties with the Grand Duchy of Lithuania, all that had ceased to exist after the Second World War.

In the last two hundred years, Russia has caused our nation a tremendous amount of harm. But we also have to remember that during the 19th century until after the First World War, many Poles had been living in Russia. They learned to appreciate

---

[1] Partition of Poland occurred in 1772, 1793, and 1795 when Poland was subdivided into three regions occupied by Russia, Prussia and Austria until 1918.

RUSSIA vis-à-vis POLAND

Russian literature and art; they loved Russian women, made fortunes in Russia, and had many Russian friends. Polish engineers built railways in Russia, and administered industry in the Don River area. Polish scientists and researchers taught at Russian universities. In the Russian Army many Poles attained the ranks of generals. Between the Insurrection of 1863 and the First World War, many influential Polish families achieved great standing in Russian society, notably; Spasowicz, Lednicki, Żukowski, Petrażycki, Waśkowski, Zieliński, Przewalski, and Grąbczewski. I still belong to the generation who had an educational background from Russian schools, and I can recite from memory more poems of Lermontov and Pushkin than poems of the Polish poets, Mickiewicz and Słowacki. Since my high school years, when I belonged to the Polish underground movement, and during the first year of the First World War when I started to become interested in politics, I was always inspired by the legend of Józef Piłsudski, but I had also learned to value the qualities of Russian culture and art.

Even in our memories from the Soviet camps and prisons during the last war, not everything was absolutely black. In Kozelsk there were several officers who had been wounded in the September campaign and who were sent, after being taken prisoner, to the hospital in Kiev. They spoke with the greatest respect about the care they received from doctors and nurses. My own observation from Soviet prisons and camps left the impression that the doctor, as a rule, was a friend of the prisoner. I have the best of memories of my comrade prisoners in the cells of Lubyanka and Butyrki because of their attitude toward me. All those things have to be put into balance when we are going to consider the case of Katyn in its historical perspective.

Obviously, the endeavor to revive the cult of Stalin is highly distressing. However, this endemic disease applies mainly to the ruling strata – Party bureaucracy – which is like a malignant growth on the body of Soviet nations, not connected organically with the economic and cultural development of the people of those countries. It is very difficult to say what the average Russian is thinking today. The word Katyn probably tells him very little. What Alexander Werth writes about the "open secret" concerns only the people oriented toward public and cultural life, and people of the older generation with whom he had been in contact. In particular, we know very little of how the young generation of present day Russia, born after the war, looks at the world, and for whom Stalin's crimes and triumphs are a question of history. But the whole world knows that among this generation there is a certain moral and artistic elite, extremely sensitive to what is a lie and what is a crime. Solzhenitsyn can be called the most outstanding representative of this elite even if Solzhenitsyn still belongs to the pre-war generation. It is quite probable that the reason why people ruling the Soviet Union cannot decide on the honorable and honest closing of the Katyn case is that they fear the danger of shock among the wide masses and mainly among the young generation when the circumstances of this crime are publicly announced. In the meantime, represented mainly by Solzhenitsyn, Sakharov, Amalrik, and the editors of the *Samizdat* (underground magazine), this moral elite may somehow neutralize the historical effect of Stalin's crimes.

When one is talking about the Soviet system of murder and terror, one thing has to be remembered. Stalin and Beria were not Russians, but Georgians. Stalin, just like Catherina II, apparently could never get rid of his foreign accent. I discovered this myself listening many times to the radio when Stalin was speaking at various

IN THE SHADOW OF KATYN

Congresses. The creator of the Soviet secret police, the one who started using murder and torture as a method of ruling, was Polish nobleman Feliks Dzerzhinsky. Second in command to Dzerzhinsky was Menzhinsky, another Pole of noble origin who later became Chief of OGPU. After the death of Menzhinsky in 1934, Genrikh Yagoda, apparently a Polish Jew,[2] became Chief of the Secret Police, renamed NKVD. Only after the fall from power and imprisonment of Yagoda in 1937, came the Russian Yezhov, and then in 1938 the Georgian, Beria. One of the most repulsive characters of Stalinist terror, Attorney General Andrei Vyshinsky, who had been the prosecutor in all the main show trials in which they sentenced old co-workers of Lenin, also admitted his Polish origin even though, as he said, he did not know the Polish language.

Present day Poland is connected with Russia, not only because together with other countries of Middle and Eastern Europe it is being held in the vise of the huge Soviet military and police machinery, but also because all the hopes for liberation are based on the possibility of some changes in Russia. Today [1976], nobody could pray for the great "spring tide of nations" (Revolution of 1848) as Mickiewicz did during the last great emigration of Poles to France after the failure of the Polish Insurrection of 1831. Alas, the future of the world is now to a great extent dependent on those who have the means of mass destruction in hand. But even if we assume that Poland will at some future time regain complete freedom to decide its own fate, one has to remember that Polish industry is almost completely dependent on Russian raw materials. Some sort of ties with Russia should be maintained. Under those conditions, it is in the interest of both sides that those ties should be based, not on fear — as it is today — but on a foundation of common respect, confidence, and trust.

The Katyn case is a festering ulcer that could poison Polish-Russian relations for centuries. If those relations are going to be developed on a healthy basis then this ulcer must be removed. The number of Jews, murdered by the Gestapo, is much larger than the number of Poles who were murdered or tortured by the NKVD, but the relations between Germans and Jews became normalized. This was possible because postwar German Governments and the whole German society utterly and irrevocably condemned the murders, performed on an unprecedented scale by Nazis on Jewish people in various European countries. In the meantime, nobody knows how many among the Soviet neo-Stalinists see the Katyn decision as one of the manifestations of Stalin's wisdom as a Statesman.

The Soviet Union condemned many murders performed on Stalin's orders: the posthumous exonerations of Marshals Tukhachevsky and Blücher, and a number of old communists who had been co-workers of Lenin. Khrushchev condemned the deportations of Crimean Tartars, and some of the Caucasus and Middle Asian nations, whereupon the deportees received at least partly the right to return to their places of origin. They executed Beria and Merkulov, the main performers of criminal acts of Stalin. However, in the case of Katyn the Soviet Union is still covering itself behind the fiction of the Commission appointed by Stalin. **This Commission was an absurdity from the point of view of logic and law, because it was not given the right to investigate who committed the murder of Katyn**. It had to accept **a priori** the assertion that Germans had committed the crime and discussion was not allowed; thus its only function was to show *how* the Germans had performed this crime – mainly on

---

[2] Hingley, R., *The Russian Secret Police*, Hutchinson, London, 1970, p. 157.

RUSSIA vis-à-vis POLAND

the basis of the material submitted by the NKVD. The lie was in the basic premise of this commission which – as it was admitted by its Chairman Dr. Burdenko – was acting under duress by personal order of Stalin. All Poles and Russians, belonging to the Party or not, who want to establish an atmosphere of common trust and cultural cooperation between Poland and Russia, have to firmly demand that the Soviet rulers take the case of Katyn from the blind alley they created by officially supporting the indefensible thesis that the Katyn massacre had been performed by the Germans. A myth which nobody believes today!

The way out of this poisonous atmosphere of deception would be to create some Polish-Soviet Commission that would investigate the collected materials of this case and determine the guilt. The determination of guilt does not mean that there have to be court cases to punish the guilty. Most likely, the main perpetrators of the Katyn massacre are no longer alive. Many of the criminal decisions of Stalin were already condemned during the 20th Congress of the Communist Party, and then at the 21st Congress, it was decided that Stalin's body be taken away from Lenin's mausoleum. Beria and Merkulov, probably the main instigators of the Katyn decision, were executed on the basis of the verdicts of the Soviet Courts. Because the proceedings were secret, we do not know if the Katyn massacre was mentioned during these trials and if they were charged with this murder. The case of Katyn is going to be closed only when the whole Russian nation condemns this hideous crime performed with full premeditation by the NKVD – and learns from this.

IN THE SHADOW OF KATYN

EPILOG

This book was published for the first time in the Polish language in 1976. In the last chapter "Russia vis-à-vis Poland" my father (author of this book) expresses his concern about how future Polish-Russian relations would be influenced by the Katyn Massacre.

Here I would like to add:

1. How the discovery of the Katyn graves was perceived by the people living in Poland when they originally heard this news.
2. The conversation I had with my father on the subject of the Katyn Massacre in June 1949.
3. The struggle of individual Russians to bring out the truth about the Katyn Massacre.

The first time I heard of the discovery of the mass grave of Polish officers at the Katyn Forest was on April 13, 1943. At that time, I was thirteen and living in Wilno (presently Vilnius), then under German occupation. On the front page of the newspaper, I read the announcement of the discovery of the graves of Polish officers stating that they were all found to be shot by a single bullet in the back of the head. In Wilno, none of us had any doubt as to who had committed this crime. Families of Polish officers received letters from their husbands, sons, and fathers between November 1939 and March 1940. Since April 1940, letters had abruptly stopped arriving and no other news was forthcoming concerning the whereabouts of the Polish prisoners of war. The anguish of those three years had now turned into deep grief and mourning for all these families.

Subsequently, when the Soviet Army arrived in Eastern Poland in the summer of 1944, we heard a different version of the Katyn massacre: The Germans were the culprits. The Polish Communist Government, while officially accepting the Soviet version about the Katyn massacre, kept very quiet about the whole affair and tried to avoid the issue. In 1948, I joined the Polish Merchant Navy Training School in Gdynia and in May 1949, I escaped from the training ship, *Dar Pomorza*, while on a visit to Sweden. In June 1949, I arrived in England to be reunited with my father after a forced separation of almost ten years.

In the Communist world the subject of Katyn had been tacitly banned, and any form of query or criticism would be met with severe punishment. Soon, my Father and I were discussing Katyn, about which he had substantial knowledge, having been close to the scene of the crime while the executions were going on. I was naturally very interested to learn about the perceptions and reactions of the Western Allies to this

EPILOG

horrible Soviet crime, and particularly how the Soviets could have explained the Katyn Massacre to the International Military Tribunal at Nuremberg. To my consternation, my father told me that at Nuremberg, the Soviets shamelessly had accused the Germans of committing this crime. He explained that the Nuremberg Tribunal could not possibly convict the Germans, for he believed that the Judges at Nuremberg knew all too well of the Soviets' responsibility. However, if they had convicted the Germans of the Katyn Massacre **(based only on the Soviet allegations)**, the entire Tribunal's historical validity would be jeopardized; therefore, the matter was not pursued. In the meantime, the Soviet propaganda machine succeeded in convincing the majority of world opinion to believe its version of the story. For the Polish people, in addition to the anguish of losing 15,000 officers, there was this further blow of knowing that the true culprits were being exonerated

I asked my father:
"Is there any hope that the true version of the Katyn tragedy will ever be exposed to the world?"
My father, who grew up among Russians and knew them well, who went to Russian schools and studied at the Moscow University, replied:
"I am sure that future Russian historians will dig up the truth of the Katyn Massacre and expose it to the world."

As my father had predicted, there were many people in the Soviet Union who could not abide the historical lie that had been perpetrated concerning the fate of those 15,000 Polish officers. In 1969, Ukrainian poet and journalist, A. Karavansky made an appeal to the Central Committee of the Soviet Communist Party to order The State Attorney's Office to conduct a new investigation of the Katyn Case. He cited the names of two prison guards who had participated in the execution of the Polish officers. This act of bravery by Karavansky was rewarded with the gift of "a sentence to the GULAG" in 1970, and he was not released until 1979.[1]

In April 1980, on the fortieth anniversary of the Katyn Massacre, a number of Soviet defenders of human rights, namely L. Alexeyeva, A. Amalrik, V. Bukovsky, B. Vail, T. Venclov, A. Ginzburg, N. Gorbanevska, Z. and P. Grigorenko, B. Jefimov, P. Litvinov, K. Lubarsky, B. Nekrasov, and others, published a prophetic declaration. They expressed their conviction that the day would come when their country [the Soviet Union] would render justice to all involved in this tragedy. The law would be applied to the perpetrators who committed this crime, and there would be restitution to the victims for their suffering. The undersigned assured the nation that not one of them has forgotten, nor is ever going to forget that: "The responsibility rests with our country for the crimes committed by its official representatives at Katyn."[2]

In 1970, Natalia Lebedeva, a post-graduate student of the Institute of General History of the Academy of Sciences of the USSR, was working on the Nuremberg Trial

---

[1] Jerzewski, Leopold, *Dzieje Sprawy Katynia,* (The History of the Katyn Question), Glos Publishing, New York, 1983, p.65.
[2] Ibid., pp. 65-66.

IN THE SHADOW OF KATYN

when she came across the Katyn problem. However, the relevant Soviet archives were still inaccessible, and therefore she could not study the Katyn Massacre. Eventually, Dr. Natalia Lebedeva found documents on the movements of the units assigned to escorting prisoners of war to their place of execution in 1940, and thereby located relevant documents concerning the Katyn case.

On March 25, 1990, Dr. Lebedeva sent her findings for publication to *Moskovskoye Novosti* (Moscow News). The subsequent publication of her work created a cataclysm for Dr. Lebedeva not unlike the explosion of a bomb. She was threatened with banishment from the archives, prohibited from ever being published again, and told that she would never be permitted to travel abroad. Despite initial attempts to quash Dr. Lebedeva's findings, on April 14, 1990, the news agency **TASS** announced that it was in fact the **NKVD**, and not the Germans, who had murdered approximately 15,000 Polish officers in the spring of 1940.

Dr. Lebedeva states that her monograph, *Katyń: zbrodnia przeciwko ludzkości,* (Katyn: a crime against humanity) is atonement by a Russian for the crimes that were committed against the best sons of Poland on her [Russian] soil.[3]

In 1992, Boris Yeltsin, the President of the Russian Federation handed Lech Wałęsa, the President of the Polish Republic, copies of the original documentation concerning the Katyn crime, confirming beyond all doubt the responsibility of the state authorities of the Soviet Union for taking and carrying out the decision to eleminate Polish officers.

WITOLD SWIANIEWICZ

Polish War Cemetery in Katyn
OPENED AND DEDICATED 28 JULY, 2000
Polish Soldiers of 21st Century

---

[3] *Zbrodnia Katyńska Po 60 Latach*, (Crime of Katyn after 60 years), Publisher: Polska Fundacja Katyńska, Warsawa 2000, pp. 120-121.

EPILOG

Медное, Осташков

ПРОСТИТЕ НАС, ПОЛЯКИ

Тверь 36-18-05 Геѳргий МАЙ, 2000г.

Copy of pamphlet distributed by Russians during the consecration of the cemetery in Mednoye, September, 2000.

Mednoye, Oshtashkow

FORGIVE US, POLES

Tver 36-18-05 Georgyi May. 2000

The search for the burial sites of the mass graves of Mednoye and Kharkov was begun in 1990, and in 1996 the location of most of the bodies had been found.

In the year 2000, sixty years after the soldiers' deaths, three war cemeteries were officiallly opened and dedicated: one in the Ukraine and two in Russia.

POLISH WAR CEMETERY AT KHARKOV	JUNE 2000
POLISH WAR CEMETERY AT KATYN	JULY 2000
POLISH WAR CEMETERY AT MEDNOYE	SEPTEMBER 2000

THE FATE OF MANY MORE POLISH SOLDIERS AND CIVILIANS REMAINS UNKNOWN

IN THE SHADOW OF KATYN

INDEX of NAMES

Abramowicz (friend of Lenin), 235
Abramowicz, Witold, 199
Adamus, Jan, doctor, 124
Ahrens, colonel, xi
Alexander I, tsar, 240
Alexander II, tsar, 240
Alexeyev, Felix, 227
Alexeyeva, L., 257
Alexandrowicz, Bohdan, 137
Alliluyeva (Stalin's wife), 79, 126
Alliluyeva, Svetlana, 79, 235
Alter, Wiktor, 162-167, 191, 193, 194, 209
Amalrik, Andrei, 253, 257
Ancewicz, Franciszek, 125, 167
Anders, Władysław, general, *passim*
Andrew, Christopher, ix
Andrzejkowicz, lieutenant, 28, 30
Antoniewicz, captain, 57, 58
Atatürk, Kemal, 136, 176

Bader, Karol, envoy, 216
Badjan, doctor, 129, 130
Bąkiewicz, Wincenty, major, 54, 219
Barnby, Lord, 227
Batory, Stefan, King, 196, 201
Beck, Józef, 4, 6, 13, 16, 17, 19, 31, 32, 95, 178, 179, 181, 200
Bela-Kun, 101, 115, 133, 249
Belina-Prazmowski, 213
Beneš, Edvard, President of Czechoslovakia, 179
Beria, Lavrenti, *passim*
Berling, Zygmunt, general, 237, 251
Bevin, Ernest, 215
Bierut, Bolesław, 251
Bismarck, chancellor, 19, 176, 178
Bissel, general, 231
Bliss-Lane, Arthur, Ambassador, USA, 225
Blücher, Marshal, 242, 254
Błeszyński, colonel, 172
Bocheński, Adolf, 2, 168, 169, 174, 177
Bogomolov, Ambassador, USSR, 216, 218
Bohatyrewicz, Bronisław, general, 59, 233
Branicki, 116
Brezhnev, Leonid I., 84
Broniewski, Władysław, 158, 170
Brooke, Alan (Alanbrooke), field marshal, 32
Brzezinski, Zbigniew, professor, 248
Brzozowski, Stanisław, 180
Budyonny, 242

Bukharin, Nikolai, 84, 93, 98, 164
Bukovsky, V. 257
Burdenko, doctor, 232, 234, 235, 255
Bychowiec, Jerzy, captain, 29, 32, 39, 70

Cadogan, Alexander, Sir, 228
Catherine II, the Great, tsarina, 118, 136, 188 197, 202, 253
Carton de Wiart, general, 171
Charles X, Swedish King, 155
Charles XII, Swedish King, 155
Chamberlain, Neville, 15, 96
Charles Martel, xiii
Chicherin, Georgi, 19, 151
Churchill, Winston, x, xi, xii, 59, 65, 96, 181-183, 210, 228
Ciechanowski, Jan, Polish Ambassador, 215, 221
Conquest, Robert, 135, 235, 249
Cripps, Stafford, Sir, British Ambassador, 191
Czajkowski, landowner, 68
Czapski, Józef, cavalry captain, 216, 232, 238
Czartoryski, Adam, Prince, 240

Dallin, Alexander, 241
Dargenfield, Irma, 228
Dąb-Biernacki, Stefan, general, 38, 52, 54, 56, 57, 230, 239
Dekanozov, Soviet Ambassador, 247
Dembiński, Henryk, 16, 120, 187
Denikin, general, 160
Deutscher, Izaak, 166
Dmowski, Roman, 168
Dostoyevsky, Fyodor, 66, 79, 127, 137
Douhet, Giulio, general, 104
Dunin-Borkowski, Piotr, captain, 56
Dzerzhinsky, Felix, 23, 79, 123, 136, 154, 235, 254
Djilas, Milovan, 93, 105, 244

Earl, George H., 231
Eden, Anthony, 228
Ehrenkreutz, Stefan, 17, 111
Ehrlich, Henryk, 162-167, 191, 193, 194, 209
Eisenhower, Dwight, 32, 215
Englicht, colonel, 111
Epstein, Julius, 235
Estreicher, Stanislaw, 20

Fajans, Roman, 159, 195
Feuerbach, Ludwig A., 236
FitzGibbon, Constantine, 236
FitzGibbon, Louis, xii, 226, 227, 229

INDEX OF NAMES

Frederick II (of Prussia), the Great, 11

Gacki, Stefan, 158
de Gaulle, Charles, general, 104
Gawlina, army bishop, 162
Genghis Khan, 20
George VI, King of England, 228
Giedroyc, Jerzy, 8, 165, 168
Ginzburg, A., 257
Godłowski, Dr., 58, 69
Gogol, 155
Gorbanevska, N., 257
Gordievsky, Oleg, ix
Gomułka, Władysław, 243
Goering, Hermann, xii, 10
Grabski, Stanisław, professor, 124
Grąbczewski (family of), 253
Grąbczewski, general, 202
Grigorenko, P., 257
Grigorenko, Z., 257
Grubiński, Wacław, 158, 170

Hagemayer, Włodzimierz, 169
Haller, Józef, general, 52
Hegel, Georg W.F., 236
Hertz, Aleksander, 11
Heydel, Adam, professor, 168, 198, 199
Hindenburg, Paul, 9
Hingley, Ronald, 235, 242, 247, 254
Hitler, Adolf, *passim*

Ibsen, 155
Igor, Prince, 55
Ivan IV the Terrible, tsar, 196, 201
Ivan III the Great, tsar, 136, 188, 201

Jadwiga, Hungarian Princess, 41, 186
Jackson, Robert, xi
Jakowicki, W. M., professor, doctor, 137
Jagiełło (Jogaila), Grand Duke of Lithuania, 41, 186
Jagiellons, 41, 155
Jefimov, B., 257
Jefremov, 126
Jędrychowski, Stefan, 186
Jędrzejewicz, Janusz, Prime Minister, 16
Jerzewski, Leopold, 257

Kalinin, 79
Kaganovich, 79
Kamenev, Lev B., 93, 164

Kamiński, Władysław, lieutenant colonel, 219
Kandelaki, David, 248
Kane, Senator (Australia), 227
Kantak, Kamil, priest, professor, 66
Karavansky, A., 257
Kautsky, Karl, 180
Kennan, George F., 249
Keynes, John M., 5, 8
Kerensky, Alexander, 102, 153
Khrushchev, Nikita S., 84, 116, 135, 136, 242-245
Kimbal, Warren, xi, 228
Kirov, Sergei M., 248
Kisselev, P., 255
Kleeberg, Franciszek, general, 45
Kobylański, Eastern Department
   of Ministry of Foreign Affairs, 111
Koc, Wacław, colonel, 124, 199
Koestler, Arthur, 113
Kolchak, Alexander, admiral, 51
Komarnicki, Wacław, professor, 65, 69, 71, 86, 129, 182, 238, 239
Korniłowicz, priest, 68
Korniłowicz, Tadeusz, lieutenant colonel, 67
Korowajczyk, Leonard, second lieutenant, 67, 68, 72
Kościałkowski, Stanisław, professor, 158, 170
Kościuszko, Tadeusz, 12, 177
Kot, Stanisław, professor, *passim*
Kowszyk, Arkadiusz, captain, 32, 33, 43, 220
Koziełł-Poklewski, captain, 63
Kozłowski, Leon, professor, Prime Minister, 167-169
Krajewski, lieutenant colonel, 222
Krivozertsov, Ivan, 225
Kropotkin Pyotr, Prince, 146
Król, second lieutenant, 35
Kruk, Wacław, lieutenant, 231
Kruk-Śmigła, lieutenant colonel, 28, 30, 32
Kucharski, O., jesuit priest, 159, 162, 181
Kuczyńska, Danuta (wife of Stefan), 234
Kuczyńska, Irena (wife of Stanisław), 234
Kuczyński, Stanisław, cavalry officer, 234
Kuczyński, Stefan, lieutenant, 234
Kukiel, Marian, general, 223
Kuminek, Henryk Bruno, second lieutenant, 231
Kutrzeba, Stanisław, professor, 20

Künstler, S., colonel, 34, 56, 57, 62, 122, 239, 240
Kwaciszewski, general, 26, 28, 30
Kwiatkowski Eugeniusz, engineer,
   vice-Prime Minister, 24, 46, 165, 172

IN THE SHADOW OF KATYN

Laternser, Hans, doctor, xi
Lawrence, Lord Justice, xi
Lebedeva, Natalia S, doctor, xi, 70, 257, 258
Lebiedziewski, Jerzy, 219
Lednicki, 253
Lenin, Vladimir Ilyich, *passim*
Lermontov, Mikhail, xv, 136, 194, 253
Libicki, Janusz, lieutenant, 67
Lipkowska, Teresa, 175, 195, 208, 209
Lipski, Józef, Polish Ambassador, 10
Litvinov, P., 257
Litvinov, Maxim M., 17
Lloyd, George, 172, 215
Lord D'Abernon, xiii
Lubarsky, K., 257
Lubodziecki, Stanisław, colonel, 108, 219
Lubomirski, Eugeniusz, Prince, 167
Ludendorff, Erich von, general, 9
Ludendorff, Matilda, Dr. of philosophy, 9
Loboda, Michal, 226
Lunacharsky, Anatoli, 140, 151

Mackiewicz Józef, author, brother of Stanislaw, 168, 225, 226, 233, 241
Mackiewicz Stanisław, newspaper editor, *passim*
Mayakovsky, Vladimir, 104
Majkowski, captain, 47, 48
Maisky, Ivan, 65, 174, 177, 179, 189, 192, 215, 220
Maliniak, Julian, doctor, 195
Maliszewski, doctor, Mayor of Wilno, 137
Mann, Thomas, author, 9
Marx, Karl, 79, 104, 180, 188
Marshall, George, 32
Masaryk, Tomas Carrigue, 156
Mazepa, hetman, 155
Merezhkovsky, Dmitri S., 66, 127, 155
Meyerhold, Vsevolod E., 116, 117
Mihailovich, Dragoljub, general, 168
Mickiewicz, Adam, author, 21, 253, 254
Menzhinsky, Vyacheslav R., 254
Merkulov, Vladimir, 79, 150, 250, 251, 254, 255
Mikołajczyk, Stanisław, xii, 190, 246
Miłosz, Czesław, 187
Mikoyan, 79
Minkiewicz, Henryk, general, 233
Miroshnikov, 113, 114, 115
Molotov, Vyacheslav M., ix, 17, 22, 79, 135, 150, 163, 164, 216, 247-249
Młynarski, Bronisław, 238
Monfort, Henri de, 235

Morawski, Kajetan, 216, 218
Moszyński, Adam, major, 57, 219
Mościcki, Ignacy, President of Polish Republic, 15, 16, 31, 179
Mussolini, Benito, 13

Nadezhda, Alekseyevna, 143, 144
Napoleon I, 65, 96
Napoleon III, 65
Neave, Airey, member of British Parliament, 227
Neckreech, A. M., 247
Nekrasov, B., 257
Neurath, Konstantin von, 248
Nebogatov, admiral, 51
Nicholas I, tsar, 94, 194
Nicholas II, tsar, 63, 175, 202
Nikolai, Metropolitan, 232
Nikon, patriarch, 126, 127
Nixon, Richard, 228
Nowak, colonel and priest, 59, 66
Nowakowski, major, 30, 31
Nowicki, cavalry officer, 24, 38
Novikov-Priboy, Aleksei S., Russian author, 51
Nowosielski, Gustaw, lieutenant.colonel, 31-33, 46-52, 54, 55, 57, 59, 60, 71, 220

Oberländer, Teodor, professor, 4, 5, 6, 7
Obertyński, colonel, 54
Okulicki, Leopold, colonel, 218
Olejniczakowski, Eugeniusz, 17
Olshansky, B., professor, 234, 235
O'Malley, Owen, Sir, British Ambassador, 228
Orlov, admiral, 114, 138
Orlov, doctor, wife of admiral, 138, 139
Orsos, professor, 225

Pawderewski, Ignacy, 6, 200
Parczewski, Alfons, rector, 178
Parnicki, Teodor, 158
Pawlukiewicz, officer cadet, 131
Pawłowski, captain, 30, 32, 35, 39, 220
Payot, 94
Pehr, Otto, 149-153, 156, 194, 217
Pełczyński, Tadeusz, colonel, 26, 27, 30, 112
Peotrovich, Nikolai, 140-145
Peszek, W., colonel, 31
Peszke, colonel, pastor, 59
Peter I the Great, tsar, 127, 188, 203, 245
Peter III, tsar, 118
Petlura, Symeon W., Cossack hetman, 17
Petrażycki, 253

INDEX OF NAMES

Piasecki, vice-Minister of Communication, 3
Piekarski, general, 39, 47
Piłsudski, Józef, marshal, *passim*
Piłsudski, Rowmund, 228
Pipes, Richard, 136
Pohorecki, judge, 238
Połujan, Józef, lieutenant, 57, 58
Postischev, 248
Pruszyński, Ksawery, 158, 166, 174-188, 192 194, 195, 197, 198, 204, 205, 207, 209, 213, 252
Prystor, Aleksander, Polish Prime Minister, 16, 167
Przedrzymirski, general, 38, 47
Przewalski, 253
Pucinski, Roman, congressman, 227
Pugachov, Yemelyan, 118, 123, 201, 202
Pushkin, Alexander, 99, 100, 104, 136, 155, 194, 252, 253
Puzyn, princes, 63

Raczkiewicz, Władysław, president, 160, 173
Raczyński, Edward, Polish Ambassador, 218
Radek, Karol, 93, 101, 126
Radowski, Consul, 3, 4
Radziwiłł, Janusz, Prince, 155
Radziwiłłs, 20
Reich, Zinaida, 116, 117
Rakosi, Matyas, 116, 133, 134, 249
Rasputin, Grigori J., 63
Razin, Stenka, 201
Rekść, 30
Remarque, Erich Maria, German author, 137
Reza Pahlavi, Shah, 206
Ribbentrop, Joachim, ix, 22, 135, 191, 247-249
Rola-Janicki, 170-177, 192, 209
Romer, Tadeusz, Polish Ambassador, 189, 193, 210
Roosevelt, Eleanor, 163, 164
Roosevelt, Franklin Delano, x, xi, 215, 228, 231
Rose, Professor, 58
Rudenko, R.A., xi
Rudnicki, Tadeusz, lieutenant colonel, 30-33, 171

Sacco, 165,
Sakharov, Andrei, xv, 253
Sadowski, corporal, 48, 49
Sawicki, general, 36
Savinkov, Boris, 102
Schacht, Hjalmar, 5, 8, 248

Schapiro, Leonard, 164, 242, 244, 248
Schulenburg, Friedrich W., 247
Seeckt, Hans von, general, 12
Seraphim, Peter Hans, 7
Serov, NKVD general, 135, 244
Severy, Frank, British Consul, 172
Shamyl, 203
Sharonov, Nikolai, ix
Sielicki, lieutenant, 34, 51, 53, 220
Sienkiewicz, Henryk, author, 22, 68, 86, 155
Sierakowski, Zygmunt, 203
Sigismund II Augustus, 41, 186
Sikorski, Władysław, general, *passim*
Singer, Bernard, 159, 165, 166, 170, 195, 198, 199 204, 205, 208, 209, 212
Skalak, Bronisław, 103, 104, 107
Skapski, chemistry, 158
Skorel, priest, 59, 66
Skrzypek, Stanisław, doctor, 124
Skulski, Leopold, Polish Prime Minister, 167
Skwarczyńska, doctor, 139
Sławek, Walery, 16, 17
Sławoj-Składkowski, Felicjan, general, Polish Prime Minister, 176,
Śmigly-Rydz, Edward, Marshal, ix, 12, 13, 15, 31, 44, 176, 179
Słowacki, Juliusz, 33, 253
Sneh, Mosze, doctor (Kleinbaum), 229, 230
Sokolnicki, Henryk, 158, 210
Solovyev, Vladimir, Russian philosopher, 66, 127
Solski, Adam, major, 56, 57, 230
Solzhenitsyn, Alexander, I., 77, 117, 140, 235, 244, 253
Sombart, Werner, 9, 112. 119
Sorel, Georges, xiii, 11
Sosnkowski, Kazimierz, general, 48, 50, 113, 114, 160, 175, 176, 215
Spasowicz, 253
Speer, Albert, 218, 249
Stahl, Zdzisław, professor, 64, 225, 226
Stalin, Joseph V., *passim*
Staniewicz, Witold, professor, 4, 10, 14
Stanislavsky, Konstantin S., 104, 116
Stankiewicz, Wacław, cavalry officer, 57
Starzewski, A., lieutenant colonel, 108
Stepanov, colonel, 70
Stolypin, Peter, A., 71, 72, 89, 175
Stresemann, Gustav, 10
Stroński, Stanisław, 200
Studnicki, Władysław, 2, 13, 17, 20, 168, 177
Sukiennicki, Wiktor, professor, 63, 125, 158, 159, 166

IN THE SHADOW OF KATYN

Swan, xiii
Swianiewicz, Stanisław, doctor, xii-xv, xxi, 87
Swianiewicz, Olimpia, xv, xvi
Swianiewicz, Witold, xv
Szamota, lieutenant, 40
Szawłowski, professor, 169
Szymanski Henry J., colonel, 231
Szyszko-Bohusz Z., general, 181
Świtalski, Kazimierz, Polish Prime Minister, 247

Telmany, Adam, lieutenant, 129, 219
Tischbein, 114, 115
Todt, Fritz, 3, 218, 225, 232
Tolstoy, Aleksei, 232
Tolstoy, Leo, 136, 155
Toynbee, Arnold, 188
Trotsky, Leon D. (Lev Bronstein), 19, 113, 125 151, 163, 166
Truman, Harry S., U.S. President, xi
Tukhachevsky, Mikhail N., marshal, 13, 15, 103 114, 138, 139, 242, 248, 249, 254
Tucholski, docent, 72
Tupolev, Andrei, N., 117
Tyszkiewicz, Michał, 211
Tyszkiewicz, Stefan, 3
Tyszyński, colonel, 56, 57, 62, 239, 240

Ulam, Adam B., professor, 235
Urbanowicz, Wacław, lieutenant, 29, 30, 31, 48

Vail, B., 257
Van Vliet, colonel, 231
Vanzetti, 165
Varga, 133
Venclov, T., 257
Vidra, Abram, 229, 230
Voroshilov, 79, 113, 242
Voznesensky, M. A., 184
Vyshinsky, Andrei, 163, 164, 193, 216, 217, 254

Wagner, xv, 40
Wałęsa, Lech, President of the Polish Republic, 258
Wania, lieutenant colonel, 57
Washington, George, 12
Wasilewska, Wanda, 99, 232
Wasilewski, Leon, 98
Waśkowski, 253
Weber, Max, 199

Weintraub, Wiktor, professor, 158, 166
Werth, Alexander, 243, 253
Weygand, Maxime, general, 58, 181
Wielopolski, Aleksander, margrave, 177, 179, 240
Wilecki, Alfred, captain, 231
Wilson, Woodrow, U.S President, 2, 6
Wirsziłło, Tadeusz, 69
Wiścicki, captain, 30
Wiśniowski, Kazimierz, general, 113-115
Witold, Grand Duke of Lithuania, 5
Witos, Wincenty, 198
Wittlin, Tadeusz, 230-232
Wojtyniak, priest, prelate, 59, 66
Wolikowski, general, 150, 159, 192, 222
Wołkowicki, general, 38, 45-47, 51-54, 58-60
Wysłouch, Seweryn, 16
Wyspiański, Stanisław, 17

Yagoda, Genrikh, 79, 254
Yegorov, marshal, 242
Yeltsin, Boris, President of the Russian Federation, 224, 258
Yenukidze, Abel, 138
Yesiennin, Sergei, A., 117
Yezhov, N., 79, 101, 104, 121, 127, 128, 132, 134, 140, 161, 162, 165, 222, 254

Zając, general, 210
Zaleski, August, 160, 215, 218
Zarubin, brigadier, 64, 69, 70, 86, 94, 122, 182, 238 239, 250
Zawadzki, Władysław, professor, 213, 214
Zawodny, Janusz, K., professor, xi, 226-228, 231, 235, 236, 246
Zbyszewski Wacław A., 2, 22, 174
Zdziechowski, Marian, 66, 239
Zieliński, 253
Zinovyev, G. I., 93, 164
Ziółkowski, priest, 66
Zwierzyński, 185
Zyndram-Kościałkowski, Marian, 17, 167
Żelisławski, colonel, 57, 119
Żukowski (family of), 253
Żukowski, Władysław, 175
Zia Ad-Din, Shah, 206

CHRONOLOGY

Century / Year		
10th	966	Poland founded as a nation.

* *

14th ↕ 16th	1385 ↕ 1572	Jagiellon Dynasty: - The combined resources of Poland and Lithuania created a most powerful unit in Eastern Europe and stopped expansion of Teutonic Order and Muscovites.

* *

16th ↕ 18th	1572 ↕ 1795	The Noble Republic: The king ruling over Polish-Lithuanian Republic elected by Nobility. Their influence was enhanced by introduction of *Liberum Veto*. This device could halt proceedings of the Sejm (Parliament) by the simple word *Veto* of a single noble member. King's power was severely limited and the Polish-Lithuanian Republic suffers prolonged and severe deterioration.
	1772	FIRST partition of Polish-Lithuanian Republic among Russia, Prussia and Austria.
	1791	Constitution May 3rd. Hereditary monarchy was restored and *Liberum Veto* abolished. However it was too late to save the Republic.
	1793	SECOND partition takes place between Russia and Prussia.
	1795	THIRD partition among Prussia, Austria and Russia, under Catherine II, take over control of their respective portions of the thrice divided Polish-Lithuanian Republic. This subjugation continued until 1918 when Poland gained independence after The Treaty of Versailles (see 1918).

* *

19th	1815	Congress of Vienna establishes The Kingdom of Poland – so-called Congress Kingdom – subjugated to Tsar of Russia.
	1830-31	November Rising - Polish army of Congress Kingdom rebels against the Tsar. After a year of fighting it culminated in defeat.
	1863-64	January Rising - Poland subject to the Tsar had no regular army. Therefore, conflict could only take the form of guerrilla warfare and ended in failure.

* *

20th	1914 1918		WORLD WAR I begins, July 28. (Austria-Hungary declare war on Serbia.) WWI ends November 11, 1918. Poland gains full independence after nearly 150 years of partition and occupation.
	1919-20		POLISH-SOVIET WAR - Poland alone under Marshal Piłsudski instills total defeat of Bolshevics in their attempt to take over all of Western Europe for conversion to Marxist ideology. Battle of Warsaw, August 1920.
	1939	Sep 1	- WORLD WAR II begins. GERMANY ATTACKS POLAND.
		Sep 3	- Great Britain and France declare war on Germany.
		Sep 17	- Soviets attack Poland.
		Sep 28	- *Lt. Swianiewicz, other Polish officers, captured by Russians.*
		Oct	- *Captured Polish officers sent to camp at Putyvl., Ukraine.*
		Nov	- *These Polish officers transferred to camp at Kozelsk.*
	1940	Mar 5	- Stalin signs an order to execute 20000 Polish officers.
		Apr 3	- Transports from Kozelsk to Katyn begin.
		Apr 29	- *Lt. Swianiewicz is transported with other officers toward Katyn.*
		Apr 30	- *By order, Lt. Swianiewicz is separated from the transport about 3 km from Katyn Forest and sent to NKVD prison in Smolensk.*
		May 5	- *Lt. Swianiewicz is transferred from prison in Smolensk to Lubyanka prison in Moscow.*
		May	- *Lt. Swianiewicz is accused of spying and is being investigated at the Lubyanka prison in Moscow.*
		Dec	- *Lt Swianiewicz is transferred to Butyrki prison in Moscow.*
	1941	*Feb*	- *Lt. Swianiewicz is sent to a transfer camp in Kotlas.*
		Mar	- *Lt. Swianiewicz arrives at Ust-Wymsk camps in North Russia.*
		[Jun 22	- GERMANY ATTACKS SOVIET UNION.]

	Jul 30	- Gen. Władysław Sikorski, president of Polish Government in exile, signs a formal agreement with Stalin.. Under this pact, all Polish prisoners are to be released from Soviet camps.
	Aug	- Lt. Swianiewicz is released from GULAG, but at the end of August 1941, he is arrested again and sent back to the GULAG. Nine month stay begins in camps under unbearable conditions.
	[Dec 7	JAPAN attacks PEARL HARBOR. United States enters WW II.]
1942	Apr 20	- Release from camps. May arrival of Lt. Swianiewicz at the Polish Embassy in Kuybyshev.
	Aug	- Final departure, rather eventful, with Ambassador Kot to Persia. Arrival at Tehran.
1943	Apr 13	- Germans announce discovery of the graves of Polish officers at Katyn Forest.
1945	May 8	- WORLD WAR II ENDS IN EUROPE.
	Aug 8	- The charter of the International Military Tribunal was signed by the United Kingdom, America, France, and the Soviet Union. The charter laid down the crimes which the tribunal was to try: "Crimes Against Peace", "War Crimes ", and "Crimes Against Humanity".
	Sep 2	- WORLD WAR II ENDS IN PACIFIC. Japanese surrender.
	Oct 18	- The indictment against German war criminals was presented in Berlin by the representatives of Great Britain, France, United States and USSR. Later it became the basis of the Nuremberg Trial. Among crimes, they also brought up the Katyn Massacre which was the Soviet version that stated: " in September 1941, 11000 Polish officers were taken and murdered in the Katyn Forest near Smolensk [by the Germans]."
1946	Feb 13	- Colonel Pokrovsky, the Soviet Prosecutor, in his speech refers to Katyn at Nuremberg Trial, charging Germans with the crime.
	July 1	- German and Soviet witnesses testifying on the Katyn Massacre before the International Military Tribunal at Nuremberg.
	Sep 30	- Final verdicts were announced by International Military Tribunal at Nuremberg, The Katyn affair was not mentioned. The charge concerning Katyn was simply omitted without any explanation.
1951	Sep 18	- The House of Representatives of the 82nd Congress of the United States, unanimously adopted House Resolution No. 390 which established "a Select Committee to conduct a full investigation and study of all facts, evidence and circumstances of the Katyn Forest Massacre, an international crime committed against soldiers and citizens of Poland at the start of World War II."
1952	Apr 16	- Select committee hearings in London; Dr. Swianiewicz testifies at the hearings.
	Dec 22	- Select committee issues a unanimous final report; it blames the Soviet NKVD for the Katyn Massacre and calls for a trial in the World Court ... but this was never pursued.
1957	Apr	- Dr. Swianiewicz meets his wife in Jogjakarta, Indonesia, after 18 years of forced separation when the Communist Regime in Poland finally allows her to leave Poland.
1975	Oct	- Dr. Swianiewicz was attacked on the street in London, England, and left uncounscious on the pavement. It was two weeks before he was to give evidence at the Sakharov hearings on violation of human rights in Russia.
1990	Apr 14	- Soviet News agency TASS announces for first time that Russia committed Katyn Massacre.
1991	Jun-Sep	- Finally, discovery of Kharkov and Miednoye sites after 50 years.

* *

| 21st | 2000 | Jul 28 | Dedication and Consecration of Katyn Cemetery on Russian site. |